CHANGING UNJUST LAWS
JUSTLY

*For my good friends
Mike + Janet,

With love + all best wishes,

Colin.*

17 September 2005.

CHANGING UNJUST LAWS
JUSTLY

PRO-LIFE SOLIDARITY WITH
"THE LAST AND LEAST"

COLIN HARTE

THE CATHOLIC UNIVERSITY OF
AMERICA PRESS • WASHINGTON, D.C.

Copyright © 2005
The Catholic University of America Press
All rights reserved

The paper used in this publication meets the minimum requirements of American National Standards for Information Science—Permanence of Paper for Printed Library Materials, ANSI Z39.48-1984.

∞

LIBRARY OF CONGRESS CATALOGING-IN-PUBLICATION DATA

Harte, Colin, 1965–

Changing unjust laws justly : pro-life solidarity with "the last and least" / by Colin Harte.— 1st ed.

p. cm.

Includes bibliographical references and index.

ISBN-13: 978-0-8132-1406-1 (cloth : alk. paper)

ISBN-10: 0-8132-1406-8 (cloth : alk. paper)

1. Abortion—Law and legislation—Great Britain. 2. Abortion—Moral and ethical aspects—Great Britain. 3. Abortion—Religious aspects—Catholic Church. 4. Pro-life movement—Great Britain. I. Title.

KD3340.H37 2004

342.4108′ 4—dc22

2004008037

*In memory of Christian
and with gratitude to his mother*

CONTENTS

Preface   xi

Acknowledgments   xv

Introduction   1

PART I. PRACTICAL REALITIES OF RESTRICTING ABORTION

1. A Denial of Solidarity   15
   General Features of Abortion Laws / 17
   Legislative Campaigns to Prohibit Late Abortions / 20
   Campaigning to Stop "Abortion on Demand" / 41
   The Exclusion of Disabled Unborn Children as a Paradigm of the Denial of Solidarity / 47
   Exclusions or Solidarity? / 54

PART II. A QUESTION OF LAW

2. Jurisprudential Options Revisited   59
   The Three Basic Jurisprudential Options / 59
   The Seven Jurisprudential Options / 72
   Legal "Permission" and Legal "Toleration" / 78

3. The Problem of Intrinsically Unjust Laws   90
   Law: Justness and Unjustness / 90
   Responding to Intrinsically Unjust Laws / 103

PART III. ETHICAL CONSIDERATIONS

4. Good Acts by Bad Acts? — 121
   Material Cooperation and Side Effects / 122
   Intentions and Consequences / 131
   Veritatis splendor, n. 78, on the Moral Object / 140
   An Analysis of Voting / 151

5. A "Special Case" Consideration — 159
   The Concept of "Anti-Abortion Politics" / 161
   "Corrupted" Systems and Oath Swearing / 168
   The Context of the Restrictive Law / 174
   A Different Kind of "Special Case" / 178
   A Return to the "Object" / 181
   Form and Matter / 184

6. Avoiding Ethical Inconsistencies — 186
   The Lesser Evil / 186
   The Principle of Totality / 202
   The Law of Gradualness / 206

PART IV. LEGISLATIVE MATTERS

7. Identifying Just and Unjust Proposals — 215
   Primary and Secondary Aspects of Abortion Laws / 218
   A Typical Abortion Act / 222
   A Range of Legislative Proposals / 235
   A Consideration of Side Effects / 248

8. Voting Opportunities — 255
   The Unborn Children (Protection) Bill of 1980 / 257
   The Unborn Children (Protection) Bill of 1982 / 263
   The Abortion Bill of 1986 / 266
   The Abortion (Amendment) Bill of 1992 / 273
   The Abortion (Amendment) Bill of 1995 / 275
   The Human Embryo (Protection) Bill of 2000 / 279
   Voting Opportunities: A Summary / 283

PART V. MAGISTERIAL TEACHING AND A CONCLUSION

9. *Evangelium Vitae*   289
   Reading *Evangelium vitae*, nn. 73 and 90, in Context / 289
   Understanding *Evangelium vitae*, n. 73 / 295
   Questions Posed by *Evangelium vitae*, n. 73 / 301
   Evangelium vitae, n. 90 / 308
   Authoritative Clarifications of *Evangelium vitae*, n. 73 / 310

10. An Overview and Conclusion   317

APPENDICES

A. The UK Abortion Law Prior to the Abortion Act 1967 / 335
B. Abortion Act 1967 / 337
C. Abortion (Amendment) Bill (January 1988) / 341
D. Abortion (Amendment) Bill (May 1988) / 343
E. Section 37 of the Human Fertilisation and Embryology Act 1990 / 345

Bibliography   347
Index   359

PREFACE

Many a man has ideas, which he hopes are true, and useful for his day, but he wishes to have them discussed. He is willing or rather would be thankful to give them up, if they can be proved to be erroneous or dangerous, and by means of controversy he obtains his end.
—Cardinal Newman, *Apologia Pro Vita Sua*[1]

The issue at the heart of this book has troubled me for some fifteen years. It should have troubled me for a year or two longer, but I was reluctant at first to let it trouble me. I can understand why readers committed to a policy of supporting restrictive abortion legislation, as part of a strategy intended to lead ultimately to a total prohibition of all abortions, may be reluctant to consider whether their commitment has been right. I understand because I too was committed to such a policy. My commitment was such that I interrupted my undergraduate studies in 1987 to work full-time for the pro-life movement in the UK, eager to do everything possible to help David Alton's Abortion (Amendment) Bill—to be discussed in Chapter 1—to become law. I did not want to hear expressions of fundamental concern about supporting the policy to which I was committed.

During the course of the Alton Bill I became aware of the considerable disquiet felt by my friend and pro-life colleague, Alison Davis. The bill excluded disabled unborn children from the protection given to those who were not disabled and, having been born with the sort of serious disability for which abortion is commonly regarded as the appropriate "solution," Alison had particular reason to be concerned about the exclusion. As the leader of a group within the Society for the

---

1. John Henry Newman, *Apologia Pro Vita Sua* (1864; reprint, London: Collins, Fontana, 1959), 298.

Protection of Unborn Children set up to promote the right to life of disabled people, she found herself in an impossible position.[2] The Alton Bill became a trial for her. I regret that I, like many others, was unwilling then to give serious consideration to her concerns.

Since 1989 I have had the privilege of being Alison's personal assistant, and not only have I come to understand her concerns, but they have become mine. This book is the culmination of those concerns. For its flaws I take full responsibility, but if it has any merit, much of this is owed to Alison's contribution. This book is the fruit of much discussion with her, much redrafting of the text—with Alison's helpful comments on several drafts—and, in particular, it is the fruit of considerable suffering on her part. Without Alison's inspiration and ongoing support this book would never have been written, and I—like the pro-life movement generally—owe her a considerable debt.

There continues to be a general consensus within the UK pro-life movement that a strategy to protect the unborn gradually, by restrictive or "incremental" legislation, is entirely justified. In the United States and some other countries there has been more controversy, with pro-life groups taking different positions on the question, some adopting a view that is broadly sympathetic to my concerns. A book of this sort cannot avoid contributing to, or even arousing, controversy. Controversy can, of course, be damaging, but if it is rightly undertaken with respect and charity for those who hold different opinions, it can be fruitful. It is my hope that this book will assist the pro-life movement in its vitally important work.

Catholics within the pro-life movement have the confidence of knowing that disputed questions, like the one discussed in this book, can be resolved by an authority whose judgment can be safely depended upon—and those whose views are judged to be erroneous or dangerous should be willing and thankful to give them up. The purpose of this book is not to convince readers of the rightness of my argument but to encourage them to consider it: to reject it if it is unsound, and to

---

2. At the time of the Alton Bill the group was called SPUC's Handicap Division. It has since been renamed No Less Human. Alison Davis has been coordinator of the group since 1983 and is recognized as one of the most compelling and authoritative speakers for the pro-life movement in the UK.

accept it if it holds. If the position promoted in this book is flawed I would be both willing and thankful to be persuaded by reasoned argument or by an authoritative judgment.

Milborne St. Andrew, Dorset.
Solemnity of the Annunciation, 25 March 2004

ACKNOWLEDGMENTS

As acknowledged in the Preface, I am indebted above all to Alison Davis. A mere expression of thanks does not do justice to her contribution to this book.

Several scholars, some of whom have expressed considerable disagreement with my line of thought, have helped me to develop the argument of this book by their comments on early drafts of different parts of the text. Particular thanks are due to Fr. Peter Bristow, Fr. Kevin L. Flannery, S.J., Fr. Jarosław Merecki, S.D.S., Richard Myers, and Fr. Martin Rhonheimer. I am especially grateful to Colin Mason, Charles Rice, Chris Tollefsen, and Helen Watt for reading the whole book and suggesting many corrections. I am also sincerely grateful to the following people—some of whom have serious objections to my general thesis—who have generously assisted my research: David Alton, Michael Baker, Bishop Christopher Budd, Theresa Croshaw, John Finnis, Fr. John Fleming, Damian P. Fedoryka, Fr. Hermann Geissler, F.S.O., Robert P. George, Robin Haig, William May, Bernard Sadler, Fr. Tadeusz Styczeń, S.D.S., and Ted Watt.

In addition to extracts from published material, the book includes extracts from recorded interviews. I am very grateful to those who agreed to be interviewed: Ruth Bailey, Agnes Fletcher, Rachel Hurst, Peter McLean, and John Smeaton.

I have benefited from the use of the libraries at the Maryvale Institute, Birmingham, and the Linacre Centre for Healthcare Ethics, London, and am grateful to the librarians and staff at these institutions for all their assistance. I am also grateful for the assistance given by the SPUC Educational Research Trust.

I am very grateful to Gregory LaNave at The Catholic University of America Press for overseeing the process from book proposal to published work. I very much appreciate his helpfulness, as well as that of

Elizabeth Benevides and Susan Needham, during the review and publication process.

Much of the material for Chapter 6 was taken from "Inconsistent Papal Approaches towards Problems of Conscience?" *National Catholic Bioethics Quarterly* 2, no. 1 (2002): 99–122, and some of the material from Chapter 9 was taken from "Challenging a Consensus: Why *Evangelium Vitae* Does Not Permit Legislators to Vote for 'Imperfect Legislation,'" in Luke Gormally, ed., *Culture of Life—Culture of Death* (London: Linacre Centre, 2002), 322–42. I am grateful to the editors of these volumes for permission to use this material. The texts of the Abortion (Amendment) Bill reproduced in the Appendices and the typographical arrangement of the text are Parliamentary Copyright. The Acts of Parliament are reproduced in the Appendices under the terms of Crown Copyright Policy Guidance issued by H.M.S.O.

As with any undertaking, the support and prayers of family and friends have been an invaluable contribution. The encouragement and support of those who have contacted me because they share my concerns has been greatly appreciated, and I am especially indebted to Patrick Delaney.

My involvement with the pro-life movement, especially with the Society for the Protection of Unborn Children (SPUC), dates back to 1983. Since then I have enjoyed many friendships with pro-life colleagues that have endured in spite of serious differences of opinion—and I hope these friendships will continue in spite of this book! I believe my critique of SPUC's (and my own former) support for restrictive legislation is fairly made, but it must also be accompanied by an acknowledgment of the impressive commitment to the pro-life cause—in some cases, for many years and at great personal cost—demonstrated by SPUC's leaders and members. In particular, I readily acknowledge the dedication of SPUC's former national director, Phyllis Bowman, and its current national director, John Smeaton. After twenty years as colleagues and friends, they know me well enough to recognize that if any aspect of my critique of SPUC's activities under their leadership is in any way unfair, it has nevertheless been made honestly and with good will toward them and the UK pro-life movement to which they have dedicated themselves.

CHANGING UNJUST LAWS
JUSTLY

INTRODUCTION

Some things are obvious. In an emergency situation like that of a burning building or a sinking ship, where lives are in jeopardy, the automatic response is to try to save lives. The value attached to human life is such that rescuers may even place their own lives at risk in order to save others. And nobody would suggest that if rescuers are unable to save all, then they should not try to save any lives. They should, rather, do their best to save as many lives as possible.

As long as it is not possible to prohibit all abortions, many pro-life individuals and organizations believe their role is to stop any that they can. The duty for many seems clear: "we must be about saving as many lives as we can."[1] It is claimed that the existence of abortion legislation poses an emergency situation analogous to that of a burning building or sinking ship in which lives are threatened. This analogy has been made frequently by pro-life leaders in the United Kingdom—for example, by Ann Widdecombe, a leading pro-life Member of Parliament (MP),[2] and by John Smeaton, the national director of the UK's oldest pro-life or-

---

1. William F. Maestri, "Abortion in Louisiana: Passion over Prudence," *Linacre Quarterly* 57, no. 4 (1990): 42.

2. "At the Second Reading we had a majority in favour of the Bill but many people who supported us at Second Reading only did so on the understanding that we would amend the Bill in Committee and we simply did not have a majority to carry the Bill through in its original form. We had to take account of the fact that 92% of all late abortions are performed on perfectly fit and healthy children and faced with a prospect of losing the Bill altogether, we had to ask whether we should lose thousands of unborn lives or whether we should make a compromise which would save 92% of those lives. If one is faced with a shipwreck and can only save some of the people on board then surely it is better to save these than not to merely because all cannot be saved. That was our situation and we adopted the clause on handicaps purely in order to save the Bill and not because we all wanted it." Ann Widdecombe, MP, to Miss M. Denney, 29 Dec. 1988. Chapter 1 provides fuller details of the bill.

ganization, the Society for the Protection of Unborn Children (SPUC).[3] An attempt to save lives is a "first consideration," says Smeaton, that is revealed by "ordinary common sense."[4] In other words, it is obvious.

The rightness of supporting restrictive abortion legislation to save lives seemed obvious to me when, in 1987–88, as an undergraduate student, I took a year out from my studies to be employed by SPUC as part of the campaign team for the UK's most significant attempt to restrict abortion. With virtually all of the pro-life movement, I was a committed supporter of the Abortion (Amendment) Bill promoted by David Alton, MP, to reduce the time limit up to which abortions could take place. Some features of the campaign for the bill will be described in Chapter 1. At that time the pro-life movement was publicly united in its support for the bill and there was no philosophical debate about the ethics of supporting such restrictive legislation because there seemed to be no case to answer. David Alton noted that among the twenty thousand or so letters he received during the campaign for his bill,[5] only three or four maintained that anything other than total repeal of the abortion law was unacceptable.[6]

In 1998, ten years after the campaign for his bill, Alton provided the ethical rationale that, in his opinion, justified the attempt to restrict the abortion time limit: "I am, myself, an 'absolutist' but the ethical rationale for the Bill supported by the Catholic hierarchy and others, was that any measure which saved a single life, reduced the total number of abortions, and re-opened the debate, was entirely acceptable from an ethical point of view."[7] The ethical rationale for supporting the bill in 1988 had not changed by 1998, and in 2004 support for restrictive legis-

---

3. John Smeaton, interview by author, 8 Aug. 1998. Smeaton made the comparison between supporting restrictive legislation and saving lives in an emergency situation during this interview.

4. Ibid.

5. David Alton, *Whose Choice Anyway?* (Basingstoke: Marshall Pickering, 1988), 69.

6. David Alton, letter to the author, 5 May 1998. He noted that no pro-life organization objected to the bill on those grounds. On the contrary, he wrote that all the pro-life groups gave him "enthusiastic and formidable support."

7. David Alton, letter to the author, 15 April 1998.

lation as a means of "saving lives" still dominates much thinking in pro-life circles in the UK, the United States, and throughout the world.[8] The Catholic hierarchy of England and Wales, to which Alton referred, still stands by the position it held in 1988, and other hierarchies take a similar view, with papal approval being claimed in support.[9] Like many others who campaigned for the Alton Bill, I believed that the efforts to enact it would have been more than worthwhile if the bill saved even a single life. Indeed, the goal of saving lives, or even one life, was regarded generally as so laudable that there was very little consideration of the legislative means being supported to achieve that end.

Having committed myself to supporting restrictive legislation, it was somewhat disconcerting to realize later on that the justification for supporting measures like the Alton Bill "to save lives" was not as obvious as it had previously seemed. Certainly pro-life legislators were trying to save some lives in a situation where they were unable to save all. But was it really analogous to the emergency situation of a burning building or sinking ship, in which it was justified to save some lives even though one might not be able to save all? I gradually acknowledged that the analogy did not hold.

The Maxim "Women and Children First"

The principal objection to the analogy was drawn to my attention by Alison Davis, whose particular contribution to this book is acknowledged in the Preface. She noted that when saving lives in any emergency situation the maxim "women and children first" is universally

---

8. The comparison between voting for restrictive abortion legislation and saving lives in difficult situations has been made recently by John Finnis, "Restricting Legalised Abortion Is Not Intrinsically Unjust," in Helen Watt, ed., *Cooperation, Complicity and Conscience* (London: Linacre Centre, 2005). Within a single paper he compares legislators voting for restrictive legislation with a group of stalwarts rescuing some—but not all—children from a desert torture camp (sec. 5), with firemen rescuing some people in a burning building (sec. 6), and with soldiers rescuing Jews and gypsies from an extermination camp (sec. 7).

9. The teaching of John Paul II at *Evangelium vitae*, n. 73, is commonly cited as approving votes for restrictive legislation like the Alton Bill. What precisely has been taught will be considered in Chapter 9.

acknowledged. Those who may be regarded in some way as "weaker" are given preferential treatment, a policy that would appear to testify to a belief in the intrinsic dignity and value of human beings: human beings are valuable for who they *are,* not for what they can *do.* The value of those who are "weaker" is no less than that of those who are "stronger." In contrast to the world's standards—which are inclined to esteem those who are higher in status, richer, more powerful, or more talented—the maxim "women and children first" is an important reminder, by giving priority to the "weaker," of the equal value and dignity of all people.

With respect to restrictive abortion legislation, however, one sees that the principle of "women and children first" is inverted. It is true that all the unborn who are threatened by abortion are vulnerable (just as all—men, women, and children alike—are vulnerable in a burning building), but some are more vulnerable than others. Laws to restrict abortion do not even protect unborn children randomly, but give priority to those who, because they have favorable characteristics, can be judged to be less vulnerable. As Chapter 1 will describe, those with the unfavorable characteristics of being disabled, younger, conceived after rape, etc., tend not to be included in laws to restrict abortions. If the existence of an abortion law were truly an emergency situation in which the maxim "women and children first" were applied, the most vulnerable of the unborn would be given first place, not last, in attempts to save some lives.

Second, we need to make a distinction between the actions of individuals, such as firefighters, whose attempts to save lives are necessarily restricted by the physical environment in which they are working, and the actions of legislators who are not performing the same sort of "individual" action for the good of *some* people but rather a public policy legislative action that, with respect to the right to life, must focus on the good of *each* and *all.* Natural disasters, carelessness, or willful disregard for public order and the rights of others are the normal causes of emergency situations, and the passing of laws to cope with an emergency situation in order to save lives and preserve public order may be required of legislators. In such instances legislators would be attempting to provide a way of helping to overcome the emergency situation. By contrast, if the existence of an abortion law constitutes an emergency situation, legislators themselves—as a group—can normally be regarded as responsible for the problem itself.[10] And if the response to the emergency situation is to pass a law prohibiting only some abortions, this suggests that such a law is an appropriate legislative response to the emergency, whereas in fact anything short of prohibiting all abortions is an inadequate *legislative* response. Much more on this could be said but, in short, it is not so "obvious" that voting for restrictive legislation is analogous to saving lives in an emergency situation like that of a burning house.

A Universal Problem

The subtitle of this book highlights a concern for *pro-life solidarity with "the last and least,"* and I argue in Chapter 1 that support for restrictive abortion legislation violates the requirements of solidarity. The problem that unjust abortion laws pose to the pro-life movement is almost universal, and this book attempts to shed light on matters that are likely to be relevant to all readers, whether in the Americas or in Europe, Africa, Asia, or Australasia. The book is not about changing the laws of any particular country, though the experience of the UK pro-life movement is sometimes presented to illustrate points that are of

---

10. In most countries legislatures have been responsible for passing abortion laws. The situation in the United States is different insofar as a "right" to abortion has been established since 1973 by judicial decree. Even if the U.S. federal legislature cannot be held responsible for that judicial decree itself, it has assumed a subsequent responsibility insofar as it has been unwilling to support a proposal for a constitutional amendment—such as a proposed Human Life Amendment—to establish the right to life of all from conception. Such an amendment would overturn the Supreme Court's *Roe v. Wade* (1973) ruling in the same way that the thirteenth and fourteenth constitutional amendments overturned the Supreme Court's *Dred Scott v. Sandford* (1857) ruling upholding slavery. However, even if particular legislatures—whether at the state or the federal level—cannot be held "responsible" for the existence of an abortion law (just as pro-life legislators who have done everything possible to uphold the right to life are not personally "responsible"), individual legislators must always fulfill their legislative responsibilities *in accordance with law*. This responsibility—which, as Chapter 5 discusses, is normally performed under solemn oath—requires fundamentally that they not support legislation that, being intrinsically unjust (even if "restrictive"), cannot be properly regarded as "law."

universal relevance. In Chapter 1 the experience of the UK pro-life movement is presented as illustrative of the problems inherent in support for restrictive abortion legislation. Though the pro-life movements in many countries have tried to restrict abortion in similar ways, the restrictions placed on state and federal legislatures by the U.S. Supreme Court's *Roe v. Wade* (1973) ruling have meant that such problems are not currently encountered in the United States. What is described in Chapter 1 will be highly relevant to the U.S. pro-life movement if (or, as is anticipated, when) the Supreme Court overturns *Roe v. Wade* and if abortion legislation then becomes the responsibility of state legislatures. William F. Maestri, envisaging the reversal of *Roe v. Wade*, indicates how state legislatures, if unwilling to protect all the unborn, may be willing to restrict abortion, and he proposes what in his view would be an appropriate (Catholic) pro-life approach: "Legislation after *Roe* may have to start with the protection of the unborn from abortion except in those cases where rape, incest and severe genetic defects are present as well as the physical life of the mother is in danger. There seems to be a moral consensus for such an approach to abortion policy. Many unborn children now aborted would be saved."[11] Maestri expresses a widely held view, but this book argues that the pursuit of such legislation, or support for it, is not an ethical option.

As noted, this book is not about changing the UK abortion law, and references in Chapter 1 to the pro-life movement's attempts to change the law should be regarded as illustrative of a general, almost universal problem. For those wanting to be more informed about the illustrations, details of the law prior to the Abortion Act 1967, as well as the text of the 1967 Act itself, are provided in the Appendices. Also provided are the texts of subsequently enacted changes and two versions of the Abortion (Amendment) Bill sponsored by David Alton, MP. The UK abortion law has remained substantively unchanged since 1990, and from that date there have been no legislative campaigns by the pro-life movement to change that law. The 1990 change in the law—which will be described—was regarded as a disaster by the pro-life move-

---

11. William F. Maestri, "The Abortion Debate after Webster: The Catholic-American Moment," *Linacre Quarterly* 57, no. 1 (1990): 52.

[handwritten: This is a crucial factor in the political calculus of the wisdom of introducing bills to limit abortion]

ment. It demonstrated how little parliamentary support existed for the pro-life movement, and subsequent parliamentary elections further eroded that support.[12] Though the UK pro-life movement has remained active on many fronts—for example, in its opposition to the morning-after pill, RU 486, embryo experiments, and euthanasia—an awareness of the diminishing number of its supporters in Parliament has been a factor in decisions not to campaign for legislation to restrict abortion. The focus in Chapter 1 on the UK pro-life movement's activities in the late 1980s and early 1990s should thus not be regarded, on account of the passing of the years, as an outdated description of the pro-life movement's attempts to change the law. It is, rather, a fully up-to-date account of attempts to change the law in the UK, and the issues described in Chapter 1 are still the relevant "battlegrounds" for many pro-life leaders.[13]

A Question of Law and Ethics

After the demonstration, in Chapter 1, of some practical realities of attempts to change abortion laws, subsequent chapters focus on some of the jurisprudential, legislative, and ethical problems encountered in such attempts. Note that David Alton maintained that "any measure"

---

12. Generally, but by no means exclusively, members of the Conservative Party have been more inclined to oppose (at least some) abortions, and the attempt to restrict abortion in the late 1980s coincided with a large Conservative majority in Parliament. In 1992 that majority was greatly reduced and in 1997 a Labour government was elected. Prime Minister Tony Blair and the Labour government have consistently supported anti-life measures.

13. Evidence that the UK pro-life movement's strategy for gradual change remains unaltered from the period discussed in Chapter 1 was provided in a recent article by Ann Widdecombe, MP, "At Last the Law on Abortion May Be Properly Upheld," in the *Times* (11 Dec. 2003). The article focused on the very issue—even to the extent of referring to a case reported in the 1980s at a Carlisle hospital—that the pro-life movement had focused on with its support for the Alton Bill: namely, that late abortions of babies capable of surviving outside the womb were particularly objectionable. And the article repeated the need to ensure—as had been sought in 1990 by Widdecombe herself, with the support of the pro-life movement—that abortion after 24 weeks should be allowed only for those babies with "serious handicaps" and not those with "minor or moderate handicaps."

that saved a single life was entirely acceptable from an ethical point of view. *Any* measure? Is no measure unacceptable? Moving away from the deceptively "obvious" focus on "saving lives," the question of changing unjust abortion laws is examined in terms of what it really is: a question of law and ethics. Chapters 2 and 3 draw attention to the fact that all "restrictive abortion legislation" (though not, as I shall explain, all legislation that might prevent some abortions) is not only unjust but *intrinsically* unjust, a key factor when considering the ethics of voting for it. Chapters 4 and 5 address the distinct ethical problem of voting to enact any legislation that is intrinsically unjust, and Chapter 6 addresses some unsatisfactory arguments—especially the claim that it is legitimate to support the "lesser evil"—that have sometimes been presented as justifying votes for restrictive abortion legislation. Concrete legislation is complex, and an analysis of ways to promote the pro-life cause by legislative means is undertaken in the two following chapters.

A range of legislative proposals that would restrict abortion or might prevent women from having abortions is considered in Chapter 7. Some of the proposals considered—such as regulations requiring counseling, informed consent, or parental consent for minors—have been generally supported by the pro-life movement in the United States and enacted in some state legislatures. Some of my pro-life friends in the United States have argued that support for such proposals is justified because the *Roe v. Wade* ruling prevents state legislatures from prohibiting abortion: were a state to pass a law *prohibiting* abortions, it would be struck down by the courts. It is claimed that the unusual situation in the States justifies support for regulatory legislation (which the courts would uphold) dealing with such matters as counseling and consent in order to prevent as many abortions as possible. In fact, such proposals have also been considered, and even enacted, in other countries, and I do not accept that the judicial restrictions imposed on state legislatures in the United States makes their acceptance of such measures a special case. I argue that the necessary consideration is whether the specific proposal under consideration is itself *just,* and that factors such as whether it is impossible to prohibit all abortions because such laws would be struck down as invalid, or because pro-life legislators are in a minority, do not justify voting for prohibitory or regulatory proposals that are in themselves unjust.

In Chapter 7 I also discuss proposals to prohibit particular methods of abortion, like partial-birth abortion (PBA), and argue that such proposals cannot be regarded as equivalent to those that would, say, prohibit abortion after the unborn child has reached a certain gestational age. Indeed, a proposal to ban the procedure of PBA could be just, and justly enacted. A proposal to ban PBA, as well as other just proposals described in the chapter—e.g., proposals to prohibit public funding for abortion, or to establish that medical and other personnel have the right not to be involved in offenses against life—could prevent some abortions, and yet not fall within the category that I label *"restrictive abortion legislation."* I use this term to refer to proposals that would in themselves restrict abortion to particular (categories of) unborn children—the proposals referring to such things as the gestational age of the unborn child, his or her state of health or disability, the circumstances of the conception, etc. Such proposals should be distinguished from other proposals that might benefit the pro-life cause. I argue that it is never licit to support *restrictive abortion legislation* (because the legislation is intrinsically unjust), but that it can be licit to support legislation that might prevent abortions (provided that the legislation is, in fact, just). I accept that the distinction between "restrictive abortion legislation" and "legislation that might prevent abortions" may not be immediately apparent, but it is a real and necessary distinction, as will be explained. At any rate, it is important to keep in mind that a precise meaning is attached to the term "restrictive abortion legislation."

The "voting opportunities" of Chapter 8 refer to the range of votes encountered at different stages of the legislative process. A simplified generic legislative system is presented in order to discuss the main considerations, and it is assumed that the legislature can freely determine its own laws. In some countries, such as the United States, legislators do not have such freedom to enact fully protective laws, but nevertheless the principles outlined in this chapter—in particular, the requirement for justness in laws—are universally applicable.

Although there is a widespread belief that in his encyclical letter *Evangelium vitae* (1995) Pope John Paul II has given his approval for restrictive abortion legislation, Chapter 9 shows that what might appear to be an "obvious" interpretation must be reconsidered. The thesis promoted in this book is that good motives and intentions can never justify voting to enact any legislation that is intrinsically unjust, and that all "restrictive abortion legislation" is, in fact, intrinsically unjust. Chapter 9 argues that this thesis is consistent with the teaching of the magisterium, including that of *Evangelium vitae*.

A Specific Focus

The pro-life movement consists of Christians of all denominations and members of all faiths and none. It is not the exclusive preserve of Roman Catholics, though the concern of Catholics to guarantee the right to life of all is well known. This book generally engages in discussion with Catholic academics and pro-life leaders, acknowledging the particular weight that must be attached to the Church's traditional teaching on law and ethics as well as recent magisterial pronouncements. Though Catholics are the leading participants in this book's discussion, the discussion itself—which is principally philosophical rather than theological—is also relevant to non-Catholic pro-lifers, irrespective of their religious belief or unbelief: whether restrictive abortion legislation is just or unjust and whether it is ethical to vote for it is determined principally by sound reason, which may or may not be associated with religious profession. Sound reason and true religion do not contradict each other,[14] and this book does not provide an argument that is applicable only for Catholics. This book restricts its attention to practical and philosophical matters, but if its argument is essentially correct there will be a range of theological matters that could also be profitably pursued.

Leaving the book's practical and philosophical focus for a moment, I would like to draw attention to two biblical passages that have been at the forefront of my mind when considering the central concern of this book, passages that fellow Christians might also want to reflect on while reading the following chapters. In view of the exclusion of the most vulnerable of the unborn in restrictive legislation, the first passage draws attention to how the unjust exclusion of some unborn children also involves an exclusion of Christ: "Truly I tell you, just as you did not do it to one of the least of these, you did not do it to me" (Matt. 25:45). The second passage serves to question the rationale underlying

---

14. See John Paul II, Encyclical Letter, *Fides et Ratio* (1998), n. 43.

support for restrictive legislation. The thinking seems to be not only that it is better to have a law permitting a limited number of abortions than a law permitting a greater number of abortions, but that it is right *to support* a law permitting a limited number of abortions in order to overturn or prevent the enactment of a law permitting more abortions. My concern is that this rationale for acting is indistinguishable from the rationale presented by Caiaphas to justify Jesus' death: was it not expedient, he argued, to allow one man to die rather than have the whole Jewish nation perish (John 11:50)? The underlying rationale for restrictive legislation would similarly appear to be: is it not expedient to allow abortion for a limited number of unborn children rather than have much larger numbers perish through abortion on demand?

This book does not, however, address these and other important theological matters. Nor does it address other areas relevant to the concerns of the pro-life movement—such as laws on euthanasia, embryo experimentation, or cloning—though the applicable principles should become clear to the reader. The book focuses on the practical, jurisprudential, ethical, legislative, and doctrinal dimensions of the question of supporting restrictive abortion laws. As a result of this focus other areas are not covered, and it is only fitting that recognition of a particular omission be noted here. For if this book is sometimes critical of the statements and actions of certain people or groups in the pro-life movement with respect to the question of restrictive abortion laws, there should also be an acknowledgment of the immense good pursued and frequently achieved by the same people and groups in their other important endeavors for the pro-life cause. This book is not a blanket criticism of the pro-life movement, but to have included an account that did justice to everything that is being done well—demonstrating commitment for the right to life of the unborn as well as compassion for women in the difficult situations of contemplating abortion, accepting a "crisis" pregnancy, or grieving after abortion—would require a book vastly longer than this one. And if, especially in the account of the UK pro-life movement's support for David Alton's Abortion Bill, this book expresses criticisms of others, I acknowledge that those same criticisms are also directed toward me for the part I also played in supporting a strategy I judge now to be indefensible.

PART I

PRACTICAL REALITIES OF RESTRICTING ABORTION

1. A DENIAL OF SOLIDARITY

Whether or not it is justified for pro-life legislators to vote for restrictive abortion legislation in a situation where there is no chance of a fully prohibitive law being enacted is ultimately resolved only by a thorough analysis of the various jurisprudential, legislative, and ethical dimensions of the question. These dimensions will be the focus of subsequent chapters. This chapter has a limited objective, focusing on the virtue of "solidarity" and, with respect to supposedly "pro-life" campaigns for restrictive abortion legislation in the United Kingdom, drawing attention to three underlying realities: (i) that laws to restrict abortion do not simply "save some lives" but always *exclude from protection* some unborn children who are also entitled to protection; furthermore, that those unborn children who are excluded can always be identified as being weaker and more vulnerable than those who are granted legal protection; (ii) that restrictive abortion laws, as well as the campaigns both within and outside legislatures to gain support for such laws, inevitably distort the truth of the pro-life perspective that "every innocent human being is absolutely equal to all others [and that] before the moral norm which prohibits the direct taking of the life of an innocent human being there are no privileges or exceptions for anyone";[1] (iii) that those unborn children excluded from legislative proposals to restrict abortion are further marginalized as a result of the campaign for the legislation as well as by any subsequent enactment.

"Solidarity" has emerged as a key concept in Pope John Paul II's social teaching. It is the virtue of committing oneself to the common good, which for legislators is achieved in the context of enacting law. St. Thomas Aquinas teaches that laws are necessary "in order that man might have peace and virtue,"[2] and a fundamental requirement of

[1]. John Paul II, Encyclical Letter, *Evangelium vitae* (*EV*) 57 (1995).
[2]. St. Thomas Aquinas, *Summa Theologiae* (hereafter *ST*) I-II, q. 95, a. 1.

peace is that the right to life of all human beings be guaranteed by law. A law, therefore, that prohibits some abortions but has the objective meaning (or intent) of specifically permitting or tolerating other abortions[3] is not only unjust; it violates what is fundamental for peace because it fails to secure the right to life of all unborn children. As John Paul II teaches in *Evangelium vitae,* there cannot be true peace unless life is defended and promoted.[4] He observes that the motto of his predecessor, Pius XII, was *Opus iustitiae pax*—peace as the fruit of justice—and notes: "Today one could say, with the same exactness and the same power of biblical inspiration (cf. *Isa* 32:17; *Jas* 3:18): *Opus solidaritatis pax,* peace as the fruit of solidarity."[5]

John Paul II defines solidarity as *"a firm and persevering determination to commit oneself to the common good; that is to say to the good of all and of each individual."*[6] The virtue of solidarity must be cultivated in order to secure peace, and laws are necessary for men and women to live in peace. In this chapter I will demonstrate that legislative support for restrictive abortion laws, frequently accompanied by protracted public campaigns by the pro-life movement, does not constitute *a firm and persevering determination to the good of all and of each unborn child,* and that support for restrictive abortion laws conflicts with true solidarity.

---

3. A law "permitting" abortion specifically authorizes abortion; it may even specify that women have a "right" to abort. A law "tolerating" abortion does not specifically authorize abortion or establish a "right" to abort; it may, however, specify that some or all abortions are "not prohibited" or are "unpunishable" acts. Such laws also violate the fundamental right to life that civil law must always recognize (see *EV* 71). Subsequent chapters highlight the relevance of the distinction between laws "permitting" or "tolerating" moral evils and explain why laws "permitting" or "tolerating" abortion are both to be rejected as unjust, even though they can be distinguished.

4. "There can be no *true democracy* without a recognition of every person's dignity and without respect for his or her rights. Nor can there be *true peace* unless life is *defended and promoted.*" *EV* 101.

5. John Paul II, Encyclical Letter, *Sollicitudo rei socialis* (1987), n. 39.

6. Ibid., n. 38.

General Features of Abortion Laws

In recent decades legislation favoring abortion has been enacted in many countries. This chapter concentrates on attempts that have been made by pro-life campaigners to change the abortion law in the United Kingdom, but the points highlighted for consideration are also relevant for those concerned about changing laws in other countries. It is possible that some of my remarks may not seem immediately applicable to some other countries. For example, some aspects of the UK experience have not yet been encountered in the United States, but it is likely that the American pro-life movement will face them in the coming years. Because of the 1973 U.S. Supreme Court judgments granting women a fairly broad "right" to abortion, state and federal legislatures have limited ability to change the abortion law. If the Supreme Court were to reverse its 1973 judgments and rule that the unborn have a constitutional right to life, then the legislatures would be similarly prevented from legislating on abortion, but in this case pro-lifers would have no objection because the legislatures would be unable to enact laws favoring abortion. The anticipated scenario is that the U.S. Supreme Court will overturn the 1973 judgments and leave legislation on abortion for individual states to decide. If this happens, the sorts of questions that have already been encountered by the UK pro-life movement, and that are described in this chapter, will emerge in states throughout the United States. The concept of "solidarity," highlighted in this chapter, has universal relevance even though it is discussed with particular reference to concrete experiences in the United Kingdom.

What, then, are the general features of abortion laws? A law granting women full freedom of access to abortion would allow abortion for any reason at any time during the 40 weeks of pregnancy, thereby denying the right to life to all unborn children. Most abortion laws, however, contain some restrictions, even if they are minimal, so that abortions are allowed subject to the fulfillment of certain criteria. If abortions are not allowed throughout the whole of pregnancy, a time limit must be established after which they cannot take place. Also, the reasons for allowing abortion can vary. For example, the law may or may not specify that abortion is allowed if pregnancy occurred as a result of rape/incest, if the child would be born disabled, if the mother lacks a supportive spouse or partner, if the mother is financially unable to support a child, if there are concerns (serious or otherwise) regarding the mother's physical or mental health, etc. The laws of a particular country may establish different time limits for different conditions, allowing, say, abortions for general health or financial reasons up to the 12th week of pregnancy, but allowing abortions after rape or if fetal disability is detected up to the 30th week.[7]

With the passing of the Abortion Act 1967 abortions became widely available in the UK. Abortions could be performed to save the life of the pregnant woman, or for the sake of the physical or mental health of the pregnant woman or any existing children, or if it were likely that the child would be seriously disabled. Up to what stage these abortions could take place was a matter of dispute. Commonly, the law was described as allowing abortion up to the 28th week of pregnancy, but pro-lifers argued that the law specified that abortions were illegal if the child was "capable of being born alive" and that, because some babies lived after being born premature at 22–23 weeks, no legal abortions could take place later than this stage.[8] The clause allowing abortion for the sake of the mother's mental health soon became interpreted so liberally that doctors sympathetic to abortion were able to cite this reason as their justification for performing abortions simply at the woman's request. The Act did not specify that pregnancy as a result of rape/incest justifies abortion, but in such a situation (as with virtually every other possible situation) abortions would be granted for the sake of the woman's "mental health."[9]

7. The discussion in this chapter focuses on the substantive (primary) part of abortion laws, which governs which abortions may or may not be procured. Later chapters will consider secondary aspects of abortion laws, e.g., regulations about how abortions will be funded, whether there are any conditions like counseling or a cooling-off period, who may perform abortions, and where they may be performed. Such secondary aspects of abortion laws may affect women's access to abortion.

8. The 1967 Act did not, in itself, set an upper limit for abortion. The upper limit was set by reference to the Infant Life (Preservation) Act 1929, which stated that anyone whose willful act caused the death of an unborn child who was "capable of being born alive" would be guilty of "child destruction." The 1929 Act specified 28 weeks of pregnancy as *prima facie* proof that the child was capable of being born alive.

9. The Abortion Act 1967 is reproduced in Appendix B.

Although the content of the United Kingdom's legislation may be different from that of other countries, attempts to restrict abortion—i.e., to prohibit certain categories of abortion[10]—in *all* countries are inevitably based on one or both of two particular factors. One factor refers to the period of time (often measured in weeks or, perhaps, trimesters) during which abortions may take place; the other refers to the particular reasons or grounds (mother's health, rape, disability, etc.) for which abortions may or may not be performed. Pro-life legislators, supported by pro-life groups, are faced with the prospect of being able to *restrict* abortion because other legislators have a variety of views about the degree to which abortion should be accepted morally and/or legally.

Nowadays abortion tends to be mostly accepted if it is performed as a means of saving the mother's life, if pregnancy occurs after rape, if the unborn child would be born disabled, and if the pregnancy is in its earlier stages. In keeping with this book's focus on the need for solidarity with "the last and least," I do not wish to overlook the tragedy of laws that allow direct abortion in either of the first two situations, where it is a tragedy not only for the child but also for the mother, who is already in a situation that calls for genuine care and compassion. In such situations the pro-life response should be to respect the inviolable dignity and value of the lives of both the mother and the child. For the purpose of demonstrating particular objections to legislative attempts to restrict abortion I shall, however, tend to give examples that focus on the last two situations—i.e., measures that would attempt to prohibit abortion later in pregnancy and when the child would not be born disabled. In many respects the status of disabled unborn children is at the crux of the issue, because one tends to find that attempts to lower the abortion time limit will be unsuccessful unless an exception is made that excludes disabled babies. The UK experience of excluding disabled unborn children from proposals to restrict abortion that are supported—if not positively promoted—by the pro-life movement can be viewed as a paradigm of the point this chapter seeks to make with respect to the

10. As note 7 said, this chapter focuses on the substantive (primary) part of abortion laws. A range of legislative proposals, discussed in Chapter 7, that address secondary considerations can also affect the abortion rate.

requirements of solidarity and the promotion of truly pro-life legislation that rejects exclusions.

Legislative Campaigns to Prohibit Late Abortions

In the years following the Abortion Act 1967 several bills, all of which failed to be enacted, were introduced in the UK Parliament in order to prohibit some (though not all) abortions. In the earlier years some of the bills sought to restrict abortions in a variety of ways, though a particular objective of most bills was to stop late abortions. The attempt to lower the time limit to 18 weeks was the sole feature of the Abortion (Amendment) Bill introduced in 1987 by David Alton, MP, and because the campaign for this bill stands out from all the other UK attempts to restrict abortion it merits particular consideration. The arguments and actions of David Alton, other pro-life legislators, and also the leading pro-life organization supporting the bill demonstrate how this sort of measure inevitably distorts the true pro-life perspective.

Recourse to False "Arguments"

The first point supporters of a measure to restrict abortion to 18 weeks have to address is *why 18 weeks?* What is so special about 18 weeks? Why choose 18 and not, say, 10, 14, or 22 weeks? David Alton acknowledged the need to address the question if he were to gain support from other legislators for his bill, and in speeches throughout the country and within Parliament he specifically raised the question, "Why 18 weeks?"[11] In the first parliamentary debate for the bill (which is, procedurally, its second reading), Alton tried to do two contradictory things. On the one hand he indicated that there was nothing special

---

11. For example, David Alton asked himself, "Why 18 weeks?" in a speech delivered during the early stages of the campaign for his bill, when speaking to a pro-life rally at the House of Commons on 27 Oct. 1987. The full text was reproduced in *Life News* 17 (winter 1987–88). The reasons he gave were similar to those he gave in statements on radio and television, in speeches delivered throughout the country, and also during the parliamentary debates to which I shall refer. I maintain that there is no good reason for choosing 18 weeks and that his persistent attempts to justify this time limit distorted the true pro-life view.

about 18 weeks; he noted that a range of limits had been suggested: "14, 16, 18, 22, or anything up to 28 weeks" and that "if an amendment [to his 18-weeks proposal] were suggested, provided it did not emasculate the Bill beyond recognition, I should be happy to accept anything that could be done to rationalise the law."[12] On the other hand, he proposed particular reasons, which need to be examined, for supporting the 18-week limit.

David Alton noted, as his first consideration, that the previous upper limit, established with reference to a statute—the Infant Life (Preservation) Act—passed in 1929, protected unborn children who were "capable of being born alive." The 1929 Act indicated, in accordance with the medical circumstances of its time, that an unborn child of 28 weeks should be regarded as capable of being born alive. David Alton argued that it was incumbent upon society to review its public policy, "given the gigantic strides in medicine and technology, where medical knowledge has increased by leaps and bounds," and that the decision to restrict abortion to 18 weeks was based on the factor of viability.[13] Alton's (pro-life) parliamentary colleague Ann Widdecombe, MP, explained the "validity" of the 18-week limit more clearly:

> Where do we draw the line? Is it at the presently recorded lowest survival rate of 24 weeks for permanent survival and 23 weeks for temporary survival, or at the point where we think medical science will move in the foreseeable future, or do we recognise as life the time when a child is fully formed, is sentient, and can feel pain and react to stimuli? We have all reached different decisions of conscience. The Bill is a valid attempt to set down a line, and I support the line that the Bill has set down.[14]

Having established the main reason, based on viability, for supporting the bill, David Alton argued: "By 18 weeks, a foetus is not just a clump of tissues, not just a blob of jelly. The child has sentience and can feel pain. If a light is shone at its mother's womb, the child will react and turn away. The child has a complete skeleton and reflexes. It pumps 50 pints of blood a day."[15]

---

12. *House of Commons Official Report ("Hansard"):* Second Reading of Abortion (Amendment) Bill (22 Jan. 1988), col. 1231.
13. Ibid., col. 1230.   14. Ibid., col. 1280.
15. Ibid., col. 1234.

In the attempt to promote a bill that they believed would save some lives, the pro-life legislators inevitably contradicted their true beliefs and thus made contradictory statements. For example, although David Alton acknowledged his personal opposition to all abortions by stating, "for me, abortion, whether late or early, whether legal or illegal, is the taking of life,"[16] elsewhere he said that "in my judgment 18 weeks is about the right time"[17] to establish an upper limit for an abortion. Ann Widdecombe urged her parliamentary colleagues: "We must decide when life is life and must be fully and absolutely respected,"[18] giving the impression that the Alton Bill and the accompanying debate had the objective of doing that. She exhorted other legislators to allow the bill to make further progress, because even if it were amended at a later stage in committee to create some exceptions to the 18-week limit (in particular, she noted a willingness to make what she acknowledged to be a "compromise" so that disabled babies could be aborted later than 18 weeks),[19] "what finally emerges will be a wise, humane, just and civilised Bill; and the present legislation [i.e., the Abortion Act 1967] fulfils none of those criteria."[20]

I deviate briefly from the main purpose of this chapter to note that Widdecombe's remarks would seem to indicate why she and other pro-life leaders fail to understand the fundamental moral objection to voting for laws to restrict abortion, an objection that depends primarily on their being intrinsically unjust, as I shall argue in later chapters. If the Alton Bill had been enacted, it would have had as a good consequence the prohibition of some abortions, but *the bill itself was intrinsically unjust*. In fact, whereas the previous legislation had regulated abortions so that those performing them "shall not be guilty of an offence under the law,"[21] the Alton Bill went further and specifically permitted abortions, saying that "A woman's pregnancy *may be terminated* . . . up to the beginning of the 18th week of gestation"[22] (my emphasis). No bill that permits or tolerates abortions can be judged to be either wise or humane or just or civilized, and Widdecombe's claim that the Alton Bill

16. Ibid., col. 1233.
17. Ibid., col. 1231.
18. Ibid., col. 1280.
19. Ibid., col. 1280.
20. Ibid., col. 1281.
21. Abortion Act 1967: 1(1).
22. Abortion (Amendment) Bill 1 (1).

exhibited these qualities—whether before or after the "compromise" to exclude disabled babies from the 18-week limit—must be rejected as false. Similarly, Alton had stated, as quoted above, that he "would be happy to accept anything that could be done to rationalise the law." "To rationalise" means "to conform to reason," and the law was incapable of conforming to reason as long as it continued to allow abortions. Support for restrictive measures like the Alton Bill would appear to be based on a fundamental error as to what is reasonable, just, wise, humane, and civilized.

The distinct impression gained from the statements made by David Alton and his parliamentary colleagues was that 18 weeks signified a decisive moment for determining the *humanity* of the unborn child, and thus the moral and legal unacceptability of abortion later than this stage. The pro-life organizations leading the public campaign to support the bill also contributed to this view. For example, the Society for the Protection of Unborn Children (SPUC) published leaflets and booklets responding to arguments against the bill. The standard response to the claim that "at 18 weeks gestation the foetus is only a potential human being" was that "by 18 weeks the unborn child is a fully formed, unique human being, with all its major organs, apart from the lungs, functioning. At this stage it is responsive to light, warmth, touch, sound and pain, and is even getting to know its mother's voice."[23] The SPUC response is similar to the statement by David Alton, already cited, and it is to be faulted for the same reason. The implication is either that "18 weeks" is a significant stage in designating the unborn child as a "fully formed, unique human being," or that at some stage *up to* 18 weeks—*by* 18 weeks—the child becomes a fully formed, unique human being. The impression is given that the existence of major organs, and being responsive to light, pain, etc., are particular reasons for stopping abortion after 18 weeks. By implication, abortion could be regarded as less objectionable before 18 weeks (if at all), or at least before the unborn child is "fully formed" and responsive to light, pain, etc. Alton's statement, quoted above, included the remark that "by 18 weeks, a foe-

23. This was stated in the booklet *Facts on the Abortion (Amendment) Bill* (1987) and also in the widely distributed leaflet *Back the Alton Bill: Fight with Fact* (1987), both of which were published by SPUC.

tus is not just a clump of tissues, not just a blob of jelly." This remark was made to gain support for his 18-week limit but undermines the truth of the pro-life view because it suggests that before 18 weeks (or at least during some stage up to 18 weeks), abortion is (more) justified, the fetus being "just a clump of tissue" or "a blob of jelly" and not truly a human being. In fact, the fetus is *never* "just a clump of tissue" or "a blob of jelly," and Alton's remark undermines the case for arguing that earlier abortions are not ethically good choices. Indeed, some supporters of the bill, like Dale Campbell-Savours, MP (sometimes cited as a leading "pro-life" MP), specifically linked support for the bill with an appeal for legislation to ensure that women would be able to have *earlier* abortions.[24]

Another argument Alton advanced to prohibit abortions after 18 weeks was the particularly unpleasant procedure of later abortions, which he described in vivid detail, noting how "it is a corrupting and degrading business for the medical staff" and that "the nature of the operation that I described can be undertaken only by a doctor and a nurse if it is undertaken so late in pregnancy."[25] By implication, earlier abortions (which were specifically permitted by his bill) would be considered less (if at all) objectionable because they were less (if at all) unpleasant. The argument implied that later abortions alone were "corrupting and degrading for the medical staff" and that earlier and/or non-surgical (i.e., chemical) abortions were morally distinguishable from the abortions after 18 weeks that his bill would prohibit.

I accept that pro-life legislators and organizations should give full information about the development of the unborn child, and the reality of abortion procedures. It is entirely legitimate for pro-life presentations to describe the development of a child from conception through

---

24. Dale Campbell-Savours, MP: "My hon. Friend the Member for Barking (Ms. Richardson) referred to a Bill that she brought before the House in 1981 [which would have enabled women throughout the country to gain access to National Health Service abortions early in pregnancy]. I agonised long and hard over that Bill. I am convinced now that in principle she is right. If we are to bring in legislation that will draw women into earlier abortions, we must set up the arrangements to facilitate that." *Hansard* (22 Jan. 1988), col. 1283.

25. Ibid., col. 1235.

the different stages of 8, 12, 18, 24 weeks, and so on, and to describe the different abortion methods. Such descriptions are, however, merely *points of information*. The *argument* against abortion is that human life begins at conception and that killing a human being is morally wrong; the other factors relating to the child's development and methods of abortion are secondary and do not constitute arguments.[26] The reason why pro-life legislators and campaigners distort the pro-life view when campaigning for restrictive legislation is that they fail to distinguish between points of information and arguments. Factors such as the unborn child's viability, ability to feel pain, possession of the appearance of a born human being (i.e., not "just a clump of tissues" or "blob of jelly"), and the unpleasantness of methods of abortion, are presented as decisive arguments in determining the legal (and hence human) status of unborn children at a particular stage of development, instead of being regarded merely as points of information relevant to the wider question of abortion. The pro-life view is distorted by the presentation of "arguments" that are not, in fact, arguments.

Excluding Disabled Babies from Legislation to Lower Abortion Time Limits

Prior to the enactment of the Abortion Act 1967, parliamentary and public debate highlighted fetal handicap as a main reason for supporting abortion legislation, and the 1967 Act contained a clause specifically allowing abortion in cases where "there is a substantial risk that if the child were born it would suffer from such physical or mental abnormalities as to be seriously handicapped."[27] Polls in subsequent decades have consistently demonstrated overwhelming support for such eugenic abortions, and measures introduced by pro-life legislators prior to the Alton Bill had taken heed of this by promoting a lower limit for abortions procured for "social" reasons than for eugenic abortions. For example, in his Abortion (Amendment) Bill 1975, James White, MP, attempted (among other things) to lower the upper limit to 20 weeks

---

26. See the distinction between arguments and points of information (with respect to a different question) made by Karol Wojtyła in *Love and Responsibility* (London: Fount Paperbacks, 1982), 276.

27. Abortion Act 1967, clause 1 (1)(b).

for most abortions but accepted a higher limit of 24 weeks if the child "would be born with a major disability, whether physical or mental."[28] Subsequent bills—*also introduced by pro-life legislators*—similarly reflected the view that a discrepancy between the legal status of disabled and able-bodied unborn children (in which the former were treated less favorably) was acceptable if lives were thereby saved. Like the White bill, some of these measures attempted to lower the limit for most (i.e., "social") abortions to 20 weeks.[29] They differed from the White bill, however, in not specifying a 24-week limit for eugenic abortions; each of these bills contained clauses excluding abortions for "seriously handicapped" unborn children from the 20-week limit, with the result that such abortions would still have been procured under the terms of the 1967 Act, arguably as late as 28 weeks. (Other, equally unsuccessful, measures had attempted to establish a general upper limit of 24 weeks.)[30]

Seen in its historical context, David Alton's bill was by no means an isolated measure but the latest in a series of measures introduced over a thirteen-year period in which campaigns had been waged with relentless consistency. The creation of a legal distinction between the status of disabled and able-bodied unborn children had been proposed by the pro-life movement over a long period, and the events that unfurled during the passage of the Alton Bill cannot be viewed as exceptional.

It is appropriate to note at this point that in the years immediately prior to David Alton's bill, SPUC had expressed serious concerns about attempts to lower the abortion time limit based on an awareness that the 1967 Act upheld some, albeit minimal, protection for some unborn children that might be undermined if an attempt to lower the time limit backfired; SPUC's concerns were thus about tactics (or "political strategy"), not ethics. When the time-limit question was finally re-

---

28. Abortion (Amendment) Bill 1975, clause 7(b).

29. Attempts to restrict social abortions to 20 weeks, which specifically excluded the abortion of "seriously handicapped" babies from this lower limit, were made in successive Abortion (Amendment) Bills: in 1977 by William Benyon, MP, in 1978 by Sir Bernard Braine, MP, and in 1979 by John Corrie, MP.

30. Bills to prohibit abortions after 24 weeks were promoted in 1980 by David Alton and in 1987 by the Anglican Bishop of Birmingham (in the House of Lords).

solved by the government-sponsored Human Fertilisation and Embryology Act 1990 (which determined that "social" abortions be allowed up to 24 weeks and that the time limit for abortions for disabled and some other babies be extended *up to birth*), the outcome was regarded as a "disaster" for the pro-life movement,[31] and some leading figures in SPUC then sought to distance themselves from the Alton Bill, which had been instrumental in leading to the disaster.[32]

While justly acknowledging its original concerns about the Alton Bill, SPUC's 1990 retrospective overlooked the fact that the organization had expressed its satisfaction with the assurances David Alton had provided, and that it had given unfailing support not only to the Alton Bill but also to subsequent similar attempts to lower the limit that culminated in the 1990 legislation. This section seeks to examine the factor of excluding disabled babies from legislation to lower the abortion time limit. And although it is only right to acknowledge that SPUC's leaders had, for some years, argued against supporting upper-limit legislation, it is also necessary to acknowledge that their concerns were not based

---

31. The decisive votes cast for the 1990 Act were reported under the main front-page headline "Disaster in Parliament," in *Life News* 22 (summer 1990).

32. See, for example, the article "Where Did Pro-lifers Go Wrong?" by Christopher Whitehouse, Parliamentary Officer of SPUC, in the *Universe* (28 Oct. 1990), in which he stated that David Alton had been "begged" to tackle a different aspect of abortion law reform, but that "once the Alton Bill had been introduced, the pro-life group in Parliament and SPUC had no choice but to back it." The following week Keith Davies, the National Campaign Coordinator of the pro-life organization LIFE, criticized as "lamentable" Whitehouse's attempt to put the blame on David Alton for the parliamentary disaster. He argued that as a paid full-time researcher to a pro-life MP, and as clerk to the All-Party Parliamentary Pro-Life Committee, Whitehouse himself bore part of the responsibility for not sounding a note of caution during the campaign in which he had played a significant part; see the *Universe* (4 Nov. 1990). A letter from Whitehouse published the following week stated (contrary to the impression given in his original article) that he had been speaking "in a purely personal capacity" and not expressing the official position of the All-Parliamentary Pro-Life Group or SPUC; see the *Universe* (11 Nov. 1990). In spite of his disclaimer, Whitehouse's article appeared consistent with the SPUC view, which was subsequently expressed widely, even ten years later, in August 1998, when I interviewed John Smeaton, who was then SPUC's national director, having been at the time of the Alton Bill SPUC's general secretary (effectively, the deputy national director).

on the ethics of supporting such legislation but on the strategy of supporting upper-limit legislation in view of the particular situation in the UK, and these concerns were overcome after discussions with David Alton. The week after Alton announced (at the annual SPUC conference in September 1987) that he would introduce his "18-weeks" bill, SPUC's view was expressed in the *Universe*. After noting that "SPUC, which in the past has had reservations about supporting a Bill concerned with abortion deadlines, warmly welcomed Mr. Alton's initiative,"[33] the reporter quoted Phyllis Bowman, then SPUC's national director:

> Our greatest fears with this kind of Bill have always been that it would undermine the 1929 Infant Life Preservation Act—which protects all babies capable of being born alive—and that it would end up a weak Bill, with a ban at, say 24 weeks, or exemptions for babies with handicaps. However, Mr. Alton has assured us that his Bill will not undermine the 1929 Act; he stands firm on 18 weeks and no exemptions, and has said that if the Bill was to become weakened through a number of amendments he would rather give it up altogether.[34]

Bowman's remarks were consistent with David Alton's public statement at the SPUC conference the previous week. A disabled delegate, aware that previous bills to lower the time limit had, from their inception, contained an exclusion for disabled fetuses, publicly asked whether Alton would accept an amendment at a later stage excluding disabled fetuses, and Alton replied that he would not. In view of the historical reasons for excluding disabled unborn children in the previous lower-limit bills, Alton's statement to the conference seems quite remarkable. Within days of announcing his bill a major criticism was that, if enacted, the bill would prohibit the abortion of disabled babies,[35] and Alton soon realized that he would not have sufficient sup-

---

33. Sandra Pajak, "SPUC, LIFE, Back Alton Abortion Bill," *Universe* (2 Oct. 1987).

34. Ibid.

35. Writing on the day that David Alton's bill was formally announced, Jane Owen wrote a full-page article in which her sole criticism of the bill was that it would prevent late abortions for "those who discover they are carrying an abnormal child" (*Daily Express,* 26 Sept. 1987). This view was expressed by reports with headlines such as "Bill

port if he were to stand by his original pledge to reject exclusion amendments. When the bill was published in December 1987 its longer title stated that it was "A Bill to limit the period within pregnancy during which an abortion may be performed, *subject to certain exceptions*" (my emphasis). Of the five exceptions to the 18-week limit, three referred to the mother's state of health and two to the condition of the unborn child, the clause relevant to the child's condition specifically allowing abortion later than the proposed limit "if . . . [i] the child is likely to be born dead or [ii] with physical abnormalities so serious that its life cannot be independently sustained."[36] In a statement accompanying publication of the bill, Alton said that under this clause abortion would be allowed for children with anencephaly, Potter's disease, and Edwards syndrome.[37]

The inclusion of the exception clause had been indicated in an earlier press statement, in which Alton acknowledged that support for his bill appeared to depend on his acceptance of exceptions for disabled babies, to which he expressed his opposition:

> I appreciate that some MPs will vote for an exclusion clause to allow for abortion on the grounds of disability. Parliament will have the opportunity to consider this specific issue but I will personally oppose such a move.

---

would bring more babies with handicaps" (*Independent*, 28 Sept. 1987). In a major article, Polly Toynbee criticized David Alton's bill. After noting that many women have late abortions because of delays in the health service, she expressed her first main objection to an 18-week limit: "The majority of late abortions, after 20 weeks, are carried out because the babies are suffering severe abnormalities which cannot yet generally be diagnosed until after the twentieth week" (*Guardian*, 1 Oct. 1987). In her article "Where David Alton Is Wrong," Annabel Ferriman wrote: "The new Bill would particularly hit those women carrying handicapped babies, since the results of most diagnostic tests are not usually available until the twentieth week of pregnancy. No exception will be made for women who find themselves carrying a fetus with Down's Syndrome, spina bifida or anencephaly, a condition incompatible with life" (*Observer*, 4 Oct. 1987).

36. Clause 1, (2)(a)(ii) of the original bill. The three other exceptions were (a) to save the life of the woman; (b) if there was immediate necessity to save the life of the woman; (c) if there was immediate necessity to prevent grave permanent injury to her physical health. In the last two instances the abortion could be performed if considered desirable by just one, not the customary two, medical practitioners. The bill, as originally presented to the House of Commons, is reproduced in Appendix C.

37. See the report "Alton Publishes Bill" in the *Guardian* (17 Dec. 1987).

Disability should not be confused with diseases like Potter's Syndrome or Anencephaly where a child does not have the organs necessary to sustain life. My Bill will obviously allow for terminations in such cases and in order to save the life of a mother or child. But there is a world of difference between Anencephaly and, for instance, muscular dystrophy. There would presumably be a public hue and cry if we allowed abortions on the grounds of colour or sex but we allow it on the grounds of disability.[38]

This statement is illuminating in two respects. First, it is consistent with Bowman's remarks, quoted above, which highlighted opposition to amendments for disabled babies. In view of Bowman's, SPUC's and Alton's undiminished public support for the bill at later stages, one should bear in mind to what extent their actions were compatible with their original statements. Second, the statement is self-contradictory and misleading in suggesting that opposition to exclusions on the grounds of disability is consistent with making an exclusion for conditions such as anencephaly and Potter's syndrome. Children with these conditions are the most profoundly disabled, yet Alton not only excludes them from his bill by denying them their status as disabled children but effectively denies them their humanity by stating that his bill would "obviously" allow for them to be aborted.[39] The exclusion of such babies within the original bill was overlooked generally by the pro-life movement, which, in the words of David Poole Q.C., the chairman of the Association of Lawyers for the Defence of the Unborn (ALDU), was "bordering on desperation for a victory, any victory" and more than willing to overlook the detail of the bill in its eagerness for

---

38. Press release by David Alton, MP, Sept.–Oct. 1987.

39. During the bill's first parliamentary debate, a pro-abortion MP, Peter Thurnham, asked David Alton's view about a baby who, according to Thurnham, was "featured on the front page of a newspaper recently which was born with two heads and is living. It is showing it is capable of independent life. Would he [i.e., Alton] force a mother to go through with such a pregnancy because the baby is capable of life?" Alton's response (to this situation which would appear to involve conjoined twins) was, "In those circumstances, of course, it would not be the intention of my Bill to force someone to carry a child." *Hansard* (22 Jan. 1988), col. 1257. The inclusion of the words "of course"—like "obviously"—would appear to indicate that Alton regarded abortion as not only a legitimate option in such circumstances but as an expected and possibly desirable option.

some legislative "success."[40] It seems that ALDU was the only pro-life organization to highlight concerns about the exclusions the bill originally contained. However, by making, first, the legal observation that "the language of the clause is alarmingly wide, and experience does not inspire confidence that the courts would interpret it restrictively,"[41] ALDU appears to indicate that the main objection to the clause was not so much that the sorts of babies Alton mentions (those with anencephaly, etc.) would be excluded from protection, but that other babies with less profound disabilities (such as those with muscular dystrophy) might also be judged to fall into the same category and therefore aborted after 18 weeks. ALDU made a valid legal observation, but the primary consideration lies in whether one can find an ethical justification for such an exclusion for *any* child.

Although the development, to be described below, of *further* exclusions for disabled babies in later stages of the bill's passage through Parliament encountered expressions of particular concern, I think it is necessary to recognize that the exclusions specified in the Alton Bill from the outset should not be regarded as a point of minor, esoteric interest, relegated perhaps to a footnote in the history of abortion law reform, but that they demonstrate the primary grounds for concern about attempts to restrict abortion. My concern that the pro-life movement unjustly excluded babies with profoundly disabling conditions such as anencephaly must, if the truth be told, be accompanied by an acknowledgment that I was as culpable as anyone else campaigning for the Alton Bill, in that I hardly observed or particularly cared about the exclusions. Contemporaneously with the Alton Bill, pro-lifers were arguing against using organs from aborted anencephalic babies for transplantation.[42] Like many others, I failed to see that the credibility of the pro-life movement with respect to that specific issue, as well as generally, was undermined by its support for the Alton Bill with the anencephaly exclusion. In my view, the statement that abortions would "obviously"

---

40. David Poole, Q.C., "Abortion and Legislation," ALDU's *News and Comment* 37 (spring 1988): 1.
41. Ibid., 2.
42. Cf. Peter McCullagh, *The Foetus as Transplant Donor: Scientific, Social and Ethical Perspectives* (Chichester: J. Wiley & Son, 1987).

be allowed for anencephalic babies constitutes a failure to acknowledge and respect the value and dignity of human beings who, precisely because their lives are so short, should be specially cherished during their brief hours or days of life.

Having established that from the outset the Alton Bill reflected a negative and discriminatory attitude toward babies with the most profoundly disabling conditions, I shall turn now to the exclusions introduced during its passage through Parliament to allow abortions more generally for disabled children, which were regarded as *the* "disability exclusions." The ethical and jurisprudential aspects of such exclusions are not the particular concern of this chapter; for now, I am simply describing, on the basis of a concrete experience of campaigning for legislation (which even today has not been acknowledged in pro-life circles as being flawed per se), the sorts of practical decisions that will inevitably be made if support for restrictive abortion legislation is considered a legitimate option.

The assertion of SPUC's national director, when the bill was announced in September 1987, that David Alton "stands firm on 18 weeks and no exemptions and has said that if the Bill was to become weakened through a number of amendments he would rather give it up altogether,"[43] was not borne out by the contents of the bill published in December 1987. The lack of consistency with assurances that had been previously given was also revealed in a letter from Alton, dated 26 November 1987, several weeks prior to the bill's publication, to a pro-life campaigner who was concerned that an amendment might be considered to make an exclusion for disabled children. Alton no longer stood by his earlier statement, which expressed his opposition to such an exclusion, but rather, after stating his view that "the provisions relating to handicapped babies are most important and I will do everything I can to ensure that no exclusion clause is put into the Bill," wrote, "However, in the event of us being defeated in a Commons vote, I do not feel that we could destroy the Bill and lose the 92 per cent of late abortions which are done on perfectly healthy children for the sake of the 8 per cent who will be handicapped. At a minimum we will seek

---

43. *Universe* (2 Oct. 1987), quoted above.

strengthened protection for the disabled."[44] David Alton's statement not only indicated his willingness to accept an exclusion but effectively indicated, consistent with the events that unfurled, that such an exclusion would inevitably be made and that he and other pro-life legislators would accept it. These developments, one notes, took place before the bill was even published and before its first parliamentary debate and vote of 22 January 1988.

During the first parliamentary debate on the bill (the "second reading"), Alton was challenged by the objection that the 18-week limit would prevent women from having abortions on grounds of fetal disability, because the results of screening tests would not be available on time.[45] Although he stated that he "disagree[d] . . . about the legitimacy of taking life on the ground of disability,"[46] Alton expressed the view from the outset of the debate that he was prepared to accept an amendment to exclude disabled babies from the 18-week limit in order to protect the greater number (92 percent) of able-bodied babies who, according to statistics, had hitherto been aborted after 18 weeks. As he put it, "Given that 92 per cent of all late abortions involve healthy children, if an exclusion clause were included in the Bill in Committee to deal with the question of disability it would still be a worthwhile measure."[47]

I am not suggesting that Alton and the pro-life organizations supporting his bill believed anything other than that disabled people have the same right to life as anyone else. By trying, however, to gain support for a bill that had no chance of being enacted without an exclusion for disabled babies, their actions and statements distorted their true view, because they effectively colluded with the prejudices of those legislators who positively favor disability abortions. Legislators regarded as "pro-life" made statements contradicting the true pro-life view by implying that aborting an able-bodied child was worse than aborting a

---

44. David Alton, MP, to Mrs. C. Perry, 26 Nov. 1987.

45. Intervention by Mr. Dafydd Wigley, MP, *Hansard* (22 Jan. 1988), col. 1231. Numerous other interventions on the same point were made; for example, by Mr. Andrew MacKay, MP (col. 1239); Mr. David Steel, MP (col. 1242); Ms. Clare Short, MP (col. 1242); Dr. Lewis Moonie, MP (col. 1249–50).

46. Col. 1231.

47. Ibid.

disabled child. For example, Sir Bernard Braine, MP, who was at that time the chairman of the All-Party Parliamentary Pro-Life Group, stated during the second reading debate:

> For over 20 years, I have been concerned at the way in which a civilised country such as ours has permitted, and indeed encouraged, the deliberate destruction every year of 150,000 unborn babies, most of whom, if born, would have been perfectly normal, healthy children.... In cases where the mother's life is in danger or where there are indications of grave and permanent damage to the child if born, the majority accept that termination is justified ... The overwhelming proportion of late abortions are performed on babies which if born, would have been normal healthy children. There is only one word for that in my book, and that is murder.[48]

Those legislators who particularly favored abortion for disabled unborn children used terms which many disabled people find offensive; they undermined the dignity and humanity of such children by rejecting them as "grossly disabled"[49] or as possessors of "severe abnormality."[50] The pro-life response did not consist of an unconditional affirmation of the value, intrinsic dignity, and right to life of all the unborn, disabled and able-bodied alike, but rather colluded with this prejudice by emphasizing that most abortions after 18 weeks were performed, in Sir Bernard Braine's words, on "perfectly normal, healthy children," which suggests that those who do not fall into this category are "abnormal" and "unhealthy," and, by implication (and as the pro-abortionists believe), inferior. In addition, Braine's remarks about "murder" do not seem to apply to the abortion of disabled unborn children. At best, the pro-life legislators (and campaigners outside Parliament) presented a mixed and ambiguous message about their view of the status of disabled people; at worst, it seemed as if they shared the same discriminatory, "eugenic" tendency as pro-abortion legislators and society generally, and that their opposition to eugenic abortion was based not on a positive attitude toward disabled people but rather on a fear that able-bodied children would also be affected by the "slippery slope" effect of a eugenic law.

48. Col. 1245.
49. Terminology used, e.g., by Andrew MacKay, MP (col. 1238).
50. Terminology used, e.g., by Jo Richardson, MP (col. 1276).

I do not wish to imply that genuinely pro-life legislators supporting the Alton Bill possessed negative or derogatory attitudes toward disabled people. However, because the measure they were supporting was so radically flawed, their statements in support of it could hardly be anything but a travesty of the true pro-life view. The language of "doublespeak" that was to become a feature of the campaign for the bill should have been apparent from the speech in which Alton first announced that he was going to introduce an abortion bill, but at this stage his words were generally overlooked by an audience (of which I was part, and no more perceptive than the majority), which in anticipation of legislative "victory" failed to observe the means that would be adopted in the attempt to achieve it. In that first speech, at the SPUC conference on 26 September 1987, Alton stated that "if you believe, as I do, that post conception a child has begun its development as a unique new individual then this overriding right to life must always take precedence over any other claimed rights,"[51] and he expressed his opposition to eugenic abortions. However, accompanying this view was the incongruous statement that "My Bill is intended to spur the N.H.S. [National Health Service] into providing better facilities and earlier tests." Newspapers could not be faulted for reporting that, in Alton's view, the reduction in the time limit need not alarm those who support abortion because his opposition to later abortions was compensated by less (if any) opposition to earlier abortions. In particular, if there were earlier tests for disabling conditions there would be even less "need" for late abortions. This was the message presented not only by the mainstream media[52] but also by pro-life organizations. For example, SPUC's booklet *Facts on the Abortion (Amendment) Bill* responded to those objecting to the bill on the grounds that it "will prevent late abortions which are mainly performed on women bearing handicapped children," with the following statement which I quote in its entirety:

---

51. The text of this speech was reproduced in Alton, *Whose Choice Anyway?* 11–16.
52. The statement in the *Sunday Times* (27 Sept. 1987) that "Alton wants his bill to spur the N.H.S. to provide better facilities and earlier tests for abortion" accurately reported what Alton had said on many occasions. If this was truly what Alton wanted his bill to achieve, neither he nor his bill should have been regarded as "pro-life."

In 1986 of 8,276 abortions after 18 weeks, 648 (only 7.8%) were performed because the child was likely to be born handicapped. Regardless of whether one believes in abortion for the handicapped or not, the fact is that the new technique of Chorion Biopsy means that any handicap formerly detected by amniocentesis late in pregnancy can now be detected at 9–10 weeks thus eliminating the need for late abortions in those circumstances.

This is quite an extraordinary response for a pro-life organization, and different strands of its contents must be considered. In the first place, the statement did not merely give factual information but also made a judgment: in stating that *only* 7.8 percent of post-18-week abortions are for handicapped babies, it implied that *one should give priority to the far greater number of non-handicapped babies* who would not be aborted if an 18-week limit were set. The SPUC response failed entirely to express positively the right to life of disabled unborn children, opting instead for the inadequate qualification "regardless of whether one believes in abortion for the handicapped or not," an expression suggesting that, at best, this was an area where SPUC held a "neutral" view. Given what followed, however, the impression was given (contrary to the position truly held by SPUC) that pro-life campaigners were not unsympathetic to the view that abortion for handicapped babies should be allowed: SPUC referred to the "need" for late handicap abortions as though this were a legitimate option, and seemed to suggest that those concerned that such babies could not be aborted under an 18-week limit need not fear—because the new technique of chorion biopsy (chorionic villus sampling) would ensure that these babies could be aborted *before* 18 weeks.[53] SPUC did not express its belief in the right to life of disabled unborn children, and the argument it presented demonstrated at best that aborting disabled children was less objectionable than aborting able-bodied children. Indeed, SPUC omitted to say whether the former was objectionable at all.

David Alton expressed virtually the same view as SPUC during the

53. The SPUC statement was not, in fact, correct. Although chorionic villus sampling could detect some disabilities, the later test of amniocentesis would still have been required if one wanted to detect disabilities like spina bifida with a view to abortion. SPUC chose to advocate an 18-week limit using a "technological argument" that not

second-reading parliamentary debate. Responding to a criticism that screening for some fetal disabilities could take place only after 18 weeks and that his bill would prevent this,[54] he said:

> The hon. Gentleman is well aware that the new developments of chorionic villus sampling, combined with ultrasound scanning and amniocentesis, mean that, increasingly, the thresholds are being pushed back. Although I have already conceded that there is an argument on the crucial question of whether or not a person has the right to decide to terminate where there is a detected disability, will the hon. Gentleman also say a word about the 92 per cent. of late abortions that occur after 18 weeks and which involve perfectly healthy children?[55]

Pro-life legislator Dame Jill Knight, MP, acknowledged rightly that "almost all the flak against the Bill has been to do with handicapped children."[56] However, instead of maintaining without compromise the principle that disabled children had an equal right to life, the pro-life legislators and campaigning organizations acted as though the flak were justified, by arguing in support of the bill that these children could be aborted earlier and by implying that their particular concern was to stop "perfectly healthy children" from being aborted.

Contrary to his earlier assertion that he would personally oppose any move by Parliament to exclude disabled babies from the 18-week limit, Alton, with other pro-life legislators and the main pro-life organizations, was instrumental in having this exclusion made in his bill. Alton had indicated his acceptance of the exclusion at the second-reading debate and announced prior to the committee stage which amendments he had decided to table.[57] In the committee, the amendment to

---

only failed to assert unequivocally the right to life of all disabled people but was also factually incorrect.

54. Intervention by Peter Thurnham, MP, *Hansard* (22 Jan. 1988), col. 1254.
55. David Alton, MP, ibid., cols. 1254–55.
56. Ibid., col. 1251.
57. The *Times*'s political reporter, Martin Fletcher, reported on the day prior to the commencement of the committee stage: "[Alton] has already announced amendments for the committee stage that will allow abortions after 18 weeks—subject to strict safeguards—for mothers whose babies are likely to be born with severe physical and mental disabilities, and for girls under 18 who have been raped" (*Times,* 22 March 1988).

exclude disabled babies from the 18-week limit was not proposed by the pro-abortion legislators but *by a pro-life legislator*—Sir Bernard Braine, MP, the chairman of the All-Party Parliamentary Pro-Life Group—and it was supported by the pro-life legislators, including Alton. After being amended by the committee and presented again to the House of Commons, Alton's bill still attempted to lower the upper limit for abortions in most instances to 18 weeks. It also specified, however, that abortions could take place "up to the end of the 28th week of gestation" if "it is likely that if the child were born it would suffer from severe physical or mental disability."[58] I have already noted that it was disputed whether the upper limit for abortion was 28 weeks or several weeks earlier, when the child could be regarded as "capable of being born alive." By specifying this "end of the 28th week" limit, the pro-life legislators were, arguably, extending the period during which some abortions could take place.

In spite of the fact that SPUC had originally indicated serious concerns about an Alton-type bill, at no stage did it waver in its public support for Alton's bill. Because of parliamentary filibustering, there was no vote at its report stage and the bill made no further progress. If by this stage the pro-life movement had recognized serious problems with the bill, the filibuster could have been regarded as a fortunate way of ending its passage, but SPUC's activities reveal that it had put aside its previous concerns. SPUC, with the ongoing backing of other pro-life organizations, continued to support the bill even after the exclusion was made for disabled babies; it organized a mass lobby of Parliament calling for parliamentary time to be made available to resolve the issue; it supported the reintroduction of the bill (with the amendments accepted in committee) by another legislator, Ann Widdecombe, in the next parliamentary session; it successfully campaigned for the Alton-Widdecombe proposal to be dealt with as part of a government bill dealing with *in vitro* fertilization. For more than two years the pro-life MPs and SPUC campaigned for the proposal that would create an upper limit of 18 weeks for most abortions and a higher limit of 28 weeks

---

58. The Abortion (Amendment) Bill as amended by standing committee, presented to the House of Commons on 6 May 1988 at its report stage. See Appendix D.

for disabled (and some other) unborn children. Although SPUC later tried to distance itself from what happened by emphasizing its original reservations, the evidence shows that, far from expressing fundamental opposition to the developments of the Alton campaign, it actively and enthusiastically continued to support the Bill and wanted it to succeed. Support for this type of legislation did not diminish before the matter was finally resolved during the passage of the government-sponsored Human Fertilisation and Embryology Act 1990, which established a 24-week lower limit for most abortions, with abortion for disabled (and some other) children being legalized *up until birth*.[59]

Although it was understandable that SPUC's national director, Phyllis Bowman, should regard the 1990 change in the law as a "terrible tragedy,"[60] one could argue that the "tragedy" lay not so much in the outcome of the vote as in the pro-life movement's contribution to this outcome. As indicated above, a key "argument" advanced by Alton and others in favor of a lower limit was the viability factor—an "argument" that had been presented for at least sixteen years (from the time of James White's bill in 1974) until the enactment of the 1990 legislation. Many pro-abortion legislators finally opted for a 24-week limit on the grounds that in their view this was the stage of viability.[61] The pro-life movement had not presented legislative proposals that accorded with the view that all unborn children have a right to life from conception but had presented a false argument, objecting in particular to the

---

59. The section dealing with abortion in the Human Fertilisation and Embryology Act 1990 is reproduced in Appendix E.

60. Phyllis Bowman to SPUC members, 2 Jan. 1991.

61. Pro-life and pro-abortion legislators alike focused on the question of viability during the parliamentary debate for the 1990 legislation. Mrs. Virginia Bottomley, MP, the minister for health, opened the debate by arguing in favor of a 24-week limit that, she said, was favored by the Royal College of Obstetricians and Gynaecologists, because in its view "24 weeks should be the age at which a foetus is considered viable" *Hansard* (24 April 1990), col. 173. In reply, David Alton argued that other sources have defined viability differently, indicating that this would justify a lower limit (ibid., col. 174). A pro-abortion legislator, Ms. Clare Short, MP, backed a 24-week limit because "viability is reached at 24 weeks" (col. 256), and another pro-abortion legislator, Ms. Harriet Harman, MP, argued against supporting "a 22-week time limit, at which, I repeat, medical opinion is agreed that the foetus is not viable" (col. 262).

abortion of *viable* babies. In essence they won the principal part of their argument that viable babies should not be aborted; they merely lost on the secondary issue of whether viability occurs by 18, 20, 22, or 24 weeks.

As for the "tragedy" of the 1990 legislation allowing abortion up to birth for disabled babies, this consisted, I suggest, in the fact that pro-life legislators and campaigners were responsible initially for promoting the view that it was legitimate to accept one upper limit for most (i.e., "social") abortions and a different—higher—upper limit for eugenic (and possibly some other "hard case") abortions. The 1990 law enacted the very distinction that pro-life legislators themselves had been prepared to promote between the status of unborn able-bodied and unborn disabled babies. The only difference was that the degree of the distinction was greater than pro-life legislators had promoted. Having, as it were, promoted a principle that a distinction was legitimate, pro-life legislators have little grounds for complaint if other legislators are prepared to accept that principle and to go somewhat further with their practical application of it. In sum, the tragedy of the 1990 legislation lies not so much in what was enacted as in the sixteen years of campaigning for a series of measures that were flawed in themselves because they unjustly made a distinction between different categories of the unborn: older/younger, viable/non-viable, disabled/non-disabled, etc.

The exclusion of disabled babies from supposedly "pro-life" bills like Alton's can be regarded as a paradigm for considering the inadequacies of any attempt to prohibit abortion by incremental or "step-by-step" legislation, and not, as SPUC's 1990 retrospective tried to indicate, a negative aspect solely to be encountered in upper-limit legislation. In his 1990 analysis asking, "Where did pro-lifers go wrong?" SPUC's parliamentary officer, Christopher Whitehouse, indicated that the difficulties encountered by the upper-limit measure would not have occurred if David Alton had heeded the advice he was given in 1987 to focus on the "grounds" under which abortions were being performed, rather than on the question of "weeks":

> David Alton was begged to tackle the gross abuse of the Abortion Act through which 90 per cent of abortions are performed upon purely social

grounds. If successful, it would not have misrepresented the then legislative position that the upper limit was the ability to be born alive and not 28 weeks, and it would not have focused debate upon the perceived need for exceptions, in the case of the handicapped.[62]

The experience of the following years revealed that Whitehouse, like SPUC generally, failed to recognize that the approach that focuses on "social" abortions (often presented as trying to curb "abortion on demand") encounters exactly the same problems and objections as those faced by upper-limit campaigns.

Campaigning to Stop "Abortion on Demand"

After the debacle of the 1990 legislation, the pro-life movement moved away from the issue of stopping later abortions, and focused instead on the "grounds" for performing abortions. Opinion polls indicated then, just as they do now, that while most people favor abortion for "serious" reasons—after rape, or if the child will be disabled, or if the mother's life or health will be genuinely put at risk—there is less support for other abortions. Most people are not totally against abortion but are inclined to think that 180,000 or so abortions per year in Great Britain are "too many": they tend to oppose abortion for lifestyle or "social" reasons, i.e., they tend to oppose "abortion on demand."

Although there have been no major legislative attempts in the UK to stop abortion on demand, the pro-life movement has steadily promoted particular opposition to that sort of abortion. A major SPUC publication, *Legal Abortion Examined: Twenty-one Years of Abortion Statistics,* was produced in 1992. The introduction to this publication and the accompanying SPUC publicity gave the impression that SPUC would not be particularly concerned if abortions were performed on a limited scale for the "hard cases" but that its main concern was that abortions were being performed virtually on demand. The accompanying, widely reported press release quoted SPUC's national director, Phyllis Bowman:

---

62. Whitehouse, "Where Did Pro-lifers Go Wrong?"

David Steel's 1967 Private Member's Bill to decriminalize abortion was supposed to benefit women in difficult circumstances—mothers of large families, women carrying handicapped children, and older women whose health was likely to be endangered by carrying a pregnancy to term. In fact, the typical woman seeking an abortion under the Act is young, single, with no previous children, and carrying a healthy baby—the very type of case which David Steel persistently claimed the Act was not intended to facilitate as it would mean abortion on request which was not the aim of his Bill.[63]

Bowman (like SPUC itself) is opposed to all abortions, but in her attempt to highlight opposition to the practice of abortion on demand she effectively indicates, among other things, that aborting a disabled baby is more acceptable than aborting a "healthy baby." *Legal Abortion Examined* and the accompanying publicity highlighted the fact that "less than 2% of abortions are actually carried out on grounds of handicap"—the reason for which society most favors abortions—and that the overwhelming majority are carried out "on request."

It is undeniable that more abortions are performed, and for a wider range of reasons, than had been claimed during the debates in 1966–67 prior to the enactment of the Abortion Act 1967. This is a fact that can be stated. The clear implication of the SPUC publicity, however, is not that abortion is unacceptable per se but that only certain sorts of abortions—those for "less serious" reasons—are unacceptable. In this publicity SPUC did not criticize the Abortion Act 1967 per se for being a fundamentally unjust law because it allows *any* abortions, but simply criticized the way the law was working in practice to allow abortion *on demand*. This certainly was the *Scotsman*'s interpretation of the SPUC publicity, and it reported the publication of *Legal Abortion Examined* under the headline "Campaigners hit at *'misuse'* of abortion law" (my emphasis).[64] Another newspaper reported that "SPUC members accept that there might be a need for abortion if the mother-to-be faces risk to her life, serious damage to her health or where the foetus is expected to be seriously deformed. But in the grey area that labels a pregnancy as

---

63. The press release was widely quoted in local newspapers throughout the country and in national papers such as the *Daily Telegraph* (8 Jan. 1992).

64. *Scotsman* (8 Jan. 1992).

'unwanted' for non-medical reasons their feelings about the growing foetus are quite clear."[65] Although this does not accurately report the true view of SPUC members, the reporter cannot be faulted given the sort of material SPUC itself was promoting. In focusing on opposition to abortion on demand SPUC members themselves appeared to condone some abortions. For example, the chairperson of a local SPUC branch was quoted elsewhere as saying, "If we did allow abortions for all rape cases and others where handicap was suspected then 98 per cent of abortions every day would not be done."[66]

This sort of remark, as well as remarks that "less than" or "only" 2 percent of abortions are of disabled babies, do not merely state statistics. The figures are presented in such a way as to highlight the large number of abortions being performed "on demand." Concerns about disabled babies—who are "only" 2 percent of the total—and other "hard case" abortions are put aside in the interest of the greater number.

Pro-life legislators echoed statements by pro-life campaigners outside Parliament. For example, Alan Amos, MP, wrote: "The risk of handicap in the child accounted for only 1.9% of the total number [of abortions]. The large majority of abortions, an incredible and alarming 98%, are the so-called 'social abortions,' or to be more accurate abortion on demand. . . . This 98% are carried out on perfectly healthy children, on demand, and for social convenience."[67] The clear impression that one receives from such statements is that the abortions one should be concerned about are those on "perfectly healthy children." Amos and other pro-life campaigners do not suggest that the number of abortions of disabled babies is "incredible and alarming"—even though compared with the number of disabled babies born, a *vastly* higher proportion are aborted.[68] This fact is, perhaps, considerably more alarming, but it tends to be overlooked while the pro-life movement concentrates on the large number of "social abortions."

 65. "Fighting to Protect the Gift of Life," *Bury Times* (11 Jan. 1992).
 66. "Anti-Abortionists Gather Strength," *Rossendale Free Press* (11 April 1992).
 67. Alan Amos, MP, "Unborn Children Denied Rights to Life and Love," *Newcastle Chronicle and Journal* (13 Jan. 1992).
 68. In Britain about 20 percent of able-bodied fetuses are aborted, whereas more than 90 percent of fetuses with conditions such as spina bifida and Down's syndrome are aborted.

In principle, SPUC is against "hard case" abortions and its committed opposition to eugenic abortions is demonstrated by its establishment of and support for a group within it called No Less Human, which is run for and by disabled people and their families to promote the right to life of all disabled people.[69] Nevertheless, SPUC's public statements have tended to focus on the question of abortion on demand, as though the performance of other abortions were of little, if any, consequence. For example, a press release issued by SPUC in May 1992 to publicize one aspect of SPUC's "Heartbeat campaign" stated: "Today there are 40 million abortions per annum worldwide which means that every time your heart beats an unborn baby dies; less than 2 per cent for genuine medical indications including trauma following rape." In this statement, SPUC is not simply stating the fact that abortion kills an unborn baby but is highlighting the vast number performed for "non-medical" reasons. By referring to the comparatively smaller number performed for "*genuine* medical indications" (which would also include abortion after detection of fetal disability), SPUC is making a distinction between different categories of abortion. In particular, one would assume that abortion for a "genuine" medical indication was considered a legitimate procedure.

There are many instances in which pro-life individuals, groups, and legislators have focused on the practice of abortion on demand—as though the other abortions could be tolerated. The parliamentary motion—an "early day motion"—promoted by pro-life legislators in April 1993 to commemorate the twenty-fifth anniversary of the implementation of the Abortion Act typically highlights the practice of abortion for "social" reasons in such a way that others are inevitably overlooked. The motion particularly noted that more than 90 percent of the abortions were "for reasons merely of social convenience" and that "only 151 abortions or 0.004% of the total were performed in emergency to save the life of the mother." From what is stated in the motion one would think that the legislators, who were promoting this motion with the support of the pro-life groups, were concerned merely that the UK

---

69. The group, having formerly been called the SPUC Handicap Division, was renamed No Less Human in June 2002.

had such "*liberal* abortion laws" and that they would not have objected if the law restricted abortion to a smaller number. The motion does not specifically register any objection to abortion for disabled or rape babies—almost certainly because fewer legislators would have supported it if it had.[70] In the same year, SPUC's journal *Human Concern* reported that twenty-three members of Parliament delivered a letter to the prime minister "protesting at the manner in which the Abortion Act is being interpreted to allow abortion on demand"[71]—but not about the practice of abortion per se. In parliamentary elections, SPUC does not judge the acceptability of candidates with respect to whether they are against *all* abortions but merely whether they are opposed to "abortion on demand."[72]

70. The full text of the early day motion, presented on 27 April 1993 to commemorate the twenty-fifth anniversary of the implementation of the Abortion Act 1967, states:

> That this House notes with sadness that the Abortion Act first came into force twenty five years ago on 27th April 1968; deeply regrets that under the authority of this Act over 3.7 million unborn children have been killed, over 90% of them for reasons merely of social convenience, that only 151 abortions or 0.004% of the total were performed in emergency to save the life of the mother; observes that such liberal abortion laws have done nothing to liberate women, or to end the social problems for which they were hailed as the panacea; expresses its sorrow that the United Kingdom law has become a model for liberal abortion laws the world over; accepts that this legislation brings shame upon the House and upon the country; and believes that the time has now come for the working of the Abortion Act to be thoroughly reviewed and for Her Majesty's Government to bring forward proposals for humane legislation which strikes a more acceptable balance between the care of the individual mother, and the inalienable right to life of the unborn child.

71. *Human Concern* (winter 1993): 5.

72. Prior to the 1992 general election SPUC did not ask its members and supporters to discover whether their parliamentary candidates were actually *pro-life* but merely to discover (i) how they would vote "on proposals to tighten the grounds for abortion to stop abortion on demand," (ii) whether they would vote "to stop abortions after 24 weeks except to save the woman's life." (Abortions for "social reasons" were illegal after 24 weeks, and abortions after that stage would take place mainly if the baby were disabled.) From the questions set, it would seem that SPUC was happy for its supporters to vote for parliamentary candidates provided that they opposed abortion on demand and abortion of disabled babies after 24 weeks. Candidates who were in favor of the "hard-case" abortions (particularly after rape and for disability) before the 24-week

In a 1997 major publication stating its "aims, ethics and activities," SPUC acknowledged that "the principal focus of the pro-life political campaign in Britain is to tighten the current law to stop the practice of abortion on demand: a realistic legislative objective which would save as many unborn lives as possible in as short a time as possible."[73] If SPUC is ultimately successful in stopping the practice of abortion on demand this will have been achieved only by a process that involves undermining the right to life of "hard case" babies. Following SPUC's publicity for *Legal Abortion Examined,* one encountered other statements (issued, perhaps, by those who were not fully aware of the implications of their remarks) that similarly undermined the status of babies who do not fall within the "abortion on demand" category. In the letters page of the *Daily Telegraph* on 20 June 1992 the Rev. Paul Sidoli wrote: "Records show that 95 per cent of these [abortions] were healthy 'humans' who were simply 'not wanted.'"[74] Five years later Professor P. M. Stell made the same point, also in the letters page of the same newspaper: "More than 90 per cent of children who are aborted are the healthy children of healthy mothers in their teens."[75] These two statements, written by individuals who would not appear to be associated with pro-life organizations, were consistent with statements issued

---

limit would seem to merit the vote of pro-life electors. Prior to the 1997 general election SPUC issued a questionnaire to be used by members questioning parliamentary candidates. The questionnaire referred not only to abortion but also to the issues of experimenting on human embryos, population-control programs, and euthanasia. There was only one question about abortion: "If elected to Parliament would the candidate vote for or against tightening the grounds for abortion to stop the practice of abortion on demand?" If the answer was "for," the candidate was acceptable. Such candidates would qualify as "pro-life" even though they might favor eugenic and other abortions. SPUC's questionnaire for the 2001 general election similarly mentioned only objection to "abortion on demand," so that parliamentary candidates did not have to say whether or not they supported other "hard-case" abortions.

73. SPUC, *Our Aims, Ethics and Activities* (London: SPUC, 1997), 27. When I interviewed him, John Smeaton, SPUC's national director, confirmed this policy: "Abortion on demand is the issue which would probably be our first choice bill. It is arguable that such a bill would save the most lives in the possible circumstances." Smeaton interview, 6 Aug. 1998.

74. *Daily Telegraph,* 20 June 1992.

75. Ibid., 26 June 1997.

publicly by the pro-life movement, and they may demonstrate the impact that pro-life publicity can have on public attitudes. I contend that an impartial reader of these statements would assume that the writers were saying that aborting "healthy" humans is worse than aborting others, though this may or may not be precisely what the writers believed and intended to convey.

It is only a short step from this to the statement made by Robert Ripamonti, press spokesman for the pro-life organization LIFE (Isle of Man), during the campaign in 1994 to oppose or at least restrict the introduction of abortion to the Isle of Man, where the law differed from that of mainland UK. He said, "If the bill is to be used only in hard cases, fine. But let us tighten it up and make it for the hard cases, so that we do not have abortion on demand."[76] Ripamonti stated explicitly a view that, as I have indicated, was implicitly presented in the statements made by pro-life groups, individuals, and legislators. I contend that it is not possible to campaign to stop a particular category of abortion without undermining the status of the babies excluded in the campaign (e.g., disabled, younger or rape babies). Legislation excluding *any* baby from the protection to which she or he is rightly entitled should be neither promoted nor supported by any pro-life legislator or campaigner. I have highlighted how legislative exclusions in the UK have reinforced negative attitudes towards disabled unborn children, and also other vulnerable babies, such as those conceived after rape or incest, for whom abortion is commonly considered desirable. Continuing to focus on abortion on grounds of disability, I shall now consider more fully how campaigns to prohibit some categories of abortion effectively deny the humanity of those who are excluded from the restrictive proposals.

The Exclusion of Disabled Unborn Children as a Paradigm of the Denial of Solidarity

As noted in the Preface, the Alton Bill was a particular trial for Alison Davis. Since the early 1980s she has been a leading spokesperson for SPUC and the coordinator of No Less Human (formerly called

---

76. *Isle of Man Examiner,* 8 Feb. 1994.

SPUC's Handicap Division)—a group within SPUC of disabled people and their families and caregivers, who are particularly concerned about the eugenic aspect of the UK abortion law. Although she supported the Alton Bill in its early stages, she considered the exclusion of disabled babies unacceptable. Alton and SPUC argued that if the concept of an incremental approach to overturning abortion laws was justified as a means of saving lives, then the disability exclusion clause was justified—by the same logic—in order to save lives. Davis rejected the view that an exclusion could be made for disabled babies, and the logic of her position led her to reject exclusions for any baby, thus challenging the incremental approach SPUC had supported since the 1967 Abortion Act. During the passage of the Alton Bill I was aware of Davis's concerns but, like others, I overlooked them in the midst of the frenetic atmosphere that prevailed as the pro-life movement hovered on the threshold of its first major legislative "success" in twenty years. Given the logic of Davis's view, the exclusion of disabled babies from the Alton Bill (and here, I am referring in particular to the exclusion made during its passage, even though the bill, when first presented to Parliament, was similarly unacceptable given its original exclusions of the most vulnerable of disabled children) can be presented as a paradigm of the unsatisfactory nature of all legislation that grants the right to life to some unborn children but not to others.[77]

I have already referred to the inherently contradictory "doublespeak" of the campaign for the Alton Bill, and an awareness of this helps one to understand the incongruence of the words and actions of pro-life legislators and others supporting the bill. For example, even though she supported the bill after disabled babies had been excluded, Dame Jill Knight had previously acknowledged how such an exclusion would be regarded in the country: "If we send out from the House [of Commons] the message that handicapped people have no right to live, that is a very serious matter, and that is what people will think. I have

---

77. For an eloquent account, from her perspective as a disabled person, of the pro-life movement's lack of solidarity exhibited in accepting exclusions for disabled and other hard-case babies in legislative attempts to restrict abortion, see Alison Davis, "Ofiara, Na Którą Można Się Zgodzić?" (An acceptable sacrifice?), *Ethos* 61–62 (2003): 214–31.

A DENIAL OF SOLIDARITY 49

talked to handicapped people outside the House—[*Interruption*]. Clearly that is the implication. If the House sticks to the idea that a handicapped person can be destroyed, many handicapped people will have cause to be concerned."[78] How is one to reconcile this well-informed statement, recognizing the serious implications of excluding disabled people, with the facts: (a) that even during the debate in which Knight was speaking, David Alton and other pro-life legislators were expressing their willingness to make such an exclusion; (b) that the "pro-life" legislators were responsible for the actual promotion of the exclusion amendment; and (c) that Knight herself, as well as the other pro-life MPs, continued to support the bill even after the exclusion had been made?

Given that the views of disabled people, including those within the pro-life movement, were overlooked at the time of the Alton Bill, it is appropriate to place on record how they regarded the provision of an exclusion for babies who, like them, had a disabling condition. A letter from Alison Davis, published in the *Times* just after the second-reading debate, expressed the degree of offense that an exclusion clause in the Alton Bill would give to disabled people:

> If David Alton is right in saying that abortion after 18 weeks is wrong, those who support him only if handicap is excluded are admitting that it is acceptable to kill on the grounds of handicap alone. Speaking as someone with a detectable, abortable condition (I have spina bifida) I find this attitude disturbing, divisive, and as morally and ethically repugnant to the disabled as apartheid is to black people.[79]

Other pro-life disabled people have expressed concerns similar to those indicated by Dame Jill Knight. For example, Peter McLean, chairman of the SPUC Handicap Division in Scotland at the time of the bill, states that there is "no justification at all" for measures like the Alton Bill, and that they "have a detrimental effect on the attitudes of able-bodied people to the disabled. . . . The message was sent out from Parliament that disabled people are second class citizens. . . . Alton

---

78. Dame Jill Knight, MP, second reading debate of David Alton's bill, *Hansard* (22 Jan. 1988), col. 1252.

79. *Times,* 8 Feb. 1988.

didn't think of the long-term consequences such as how disabled people are seriously affected."[80]

Some campaigners for the rights of disabled people who are not involved with pro-life groups have expressed similar concerns. For example, Rachel Hurst, vice chair of Disabled People's International, says that by trying to stop some social abortions but not eugenic abortions, pro-life groups "are being extremely discriminatory and obviously show eugenic tendencies, even though they would refute them." She says she views "with absolute horror" attempts to stop social abortion that by their nature exclude disability abortions because "this is making scapegoats of disabled foetuses."[81] With specific reference to the exclusion for disabled fetuses in the Alton Bill (and subsequent legislation), Hurst argues that the lower status given to disabled fetuses reflects a view that "disabled people are not seen as human beings." Echoing the statement made by the pro-life legislator, Ann Widdecombe, MP, during the second-reading debate on the Alton Bill ("We must decide when life is life and must be fully and absolutely respected"),[82] Hurst expressed her view that the public debate to decide the time limit sought to address the question "when a foetus becomes a human being and when it is not." Whatever limit was chosen signified society's view that a human being exists at this stage and should be protected. If abortion for disabled fetuses is permitted after the chosen time limit, says Hurst, this signifies a view that that the possession of disability constitutes *a lack of humanity.* Thus, in Hurst's view, the exception for disabled fetuses in the Alton Bill "is complete discrimination about our humanity."[83]

Ruth Bailey, a disabled woman active in the disability rights movement, is not opposed to abortion generally but is concerned about the 1990 Act, which made a distinction between the status of disabled and able-bodied fetuses: "The concern here is one of principle—that impairment has become reason for affording a foetus less protection, and less value before the law. . . . How can disabled people be confident that

80. Peter McLean, interview by author, 7 Sept. 1999.
81. Rachel Hurst, interview by author, 2 Aug. 1999.
82. *Hansard* (22 Jan. 1988), col. 1280.
83. Hurst interview.

they will be protected from the implications or risks of new reproductive technologies?"[84] Bailey is not pro-life, but one wonders to what extent this may be due to a belief—similar to Hurst's view that support for legislation like the Alton Bill shows the pro-life movement's "eugenic tendencies even though they would refute them"—that the pro-life movement is not concerned about the rights of disabled fetuses or adults. Bailey says, "The anti-abortion position is disingenuous. They say, 'We are against abortion because it is the taking of a life.' But then they imply by their actions that some lives don't matter."[85]

I am not suggesting that *all* disabled people—whether within or outside the pro-life movement—are deeply offended by or feel excluded by the policy aimed at prohibiting social abortions,[86] but I believe that the pro-life movement must acknowledge the ineluctable fact that its strategy has caused considerable distress and dismay to many disabled people whose status is already undermined by negative discriminatory attitudes within society, attitudes that are in turn reinforced by the eugenic aspects of abortion laws. The deep hurt and sense of dismay felt by one pro-life disabled woman was expressed in a letter in which she explained why she could no longer remain a member of SPUC, the principal campaigning pro-life organization:

> I can't live with the fact—at least I do live with it very uncomfortably—that the pro-life movement remained silent about my right to life. My grandchildren's life and great grandchildren were told to wait their turn, there's a queue, you're on the end. Now and since that decision [to support legislation making a distinction between the upper time limits for aborting

---

84. Ruth Bailey, "Prenatal Testing and the Prevention of Impairment: A Woman's Right to Choose?" in *Encounters with Strangers: Feminism and Disability,* ed. Jenny Morris (London: Women's Press, 1996), 160.

85. Ruth Bailey, interview by author, 10 Aug. 1999.

86. For example, Agnes Fletcher, the parliamentary officer for the Royal Association for Disability and Rehabilitation (RADAR), speaking from a "pro-choice" perspective, did not share Rachel Hurst's view that the pro-life movement's policy to stop social abortions suggested that pro-life legislators and campaigners had "eugenic tendencies." Her opposition to attempts to stop social abortions was primarily because she opposes any measure that limits a woman's choice of having an abortion. However, she expressed the view that "my secondary opposition to it would be the eugenic implication of the law." Agnes Fletcher, interview by author, 20 Aug. 1999.

52   PRACTICAL REALITIES OF RESTRICTING ABORTION

disabled and able-bodied babies] there has been a holocaust of all children, but disabled, handicapped and mentally handicapped are *first* in the queue for death. People [i.e., those in SPUC] who could not give you justice or defend your right to life—that which is your due—will never give you charity. We could never proceed together [in the pro-life movement] until we have grieved over our grave omission.[87]

Although this letter was written in response to the pro-life movement's support for "upper-limit" legislation that made a distinction between the limits for disabled and able-bodied fetuses, legislation to restrict social abortions (or "abortion on demand") would similarly marginalize disabled people.

It is no wonder, then, that some people believe that the pro-life movement positively favors eugenic abortions. From the perspective of one young woman, Cathy Rafferty—whose view is particularly noteworthy because she is both opposed to abortion and disabled (she has cerebral palsy)—it seems as though eugenic abortion is supported not only by pro-abortion but also by pro-life campaigners. An article in which her view is expressed contains an introductory note stating: "Pro and anti-abortionists only seem to agree on one thing—that a different set of rules and morality apply when terminating disabled fetuses." Cathy Rafferty herself remarks: "How the hell do you think it feels when you're a teenager who's disabled. You're trying to cope with all the normal teenage problems *and* being disabled—and you see these two factions literally at war over abortion and the only thing they seem to agree on is that you are not wanted and your life is worthless. You tell me how you think that feels!"[88]

By focusing in its subtitle on the need for solidarity, this book draws attention to the reality that any attempt to restrict abortion cannot simply be regarded as a means of "saving lives," but always specifically involves the exclusion of some unborn children who are entitled to the

---

87. The letter was written as a personal letter in Sept. 1991 to Mrs. Janet Thomas, an employee of SPUC, and not as a public statement. Because its author has severed her contact with SPUC it has been impossible to contact her, and I therefore do not identify her. The letter expresses an important view that tends to be overlooked, and I have taken the liberty, with the consent of Mrs. Thomas, of quoting from it.

88. Amanda Seller, "Quality Control," *Young People Now* (December 1990): 25–28.

protection of the law. And the problem of supporting restrictive legislation is compounded by the fact that those excluded are always those who can in many ways be considered the most unwanted, the most vulnerable, the weakest—in short, those who are often viewed as "the last and least."

I have highlighted the exclusion of disabled fetuses as a paradigm of the problems inherent in *any* attempt to restrict abortion. Cathy Rafferty's statement provides the pro-life movement with an opportunity to consider more profoundly the different levels at which the question of exclusion must be addressed. At a basic level, Rafferty is concerned with the reality that the policies of the pro-life movement exclude disabled fetuses; this exclusion, however, rises to a higher level in so far as she views this exclusion as symptomatic of the view—which she believes also to be the pro-life view—that such fetuses are considered worthless. At a still higher level, through her sense of identification with these disabled fetuses, she considers *herself* to be excluded, unwanted, and judged "worthless." A pro-life supporter of restrictive legislation might reply that Cathy Rafferty fails to understand that the pro-life movement does, in principle, uphold the right to life of disabled people, and might inform her that the movement's support for the exclusion of disabled fetuses is merely a "political strategy" undertaken in order to save some other lives. This sort of interjection, however understandable and sincere, fails to understand the higher-level lessons to which Rafferty's statement points.

The salient aspect of Rafferty's statement is that she identifies exclusion and rejection of unborn disabled children with exclusion and rejection of herself. One notes that statements, such as those from other disabled people quoted above, also indicate that attitudes toward unborn disabled children cannot be dissociated from attitudes toward disabled children and adults. This identification —which is also detected in statements made by disabled women who are not necessarily against abortion per se[89]—enables one to consider more profoundly who is be-

---

89. When interviewed, Rachel Hurst emphasized that the disability movement did not take a position on abortion. In line with this she preferred not to express her personal view on abortion itself, but she consistently expressed opposition to eugenic abortions; Ruth Bailey described herself as "pro-choice" but expressed particular concern

ing excluded. On one level Cathy Rafferty, not being an unborn child, self-evidently is not being excluded by incremental measures; yet exclusion of babies with whom she particularly identifies means that on a metaphysical level she considers herself to be excluded just as much as the disabled unborn children themselves. In identifying attitudes toward and treatment of unborn children with attitudes toward and treatment of herself, Rafferty demonstrates the radical spirit that forms the basis for true solidarity. She has a "spirit of solidarity" with unborn disabled children because she shares the common factor of a disabling condition.

Developing the logical implications of this idea, one comes to realize that Rafferty's "spirit of solidarity" with unborn disabled children should also entail a spirit of solidarity with those unborn children who are not disabled, because she shares the factor of a common humanity with all unborn children. And, indeed, disabled and able-bodied people alike should have a spirit of solidarity with *all* their unborn fellow human beings—simply by virtue of a shared humanity. This spirit of solidarity requires an attitude of mind that rejects any attempt to exclude even one unborn child from the legal protection to which he or she is entitled.

Exclusions or Solidarity?

Martin Rhonheimer notes that "the culture of death is an alternative to that of solidarity, of *unconditional* respect for life."[90] In itself, restrictive abortion legislation represents a *conditional* respect for life; it protects the unborn provided they have reached a certain stage of de-

---

that disabled fetuses are discriminated against and given less protection; Agnes Fletcher, also speaking from a "pro-choice" perspective, according to which "my aim would not be to outlaw abortion, nor would it be to outlaw abortion on grounds of disability," replied similarly when asked whether the issue of abortion was of particular relevance to people with disabilities: "Yes, it seems self-evident that it is highly relevant, given the number of tests for impairments that are available and strongly urged on women during pregnancy. So obviously the two are quite strongly linked."

90. Martin Rhonheimer, "Fundamental Rights, Moral Law, and the Legal Defense of Life in a Constitutional Democracy," *American Journal of Jurisprudence* 43 (1998): 174.

velopment, or are not disabled, or are "wanted," etc. By voting to enact such conditional legislation, pro-life legislators associate themselves with the "culture of death" and fail to uphold the requirements of solidarity. By supporting bills that permit or tolerate some abortions, legislators are committing themselves—for that period of time, which may be several months or even many years, as the experience of legislative campaigns in the UK demonstrates—to the good of some unborn children, but not of others. Solidarity requires that legislators have a firm and persevering determination to commit themselves to the good of each unborn child, and this is necessarily lacking in legislative campaigns and votes to enact bills that exclude the basic good of legal protection for some unborn children.

Further philosophical and even theological reflections could profitably be made about the virtue of solidarity with respect to abortion legislation, but this first chapter has had only the modest objective of focusing attention on the lack of true solidarity manifested in the practical actions of the pro-life movement. In directing attention to the true requirements of solidarity, this chapter has sought to highlight the need to avoid "a questionable solidarity which eventually leads to discriminating between one life and another and ignoring the dignity which belongs to every human being."[91]

91. John Paul II, Apostolic Letter, *Novo millennio ineunte* (2001), n. 51.

PART II

A QUESTION OF LAW

2. JURISPRUDENTIAL OPTIONS REVISITED

The Three Basic Jurisprudential Options

In Western societies abortion was generally regarded as a criminal offense until the 1960s if not later, so the question of how to respond to abortion laws is still a fairly new one. In this chapter I challenge some ideas that have been widely accepted in pro-life circles since the 1960s and 1970s, with a view to establishing a sound jurisprudence on abortion.

In an article published in 1970 entitled "The Jurisprudential Options on Abortion," Robert F. Drinan, S.J., asserted that "there are only three ways by which the law can operate with regard to abortion."[1] It can prohibit all abortions,[2] prohibit no abortions, or settle for a "compromise"[3] such as one that "would prohibit all abortions except in instances where the pregnancy threatens the physical or mental health of the mother, or where pregnancy results from rape or incest, or where the fetus is predictably deformed."[4] Although this is the sort of compromise envisaged by Drinan, the "compromise option" covers any degree of compromise that falls anywhere along the scale between prohibiting all and prohibiting no abortions. An article by John Finnis, "Three Schemes of Regulation,"[5] also published in 1970, takes a broad-

---

1. Robert F. Drinan, S.J., "The Jurisprudential Options on Abortion," *Theological Studies* 31 (1970): 161.
2. Ibid. Drinan makes an exception to this prohibition when the mother's life is at stake.
3. Ibid., 164.   4. Ibid., 161.
5. John Finnis, "Three Schemes of Regulation," in John T. Noonan Jr. ed., *The Morality of Abortion: Legal and Historical Perspectives* (Cambridge: Harvard University Press, 1970), 172–207.

ly similar view that abortion laws will be set according to one of three options: abortions will be either all prohibited or all permitted, or permitted "when authorized by independent officials under defined but ampler categories of medical, psycho-medical, or quasi-medical conditions."[6] This last option would inevitably include the sorts of abortions in Drinan's "compromise" option, and Finnis acknowledges that this option often attracts favor "as a moderate, pragmatic compromise" between what are regarded as the "extremes" of the two other options.[7] Although Finnis seems to suggest that this option need not be regarded as a compromise, being, as he describes it, an option different in character from the other two "with the distinct aim of preserving representative medical-psychiatrical standards,"[8] he acknowledges nevertheless that it is commonly regarded as a compromise and in my view, given that those "representative medical-psychiatrical standards" are not consistent with true ethical principles, it is rightly regarded as a compromise.

Which option or options can pro-life legislators legitimately choose? We shall consider the sorts of arguments that have been presented for each of the three options in turn.

Option 1: Prohibiting All Abortions

For those who recognize that direct abortion kills a living human being at an early stage of his or her life, nothing other than a law prohibiting all abortions might seem acceptable. If human life is inviolable (or precious, sacred, a basic good, etc.), the protection of all unborn children is a clear witness to this. A judgment that, as a matter of principle, human law *must* prohibit all abortions would seem to suggest that any law failing to prohibit all abortions is unprincipled and unworthy of support. An alternative view is that a totally prohibitive law should be regarded as an "ideal" but that other options could be legitimately chosen.

Both Finnis and Drinan include, within the option of laws prohibiting all abortions, an exception when abortion is performed to save

6. Ibid., 173.
7. Ibid., 193.
8. Ibid., 194.

the life of the pregnant woman.⁹ It is not entirely clear why this exception should apply, though it is, of course, true that many people might consider a law that prevented an abortion in such circumstances unduly burdensome for the woman. If such abortions can be judged to be morally permissible, as Finnis (with Germain Grisez and Joseph Boyle) seems to suggest, because they are unintended (or "indirect"),[10] then the category of "prohibitive law" would be absolute insofar as it would refer to all abortions considered to be immoral choices. If abortions to save the mother's life were truly performed in accordance with the double-effect principle (as Finnis et al. suggest), there would be no need to establish in law that this category of abortion be allowed because the action giving rise to the death of the child would not focus directly on "abortion" so much as on what would be regarded as a legitimate medical life-saving action. Thus, such indirect abortions—if they are truly such—would not be exceptions to a general prohibition of abortion. If, however, they are *direct* abortions, and contrary to the moral law's prohibition of all direct abortions, then it would seem more appropriate to include them within the category of "compromise" legislation.

Some of the possible shortcomings of this prohibitive option are given as reasons to support one of the other two options, which we now consider.

---

9. Drinan, "Jurisprudential Options," 161; Finnis, "Three Schemes of Regulation," 173.

10. See John Finnis, Germain Grisez, Joseph Boyle, "'Direct' and 'Indirect': A Reply to Critics of our Action Theory," *Thomist* 65 (2001): 1–44. After acknowledging (and noting their acceptance of it as a truth of the faith) the Church's teaching that direct killing of the unborn, even to save the life of the mother, is always wrong, they express their opinion "that a doctor could do a craniotomy [to save the life of the mother] even one involving emptying the baby's skull, without intending to kill the baby—that is, without the craniotomy being a direct killing" (27). It is not clear whether they believe all abortions performed "to save the life of the mother" could be justified as indirect (unintentional) killing. Elsewhere, however, Finnis writes that "a just law forbidding the killing of the unborn cannot, I believe, admit an exception 'to save the life of the mother.'" See "The Legal Status of the Unborn Baby," *Catholic Medical Quarterly* (Aug. 1992): 9.

Option 2: "Compromise" Legislation

Rather than legislate strictly for the pro-life position by prohibiting all abortions, could pro-life legislators support "compromise" legislation? The range of compromise can vary: it might be that abortion to save the mother's life is not prohibited, and/or abortion after rape, and/or abortion if fetal disability is suspected, and/or if the woman has been pregnant for fewer than 8 or 12 or 16 or 20 weeks. All legislation falling between the boundaries of "total prohibition" and "no prohibition" would constitute compromise legislation.

A "Principled" Compromise

There would appear to be two sorts of compromise legislation. The first sort, based on what might be regarded as a "principled" compromise, would be made by legislators who, though sincerely opposed to all abortions and supportive of a law enforcing this position, believe that legislation should be based not on their individual convictions but on a wider assessment of the prevailing attitudes in society. Given the pluralistic nature of modern society and its broad range of views about abortion, these legislators would not support an absolutely pro-life or a contentiously restrictive bill, even if it had a realistic prospect of being enacted, if in their view it would be widely flouted or held in contempt, or would create social unrest and/or be the subject of ongoing and possibly bitter controversy which, among other things, could perhaps undermine respect for the law generally. M. Cathleen Kaveny seems to argue in favor of this sort of "principled" compromise legislation, with respect to the prospect of states in the United States enacting different abortion laws:

> A series of checkerboard-like abortion laws, dependent on the vicissitudes of local politics, would serve only to undermine respect for law as such. Moreover, it might very well erode respect for unborn life as well, even in the "conservative" states. Rather than looking seriously at the moral message undergirding extremely strict legislation, many will dismiss it as simply the political spoils of a conservative coalition, to be unceremoniously replaced with a change in the prevailing political wind. Pro-lifers would do better, therefore, to start with a stable moral consensus and attempt to

augment it over time rather than to take advantage of ephemeral political opportunities.[11]

A "Pragmatic" Compromise

The second sort of compromise might be regarded as a "pragmatic" compromise, whereby a legislator supports a more restrictive law solely because it is not possible to enact legislation prohibiting all abortions. Commonly this sort of compromise is viewed as "choosing the lesser evil,"[12] and a compromise law might have a variety of benefits. First, it would grant legal protection to some unborn children who would otherwise not have protection, thus potentially saving lives; second, its enactment as part of a "pro-life" campaign might help to promote the view that abortion (or at least, more "liberal") laws are a matter of public concern for which society must be called to account. Mary Ann Glendon, addressing an imaginary pro-life friend who would support nothing less than a law prohibiting all abortions, presents the case for compromise legislation:

> Over time, I would say to my pro-life friend, compromise legislation may aid your cause, because it is what goes on in people's hearts and minds that you really care about. The mores, not the law, are the best protection of the weak and dependent. A law which communicates that abortion is a serious moral issue and that the fetus is entitled to protection will have a more beneficial influence on behavior and opinions, even though it permits abortion under some—even many—circumstances, than a law which holds fetal life to be of little or no value and abortion to be a fundamental right.[13]

A distinction between a principled and a pragmatic compromise is valid given the different motivations and reasons for voting for compromise legislation. The complexity of motivations can, however, lead at times to a merging of the two. Thus Richard McCormick, S.J., when expressing his belief that "the most equitable law would be one that

---

11. M. Cathleen Kaveny, "Towards a Thomistic Perspective on Abortion and the Law in Contemporary America," *Thomist* 55 (1991): 392.

12. For a fuller discussion of the question of the "lesser evil," see Chapter 6.

13. Mary Ann Glendon, *Abortion and Divorce in Western Law* (Cambridge: Harvard University Press, 1987), 60.

protects fetal life but exempts abortion done in certain specified conflict situations,"[14] presents (i) what can be regarded as a "principled" compromise (in this case, a "procedural" solution that, taking into account America's "pluralistic atmosphere," would help to avoid legal provisions on abortion being traced back to a "moral" position, whether this be Vatican II or the U.S. Supreme Court),[15] as well as (ii) what can be regarded as a "pragmatic" compromise (an acknowledgment that the compromise is "for the present" and "must be accompanied by hesitation and a large dose of dissatisfaction"; that it "is one means—but only one—that will allow us, as a nation, to arrive at a position that is compatible with the fundamental moral principles undergirding our republic").[16] The wide acknowledgment that support for legislation which fails to prohibit all abortions is a compromise seems to indicate that this is not ideal, and that a law prohibiting all abortions would be preferable.

The arguments favoring a compromise option are not homogenous and this is due not only to the distinction between "principled" and "pragmatic" compromises but also to the different legislative situations that exist and to which legislators must be attentive when considering votes for legislation that falls within the compromise category. Reasons for supporting a compromise may differ depending on whether the law previously allowed no abortions, all abortions, or a greater number than the proposed legislation. If women have a legal right to abortion (as they do in the United States) a UK-type law that does not establish such a right (legislation writers like Glendon categorize as "compromise legislation")[17] may seem beneficial to the pro-life cause—even

14. Richard A. McCormick, S.J., "Notes on Moral Theology: The Abortion Dossier," *Theological Studies* 35 (1974): 358.

15. Ibid.

16. Ibid., 358–59.

17. Other writers, by contrast, suggest that the UK law is one that prohibits no abortions. John Finnis lists it within his "third scheme of regulation," in which "abortion is either formally or in practical effect permitted whenever it is performed by a qualified physician" ("Three Schemes of Regulation," 197). As I shall argue, one must note that there is a distinction between what a law "formally" states and its "practical effect," the identification of which point is necessary to a sound jurisprudence on abortion. A consideration of laws primarily in terms of their practical effects seems to be

though the legislation may be interpreted so liberally as to be practically ineffective. Glendon argues:

> I would point out that a legal norm, even though it seems ineffective, can help to create a climate of opinion which impedes more extensive violations of the norm. One may think here of speed limits and no-smoking signs.... At a minimum, replacing the right to abortion with a compromise should help to replace strident discord with reasoned discussion about the grounds and conditions under which abortion might be permitted.[18]

Norman St. John Stevas, the Catholic member of the UK Parliament, who was one of the leading opponents of abortion during the passage of the bill that became the Abortion Act 1967, presents a different perspective on compromise from that of Glendon. He acknowledges that the pro-life parliamentarians, taking into account what he presents as a Catholic understanding of social pluralism, had taken a "middle position as regards the law," i.e., a compromise:

> As a result of our efforts, although we have not defeated it, the bill is greatly improved from its original form. Nothing would have been achieved, however, had we not taken up our position on the middle ground, accepting the need for some measure of abortion law reform but seeking to get a bill that was well drafted and limited in scope.... In any case, in a pluralist society, while Catholics are fully entitled to voice their views and work for their implementation, prudence requires that they take into account the prevailing climate of moral opinion in the country.... By taking up a middle position as regards the law, Catholics are not abandoning their principles but recognizing facts. Abortion is an evil, but it does take place, and a regulatory law that would allow some abortions to take place under proper medical conditions would not be contrary to Catholic faith.[19]

St. John Stevas was writing after the enactment of the 1967 legislation but prior to its implementation in April 1968, and he clearly did

---

why Finnis, unlike Glendon, fails to judge correctly that the UK law falls into the category of "compromise" legislation.

18. Glendon, *Abortion and Divorce in Western Law*, 60.

19. Norman St. John Stevas, "The English Experience," *America* 117 (9 Dec. 1967): 709, quoted in Daniel Callahan, *Abortion: Law, Choice and Morality* (London: Collier-Macmillan, 1970), 435.

not envisage the extensive practical effect of the legislation, which, in spite of his objections to abortion, he believes to be "well drafted and limited in scope" and "not . . . contrary to Catholic faith." As he was regarded as the leading Catholic pro-life legislator during the passage of the 1967 legislation, St. John Stevas's remarks now seem surprising and somewhat disturbing. Today, few if any Catholics in the UK or elsewhere would defend the Abortion Act 1967 as not contrary to Catholic faith.[20] St. John Stevas's position and its possible influence on the pro-life movement could be profitably examined further, but this is not the place for it. For now, my remarks are generally restricted to presenting some of the different approaches that have been suggested with respect to the concept of compromise. In the same year in which St. John Stevas was writing about the UK situation, Robert H. Springer, S.J., applied a similar analysis, taking into account social pluralism, to the prospect of legislation in the United States: "There must be recognition of the pluralisms that divide us. . . . In the last analysis, the hard demands of political reality may mean that we will have to support a compromise measure in place of a given abortion bill."[21]

Given the range of compromise legislation, a more restrictive compromise might be proposed in place of a less restrictive one, but both pieces of legislation would fall into the category of compromise legislation. The reasons for replacing one compromise law with a more restrictive compromise law would inevitably differ from those governing a decision to support a compromise law to replace one that previously prohibited either all or no abortions.[22]

---

20. Some who profess to be Catholic may, of course, defend the Abortion Act 1967, but they would do so in defiance of Catholic teaching, aware that such legislation is contrary to Catholic faith, which, especially in *Evangelium vitae,* has been clearly stated.

21. Robert H. Springer, S.J., "Notes on Moral Theology," *Theological Studies* 28 (1967): 354–55.

22. For an account of some different aspects of "a strategy of compromise," see Hans Lotstra, *Abortion: The Catholic Debate in America* (New York: Irvington Publishers, 1985), 233–37; also Thomas R. Ulshafer, S.S., "On the Morality of Legislative Compromise: Some Historical Underpinnings," *Linacre Quarterly* 59, no. 2 (1992): 10–26.

Exclusions in Compromise Legislation

The preceding remarks give an indication of the different reasons or motives for supporting compromise legislation and show that, given the different sorts of compromise and different attendant reasons, it is too simplistic to give just one all-encompassing reason to justify supporting this sort of legislation. I suggest that it would, in fact, be more illuminating to consider the features of this sort of legislation, rather than the motives for supporting it. By doing so we will be better able to identify some of the shortcomings of choosing legislation that falls within this category.

In my view, the relevant consideration is not that compromise legislation (at least legislation based on a "pragmatic" compromise) will achieve the end of prohibiting some abortions that might otherwise take place, but rather that it will *always fail to protect some* unborn children. There is, moreover, a sliding scale of compromise such that efforts will be focused on prohibiting those abortions that could be more easily prohibited by a compromise—notably those performed on older unborn children or those performed for "less serious" reasons—while there would be less, if any, prospect of compromise that would help to protect younger unborn children, those conceived after rape, or those likely to be born with a physical or mental disability. This factor of exclusion was highlighted in the previous chapter, but it is normally overlooked in many of the arguments favoring compromise legislation, for example, in those presented by Mary Ann Glendon. Indeed, if the pro-life movement were to adopt the strategy Glendon suggests of turning its attention away from the fetus as the victim of abortion and toward a consideration of how those who perform or have abortions are damaged by the process, the exclusion factor could easily be dispensed with.[23] In view of this prospect, a focus on "exclusion" is, perhaps, of particular relevance.

---

23. See Glendon, *Abortion and Divorce in Western Law,* 60–61. Those engaged in promoting the right to life should certainly heed the Second Vatican Council's teaching that abortion and other actions against life "do more harm to those who practice them than to those who suffer from the injury" (*Gaudium et spes,* n. 27) and, accordingly, treat those who are commonly regarded as their opponents with respect, compassion,

Overlooking the factor that some unborn children are excluded in compromise legislation, Glendon suggests that such a law "communicates that abortion is a serious moral issue and that the fetus is entitled to protection."[24] The counterargument is that such a law manifestly fails to do this; rather it communicates that *some* abortions pose serious moral problems and that *some* fetuses are entitled to protection while others are not. Kaveny, an admirer of Glendon's approach,[25] similarly suggests that compromise legislation can be justified on the basis of "the pedagogical function of the law in supporting and gradually extending a pro-life consensus." But what sort of pedagogy does this sort of legislation provide? Kaveny acknowledges that early abortions will be among those not prohibited by such legislation, so what does this teach? It may be that Kaveny intended it to teach something different, but what it actually teaches is that later abortions should be prohibited but that earlier ones need not be, i.e., that aborting earlier in the pregnancy does not pose the same (if any) ethical objections as aborting at a later stage. One is certainly being taught something, but is it a pro-life pedagogy? It would be, to say the least, a potential source of confusion that, to make things worse, might even militate against the pro-life position; having effectively taught that "later abortions are bad, earlier abortions are better (if not good)" the pro-life movement would have to encourage society to "unlearn" what it had been taught and to learn to accept a different view—one that this time might perhaps be consistent with the true pro-life view but that might alternatively be yet another compromise in line with an incremental approach toward a total prohibition—which, as a consequence of such false teaching, might be even harder to achieve.

---

and love. It is right for the pro-life movement to be actively concerned for women who might be contemplating abortion, as well as those who have aborted. However, as I shall explain below, the primary subject of a jurisprudence on abortion is the unborn child whose right to life is threatened by abortion legislation. This traditional view, endorsed by *Evangelium vitae,* is entirely consistent with the teaching of *Gaudium et spes,* n. 27.

24. Glendon, *Abortion and Divorce in Western Law,* 60.

25. "To my mind Glendon provides the most perceptive and judicious analysis of the interrelationship between law, public sensibilities and morality in the case of

The Glendon-Kaveny view provokes objections on various levels. How is one to engage, as Glendon suggests, in "reasoned discussion about the grounds and conditions under which abortion might be permitted" if the pro-life view, based on natural law, rejects as contrary to reason the positing of any grounds or conditions for abortion? How can pro-lifers adopt an incrementalist approach that starts, as Kaveny suggests, "with a stable moral consensus," if the consensus—which fails to protect some of the unborn—is fundamentally immoral? A commendable effort to engage in respectful and fruitful dialogue with those who do not share the pro-life view requires an honesty that is lacking in the suggestion that compromise legislation, which fails to protect some (possibly many) unborn children, is consistent with either reason or morality.

Unlike some writers, Kaveny acknowledges that a compromise excluding disabled unborn children from protection poses a particular difficulty to pro-life sensibilities; in many respects such children can be viewed, she acknowledges, as "the weakest of the weak" and to compromise in their regard seems inimical to pro-life convictions. Nevertheless, Kaveny resolves what she calls a "wrenchingly difficult situation" by accepting a compromise.[26] Her attempts to soften the blow, however, are unsatisfactory. First, her suggestion that "the first response of pro-lifers . . . should be to increase substantially aid for families with mentally or physically damaged offspring"[27] holds true irrespective of the law on abortion and is thus to be regarded as an ordinary concern of pro-lifers and not a particular response to a eugenic abortion law. Second, she suggests that "in the grim meantime, the law should certainly make clear that its refusal to implement criminal penalties in such cases is a matter of excuse, not justification."[28] In the following chapter I shall discuss the factor of "justness" in law, this factor—considered both intrinsically and extrinsically—being the justification for any law. To suggest that the law itself may be not justified, though excusable, is to embrace a jurisprudence that, I shall argue, is

---

abortion to appear in many years." Kaveny, "Towards a Thomistic Perspective on Abortion," 363n15.

26. Ibid., 393, including note 54. 27. Ibid., 393–94.
28. Ibid., 394.

alien to the natural law tradition, which considers the justness (or justification) of particular laws. Legislative Acts may include relevant background information to "make clear" the reasons for the law proper, i.e., the part or parts that prohibit, tolerate, permit, or obligate certain actions. This background information cannot explain (or rather "explain away") the inclusion qua "law" of something that, being without justification, has no rightful place within a law. Kaveny acknowledges that there is a problem with a law that fails to protect disabled unborn children, but her attempt to resolve that problem does not hold.

Option 3: Prohibiting No Abortions

The false pedagogy that the sort of compromise legislation favored by Glendon and Kaveny invites is acknowledged by Drinan, who, having previously thought that a law permitting abortion in the cases of rape, incest, or predicted fetal handicap was preferable to a law legalizing abortion generally,[29] subsequently reversed his judgment. Arguing against his former view, he maintained that such a compromise law "clearly teaches the principle that healthy and productive human beings are much more desirable for society than retarded and unproductive individuals would be."[30] Although his 1970 article does not express unequivocal support for a withdrawal of criminal sanctions in the case of *all* abortions, Drinan soon became identified with the so-called "no law" position on abortion.[31] The benefit of this position, as he acknowledges, is that it "would clearly keep the state out of the business of establishing standards or reasons with regard to what kinds of fetuses may have their life extinguished and what type must be given the right

---

29. Robert F. Drinan, S.J., "Strategy on Abortion," *America* 116 (4 Feb. 1967): 179.
30. Drinan, "Jurisprudential Options," 165.
31. See, for example, Callahan, *Abortion: Law, Choice and Morality,* 436–37. Callahan notes the various shifts in thinking in Drinan's position in the late 1960s. His position subsequently changed again. Having been regarded as a leading "pro-choice" congressman in the 1970s and an advocate for the "pro-choice" view after leaving office, Drinan signed a 1997 statement that displayed yet another remarkable shift of view: "I . . . stand ready to promote laws and public policies that aim to protect vulnerable human life from conception until natural death" (quoted in Robert P. George, "Bioethics and Public Policy: Catholic Participation in the American Debate," in *Issues for a Catholic Bioethic,* ed. Luke Gormally, [London: Linacre Centre, 1999], 279).

to be born."[32] However, in avoiding the sort of discrimination that might be applied to some categories of the unborn, such legislation would still be discriminatory because it would deny unborn human beings the protection afforded by the law to born human beings. The "no law" option would (among other reasons for concern) merely shift the boundaries of discrimination.

The Three Basic Options: An Assessment

An analysis based on the three basic jurisprudential options considered above may suffice if, from a pro-life perspective, one's concern lies with restricting—as far as possible at any moment in time—the scale of abortion, or with challenging the extent to which abortion may be viewed as desirable or beneficial or as a "right," either generally or in specific instances. If the purpose of voting for relevant legislation is to shape society's attitudes so that fewer (if any) abortions will be performed, or so that certain categories of the unborn will not be subject to particular discrimination, or to promote the pro-life view, then it would seem that pro-life legislators could justifiably vote, depending on their assessment of the situation, to prohibit either all abortions or no abortions or for some compromise position in between. In his acceptance of this sort of analysis, Charles Curran remarks that in practical terms "there is no such thing as *the* one Roman Catholic approach to abortion legislation."[33] In other words, having identified these three basic options, he maintains that each of them has its own validity, and he indicates that Catholic and other pro-life legislators could legitimately choose any of them.

Can one, then, claim that a choice of any one of these three basic options is consistent with the Roman Catholic (and, by implication, a natural law) approach? There are, I suggest, two main reasons why one cannot. The first is based on a recognition that a sound jurisprudence on abortion focuses not, in the first place, on abortion but rather on jurisprudence. And the object of interest is not a sociological, pedagogical, pluralistic, positivist, or even what might be termed a "pro-life" ju-

---

32. Drinan, "Jurisprudential Options," 167.
33. Charles E. Curran, *Ongoing Revision: Studies in Moral Theology* (Notre Dame: Fides, 1975), 135.

risprudence; rather it is a natural law jurisprudence with respect to which legislation on abortion should be examined. A natural law jurisprudence acknowledges *justness* as an essential property of any law and the property of justness is overlooked in the "three basic options" analysis I have outlined. The second reason is that the "three basic options" analysis is not merely "basic" but seriously inadequate, because it fails to identify the full range of relevant options. An awareness of the full range of jurisprudential options, which I shall now present, leads to an understanding of the importance of the concept of an *intrinsically unjust* abortion law, which will be the focus of my attention in subsequent chapters.

The Seven Jurisprudential Options

Although Robert Drinan's and John Finnis's accounts of the three basic options seem similar, let us consider more closely how they themselves describe those options in their 1970 articles. Drinan describes the "only three ways by which the law can operate with regard to abortion" as follows: (D1) "The first way ... prohibits all abortions";[34] (D2) "The second way ... would prohibit all abortions except in instances where the pregnancy threatens the physical or mental health of the mother, or where pregnancy results from rape or incest, or where the fetus is predictably deformed"; (D3) "The third way is to withdraw all criminal sanctions and to allow licensed physicians to terminate pregnancies for any reason deemed satisfactory by them." Finnis's three options are: (F1) "the prohibition of all abortions";[35] (F2) the "permission" of *some* abortions under defined conditions (usually categorized in medical or quasi-medical terms);[36] (F3) "the permission of all abortions."[37] If legal-

---

34. As noted above, Drinan makes an exception to this prohibition where the mother's life is at stake ("Jurisprudential Options," 161).

35. Like Drinan, Finnis makes an exception to the prohibition in cases where the life of the mother is threatened ("Three Schemes of Regulation," 173).

36. Finnis's description is "the permission of abortion when previously authorized, by independent officials, under defined but ampler categories of medical, psycho-medical, or quasi-medical conditions" ("Three Schemes of Regulation," 173).

37. Finnis's remark that the performance of these abortions in his model scheme

ization of abortion is viewed solely in terms of "prohibition," then Drinan and Finnis do identify accurately the only three possible options, namely: (1) to prohibit *all* abortions; or (2) to prohibit *some* abortions (whether this should be "few" or "many" constitutes a variable within this option); or (3) to prohibit *no* abortions. However, the similarity between their views only applies with respect to the *prohibitive* function of law, and their stated options require further consideration.

Law does not fulfill merely a prohibitive function. St. Thomas Aquinas, for example, classifies laws according to whether they permit *or* prohibit (forbid) *or* punish,[38] and indeed further classifications are possible. Some laws may be enacted that specifically authorize (i.e., permit) an action; other laws may remove a previous prohibition without specifically permitting, and these laws can be said to "tolerate" actions; in addition, some laws may be formally "prohibitive" but refrain from applying penal sanctions and can thus also be said to "tolerate" actions. Punishment is an essential component of some laws that, because they require the performance of an action (e.g., the payment of income tax), have an obligatory character. The distinctions of obligating (or commanding), permitting, tolerating, prohibiting, punishing, etc., are relevant to all laws and not merely those concerning moral issues like abortion. However, the relevance of the distinctions with respect to abortion legislation, to be considered in more detail below, can be shown simply by contrasting the legislation of the United States and the United Kingdom. These two nations can both be said to have laws favoring abortion, but whereas the 1973 U.S. Supreme Court ruled that women have a "right" to abortion (i.e., it permitted abortion), the U.K. 1967 legislation removed the penal sanctions and prohibition previously attached to abortion, without establishing that women have a right to abortion (i.e., it can be said to have "tolerated" rather than "permitted" abortion).[39]

---

would be carried out only by persons qualified to carry out the medical procedures would, I suggest, constitute not an "exception" but merely a condition. Ibid., 173–74.

38. *ST* I-II, q. 92, a. 2. Aquinas quotes with approval the view of St. Isidore of Seville: "Every law either permits something, as: 'A brave man may demand his reward'; or forbids something, as: 'No man may ask a consecrated virgin in marriage'; or punishes, as: 'Let him that commits a murder be put to death.'"

39. If conditions are included as part of a law that, strictly speaking, only tolerates an action, this can give the appearance of "permission," as is the case with the UK law.

Obligating, Permitting, Tolerating, and Prohibiting

I suggest that the appropriate distinctions, especially relevant for a consideration of an abortion jurisprudence, are not those which refer to permitting, prohibiting, and punishing, but rather those which refer to *obligating, permitting, tolerating,* and *prohibiting*. A sound jurisprudence on abortion, the concrete applicability of which will be readily evident to those engaged in seeking the public good amid the complexities of different juridical and legislative systems, can be developed by understanding the way in which the terms *obligating, permitting, tolerating,* and *prohibiting* are employed:

i. A law "obligating" (or commanding) abortion makes abortion compulsory. Unless a society were to develop in accordance with the models of Huxley's *Brave New World* or Hollywood's *Logan's Run* (in which baby banks replace the need for human gestation), or were to set itself on a course of self-annihilation, it is unlikely to legislate that abortion be compulsory for *every* pregnant woman. One need not, however, look to the realm of science fiction or contemplate the likelihood of there being a society willfully journeying toward self-extinction to recognize the real prospect of societies' enacting laws to make abortion compulsory in *some* circumstances, for example, as part of a program to restrict population growth, or for eugenic reasons. Indeed, compulsory abortion is already a feature of China's population policy. The effectiveness of an "obligating" law is dependent on its specification of penalties for those who violate it.

ii. A law "permitting" abortion specifically authorizes abortion, possibly even specifying that women have a "right" to abort.[40] The law itself does not have an obligatory character,[41] although an *effect* of the law may be to alter society's attitudes, creating as it were a (nonlegal)

---

40. One could make a further classification and distinguish laws granting a "right" from those that "permit," insofar as it can be argued that permission is not required to do what one has a right to do, but I think it is appropriate, in the present discussion, to regard the positing of a legal right as equivalent to legal permission.

41. By this I mean that the law itself does not oblige women to abort. I am not referring to whether it imposes obligations on others, such as doctors or health authorities, to assist women who choose to abort.

social or cultural norm which may in practice have a quasi-obligatory character. Commonly the notion of a "permissive" abortion law is construed as meaning an extensive or "liberal" law, but this is not the sense in which I am using the term. (Indeed, this notion of "permissive" law is frequently employed when the law itself does not "permit"—in the precise sense I am using the term—but rather "tolerates" abortion.) A "permissive" abortion law (or, equivalently, a law "permitting" abortion) refers to the character of the law rather than to the scale of abortion which the law allows.

iii. A law "tolerating" abortion does not specifically authorize abortion or establish a right to abort. Such a law, especially if it is enacted subsequent to a law which prohibited abortion, may rather specify that some (or all) abortions are "not prohibited," or that there is no punishment attached to some (or all) abortions. Abortions, in such cases, may not be regarded precisely as "legal" but could be performed without incurring any penalty. In terms of their practical effect, laws "tolerating" and "permitting" abortion may be indistinguishable, and contrary to the formal content of a law that "tolerates," abortion may be commonly considered to be a right. The view I am presenting of the legal toleration of abortion is consistent with an understanding of toleration as the principle of *"non impedire"*;[42] such a law does not "permit" or "authorize" or *in itself* grant approval of or encouragement for an action, but it does not impede its performance. The range of legislation that might be said to "tolerate" abortion can be quite extensive, as I shall demonstrate in Chapters 7 and 8. Some of the complexities of abortion legislation are not adequately revealed in illustrations of such legislation; for example, legislation of the form "Abortion is prohibited after 10 weeks" must be understood as *tolerating* abortion prior to 10 weeks, a point which may not be immediately apparent but which will be demonstrated in later chapters.

---

42. Pius XII uses the term *non impedire* to signify the meaning of "toleration" in his Discourse to the Fifth Convention of Italian Catholic Jurists, 6 Dec. 1953, published in the *Catholic Mind* (April 1954): 247. More recently, Janet E. Smith has used the same term to signify toleration in *Humanae Vitae: A Generation Later* (Washington, D.C.: Catholic University of America Press, 1991), 93. For further consideration of the question of "toleration," see Chapter 6.

iv. A law "prohibiting" abortion signifies that abortion is neither permitted nor tolerated. This being so, such a law must punish those who violate it, because failure to punish violators constitutes legal toleration. (The question of who should be punished—whether it should be the woman and/or a third party who performs the abortion—is not my concern at present.) One further specification must be made: a law "prohibiting" abortion is necessarily a law that prohibits *all* abortions. If it prohibits some abortions but not others, the law itself must be recognized objectively as a law that (at least) tolerates abortion of those unborn children who are entitled to be protected within the scope of that law but who have been excluded.

The four functions of law—obligating, permitting, tolerating, and prohibiting—are mutually exclusive. The complexities of much legislation may seem to indicate that particular laws frequently possess more than one of these functions, but this holds only insofar as the legislation may refer to different acts. Considered simply with respect to a specific act, a law can be typified as either obligating *or* permitting *or* tolerating *or* prohibiting. The ability to make these distinctions is essential to an objective identification of the sort of abortion law one is dealing with, such an identification being a prerequisite to any judgment on the decisive point concerning the justness of the law.

Returning, then, to Drinan's claim that "there are only three ways by which the law can operate with regard to abortion" and Finnis's consideration of the "three schemes of legal regulation," it is clear not only that an identification of just three classifications fails to cover the range of jurisprudential options but even that, when the Drinan and Finnis options are compared, the possibility of a wider range of options is evident. Drinan proposes a coherent view that the options for law are that it could prohibit either all abortions (D1), or some abortions (D2), or no abortions (D3). Finnis's approach, though on similar lines and no less coherent, is in fact different: his first option refers to prohibiting all abortions (F1) and is identical with Drinan's first option (D1), but his two other options refer to *permitting* some abortions (F2) or all abortions (F3). Finnis does not seem to use the term "permit" in the precise way that I have used it above, but seems rather to use it loosely in the sense that the law may be said to "allow" abortion—making no distinction between "toleration" and "permission." Drinan's options D2 and D3, insofar as they refer to not prohibiting or not punishing all or some abortions, correspond to the sort of legal "toleration" I have described.

As a result of focusing exclusively on the prohibitive function of law, without taking into consideration precisely how this correlates with the law's "permitting" or "tolerating" functions, Drinan proposes a jurisprudential model that refers solely to the prohibition of all or some or no abortions. Inevitably, his options require reassessment in light of his failure to identify the full range of options. Because the obligating, permitting, tolerating, or prohibiting functions of law are mutually exclusive, a law "prohibiting some" or "prohibiting no" abortions would not, in fact, classify the law as "prohibitive" (a point borne out by the fact that a law "to prohibit no abortions" can in no meaningful sense be said to be prohibitive!); rather, the law would be classified as at least "tolerating" if not in fact "permitting." Bearing in mind that there is only one sort of "prohibitive" abortion law—one that prohibits (i.e., and punishes) *all* abortions—the full range of the *mutually exclusive jurisprudential options* on abortion would appear to be:

 i. A law that prohibits all abortions.
 ii. A law that tolerates some (whether few or many) abortions.
 iii. A law that tolerates all abortions.
 iv. A law that permits some (whether few or many) abortions.
 v. A law that permits all abortions.
 vi. A law that obligates some (whether few or many) women to abort.
 vii. A law that obligates all women to abort.

A short-hand description of abortion laws inevitably has shortcomings because it may seem to highlight inappropriately as the primary subject matter of the legislation what may not in fact be the primary subject matter. For example, a law "that obligates some women to abort" might refer primarily to women over a certain age (the subject of the discrimination being the woman), or it might refer primarily to a child, characterized with respect to disability, or, perhaps, gender (in which case the subject of the discrimination is the unborn child). However, notwithstanding their acknowledged limitations, these shorthand descriptions would appear to represent accurately the full range of jurisprudential options.

Legal "Permission" and Legal "Toleration"

Of the seven identified jurisprudential options, two refer to laws "obligating" abortion, options that Drinan and Finnis may have excluded as not relevant to the sorts of legislation being promoted in 1970. Today, too, particularly in the midst of our culture of "choice," even those who have no moral objection to abortion would generally regard these options as unacceptable, and I shall not dwell on them now. I have, however, indicated a distinction between Drinan's and Finnis's options with respect to legal "permission" and "toleration," a distinction that requires further consideration.

Permitting and Tolerating Moral Evil in Human Law

Human law[43] is not expected to prohibit everything that is contrary to the natural or moral law, as Aquinas teaches:

> Human laws do not forbid all vices from which the virtuous abstain, but only the more grievous vices from which it is possible for the majority to abstain; and chiefly those that are to the hurt of others, without the prohibition of which human society could not be maintained: thus human law prohibits murder, theft, and suchlike.[44]

Elsewhere Aquinas teaches:

> The human will can, by common agreement, make a thing to be just provided that it be not, of itself, contrary to natural justice [*naturalem iustitiam*], and it is in such matters that positive right [or positive law, *ius positivum*] has its place. . . . If, however, a thing is, of itself, contrary to natural right [*ius naturale*] the human will cannot make it just, for instance, by decreeing that it is lawful to steal or to commit adultery. Hence it is written: "Woe to them that make wicked laws" (Isaiah 10:1).[45]

---

43. It will be clear from the citation of various texts that "human law" is also frequently called, without any distinction being intended for the purpose of the present discussion, "positive law" or "civil law" or "criminal law."

44. *ST* I-II, q. 96, a. 2.   45. *ST* II-II, q. 57, a. 2, ad 2.

Commenting on the first of these passages, Robert George remarks, "In certain cases it is better for the civil and criminal law of a community to permit immoral acts, lest the legal prohibition of those acts bring about worse consequences for society than a policy of legal toleration."[46] George's remarks demonstrate how the verb "to permit" (understood nowadays as having an active meaning signifying authorization or approval) is frequently—and regrettably—used interchangeably with the verb "to tolerate" (which has a passive meaning of *non impedire* as discussed in the previous section). Unfortunately, Aquinas's use of "to permit" has perhaps contributed to a blurring of the distinction between the two terms. For example, Aquinas says that human law "is said to permit [*permittere*] certain things, not as approving of them, but as being unable to direct them," it being clear that by "to permit" he means not "to approve" but rather "to tolerate."[47] Similarly, in his teaching that "God . . . neither wills evil to be done, nor wills it not to be done; but He wills to permit [*permittere*] evil to be done, and this is a good,"[48] Aquinas does not mean that God wills to approve or authorize evil, but that he wills not to impede it; i.e., he wills to *tolerate* it. The verbs "to tolerate" and "to permit" have different meanings, and each should be used with precision. It must be admitted, however, that the Latin *permittere* does not possess the active meaning of approval or authorization that the English "to permit" does today. Rather, it has a more ambiguous meaning encompassing both an active and a passive sense, similar perhaps to the current meaning in English of "to allow." In the main English translation of Leo XIII's encyclical letter *Libertas praestantissum* (1888), Aquinas's teaching, quoted above, is presented as a summary of the doctrine of "the permission of evil." The Latin text of Leo's commentary on Aquinas's teaching refers, however, not to "permission" (in spite of Aquinas's use of *permittere*) but to *tolerantia*.[49] Sim-

---

46. Robert P. George, "The Gospel of Life: A Symposium," *First Things* 56 (Oct. 1995): 32–38, viewed at http://www.firstthings.com/ftissues/ft9510/articles/symposium.html.

47. "Ad tertium dicendum quod lex humana dicitur aliqua permittere, non quasi ea approbans, sed quasi ea dirigere non potens. . . . Secus autem esset si approbaret ea quae lex aeterna reprobat." *ST* I-II, q. 93, a. 3, ad 3.

48. *ST* I, q. 19, a. 9, ad 3.

49. Leo XIII, Encyclical Letter, *Libertas praestantissimum*, 20 June 1888, Acta, tom.

ilarly, although the English translation states that "God ... permits evil to exist in the world," Leo's Latin text states: *"Deus . . . sinit tamen esse in mundo mala,"*[50] the verb *sinere* possessing the more vague, if not precisely passive, meaning attributable to "to allow." Leo's Latin text not only frequently speaks of *toleratiam* but emphasizes the word in italics. The principle, relevant to the present discussion, is clearly articulated: "The authority of man is powerless to prevent every evil.... But if ... human law may or even should tolerate evil [*ferre toleranter malum*], it may not and should not approve or desire evil for its own sake [*probare aut velle per se*]."[51]

Robert George employs the verbs "to permit" and "to tolerate" as though they were synonymous, whereas the first and second statements of Aquinas quoted at the beginning of this section reveal the clear distinction between the verbs.[52] Traditionally, adultery has been regarded as one type of immoral act that, in accordance with Aquinas's first statement, need not be forbidden by human law (i.e., human law can tolerate such acts); however, in his second statement Aquinas specifically says that it cannot be made lawful to commit adultery (i.e., the law cannot permit it). "To not forbid" is not synonymous with "to make lawful," and Aquinas's two statements are by no means inconsistent, though the use of the verb "to permit" as a synonym for "to tolerate" would suggest that they are.

I have, of course, indicated the distinction between legal toleration and legal permission in the previous section. In spite of some unfortunate problems with the terminology, which has failed to distinguish sufficiently between "permission" and "toleration," the tradition nevertheless clearly shows that this distinction is valid and apposite to the question being considered; i.e., human law need not prohibit every moral evil but can tolerate, without permitting, some moral evils.

More recent statements from the magisterium have repeated this teaching. Pius XII teaches that "no human authority ... can give a pos-

---

20, fasc. 240, 610. English translation published by the Catholic Truth Society in *The Pope and the People* (London: CTS, 1943), 89.

50. Ibid., 609, CTS translation, 89.
51. Ibid., 610, CTS translation, 89.
52. Aquinas's teaching at *ST* I-II, q. 96, a. 2, and *ST* II-II, q. 57, a. 2, ad 2.

itive command or positive authorization to teach or to do that which would be contrary to religious truth or moral good," but he accepts that in some circumstances "*'non impedire'* or toleration is permissible."[53] The Congregation for the Doctrine of the Faith acknowledged that "It is true that civil law cannot expect to cover the whole field of morality or to punish all faults. No one expects it to do so. It must often tolerate [*tolerare*] what is in fact a lesser evil, in order to avoid a greater one."[54] This toleration refers to such things as "not punishing" immoral acts, without giving them legal approval: "Human law can abstain from punishment [i.e., tolerate], but it cannot declare to be right [i.e., permit] what would be opposed to the natural law."[55]

John Paul II's teaching in *Evangelium vitae* follows a similar line. Civil (i.e., human) law is not expected to prohibit everything prohibited by the moral law ("the purpose of civil law is different and more limited in scope than that of the moral law"),[56] but it cannot permit that which is prohibited by the moral law because this would contradict "the doctrine of the necessary conformity of civil law with the moral law."[57]

Permitting and Tolerating Abortion in Human Law

In line with the tradition that human law cannot permit but can tolerate some moral evils, we can accept, at least, that human law cannot *permit* abortion. Can it, then, tolerate abortion? In his commentary on *Evangelium vitae* Richard McCormick, S.J., points to the possibility of this being a valid option, noting the distinction between laws that legitimize, authorize, or state a right to (i.e., permit) and those that leave unpunished (i.e., tolerate):

> The encyclical repeatedly refers to laws that "legitimize" or "authorize and promote" or "favor" abortion and euthanasia. It seems to use these terms in the sense of "state a right to." Would its strictures on laws on abortion and euthanasia as unjust laws be the same if these laws were un-

---

53. Pius XII, Discourse to Italian Jurists, 247; see also 248–50.
54. Congregation for the Doctrine of the Faith (CDF), *Declaration on Procured Abortion* (1974), n. 20; Latin text in AAS 66 (1974): 730–47.
55. Ibid., 21.   56. John Paul II, *EV* 71.3.
57. *EV* 72.1.

derstood not as promoting, but as "leaving unpunished"? It is one thing to "grant a right to"; it is another to "leave unpunished." It is unclear whether the Pope views these as virtually identical.[58]

McCormick is not alone in making the distinction between "permitting" and "tolerating." When Poland's 1956 Communist-era "abortion on demand" law was overturned in 1993, the new law prohibited most abortions but made exceptions in some circumstances (notably if pregnancy resulted from rape or if the unborn child would be born with a serious and permanent disability).[59] Some pro-life campaigners, expressing their regret about the exceptions, emphasized—as if to justify their support for its enactment—that the new law did not make abortion "legal" in those instances, but rather it simply did not punish (i.e., it tolerated) those abortions, and that technically the law affirmed the right to life of those unborn children who, nevertheless, could be aborted.[60] Martin Rhonheimer makes a point similar to McCormick's when he contrasts the abortion laws in Germany (where aborting some unborn children is legally tolerated even though the federal constitutional court has affirmed that they possess the right to life), with those of the United States (where the question of the personhood and any subsequent acknowledgment of the right to life of unborn children is

---

58. Richard McCormick, S.J., "The Gospel Of Life How To Read It," *Tablet* (22 April 1995): 492–93.

59. The Polish text of "The Family Planning, Protection of the Human Conceptus, and the Conditions for the Permissibility of Termination of Pregnancy Act," 7 Jan. 1993, is in *Dziennik Ustaw Rzeczypospolitej Polskiej,* Warszawa, 1 March 1993, no. 17.

60. This view was expressed by Dr. Kazimierz Janiak, vice president of Solidarity, in a presentation entitled "Learning from the Polish Experience," delivered to the annual conference of the Society for the Protection of Unborn Children in the UK, 13 Sept. 1997, at which I was present. The distinction, relevant to the point being considered, between laws tolerating and permitting immoral acts, does not, however, appear to be widely acknowledged. For example, the pro-life president of the Polish Senate, Alicja Grześkowiak, speaks of the 1993 Polish legislation as having *legalized* some abortions (as if to say "permitted"). She does not suggest that the Polish legislators were justified in supporting the law, with exceptions, on the grounds that they were merely "tolerating" some abortions; rather, she cites the passage from *EV* 73, which, she claims, teaches that such a compromise can be made. See Alicja Grześkowiak, "Difesa della Famiglia e della Vita nell'Est dell'Europa," *Familia et Vita* 3, no. 3 (1998): 75–76.

overlooked, favoring the mother's "right of privacy," which is taken as including a right to abort). With respect to these different legal situations, and also to the teaching of *Evangelium vitae,* Rhonheimer maintains that "it is important to clarify the difference between the 'decriminalization' ('depenalization') of certain acts and their 'legalization' or 'justification.'"[61] In other words, he is emphasizing the "tolerating" *versus* "permitting" distinction, the importance of which has also been the focus of my remarks. Human law may justly tolerate some immoral actions—uncharitable gossiping, temper tantrums, envy, greed, sloth, lust, masturbation, adultery, prostitution, etc.—even though it cannot justly permit them. Can the moral evil of abortion be similarly tolerated in human law?

Let us return to Aquinas's teaching from the *Summa Theologiae* I-II, q. 96, a. 2, from which the present discussion about human law tolerating some moral evils began.[62] Aquinas notes that human law prohibits (i.e., does not tolerate) those moral evils that harm others, and his first example of such an evil is murder. The reason why human law does not tolerate such evils is fundamental to the legal system itself: human law is necessary "in order that man might have peace and virtue."[63] A system of human law that fails to prohibit murder fails to guarantee what is fundamental for peace, the need for which was the reason the system was established.

Does the legal prohibition of murder also include abortion? Martin Rhonheimer considers the question: "It is insufficient simply to underline the immoral character of procured abortion, or of what is called 'active euthanasia,' in order to establish the need for a corresponding legislative, even penal, rule. We could then ask why the state must protect the life of the unborn, when its abstention from taking any meas-

---

61. Rhonheimer, "Fundamental Rights, Moral Law," 173.

62. "Human laws do not forbid all vices from which the virtuous abstain, but only the more grievous vices from which it is possible for the majority to abstain; and chiefly those that are to the hurt of others, without the prohibition of which human society could not be maintained: thus human law prohibits murder, theft, and such like."

63. *ST* I-II, q. 95, a. 1. See also q. 98, a. 1: "The end of human law is temporal peacefulness in society, an end for which it is sufficient that the law prevent those evils that may disturb the peaceful conditions of society."

ure in that regard would not constitute any threat to peaceful coexistence among men."[64] There is no problem with Rhonheimer's first assertion insofar as a general judgment that an action is immoral does not mean it should be legally prohibited. (I leave aside the question of whether Rhonheimer is asserting specifically that abortion and euthanasia, though immoral, need not be legally prohibited.) However, his question whether the state must protect the right to life rests on a premise that laws allowing abortion do not constitute "a threat to peaceful coexistence among men." One may ask who is included within Rhonheimer's category of "men"? It is not clear, but at any rate Rhonheimer would appear to be excluding those unborn children threatened by abortion laws, whose peace would be violated, and who, as members of the human race, deserve to be numbered among those called "men." Contrary to this view is the teaching of *Evangelium vitae* (which Rhonheimer also later acknowledges)[65] that there cannot be true peace unless human life is defended.[66]

The law's failure to protect all (innocent) human life, whether by failing to punish practices against life or even by specifically legalizing them, is a relatively recent phenomenon. In acknowledging this point in *Evangelium vitae,* John Paul II shows that, contrary to Richard McCormick's critique, he is aware of the distinction between laws that "grant a right to" (i.e., permit) and those that "leave unpunished" (i.e., tolerate) abortion, and that both are causes for concern.[67] Although they sometimes lacked precision, earlier statements of the magisterium, which acknowledged the state's duty to protect the inalienable rights of the person,[68] paved the way for the clear teaching of *Evangelium vitae:*

64. Rhonheimer, "Fundamental Rights, Moral Law," 143.

65. Ibid., 172.

66. "Only respect for life can be the foundation and guarantee of the most precious and essential goods of society, such as democracy and peace. There can be no *true democracy* without a recognition of every person's dignity and without respect for his or her rights. Nor can there be *true peace* unless *life is defended and promoted*" (*EV* 101).

67. "The fact that legislation in many countries . . . has determined not to punish these practices against life, and even to make them altogether legal, is both a disturbing symptom and a significant cause of grave moral decline. Choices once unanimously considered criminal and rejected by the common moral sense are gradually becoming socially acceptable" (*EV* 4).

68. The CDF's *Declaration on Procured Abortion* (1974) has a section on "Morality

"civil law must ensure that all members of society enjoy respect for certain fundamental rights which innately belong to the person, rights which every positive law must recognize and guarantee."[69]

McCormick rightly observes that the section of the encyclical that addresses the relationship between the moral law and civil law (*Evangelium vitae,* nn. 68–74) frequently speaks of laws "legitimizing" or "authorizing" abortion. There is inevitably a difficulty with establishing a vocabulary that conveys, without the need for frequent repetition, the juridical "meaning" of the different sorts of law that fall under the umbrella of "laws against life." It is perhaps unfortunate that a more developed vocabulary was not used to clarify John Paul II's teaching so that, when speaking about abortion legislation, verbs employed to convey the notion of "permitting" were also understood to convey "tolerating." Nevertheless, there is ample evidence that the pope had as the focus of his teaching laws that "permit" and also those that "tolerate"

---

and Law" (nn. 19–23). At times it makes points about legislation on questions of morality that are valid generally (e.g., that law may tolerate an evil to prevent a greater evil, n. 20) without, however, explaining with sufficient clarity why this attitude of toleration does not apply to abortion. The declaration states: "It is true that civil law . . . must often tolerate what is in fact a lesser evil, in order to avoid a greater one. One must, however, be attentive to what a change in legislation can represent. Many will take as authorization what is perhaps only the abstention from punishment. Even more, in the present case [of abortion], this very renunciation seems at the very least to admit that the legislator no longer considers abortion a crime against human life, since murder is still always punished" (n. 20). One might wonder whether this is to be regarded as a principled or a practical objection to laws tolerating abortion. The CDF *Declaration* judges a law which would admit in principle the liceity of abortion *(si lex feratur quae principium liceitatis abortus recipiat)* to be "in itself immoral" *(intrinsece inhonestae)* (n. 22), though readers may perhaps query whether this judgment also includes laws "tolerating" abortion. Elsewhere, however, the document clearly rejects the legal toleration (and not only the permission) of abortion. For example: "It is at all times the task of the State to preserve each person's rights and to protect the weakest" (n. 21). A section on "Moral and Civil Law" is included in the CDF document *Donum vitae* (1987), which rejects the legal toleration of abortion: "[C]ivil law . . . must sometimes tolerate, for the sake of public order, things which it cannot forbid without a greater evil resulting. However, the inalienable rights of the person must be recognized and respected by civil society and the political authority" (Section III) (Quebec: Editions Paulines, 1987, Vatican translation), 48.

69. *EV* 71.

abortion, euthanasia, or any other action against human life. For example, after referring to laws that "legitimize" offenses against life, the pope continues with the rejection of an argument in favor of the "legal toleration" of abortion or euthanasia *(quod autem ex lege abortum et euthanasiam tolerat)*.[70] Elsewhere he makes an explicit distinction between laws that "permit" *(permittunt)* and those that "support" *(favent)* abortion. The distinction is not properly noted by the English translation, and perhaps a wider meaning than "tolerate" can be given to the verb "support"; nevertheless, the addition of *favent* here shows that the pope is not considering only those laws that *permittunt*.[71] (Moreover, if the pope used the verb *permittere* to convey the meaning Aquinas attributed to it, as discussed earlier, then his rejection of laws *permitting* abortion would include laws *tolerating* abortion.) John Paul II's rejection of laws that either permit or tolerate abortion (or support it in any other way) is evident, above all, in his unequivocal affirmation of "the dignity of every human person, respect for inviolable and inalienable human rights [that are] certainly fundamental and not to be ignored."[72] The notion of a "right to life," expressed within the encyclical[73] and consistently in John Paul II's other teachings,[74] is incompatible with the acceptance of laws either permitting *or* tolerating abortion.

The point of this section has been labored, but there has been so

70. Ibid.

71. The English translation reads: "Laws which authorize and promote abortion and euthanasia [*Leges igitur quae permittunt euthanasiam abortumque iisque favent*] . . . are completely lacking in authentic juridical validity" (*EV* 72). Laws that tolerate abortion can be said to support *(favent)* abortion even though they do not permit, authorize, or promote it. The verb "to support" can also refer to other laws that in themselves can perhaps be said neither to permit/authorize nor tolerate nor promote abortion, e.g., a law that provides public funding for abortion.

72. *EV* 70.

73. The focus on the requirement for human law (frequently called "civil law" in the encyclical) to respect inviolable human rights—principally the right to life—is maintained throughout *EV* 70–72.

74. For example: "[T]he personal dignity of every human being demands *the respect, the defence and the promotion of the human person*. It is a question of inherent, universal and inviolable rights. No one, no individual, no group, no authority, no State, can change—let alone eliminate—them because such rights find their source in God himself." John Paul II, Apostolic Exhortation, *Christifideles laici* (1988), n. 38.

much imprecise thinking in this area that it seemed to me to need to be labored. For example, Anthony Zimmerman, S.V.D.,[75] a teacher of moral theology for more than thirty years,[76] refers to Aquinas's teaching that human government can tolerate some evils, such as prostitution:

> I answer that human government is derived from the Divine government, and should imitate it. Now although God is all-powerful and supremely good, nevertheless He allows certain evils to take place in the universe which He might prevent, lest, without them, greater goods might be forfeited, or greater evils ensue. Accordingly in human government also, those who are in authority rightly tolerate certain evils, lest certain goods be lost, or certain greater evils be incurred: thus Augustine says (*De Ordine* 11,4): "If you do away with harlots, the world will be convulsed with lust."[77]

Zimmerman says that he "wrestled with that" but that "after much thought" accepted it. Having accepted that the moral evil of prostitution can be legally tolerated, Zimmerman draws a parallel with all other moral evils, including abortion, and says, "I also accept that, in principle, 'those who are in authority rightly tolerate certain evils' [of abortion) [*sic*], 'lest certain goods be lost, or certain greater evils ensue.' We can accept that principle, without in any way compromising the Laws of God." Two sentences later Zimmerman writes, "God, then, approves that governments legally permit some evil [abortion] [*sic*] when the common welfare is better served by such action. It would be wrong, then, to appeal to divine law to exclude all LEGAL [*sic*] abortion, which nevertheless is, and remains evil, even if legally permitted."

Zimmerman, as can be seen, fails to discern the distinction between "tolerating" and "permitting" and also fails to understand that the moral evils of prostitution and abortion cannot be treated identically in human law. On the contrary, this section notes: (i) that there is a distinction between laws that permit and those that tolerate some moral

75. Anthony Zimmerman, S.V.D., *Allowing Exceptions in Abortion Laws* (1990), at http://zimmerman.catholic.ac/1-23-except.htm (viewed 12 March 2001).
76. Zimmerman mentions this himself in his text, with the apparent purpose of showing that he is expressing a considered view, reached after many years of reflection.
77. *ST* II-II, q. 10, a. 11.

evils; (ii) that the distinction, though it applies validly to some moral evils, does not apply to laws that violate the right to life.

Intrinsically Unjust Laws

The *Catechism of the Catholic Church* (CCC) defines "justice" as "the moral virtue that consists in the constant and firm will to give their due to God and neighbour,"[78] and notes that "Justice towards men disposes one to respect the rights of each and to establish in human relationships the harmony that promotes equity with regard to persons and to the common good."[79] Traditional teaching that human law can tolerate but never permit or obligate some moral evils (such as prostitution or adultery), and that it can neither tolerate nor permit nor obligate other moral evils (notably offenses against human life), is based on a consideration of what is just.

On any number of matters legislators may freely choose whether or not to have actions obligated, permitted, tolerated, or prohibited. Whether a law should obligate or permit or tolerate or prohibit such actions as the wearing of seatbelts, the purchase of alcohol, or the attendance at certain educational establishments, depends entirely on the circumstances in which the law is being considered. The justness (or justice) of such laws cannot be discerned in the abstract. In a particular instance one might make a judgment that to obligate, or to permit, or to tolerate, or to prohibit any of these actions is *unjust,* but legislation on any such matter can never be regarded as *intrinsically* unjust; laws on such matters cannot be regarded as unjust *in themselves* because any such judgment depends not solely on the particular legislation but on a consideration of circumstantial (extrinsic) factors.

By contrast, this chapter has argued that some laws are in themselves objectionable. The Church has consistently held the view that human law need not prohibit every moral evil; it can tolerate some moral evils but it cannot permit or obligate them. A law *tolerating* some moral evil does not violate God's law, but a law *permitting* or *obligating* that evil does do so; it *contradicts* God's law and, in failing to give what is due to God, can be judged to be intrinsically unjust. Offenses against

78. *Catechism of the Catholic Church* (hereafter *CCC*), n. 1807.
79. Ibid.

human life itself, such as abortion, fail to respect the rights of individuals; any law that either tolerates or permits or obligates such offenses fails to respect the rights of individuals and can be judged to be not only unjust but intrinsically unjust. The concept of intrinsic unjustness in law is implied in the Church's traditional teaching and, as I shall demonstrate, is articulated in recent magisterial teachings. The concept of the intrinsic unjustness of restrictive abortion legislation is central to my argument that it is unethical to vote for it.

3. THE PROBLEM OF INTRINSICALLY UNJUST LAWS

Law: Justness and Unjustness

As Chapter 1 recounted, the British pro-life movement's most concerted attempt to change the abortion law was made between 1987 and 1990, beginning with its support for the Abortion (Amendment) Bill, introduced by David Alton, MP, to reduce the upper limit for abortions to 18 weeks. The anticipated life-saving consequence (or effect) of the bill's enactment was sufficient for most pro-lifers to support the bill long in advance of its being published. David Poole, Q.C., the chairman of the Association of Lawyers for the Defence of the Unborn (ALDU) criticized such rash support for proposed legislation that had not even been drafted: "Lawyers usually prefer to read contracts before signing them, or advising their clients to sign. And we were a little surprised at the enthusiasm of some of our friends to sign and endorse the Bill before they had seen or read it."[1]

Ten years after the campaign for the Alton Bill I interviewed John Smeaton, the national director of SPUC, the political arm of the British pro-life movement that had been the main supporter of the Alton Bill. I was keen to discover whether the pro-life movement was, by that time, attentive to the legislative norm it was choosing to support, or whether, as at the time of the Alton Bill, it focused primarily, if not exclusively, on the consequences of legislation. In SPUC's attempts to restrict abortion, I asked, did it matter whether the endorsed bill stated, for example: (i) "Abortions will be permitted up to 10 weeks and prohibited after 10 weeks," or (ii) "Abortions will be prohibited after 10 weeks," or (iii) "Abortion before 10 weeks will not be subject to punishment under the law"?

---

1. David Poole, Q.C., *ALDU News and Comment* 37 (spring 1988): 1.

Smeaton's response was significant, given that he has had a leading decision-making and organizational responsibility[2] for SPUC's legislative campaigns:

> First of all, this is not a question I have really thought about before. And I suppose the reason I have not particularly thought about it before is because I would have automatically supposed that it is the effect that matters. I suppose the counterargument to that would be: is there a danger that a particular form of words would set some sort of legislative principle which could be built on in a negative way in the future? I think this is a political consideration we would be bound to think about. Overall, generally, I would say that it is the effect of the law that matters.[3]

Smeaton's response to my question showed not only that he (and, by implication, the pro-life movement that he led) focuses on the consequences of enacting legislation rather than on the legal norm being supported, but furthermore that there had been no previous consideration of the possibility that there might be a need to address specific legal (in fact, both legislative and jurisprudential) dimensions of the question. If one considers only the consequences (effect) of enacting a law, then the distinction, made in the previous section, between permitting and tolerating moral evils becomes redundant, because the distinction between a law permitting and a law tolerating some immoral acts (say, adultery) resides in the legislation itself and not in the behavior exhibited subsequent to the law's enactment. I contend that Smeaton's response, a response typical of the attitude of large sections of the pro-life movement both in Britain and elsewhere, overlooks the requirements of law. What is law? What is required when judging the suitability of a legislative proposal? How important is the factor of justness in laws? What is meant by an unjust, or even an intrinsically unjust, law? Can one ethically enact unjust laws? Such questions have been generally overlooked by the pro-life movement, but they require careful consideration.

---

2. John Smeaton has been national director of SPUC since 1996 and before that, from the late 1970s, he was its general secretary (in practice, the deputy national director).

3. Smeaton interview, 6 Aug. 1998.

The Essence of Law

What is law? St. Thomas Aquinas defines law as "nothing else than an ordinance of reason [*rationis ordination*] for the common good, made by him who has care of the community, and promulgated";[4] law is "nothing else but a dictate of practical reason [*dictamen practicae rationis*] emanating from the ruler who governs a perfect community."[5]

A more elaborate definition is given by John Finnis, who uses the term "law":

> [T]o refer primarily to rules made, in accordance with regulative legal rules, by a determinate and effective authority (itself identified and, standardly, constituted as an institution by legal rules) for a "complete" community, and buttressed by sanctions in accordance with the rule-guided stipulations of adjudicative institutions, this ensemble of rules and institutions being directed to reasonably resolving any of the community's co-ordination problems (and to ratifying, tolerating, regulating, or overriding co-ordination solutions from any other institutions or sources of norms) for the common good of that community, according to a manner and form itself adapted to that common good by features of specificity, minimization of arbitrariness, and maintenance of a quality of reciprocity between the subjects of the law both amongst themselves and in their relations with the lawful authorities.[6]

This definition of law (if it can be regarded as a definition)[7] is presented "above all" as a "focal meaning" construct.[8] Law, in the focal sense of the term, is fully instantiated only when each of the component terms is fully instantiated,[9] but the definition does not, says Finnis, rule out as

---

4. ". . . definitio legis, quae nihil est aliud quam quaedam rationis ordinatio ad bonum commune, ab eo qui curam communitatis habet, promulgata." *ST* I-II, q. 90, a. 4.

5. ". . . nihil est aliud lex quam quoddam dictamen practicae rationis 'in principe' qui gubernat aliquam communitatem perfectam." *ST* I-II, q. 91, a. 1.

6. John Finnis, *Natural Law and Natural Rights* (Oxford: Clarendon Press, 1980), 276–77.

7. Although it seems that Finnis presents this as a "definition" of law (cf. 278, and also the heading of the section from which I have quoted: "A definition of law," 276); his inclusion at the beginning of the sentence quoted here of the word "primarily" suggests that this sentence is not perhaps to be regarded as a complete definition.

8. Finnis, *Natural Law and Natural Rights,* 277.

9. Ibid.

"non-laws" laws that fail to meet, or meet fully, one or more elements of the definition.[10]

Finnis's definition is more expansive than that of Aquinas, but what, if anything, can be said to be the "essence" of law? Both Finnis and Aquinas include within their definitions the notion of law being a rule made by authority to be adhered to by those subject to authority; it is self-evident, then, that law must be both made by authority and, in order to gain due observance, promulgated. These elements of the definition would seem to be more appropriately described as constituent parts of the legal process (within which "law" is posited) rather than the essence of law itself. The essence of law, as posited authoritatively in accordance with the community's legal processes, would seem to be what Aquinas describes as "an ordinance of reason for the common good."[11] An "ordinance" is precisely that which is ordained by authority, and the essence of law is an ordinance in accord with reason. This notion of law as an "ordinance of reason for the common good" is consistent with Finnis's more elaborate definition, which contains within it a reference to "rules" made by an "authority" which are directed to "reasonably resolving any of the community's co-ordination problems . . . for the common good." If, as it would seem, "reasonableness" is the essence of law, could one—or indeed should one—hold the view that, contrary to Finnis's definition of law as constructed with a focal meaning, a law that lacks reasonableness is "not a law"? I shall return to this question.

In an article on Aquinas's view of the essence of law, Edward Damich focuses not on reasonableness but on law's justness.[12] The two

---

10. Ibid., 278.

11. For a more detailed analysis that essentially makes the same point I am making, see Norman Kretzmann, "Lex Iniusta Non Est Lex: Laws on Trial in Aquinas' Court of Conscience," *American Journal of Jurisprudence* 33 (1988): 110–14. From Aquinas's definitions of law at *ST* I-II, q. 90, a. 3, and q. 91, a. 1, Kretzmann extracts seven inclusion conditions for law. The two conditions that law is (A) a directive of reason and (B) aimed at the common good are, he says, evaluative (moral) conditions of inclusion among full-fledged laws; the other conditions set out non-evaluative (formal) conditions.

12. Edward J. Damich, "The Essence of Law According to Thomas Aquinas," *American Journal of Jurisprudence* 30 (1985): 79–96.

terms are, however, used synonymously. When referring to Isidore's description of positive law as "just" Aquinas says that this means it depends "on the order of reason."[13] Furthermore, Aquinas observes, "laws framed by men are either just or unjust."[14] Establishing whether laws to restrict abortion are just or unjust is critical, yet this fundamental question is commonly overlooked or fudged. It is noteworthy that many writers supporting restrictive abortion legislation have been reluctant to specify whether the legislation they are supporting is in fact just or unjust; instead, they have introduced the terminology of "imperfect" laws.[15] Robert George has described restrictive legislation as being "imperfectly just" and then has acknowledged it, two sentences later, to be "objectively unjust."[16] Descriptions like "imperfect" law should have no place in serious discussions of this question, and restrictive abortion laws should be identified for what they are—either "just"

13. *ST* I–II, q. 95, a. 3, c.

14. *ST* I-II q. 96, a. 4, c.

15. The term was used most notably as the title of a symposium ("Catholics and Pluralist Society—The Case of 'Imperfect Laws'") arranged by the Congregation for the Doctrine of the Faith in Rome, 9–12 Nov. 1994. The proceedings were published in Italian: Joseph Joblin and Réal Tremblay, eds., *I Cattolici e la Società Pluralista: Il Caso delle "Leggi Imperfette"* (Bologna: Edizioni Studio Domenicano, 1996). The term "imperfect legislation" is now commonly used in general pro-life literature and defined in one text as "a law which forbids some injustices but permits others." See Helen Watt, *Abortion* (London: CTS/Linacre Centre, 2001), 38–39, 46.

16. "The Pope does not provide an extensive argument in behalf of his teaching about the permissibility of sometimes supporting imperfectly just laws.... While it can never be fair to will that members of a disfavored class—whether the unborn, the disabled, or members of some racial or religious minority group—be excluded from legal protections one wills for oneself and those dear to one, a legislator or voter is personally responsible for no unfairness to the victims of an objectively unjust law where he supports that law precisely, and only, because the alternative is even less protective of its victims." Robert P. George, "The Gospel of Life." Elsewhere, in a paper published by the National Conference of Catholic Bishops/United States Catholic Conference, George refers to the same category of restrictive law as "not perfectly just" but "less unjust" than other laws, in such a way that he seems to be unsure whether one should focus on their justness or unjustness. See Robert P. George, "Political Action and Legal Reform in *Evangelium vitae*," at http://www.nccbusc.org/prolife/programs/rlp/96rlpgeo.htm (viewed 25 May 2000). Although a vessel may be legitimately described as half full or half empty depending on one's perspective, the judgment as to whether a restrictive abortion law is just or intrinsically unjust is not a matter of perspective.

or "unjust."[17] During the discussion period prior to the publication of *Evangelium vitae* (*EV*), the Pontifical Council for the Family noted that "the iniquity of pro-abortion laws is not only derived from their consequences, but also from the destruction of the very concept of law."[18] More recently Cardinal Ratzinger has expressed a similar concern that within the framework of juridical positivism accepted by the contemporary world "the very concept of law is losing its precise definition."[19] He acknowledges—consistent with the view I am advancing—that the problem is that of *"recta ratio"* and that "this right reason must try to discern what is just—the essence of law."[20]

It would appear that those who are actively engaged in attempting to promote the right to life are also losing sight of the very concept of law: the essence of law is its justness, and the unjustness of restrictive abortion laws is a factor that must be acknowledged and considered further.

Unjust Laws

Laws (i.e., positive or human or civil laws) are *just,* says Aquinas, (i) when they are ordained to the common good, (ii) when they are within the lawmaker's limits of power, and (iii) when the burdens imposed are in due proportion with a view to the common good. A judgment can be made that laws failing to meet these conditions are *unjust.* In particular, however, Aquinas specifies laws to be unjust (i) by being contrary to the divine good, and (ii) by being contrary to human good.[21]

---

17. The notion of "imperfect" law is, in any case, imprecise and could refer to a wide range of laws, some of which might be just, others unjust; see Colin Harte, "Challenging a Consensus: Why *Evangelium Vitae* Does Not Permit Legislators to Vote for 'Imperfect Legislation,'" in *Culture of Life—Culture of Death,* ed. Luke Gormally (London: Linacre Centre, 2002), 340.

18. The Pontifical Council for the Family, *In the Service of Life* (Instrumentum Laboris), (Vatican City: Libreria Editrice Vaticana, 1992), part 4, p. 17.

19. Joseph Cardinal Ratzinger, "Contemporary Crisis of Law," (address given on the occasion of his receiving the degree of *Doctor Honoris Causa* from the LUMSA Faculty of Jurisprudence in Rome, 10 Nov. 1999), viewed at http://www.culture-of-life.org/law_crisis.htm (29 Oct. 2000).

20. Ibid.

21. *ST* I-II, q. 96, a. 4. Aquinas presents these in the opposite order.

Aquinas's treatment of the two types of unjustness in law follows from his earlier treatment of the two aspects of human law, which he calls the *ius gentium* and *ius civile*.[22] He teaches that every human law has the nature of law only insofar as it is derived from the natural law, and he specifies the two ways in which human law can be derived: (i) the *ius gentium* refers to those laws that, being derived from the natural law "as a conclusion from premises," are the "moral" content of human law; hence laws prohibiting killing, stealing, and such things;[23] one can, to some extent, speak of such laws as being *established* by the natural law; (ii) the *ius civile* refers to those laws that are made "by way of determination of certain generalities" and are the strictly "political" content of human law; one can perhaps speak of such laws not as being established by the natural law but as being determined by human reasoning, a reasoning that cannot, of course, contradict the natural law, which is itself a law of reason. All human law is positive law, but whereas the *ius civile* is solely positive law, the *ius gentium* also has the force of natural law.

The *ius gentium* component of human law, then, consists of those matters established by natural law, such as the prohibition of murder (including abortion), bigamy, stealing, etc. The punishment for violation of these laws is not established by the natural law; rather, punishments are aspects of the *ius civile,* the determination of which is the task of legislators using their own prudential judgments. Also part of the *ius civile* is the very broad range of matters for which decisions must be made with respect to such things as economics, transport, health, education, agriculture, the environment, law and order, and so on, i.e., those areas for which a diverse range of legitimate political judgments is possible, the questions under consideration concerning "political" and not, strictly speaking, "moral" issues (notwithstanding the fact that values such as justice and fairness should be the basis upon which legislators make their decisions). Although the very need for a human authority established primarily "in order that man might have peace and virtue"[24] and to resolve a community's coordination problems is in itself established by the natural law (i.e., *ius gentium*), the determinations of

22. *ST* I-II, q. 95, a. 4. 23. *ST* I-II, q. 95, a. 2.
24. *ST* I-II, q. 95, a. 1.

the actual forms of government, with their different layers, systems, processes, checks and balances, etc., which formally constitute the "rule of law," are aspects of the *ius civile*.

Let us return, then, to Aquinas's classification of the two types of unjust law. He lists, first, those laws that are "contrary to human good" and are unjust for various reasons, e.g., the ruler enacts laws burdensome to his subjects for his own advantage, or on matters for which he does not have authority[25] or in such a way that burdens are distributed unfairly.[26] In other words, this category of unjust laws refers to unjustness with respect to the *ius civile*. The second type consists of those laws that are unjust "through being opposed to the divine good."[27] In providing an illustration of such a law Aquinas writes: "such are the laws of tyrants inducing [*inducentes*] to idolatry or to anything else contrary to the divine law," a legitimate illustration, although it has unfortunately led to a misunderstanding. It is appropriate that Aquinas should have described this category of unjust laws as constituting those things contrary to the divine law and not simply the natural law, it being understood that the divine law includes all the precepts of the natural law as well as those of a specifically religious character (such as observing holy days) that are not part of the content of natural law. The unfortunate aspect of Aquinas's illustration lies in his choice of a law regarded as unjustly *obligating* (or *commanding*) something. Thus Martin Rhonheimer asserts that "the doctrine of the law that is unjust because it goes against natural law is applicable only in those cases in which civil law *commands* or *orders* something to be done that is immoral. In the case of abortion, this is not the fundamental problem. No one defends the right of the legislator to order the carrying out of abortions."[28]

Rhonheimer's assertion would appear to be based on Aquinas's il-

25. In this instance Aquinas appears not to refer to laws that are contrary to the natural law (and hence beyond the competence of the lawmaker's authority) but simply to laws concerning matters that exceed the lawmaker's constitutional powers. This also seems to be John Finnis's reading of this section in "Is Natural Law Theory Compatible with Limited Government?" in Robert P. George, ed., *Natural Law, Liberalism, and Morality* (Oxford: Clarendon Press, 1996), 2, 19n10.

26. *ST* I-II, q. 96, a. 4. c.

27. Ibid.

28. Rhonheimer, "Fundamental Rights, Moral Law," 149n40.

lustration and not on the actual classification of this sort of unjust law. In his account of the two categories of unjust laws, John Finnis includes within this second category (rightly in my view) not only those laws that *command* subjects to do things they should not do but also laws that "authorize" immoral acts.[29] In other words, this category of unjust laws generally corresponds with unjustness with respect to the *ius gentium* (while also including unjustness with respect to matters covered by divine though not natural law).

I shall leave to one side those laws which violate the divine law on matters, such as observance of holy days, that are not contained within natural law, and consider the question of unjust laws insofar as they are unjust with respect to the *ius civile,* i.e., where the unjustness is of a strictly "political" nature ("unjust-I" laws)[30] or with respect to the *ius gentium,* i.e., where the unjustness is of a "moral" nature ("unjust-II" laws).[31] The two radically different types of unjustness reveal the need to identify laws not simply as just or unjust but as either just or unjust-I or unjust-II, this further distinction being relevant to the way unjust laws are viewed and responded to.

How, then, should we view unjust laws? If, as it seems, justness is the essence of law, is an unjust law then "not a law"? Positivists, following John Austin, might say it is "stark nonsense" to suggest that an unjust law is not a law;[32] qua "law" subjects are variously permitted to do

29. John Finnis, *Aquinas: Moral, Political, and Legal Theory* (Oxford: Oxford University Press, 1998), 272. To illustrate his point Finnis cites Aquinas at *ST* II-II, q. 57, a. 2, ad 2: "The human will can, by common agreement, make a thing to be just provided that it be not, of itself contrary to natural justice [*naturalem iustitia*], and it is in such matters that positive right [or positive law, *ius positivum*] has its place. . . . If, however, a thing is, of itself, contrary to natural right [*ius naturale*] the human will cannot make it just, for instance, by decreeing that it is lawful to steal or to commit adultery. Hence it is written: 'Woe to them that make wicked laws' (Isaiah 10:1)."

30. The description of "unjust-I" and "unjust-II" laws is taken from Kretzmann, "Lex Iniusta Non Est Lex," 118.

31. Because they refer to laws that violate the divine and not only the natural law, unjust-II laws are not solely those that are unjust with respect to the *ius gentium* aspect of human law.

32. "Now, to say that human laws which conflict with the Divine law are not binding, that is to say, are not laws, is to talk stark nonsense. The most pernicious laws, and therefore those which are most opposed to the will of God, have been and are continu-

or prohibited from (and punished for) doing whatever the law specifies can or cannot be done. Even those who recognize that human law must be in accord with the natural law are often reluctant to judge an unjust law to be "not a law." Edward Damich, for example, observes that Aquinas says that an unjust law only *seems (videtur)* not to be a law,[33] and John Finnis notes that "Aquinas avoids saying flatly that 'an unjust law is not a law: *lex iniusta non est lex*.'"[34] These arguments against the *"lex iniusta non est lex"* position can be easily dealt with: (i) the fact that one is legally free to perform a moral evil that should be punished or that one is wrongly punished by an unjust law for performing a good act, does not mean that the particular "law" *is* a law, merely that authority is treating it *as though it were* a law; (ii) Aquinas (quoting Augustine) does not necessarily say that an unjust law only *seems* to be a law *("non videtur esse lex, quae iusta non fuerit")*;[35] the Latin *videtur* could be translated differently with the meaning of "is seen," "is evidently," "is right," or "is thought";[36] (iii) although Aquinas does not say that an unjust law *is not* a law *(non est lex),* he does say that any law at variance with the natural law *will not be* a law *(non erit lex)* but rather a corruption of law.[37] The view that an unjust law is not law in its fullest sense (i.e., *simpliciter*) but is law in some respects (i.e., *secundum quid*)[38] can to some extent overcome part of the difficulty with the *lex iniusta non est lex* formula. It seems to me, however, that the key question is not so much whether one identifies an unjust law as "not a law" or as a "law *secundum quid*"; it is more relevant to establish in what way a law is unjust, and accordingly to determine an appropriate response to it.

---

ally enforced as laws by judicial tribunals." John Austin, *The Province of Jurisprudence Determined* (1832; reprint, Cambridge: Cambridge University Press, 1995), 158.

33. Damich, "Essence of Law According to Aquinas," 91.
34. Finnis, *Natural Law and Natural Rights,* 364.
35. *ST* I-II, q. 95, a. 2.
36. The query about the translation is made by Kretzmann, "Lex Iniusta Non Est Lex," 102.
37. *ST* I-II, q. 95, a. 2.
38. See Finnis, *Natural Law and Natural Rights,* 363–66.

Extrinsic and Intrinsic Unjustness

We have already identified, following Aquinas's teaching, two distinct categories of unjust law: laws that are contrary to either the human good or the divine good. I have suggested that, with some qualification, the distinction can also be described in terms of whether they are unjust with respect to the *ius civile* or the *ius gentium*. The distinctions can also be viewed, as I shall explain, in terms of the extrinsic or intrinsic unjustness of laws.

The three illustrations Aquinas gives of laws that are contrary to the human good[39] *(ius civile)* are of laws that are extrinsically unjust, i.e., the unjustness is not found in the law considered in itself but requires a consideration of extrinsic (i.e., circumstantial) factors. A law that substantially increases taxes imposes burdens on taxpayers, but the unjustness of such a law, as in Aquinas's example, derives not from the burden per se but rather from its imposition for the ruler's own advantage. The same burden would be imposed if the proceeds of the taxes were used to build hospitals or to alleviate the suffering of starving people in other countries, but this sort of burden could be judged to be a just imposition, and the law imposing it a just law. Similarly, if a ruler legislates on matters outside his competence (it being understood in Aquinas's illustration that the legislation does not violate the moral law but rather, for example, affects some aspect of an education policy beyond his remit), then the unjustness of the legislation is not found in the law per se but rather in the extrinsic factor of its being beyond the legislator's competence. The unjustness of a law distributing burdens unfairly is discerned, likewise, not so much by that single law as by that law in the context of other laws and social conditions, i.e., by extrinsic factors. All laws within this category judged to be unjust are not unjust per se but always with respect to extrinsic factors.

By contrast, laws that are contrary to the natural or divine law must be judged to be *intrinsically unjust*.[40] A law specifically "permitting" (in the precise sense proposed in Chapter 2) abortion, adultery, homosexu-

---

39. *ST* I-II, q. 96, a. 4.

40. John Finnis would also seem to accept the view that laws within this second category, unlike those within the first, are *intrinsically* unjust. He refers to "unjust

al acts, theft, slander, or idolatry can be judged to be not only "unjust" but "intrinsically unjust." The law itself requires that such a judgment be made without any consideration of extrinsic factors, and a consideration of extrinsic factors cannot reverse this judgment.

The subject of the present discussion is abortion laws, and it must be acknowledged that we are dealing with *intrinsically unjust* legislation. A law commanding or permitting abortion can easily be seen to be contrary to the natural and divine law and hence to be intrinsically unjust, but can the same be said of a law *tolerating* abortion? Certainly, one might think, there is unjustness if the law does not prohibit some or even all abortions—because those human beings for whom abortion is not prohibited are denied the protection afforded by the law to other human beings. If, however, a law does not say precisely that it is licit or "permitted" to abort, can one say that such a law tolerating abortion is *violating* the natural law and thus intrinsically unjust? If a law can tolerate other immoral acts like adultery or prostitution without violating the natural law, why cannot the same be said for laws tolerating abortion? I argued in Chapter 2 that human law cannot tolerate abortion because humanity's need for peace is the foundation of human law.[41] Although the systems of human law are a matter of human determination *(ius civile)*, the actual requirement of a system is rooted in natural law *(ius gentium)*, and the fundamental element of that system—peace, protection of human life from attack—entails by logical necessity that

---

positive laws—and above all, a law whose injustice is not merely a matter of improper motivations or procedural improprieties, but intrinsic." See his "Natural Law—Positive Law," in *"Evangelium Vitae" and Law,* ed. Alfonso Lopez Trujillo, Gonzalo Herranz, and Elio Sgreccia (Vatican City: Libreria Editrice Vaticana, 1997), 209. Martin Rhonheimer refers to "the intrinsic injustice of a law, the fact that the law may *command* something contrary to natural or divine law, or that it may impose excessively onerous obligations or burdens on citizens" in "Fundamental Rights, Natural Law," 143. I contend that Rhonheimer is wrong to focus solely on laws that "command" something contrary to natural or divine law, and that laws permitting (and, in some instances, those tolerating) immoral actions are also intrinsically unjust. Furthermore I maintain that laws imposing excessively onerous obligations are extrinsically and not intrinsically unjust. Rhonheimer does, however, acknowledge the concept of an intrinsically unjust law.

41. Cf. *ST* I-II, q. 95, a. 1. See the section on "Permitting and Tolerating Abortion in Human Law" in Chapter 2.

no abortion or other direct attack against (innocent) human life be legally tolerated, let alone permitted or commanded. A law, then, that tolerates abortion is a violation of the natural law.[42] John Paul II cites Aquinas's teaching that any law that is in any way opposed to the natural law is not really a law but rather a corruption of the law[43] and immediately follows this with remarks revealing that a law that tolerates abortion violates the natural law: "Now the first and most immediate application of this teaching concerns a human law which disregards the fundamental right and source of all other rights which is the right to life, a right belonging to every individual" (*EV* 72.2). Indeed, the "violation of the right to life" (by a law tolerating or permitting or commanding abortion) can equally be described as a "violation of the natural law," as the English translation of the Latin text of *Evangelium vitae* indicates: "A law which violates an innocent person's natural right to life [*norma quae naturalem legem violat ad vitam cuiusdam innocentis pertinentem*] is unjust and, as such, is not valid as a law" (*EV* 90).

The concept of the intrinsically unjust law is acknowledged in the Congregation for the Doctrine of the Faith's *Declaration on Abortion* (1974), which refers to a law "which would admit in principle the liceity of abortion" as an example of "a law which is in itself immoral" *(legi intrinsece inhonestae),*[44] and in *EV* 73.2, which refers to "a law permitting abortion or euthanasia" as an example of "an intrinsically unjust law" *(de lege ... suapte natura iniqua).* (The encyclical refers to a law "permitting" abortion or euthanasia, such a law being merely an illus-

---

42. In his description of Aquinas's account of how positive law is derived from the natural law, and in his acceptance that "the positive law must prohibit (and punish)" the killing of innocent persons, Robert George would also appear to accept that abortion must be prohibited (and punished)—i.e., not tolerated—in positive law, and that the toleration of the killing of innocent persons (including the unborn) is contrary to natural law. See Robert P. George, "Natural Law and Positive Law," in *The Autonomy of Law,* ed. Robert P. George (Oxford: Clarendon Press, 1996), 328. See also Wolfgang Waldstein, "Natural Law and the Defense of Life in *Evangelium Vitae,*" in *Evangelium Vitae: Five Years of Confrontation with the Society* (Proceedings of the Sixth Annual Assembly of the Pontifical Academy for Life, 11–14 Feb. 2000), ed. Juan di Dios Vial Correa and Elio Sgreccia (Vatican City: Libreria Editrice Vaticana, 2001), 223–42.

43. *EV* 72.1, citing *ST* I-II, q. 95, a. 2.

44. CDF, *Declaration on Procured Abortion,* n. 22.

tration of the point it is making about intrinsically unjust laws. It is clearly a misreading of the encyclical to suggest that laws that do not "permit" but merely "tolerate"—let alone those that "obligate"—abortion or euthanasia are not to be included within the category of intrinsically unjust laws. Of course, if the encyclical uses the verb *"permittere"* to convey Aquinas's meaning, then the illustration covers laws that tolerate abortion too.)[45] The identification of some laws as "intrinsically unjust" must precede any consideration of one's response to such laws.

Responding to Intrinsically Unjust Laws

It is not possible to answer how one should respond to unjust laws without establishing whether one is dealing with extrinsically unjust (unjust-I) or intrinsically unjust (unjust-II) laws. Although Aquinas says, with respect to unjust-I laws, that they seem not to be law *(lex esse non videtur, quae iusta non fuerit),* nevertheless such laws may sometimes oblige one in conscience "to avoid scandal or disorder."[46] Thus, although a consideration of extrinsic factors might lead to a judgment that some laws are unjust—say, by imposing excessive tax burdens, or by unfairly restricting one's employment prospects, or by restricting (e.g., by curfew) one's movement—nevertheless in order to avoid scandal or disorder (i.e., for the common good) one might be obliged to observe those "laws." One notes that in accepting the burdens or restrictions of such laws one is *not doing evil;* furthermore, one's actions do not constitute a judgment that the law is just or even that the law "is a law" even though it is being treated as though it were a law.

Aquinas's response to intrinsically unjust laws—i.e., to those laws that include abortion laws—is notably different. There is no suggestion that such laws can ever oblige in conscience, but rather "laws of this kind must nowise be observed *(tales leges nullo modo licet observare)* because, as stated in Acts 5:29, 'we ought to obey God rather than men.'"[47] In *Evangelium vitae* John Paul II teaches that (intrinsically un-

---

45. See the discussion in the previous chapter, in which I argued that verb *permittere* as used by Aquinas has a modern translation of both "to permit" and "to tolerate."
46. *ST* I-II, q. 96, a. 4.
47. Ibid.

just) laws permitting or supporting abortion and euthanasia "are completely lacking in authentic juridical validity" and are not "true, morally binding civil law[s]."[48] Abortion (like euthanasia) is a crime, says John Paul II, that "no human law can claim to legitimize" *(potest rata facere),* and such laws not only do not bind one in conscience but, on the contrary, "there is a grave and clear obligation to oppose them by conscientious objection."[49] A law, he emphasizes, that violates the right to life of even one innocent person *(norma quae naturalem legem violat ad vitam cuiusdam innocentis pertinentem)* is "unjust" and "not valid as a law" *(legis momentum habere non potest; EV* 90.3).

Immediately prior to the section that deals with the "problem of conscience" encountered by a legislator who is unable to prohibit all abortions *(EV* 73.3), is a short paragraph specifying how one should respond to intrinsically unjust laws: "In the case of an intrinsically unjust law, such as a law permitting abortion or euthanasia, it is therefore never licit to obey it, or to 'take part in a propaganda campaign in favour of such a law, or vote for it.'"[50] With good reason John Finnis asks, "But how could one *obey* a law which merely permits?"[51] He notes that the Italian text *"non e mai lecito conformarsi ad essa"* and the Latin ". . . eidem se accommodare" (i.e., the concepts of not conforming or accommodating oneself to intrinsically unjust laws), are more readily intelligible. The concept of "not accommodating oneself" to an intrinsically unjust law includes, but goes beyond, merely "obeying" such a law, though English texts frequently use, in this context, the more restricted verb "obey." Aquinas, for example, does not say that intrinsically unjust (unjust-II) laws should not be *obeyed* (although this is how he is sometimes translated)[52] but that they should not (as acknowledged by some more

48. "Leges igitur quae permittunt euthanasiam abortumque iisque favent . . . iuridiciali carent vera vi." *EV* 72.3.

49. "Huiusmodi leges non modo conscientiam non devinciunt, verum graviter nominatimque compellunt ut iisdem per conscientiae repugnantiam officiatur." *EV* 73.1. The English translation unsatisfactorily speaks of there being no obligation "to obey" such laws, a point I shall take up below.

50. *EV* 73.2. The quotation within the paragraph is from the 1974 CDF *Declaration on Abortion,* n. 22.

51. Finnis, "Natural Law—Positive Law," 206.

52. J. G. Dawson translates the Latin *Et tales leges nullo modo licet observare* as

accurate translations) be in any way *observed:* tales leges nullo modo licet *observare*.⁵³ Elsewhere in *Evangelium vitae* the English translation says that "there is no obligation in conscience to obey such [intrinsically unjust] laws," the Latin text introducing the wider concept of not binding in conscience: *"Huiusmodi leges ... conscientiam non devinciunt"* (*EV* 73.1).

The short paragraph (*EV* 73.2) is open to the charge of being tautologous, because if it is not licit to "accommodate oneself" to an intrinsically unjust law, then it would appear to follow automatically that one cannot take part in a propaganda campaign in favor of an intrinsically unjust law or vote for it, because actions of this sort signify an accommodation with the law. At any rate, the paragraph—repeating the teaching of the CDF's 1974 declaration—states unambiguously and significantly that it is *never licit to vote* for an intrinsically unjust law. I shall return to the question of one's response to unjust laws.

Legislative Votes Based on a Natural Law Jurisprudence

In the previous chapter I noted that judgments about how to vote on abortion legislation should not be based on a sociological, pedagogical, pluralistic, positivist, or even "pro-life" jurisprudence, but rather on a natural law jurisprudence. Deliberations as to whether a legislative measure may or may not be favorable to the pro-life cause are beside the point if the measure itself can be judged to be intrinsically unjust and thus contrary to the natural law. The natural law is the touchstone to which legislators must appeal in the value judgments required in making good law,⁵⁴ and the factor of intrinsic unjustness in any measure confronting legislators should be sufficient to tell them that the decision to vote to enact it is not consistent with ethical lawmaking.

Evangelium vitae teaches that a law violating the right to life of an

---

"Such laws may under no circumstances be obeyed." *ST* I-II, q. 96, a. 4, in *Aquinas, Selected Political Writings,* ed. A. P. D'Entrèves (Oxford: Basil Blackwell, 1948), 137.

53. "Laws of this kind must nowise be observed," as given by the Fathers of the English Dominican Province in their translation of the *Summa Theologiae* (London: Burns, Oates and Washbourne, 1920).

54. See Ernest Caparros, "Some Myths and Some Realities in the Contemporary World of Law," *American Journal of Jurisprudence* 35 (1990): 100.

innocent person (e.g., a law that tolerates, permits, or obligates abortion) is "unjust" and "not valid as a law" (*EV* 90). A *just law* on abortion must prohibit all abortions: as John Finnis notes, "A just law forbidding the killing of the unborn cannot, I believe, admit an exception 'to save the life of the mother.'"[55] However, Finnis does not reject as immoral the act of voting in favor of restrictive legislation; on the contrary, he claims that a legislator could rightly vote for a law of the form, "Abortion is lawful up to 16 weeks," if a previous law (or a law that would otherwise be enacted) were to say, "Abortion is lawful up to 24 weeks."[56] In the next chapter I shall pay particular attention to John Finnis's defense of such legislative votes and argue that his position is philosophically unsound. For the moment, I wish merely to draw attention to what Finnis rightly acknowledges to be a just abortion law (i.e., one that prohibits all direct abortions and does not make an exception even to save the life of the mother), and to note that my main objection to his support for restrictive legislation such as the 16-week law he proposes is that the legislation itself is unjust: more precisely, intrinsically unjust. The touchstone to which legislators must appeal when judging the justness of a law is the natural law that prohibits all abortions; a law cannot be judged just by considering the context, i.e., whether the previous law permitted or tolerated more abortions, or whether a different law permitting or tolerating more abortions might be enacted if the one subject to a vote is not passed.

One argument against voting for restrictive legislation tolerating or permitting abortion is that, being intrinsically unjust and contrary to natural law, it is not valid as law and is even 'not a law." This sort of restrictive legislation is, objectively, a "law against life" even if a legislator chooses to vote for it in order to stop some abortions and thereby save some lives. Tadeusz Styczeń, S.D.S., describes a "law against life" as

---

55. John Finnis, "The Legal Status of the Unborn Baby," *Catholic Medical Quarterly* (Aug. 1992): 9.

56. John Finnis, "Unjust Laws in a Democratic Society: Some Philosophical and Theological Reflections," *Notre Dame Law Review* 71, no. 4 (1996): 595–604. See also Finnis, "The Catholic Church and Public Policy Debates in Western Liberal Societies: The Basis and Limits of Intellectual Engagement," in Gormally, *Issues for a Catholic Bioethic,* 268–69.

"an anti-law acknowledged as a law; it is lawlessness identified with lawfulness; in the language of logic it may only be described as contradiction: (p · ~ p), while in everyday language it is called the absurd."[57]

One might assume, although Styczeń does not state it explicitly, that the "anti-law" of a law against life can also be identified as "not a law." (In fact, the label "not a law" lacks some of the force of Styczeń's judgment that a law against life is *not merely* "not a law" but the very antithesis of law.) The absurdity of voting for that which is "not a law" to be enacted as "law" is as manifest as the absurdity of voting to enact an "anti-law" as "law," and Styczeń's negative view of a law against life is consistent with, although expressed in stronger terms than, John Paul II's rejection of such a law being "not really a law" *(non erit lex),*[58] and not a "true ... law"[59] and "not valid as law."[60] A recognition of the intrinsic unjustness of legislation that in itself restricts abortion to some unborn children but not others, and the absurdity of voting for it, seems to me a satisfactory basis on which to base a moral argument against voting for it: it is hardly reasonable to choose an absurdity.

The foregoing remarks should not be construed, however, as suggesting that my argument can be reduced to a simple syllogism of the form:

> legislators have the authority to enact law and only law;
> X (a law against life) is "not a law";
> therefore, legislators do not have the authority to enact X.

A law against life, one might object, is not a law *simpliciter* (i.e., in the focal sense as Finnis describes it) but is a law in some sense, i.e., *secundum quid*. If this is accepted, the syllogism can be faulted as too simplis-

---

57. Taduesz Styczeń, S.D.S., "Ethics as the Theory of Natural Law Facing the 'Law against Life,'" in *Medicine and Law: For or against Life?* ed. Elio Sgreccia, Tadeusz Styczeń, S.D.S., Dorota Chabrajska, Jarosław Merecki, S.D.S. (Vatican City: Libreria Edictrice Vaticana, 1999), 219.

58. *EV* 72.1, quoting Aquinas, *ST* I-II, q. 93, a. 3, ad 2.

59. *"veram ... legem." EV* 72.3.

60. *"legis momentum habere non potest." EV* 90.3. See also *EV* 72.3, which says such laws "are completely lacking in authentic juridical validity."

tic. Although I think the syllogism has merit, I shall accept the objection to it. In my view the argument against the objection provides more compelling grounds for rejecting as unethical votes for (intrinsically unjust) restrictive abortion legislation. My argument is that it is precisely because an intrinsically unjust law *is in some sense law* that one should not vote to enact it, a point I shall now try to explain.

The Moral Problem Associated with the Recognition That an Unjust Law Has Some Character of Law

To help explain why the objection to voting to enact (intrinsically unjust) restrictive abortion legislation does not depend on a judgment that it is "not a law," I shall consider a very different, albeit analogous, hypothetical situation: that of "Mr. Smith," a divorced Catholic who contracts marriage for a second time while his first wife is still alive and who does not qualify for a declaration of nullity with respect to his first marriage. By marrying a second time is he contracting "marriage" or "not a marriage"? Marriage being an indissoluble union, a civil divorce cannot break that union: the Church teaches that a civil marriage after a civil divorce "cannot be recognized as valid" if the first union was so.[61] If Mr. Smith's first marriage is indissoluble, and if a man cannot be married to more than one woman at a time, it might seem logical to regard any subsequent marriage as "not a marriage." However, although the subsequent marriage is objectively not valid on a religious or moral level it is recognized as valid *legally;* the man and woman would be legally entitled to the status and benefits attributed to those judged legally married. An Austinian judgment to the effect that it is stark nonsense to say that a divorced Catholic who remarries is not married inevitably follows. And even the Church herself, one can argue, does not claim that the divorcee's second marriage is not a marriage in *any* sense. After all, she labels such people as "remarried"[62] and is likely to

---

61. *CCC*, n. 1650.

62. For example, in the title of the document from the CDF, *Letter to the Bishops of the Catholic Church Concerning the Reception of Holy Communion of Divorced and Remarried Members of the Faithful* (1994). John Paul II also refers to the divorced and "remarried" in *Familiaris consortio* (1981), n. 84, and *Reconciliatio et paenitentia* (1984), n. 34.

call Mr. Smith's second wife by the name to which she is legally entitled—Mrs. Smith—notwithstanding the judgment that the marriage is not valid and that the "real" Mrs. Smith is an entirely different person.

In other words, marriage contracts and legislation can both be viewed as "focal meaning" constructs; i.e., the absence of a particular element of a definition of marriage or of legislation does not lead to an unequivocal judgment of "not a marriage" or "not a law." Mr. Smith's second marriage is not a marriage *simpliciter* (i.e., it is not a marriage that fulfills *all* the moral and formal conditions of marriage), but it is a marriage *secundum quid* (i.e., it is a marriage *in some respects* because it fulfills some of those conditions), just as an intrinsically unjust abortion law is not a law *simpliciter* even if it is a law *secundum quid*.

In my view, it is precisely because Mr. Smith's second marriage is a marriage in some respects that his second act of "getting married" (which I shall refer to as "instantiating" the marriage) can be judged to be an intrinsically immoral action. Similarly, it is precisely because an intrinsically unjust restrictive abortion law is a law in some respects that a legislator's act of voting to enact that law (which I shall refer to as "instantiating" the law) can be judged to be an intrinsically immoral action. The instantiation of Mr. Smith's "second marriage" cannot be likened to an actor "marrying" in a stage drama, an act that lacks both the formal and moral conditions of a marriage and is uncontroversially "not a marriage," even if it possesses externally some of the characteristics of Mr. Smith's action; rather, Mr. Smith's action is a public act that as such is publicly presented as being a valid instantiation of marriage. Insofar as Mr. Smith is not morally free to instantiate the second marriage, his action, which has an objective public signification or meaning, can be judged to be "a lie": he is participating in a public act that as such purports to be "valid" but that, because of a moral defect, is necessarily "invalid."

Let us be clear. I am not arguing that the instantiation of Mr. Smith's second marriage is immoral because it is likely to lead to further immoral sexual actions, or because it may contribute to the breakdown of the nuclear family as the basis for society, or because it may negatively affect the children from his first marriage, or for other reasons. Even if there were no negative consequences or further immoral actions resulting from the "marriage," the act of instantiating it would be wrong in itself because the act of instantiating the marriage would be "a lie." That which is legal is properly based on that which is moral: the instantiation of Mr. Smith's second marriage would purport to instantiate as valid that which cannot, at the level of morality which has precedence, be accepted as valid.

With respect to the instantiation of intrinsically unjust restrictive legislation the same argument applies. A vote to enact any human law has an objective public meaning such that it is understood and presented as being a valid instantiation of law. The "moral" validity of a law has precedence over its "legal" validity because the moral (natural) law is the source of all human law, and the judgment of "validity" adhering to any law is understood as applying, first, to its moral validity, and only second to its legal validity. If a law is intrinsically unjust (i.e., if it is not an ordinance of reason for the common good), it lacks the essence of law and is essentially "invalid" even if it has some properties of "legal validity." The objection is not so much that one is voting to enact "not a law" as "law" as that one is trying to enact as law that which is "intrinsically unjust" and, equivalently, "contrary to reason"—when the factors of being "just" and "in conformity with reason" are moral conditions for determining the validity of law.

Insofar as a vote to enact intrinsically unjust restrictive legislation possesses the character of being, as such, a public act with the objective meaning of being a valid instantiation of law, one cannot discount what is objectively required for any instantiation of law; in particular, the moral conditions (essentially justness) must be satisfied. One cannot argue, as I shall explain in Chapter 5, that *normally* justness is required for any instantiation of law to be judged morally good, but that the situation of voting for restrictive abortion legislation is a "special case" in which one's actions should not be identified in terms of voting for an intrinsically unjust law (an evil) but rather in terms of prohibiting some abortions and saving the lives of some unborn children (a good). Leaving aside the fact that this sort of argument fails to distinguish properly between means and ends, objects and intentions (as I shall explain in Chapter 4), it is entirely illegitimate to maintain that the norms of lawmaking be suspended in this particular instance of lawmaking in order to justify one's preferred choice of action. Let me make my point by returning again to an analogous dilemma that confronts a different hypothetical character—"Mr. Brown."

Mr. Brown is a divorced and faithful Catholic who has not qualified for a declaration of nullity with respect to his first marriage and has not remarried. He believes that human life is an inviolable good, that human rights and dignity should be defended, and that vulnerable people should be assisted as much as possible (beliefs, one observes, that parallel those of pro-life legislators voting for restrictive legislation). While working for some time in a foreign country he finds himself in the middle of a bloody civil war, one side violently oppressing and killing thousands upon thousands of its opponents. He is given a short period of time in which to leave the country (or face death if he stays) and is torn by the fact that he will be leaving people behind, including some close to him, who have no means of escape and who face certain death as the regime continues to exact vengeance on its opponents. Can he do anything to help those whose lives are so unjustly threatened by this murderous regime? Suddenly, he realizes that he can save one life and even more because the decree permitting foreign workers to leave the country applies not only to them but also to their wives and families. If he marries a woman (and particularly one who already has children) otherwise destined to be killed at the hands of the regime, she (and her children) would be able to exit the country safely with him. Mr. Brown discovers that the marriage could be arranged and all the relevant legalities completed that same day.

Could Mr. Brown instantiate such a marriage? He reasons that because his first marriage is indissoluble (the divorce being merely a civil matter) he cannot be said to be "marrying again" because the first marriage alone counts; logically, he maintains, this "marriage" will in fact be "not a marriage" but a legal fiction. Furthermore, he and the woman he "marries" would not engage in "marital acts," and the "legal technicalities" would be resolved once he left the country so that the "marriage" would be "dissolved." Far from doing anything immoral, he reasons, he would be doing something very good: saving a human life.

One may well have sympathy with Mr. Brown's favored course of action and, indeed, his good intentions and compassion for those in such a desperate situation could be judged admirable. However, the moral question remains, and at the heart of it is the recognition that it is too simplistic to judge the proposed "marriage" to be "not a marriage." The proposed marriage cannot be dismissed as a "legal fiction" because it is an actual participation in a real legal process (the instantiation of a marriage contract) which has the *objective public meaning of being* a proper (hence morally valid) marriage. Not only is the instantiation of the marriage itself a public act (however few people are aware of it) but also its real effectiveness is such that the woman he "marries" will become his "wife" for whom safe conduct will be guaranteed and for whom this would not be possible if she were not his "wife." Notwithstanding his good intentions and the extreme circumstances in which he finds himself, Mr. Brown's public action of instantiating the marriage would have the same objective meaning that applied in the case of Mr. Smith, considered above. In instantiating the proposed marriage Mr. Brown, like Mr. Smith, would be participating in "a lie." His action would violate what is required for the instantiation of marriage to be judged morally good.

I regard this illustration of Mr. Brown's instantiation of "marriage" to be analogous to the situation of voting for restrictive legislation, though I anticipate an objection. John Finnis has argued that a pro-life legislator's vote for restrictive legislation is one that "formally" grants protection to some unborn children; the continued support for the other abortions can be regarded, he says, as a "side effect" of the pro-life legislator's action even though the "side effect" is as immediate as the restriction.[63] By contrast, it might be claimed that the double-effect principle cannot be invoked to justify Mr. Brown's action and that it can be judged, in itself, to be a bad means pursued for a good end. Such an objection, however, depends (as I shall argue in the following chapter) upon an unsound theory of legislative voting, which focuses on the legislator's intention and side effects (i.e., the double-effect principle), rather than on a consideration of the justness of the norm being enact-

---

63. Finnis, "Unjust Laws in a Democratic Society," 601; "Catholic Church and Public Policy Debates," 268–69.

ed. By contrast, I maintain that because both situations refer to the instantiation of a legal entity that is based on moral presuppositions (the natural law), and are thus subject to moral conditions, the analogy holds.

Arguments against voting for (intrinsically unjust) restrictive abortion legislation hold, irrespective of whether one's judgment is that such legislation is "not a law" *(non est lex)* or is law "in some respects" *(secundum quid)*. With respect to the "not a law" position, one might perhaps argue that pro-life legislators *could* vote for such restrictive legislation because in voting for "not a law" they would not in fact be making law and would therefore not be bound by the norms of lawmaking—in particular, the norm of justness as a moral condition for law's validity. Supporters of restrictive legislation have not expressed this argument, and because it lends itself to various absurdities I suspect it is an argument few would be rash enough to adopt. While acknowledging the sense in which an intrinsically unjust law can be said to be "not a law," I think that the recognition that it is law "in some respects" provides clear grounds for holding that it would be unethical to vote for it: the essential condition of good lawmaking refers to the justness of the legislation, a condition which is insuppressibly absent in votes for intrinsically unjust legislation.

The "Observation" of Intrinsically Unjust Laws: A Final Consideration

Aquinas teaches, as noted above, that intrinsically unjust laws should not be in any way "observed": *tales leges nullo modo licet observare*.[64] What does he mean by that? Should one refuse to call the UK Abortion Act 1967 a "law" because this might suggest one is "observing" it as a valid and just law? I do not think this necessarily follows from Aquinas's statement: he is referring not so much to the descriptive "observations" of such laws as to the way they might be "observed" at the level of moral action. In his consideration of the teaching of *EV* 73.2, which refers to the illegitimacy of accommodating oneself to (and not merely, as the translation reads, "obeying") an intrinsically unjust

64. *ST* I-II, q. 96, a. 4.

law, as noted above, John Finnis considers how one might be tempted to accommodate oneself, illicitly, to an intrinsically unjust law. Finnis had noted in his chapter on unjust laws in *Natural Law and Natural Rights* that his remarks were passing over various relevant questions such as the dilemmas faced by conscientious officials charged with the administration of unjust laws.[65] His later consideration of this point is illuminating and, I suggest, has a wider significance. He writes:

> How, then, might one be tempted to accommodate oneself, illicitly, to an intrinsically unjust positive law? One way arises from the inter-connectedness of the norms of a legal system. Health care professionals, for example, have a legal duty, whether it be founded on contractual or delictual rules, to provide all efficacious and lawful procedures to their patients. So criminal law's permission of abortion and euthanasia imposes upon such professionals, by juridical implication, a legal duty to perform (and/or to refer their patients to a professional who is willing to perform) abortions and assist in suicide or euthanasiast murders. Conscientious judges, however, are bound to deny the premise upon which that implication is founded, for to accept it is to conform and accommodate themselves to—in a sense, to obey—the intrinsically unjust criminal law, and is to treat as valid what is properly speaking a nullity.[66]

At the level of moral action a conscientious judge cannot, maintains Finnis, treat qua "law" an intrinsically unjust positive law (such as an abortion law). He cannot accept the law's toleration or permission of abortion (for example, in a ruling about the rights or duties of health care personnel, local authorities, or others implicated in such legislation), because to do so would be to treat as valid what is properly speaking a nullity. But surely, one might think, if this applies to the actions of judges when considering *the implementation* of a "law," it would also apply to their actions when making a judgment (such as the 1973 U.S. Supreme Court judgment) that forms the basis of the legality of abortion; such a judgment must surely be an action of treating as valid what is properly speaking a nullity. And, equally, the legislative act of voting for an intrinsically unjust abortion law (whether this be the original

---

65. Finnis, *Natural Law and Natural Rights,* 362.
66. Finnis, "Natural Law—Positive Law," 207.

law allowing abortion or a law making abortion more widely available or a law restricting abortion) also constitutes a moral action of treating as valid what is properly speaking a nullity. If one is to accept Aquinas's teaching that laws contrary to the divine law (i.e., intrinsically unjust laws) cannot be in any way "observed," surely this must also include their very enactment.

John Finnis has argued—as the following chapter describes—that restrictive abortion legislation can be legitimately supported in accordance with an "intentional" theory of voting that fails to correspond to the reality of what a legislator does; moreover, it contradicts the principles he states elsewhere. His view that a pro-life legislator can vote not only to restrict abortion but also to enact an abortion law (when previously all abortions were prohibited) in order to prevent the enactment of a law allowing more abortions,[67] contradicts the principle he rightly acknowledges:

> Promulgation of a law is always, willy-nilly, an act of teaching which purports to give an account of what natural law and human nature and dignity invite if not require. Unjust positive laws—and above all, a law whose injustice is not merely a matter of improper motivations or procedural improprieties, but intrinsic—are, then, false teachers. The intrinsic injustice of their immediate invitations to cooperate in wrongful conduct is compounded by the falsehoods they propose and insinuate: an academy of further and wider violations of human good for all who do not instead recoil from error's tentacles and conscientiously find their way back to true principles.[68]

Finnis rightly acknowledges that the promulgation of a law is *always* an act of teaching that purports to give an account of what natural law and human nature invite or require. The promulgation of a law to restrict abortion (which follows directly from a legislator's vote to enact it and, perhaps, a campaign by pro-life groups in support of it) provides, however, a false account of what the natural law requires. The

---

67. Finnis maintains that John Paul II has taught in *EV* 73 that "a Catholic elected legislator ... can ... licitly give his or her support to a bill for a law which permits abortion but less permissively than the existing law or than a bill which will otherwise be passed and become law." See "Catholic Church and Public Policy Debates," 268.

68. Finnis, "Natural Law—Positive Law," 209.

judgment that a law is intrinsically unjust is the decisive factor in one's response to it (i.e., that it should not be observed in any way, not only by those "subject" to it, but also by conscientious judges making a ruling with respect to it or by whoever is responsible for its promulgation). The notion that a "pro-life intention" somehow justifies "observing" such an intrinsically unjust law (i.e., by voting for it if the consequence of doing so is regarded as better than the consequence of not voting for it) is flawed, as I shall demonstrate in Chapter 4, and no support for it can be found in the teaching of the magisterium. Even if one were to argue that votes to enact legislation do not constitute "observing" it, Popes Paul VI and John Paul II have both specifically affirmed, as mentioned previously, the illicitness of voting for intrinsically unjust legislation,[69] and the "absoluteness" of the prohibition of voting for a law that commands or authorizes a moral evil is taught by Pius XII:

> [I]t must be clearly stated that no human authority, no state, no community of states, whatever be their religious character, can give a positive command or positive authorization to teach or to do that which would be contrary to religious truth or moral good. Such a command or such an authorization would have no obligatory power and would remain without effect.... Not even God could give such a positive command or positive authorization, because it would be in contradiction to His absolute truth and sanctity.[70]

---

69. CDF, *Declaration on Procured Abortion,* n. 22. This document was confirmed by Paul VI, 28 June 1974; John Paul II, *EV* 73.2.

70. Pius XII, Discourse to Italian Jurists, 247. The text quoted does not refer to a law "tolerating" evil, but it is not reasonable to infer that Pius XII was trying to make a distinction between laws "authorizing" and those "tolerating" such acts as abortion. Rather, Pius is considering the more general question of legislating on questions concerning morality and religion and noting that although some actions can be tolerated they can be neither permitted nor commanded. The questions concerning abortion legislation or other actions against human life had not properly emerged when he was writing (1953) and his text would not have been expected to cover these questions specifically. (God can, of course, make exceptions to his laws, by commanding or authorizing someone to inflict death on another person irrespective of whether that other person be innocent or guilty, or by commanding or authorizing someone to have intercourse with a woman to whom he is not married, or to take the property of another. But these commands or authorizations would apply to specific individuals or groups as

The teaching of John Paul II in *Veritatis splendor* is also directly relevant to this question. The norm respecting the right to life of all cannot be violated, even if a good "pro-life" intention is present:

> The fundamental moral rules of social life thus entail *specific demands* to which both public authorities and citizens are required to pay heed. Even though intentions may sometimes be good, and circumstances frequently difficult, civil authorities and particular individuals never have authority to violate the fundamental and inalienable rights of the human person. In the end, only a morality which acknowledges certain norms as valid always and for everyone, with no exception, can guarantee the ethical foundation of social existence, both on the national and international levels.[71]

---

exceptions to his laws, the law itself being neither contradicted nor violated. Cf. Aquinas, *ST* I-II, q. 94, a. 5, ad 2.)

71. *Veritatis Splendor,* n. 97.

PART III

ETHICAL CONSIDERATIONS

4. GOOD ACTS BY BAD ACTS?

Even though all laws tolerating or permitting abortion can be identified as intrinsically unjust, as the two previous chapters have shown, and even though a negative judgment has been traditionally made against such laws, is it possible to argue that it can be ethically good (a good act) to vote for an intrinsically unjust law (a bad Act) if one is doing so for the purpose of restricting abortion?

Any judgment about the goodness of a human action depends upon the soundness of one's theory of action, and it must be acknowledged that among those who support restrictive abortion legislation are adherents of action theories rejected as erroneous and dangerous by Pope John Paul II in *Veritatis splendor (VS)* (n. 83). Support for restrictive abortion legislation also comes, however, from some philosophers who are generally regarded as favoring a sound ethic, consistent with the teaching of *Veritatis splendor*, and who believe that the teaching of that encyclical demonstrates the correctness of their view. Among these philosophers is John Finnis, whose argument will be subject to particular attention in this chapter. I shall address Finnis's argument that votes for (unjust) restrictive legislation can be justified as material cooperation in evil, the evil associated with the act of voting being regarded as a "side effect" of the legislator's action, and I shall show that his argument is based on an incorrect analysis of the act of legislative voting. I shall argue that Finnis's analysis is based on the legislator's intention and the consequences of his vote, and that it fails to specify accurately the "object" of his act. In particular, I shall challenge Finnis's claim that *VS* 78, which specifies what is meant by the "object" of a moral act, provides a philosophical justification for his argument.

This chapter will attempt to get to the heart of the ethical problem: does the act of voting to enact an intrinsically unjust law depend upon a consideration of the circumstances, the consequences, and the legislator's intentions? Or is the identification of a legislative proposal as intrinsically unjust sufficient in itself to judge that a lawmaker acts immorally in voting to enact it?

Material Cooperation and Side Effects

Material Cooperation in Legislative Votes

John Finnis argued, in a paper delivered in 1994 and published in 1996,[1] that the principles of formal and material cooperation apply to the question of whether legislators can licitly vote to enact unjust restrictive legislation:

> In a state in which abortion is legally permitted up to (say) 24 weeks gestation, it is not necessarily unjust for a legislator to support a proposal to enact a bill of the form "Abortion is permissible up to 16 weeks." For it is possible to support such a proposal precisely as a proposal to extend legal protection to the life of unborn children after the 16th week. That is the proposal whose adoption a legislator of upright conscience may rightly support. Such support is formal cooperation in making a just change in the law, but not in the retaining of the unjust denial of legal protection to unborn children up to 16 weeks. (One cooperates "formally" with A's action X just to the extent that one intends or chooses—not merely accepts as a side-effect—that A shall accomplish something that A intends or chooses in choosing to do X.)[2]

Now of course, such a legislator's support for the bill is also *material cooperation*[3] in something unjust, namely the legislative act of continuing

---

1. Finnis, "Unjust Laws in a Democratic Society." This paper was originally given at a symposium "Catholics and the Pluralist Society—The Case of 'Imperfect Laws,'" organized by the Congregation for the Doctrine of the Faith (Rome, 9–12 Nov. 1994). The proceedings of the conference, including Finnis's paper, were published in Italian; see Joblin and Tremblay, *I Cattolici e la Società Pluralista*.

2. At this point Finnis inserts a footnote (n. 14) quoting directly from *EV* 74, which deals with formal cooperation *in evil:* "Indeed from the moral standpoint, it is never licit to cooperate formally in evil. Such cooperation occurs when an action, either by its very nature or by the form it takes in a concrete situation, can be defined as a direct participation in an act against human life or a sharing in the immoral intention of the person committing it" (*EV* 74).

3. Here Finnis inserts a footnote (n. 15) about material cooperation in evil:

the existing unjust legal permission of abortion *up to* the 16th week, i.e., the abandonment of such children to the power and desire and unjust choice of their mother and others. The one piece of behavior—say, voting for the bill at its final stage—is chosen by the upright legislator *as* an act of *making a just change in the law,* accepting as a bad side-effect the simultaneous *continuation of unjust law.* Can such material cooperation in very serious injustice be justified?[4]

Finnis considers the question posed at the end of the passage before answering that the "cooperation" can be justified: "But it seems to me that the choice to cooperate in saving the lives of unborn children between (say) 16 and 24 weeks is a good choice in relation to which it *can* be fair and reasonable to accept the bad side-effects."[5]

Although one must always do good and avoid doing evil, it sometimes happens that the performance of a good action assists another person or other persons to do evil: in such instances, the person performing the good act is said to be cooperating materially in the evil done by the other person or persons.[6] With his inclusion of the two footnotes in the text quoted above, Finnis indicates that his argument is based precisely on the principles of cooperation in evil and therefore he rightly distinguishes between formal and material cooperation: one

---

"'Material cooperation' with action X is any cooperation (participation, assistance, etc.) which does not constitute formal cooperation as defined in the text at note 14 above."

4. Finnis, "Unjust Laws in a Democratic Society," 601.

5. Ibid., 602.

6. As Germain Grisez notes, the actions of a grocer providing food to someone who acts gluttonously, of a postman delivering mail that contains pornographic material, or of a taxpayer whose government is engaged in unethical activities may all be regarded as possible examples of permissible material cooperation in evil; see Germain Grisez, *Difficult Moral Questions,* vol. 3 of *The Way of the Lord Jesus* (Quincy, Ill.: Franciscan Herald Press, 1997), 871. In each instance the action of the "cooperator" is good but it is abused by another to perform an evil act. He notes: "Obviously, if the act by which a person materially cooperates is itself sinful, the material cooperation is also sinful." See Grisez, *Living a Christian Life,* vol. 2 of *The Way of the Lord Jesus,* 441. This view of material cooperation is consistent with the formulations of the manualists, e.g., "Material cooperation is in itself a good act which is abused by another in order to commit sin." Dominic Prümmer, O.P., *Handbook of Moral Theology* (Cork: Mercier Press, 1956), 104, n. 233.2.

may never cooperate formally in evil,[7] but some forms of material cooperation may be permitted.[8]

Cooperation problems refer to evil being performed by someone else, and if voting for unjust restrictive legislative is a cooperation problem, one question must be clearly answered: *in which evil, performed by which person or persons, is the pro-life legislator cooperating?* Is it, as some claim, the evil *of abortion?*[9] There is a *prima facie* case for considering whether the action of voting for unjust restrictive legislation constitutes permissible material cooperation in abortion (i.e., in the evil act of the abortionist or of the woman undergoing the abortion), just as there is a *prima facie* case for considering whether other actions, such as that of a fetal ultrasound technician detecting whether an unborn child has a disabling condition or that of a pro-life worker who issues a counseling certificate that may then be used to procure an abortion, might be permissible material cooperation *in abortion*.[10] Of course, if one were to consider whether a legislator's action of voting to enact unjust restric-

---

7. This was clearly stated in *EV* 74, quoted in Finnis's footnote, reproduced in note 2, above.

8. "The traditional teaching on material cooperation, with its appropriate distinctions between necessary and freely given cooperation, proximate and remote cooperation, remains valid, to be applied very prudently when the case demands it." CDF, *Haec sacra congregatio* (On sterilization in Catholic hospitals) (13 March 1975), n. 3.

9. For example, Bishop John Myers of Peoria, Illinois, says that a legislator who votes for legislation "permitting some abortions in order to prevent the enactment of legislation permitting even more" is engaged in an acceptable form of "material cooperation in abortion." See his pastoral statement, "The Obligations of Catholics and the Rights of Unborn Children," in *Origins* 20, no. 4 (14 June 1990): 70.

10. Whether a fetal ultrasound technician's action should be judged as good or evil would depend primarily on the object of her act, and secondly on her intention. The act of detecting a fetal disability is not in itself a moral evil. Although the technician's action might be performed for the bad purpose (and/or with a bad intention) of enabling a woman to discover if her child were disabled with a view to abortion, it might alternatively be performed for the good purpose (and with no bad intention) of detecting whether the child had a condition which could benefit from life-saving or life-enhancing prenatal intervention (even surgery) or specialist immediate postnatal care. A technician who performed her action for the latter purpose (and with no bad intention) might subsequently find that her good action was abused and that she had materially cooperated in the pregnant woman's abortion of a disabled child, whereas a technician who performed her action for the former purpose would have formally cooperated in

tive legislation is permissible material cooperation *in abortion,* one would have to analyze whether it is in itself a good action. This analysis must take place in due course, but not in the context of Finnis's cooperation argument. This is because if one turns again to Finnis's argument, one sees that he is not, in fact, referring (as others have) to cooperation *in abortion.* Rather, he is speaking of *cooperation in making a change in the law* (which is concerned with abortion).[11] In a later paper, published in 1999, Finnis uses the same illustration of reducing abortions from 24 to 16 weeks' gestation and speaks of "the [pro-life] legislator's non-formal but obviously real material cooperation in enacting the new law which does in fact permit abortion up to 16 weeks."[12]

---

the evil of abortion (if she intended abortion) or cooperated materially but impermissibly (if she did not in fact intend abortion).

Prior to letters in January 1998 and June 1999 from Pope John Paul II to the German bishops, in which he instructed them not to allow Church counseling centers to issue counseling certificates that could then be used to obtain an abortion, Grisez had argued that such counseling certificates could be issued. He began his analysis of the question by saying that "This question concerns cooperation in abortion" and argued that the act would be permissible material and not formal cooperation (Grisez, *Difficult Moral Questions,* 381). One can only assume that in differing from Grisez's conclusion the pope also did not agree with the argument based on material cooperation. Other commentators have also explicitly linked the questions of issuing counseling certificates with votes for restrictive abortion legislation; see, for example, Gary Lysaght, "The Lesser Evil: A Moral Quagmire?" *Catholic Medical Quarterly* (May 1997): 10. It has also been reported that the German bishops argued that their understanding of the teaching of *EV* 73 and its reference to "limiting the harm" of abortion legislation provided a justification for issuing the certificates; see Arthur F. Utz, O.P., "Das Unheil der Nr 73/74 der Enzyklika Evangelium Vitae," *Theologisches* 28 (June 1998): 308. I suggest that a faulty understanding of what *EV* 73 teaches about voting for abortion legislation resulted in a false (and rejected) view of the application of the teaching to the question of the counseling certificates.

11. If Finnis's argument had been based on material cooperation *in abortion* he could have spoken of such cooperation occurring *by* passing (or making a change in) a law, but he speaks rather, as quoted above, of material cooperation *in the legislative act:* "material cooperation in something unjust, namely the legislative act of continuing the existing unjust legal permission of abortion *up to* the 16th week." An analysis of the goodness or otherwise of the act of voting for the legislation must be undertaken irrespective of whether the action is viewed as material cooperation in abortion or material cooperation in the legislative act, and this analysis will be undertaken later in the chapter.

12. Finnis, "Catholic Church and Public Policy Debates," 269.

Finnis's account of the pro-life legislator's material cooperation regards the evil act as that of enacting the new restrictive law. In any forum of collective lawmaking, the vote of an individual legislator "to enact a law" does not necessarily constitute "an act of enacting." A legislator voting for a bill at its final stage is performing an action expressive of "willing its enactment," and his or her action is, properly speaking, only "an act of enacting" if it transpires that the required number (normally a simple majority) of fellow legislators votes similarly that the bill be enacted, and if other required conditions for enactment are fulfilled, such as the assent of the head of state. Any discussion of an individual legislator's "enactment of a law" must be understood as referring to the casting of a vote expressive of willing the enactment of that law, and a consideration of whether a legislator is or is not cooperating materially (in evil) in "enacting the new law which does in fact permit abortion up to 16 weeks" must be based on an accurate understanding of what an individual legislator is doing. How, precisely, Finnis regards this as a "cooperation" matter is not clear, but he would appear to be saying one of two things, neither of which is plausible.

The first possibility is that Finnis is saying that pro-life legislators, who are themselves voting for the 16-week law, are "materially cooperating in the evil of their own action." The concept of material cooperation requires that the evil to which the cooperation refers be that of another person, so this option is hardy plausible; and if the evil refers to a pro-life legislator's own action, then his or her action must itself be evil and therefore impermissible.

The second possibility is that Finnis is making a distinction between the acts of different groups of legislators who, though voting for the same law, would be (in his view) performing very different acts. Finnis maintains that, though they are voting for a law "which does in fact permit abortion up to 16 weeks," pro-life legislators are choosing to vote for it as "a law which restricts abortion" (i.e., as a law that reduces abortion from 24 weeks).[13] Though the law does permit abortion up to 16 weeks, they are not, maintains Finnis, voting for it "*as permitting, precisely to permit, abortion,*"[14] and their action can be judged to be good, not evil. In order to restrict abortion in such an instance, pro-life

13. Ibid., 269. 14. Ibid.

legislators would normally require the support of abortion-favoring legislators who are willing to lower the upper limit for abortions but who believe abortions should be permitted up to 16 weeks. According to Finnis, their votes would be for a law "*as permitting,* precisely *to* permit, abortion [up to 16 weeks]," and these legislators, unlike the pro-life legislators voting for the same bill, would be doing evil. Is Finnis suggesting that pro-life legislators are materially cooperating in the evil act of the abortion-favoring legislators? If he is, and if the "cooperation" is material, one must still ask if it fulfills the conditions for being permissible material cooperation. Is, for example, the cooperation proximate or remote? A possible answer to this question is that the actions of pro-life and other legislators are so proximate that, even if the "cooperation" of pro-life legislators is material (and not formal), nevertheless it cannot be regarded as *permissible* material cooperation. A more pertinent question, however, is: in what way does the action of one legislator contribute to the action of any other legislator voting for the legislation? Certainly the actual enactment of legislation is a collective act: it depends on a majority of legislators expressing, by their votes, that they will the enactment, and in this sense enacting law is a "collaborative" task. "Collaboration" and "cooperation" may be used interchangeably in common discourse, but ordinary "collaboration" should not be confused with the precise meaning attached to "cooperation" as applied to the formal or material assistance given to another person's evil acts. All legislators voting for a bill are performing entirely separate, individual acts—their individual acts expressive of willing the enactment—that are in no way dependent upon the actions of other legislators voting for the same bill. Legislators are engaged in a collective, "collaborative" activity insofar as the actual enactment of the bill will depend upon a calculation of the numbers who expressed, by voting, their will that the bill be enacted. In no way, however, does a pro-life legislator assist the action—the vote—of an abortion-favoring legislator, or vice versa. It is false to say that one legislator's act of voting for a law contributes to the performance of another legislator's act of voting for the same law, and that voting for a bill like "Abortion is permissible up to 16 weeks" can in any way be regarded as the sort of "cooperation" matter that Finnis suggests.

An appropriate illustration of possible material cooperation in the (evil) act of voting for an unjust law would refer not to someone actually voting for the law but, as William May has suggested, to the actions of someone like a secretary working for a legislative drafting committee creating the law.[15] Despite the terminology he adopts, Finnis's argument is clearly not based on formal and material cooperation in evil, as it is properly understood. The double-effect principle is associated with the principles of cooperation, and Finnis has referred to "the simultaneous continuation of unjust law" as a "bad side-effect" of a pro-life legislator's vote to restrict abortion.[16] Could it be that voting for restrictive legislation is not a matter of cooperation but is justified by ordinary double-effect reasoning?

Double-Effect Reasoning

One might say that voting for unjust restrictive legislation has a good effect (the legal prohibition of some abortions) and a bad effect (the legal permission or toleration of other abortions). However, an act is not justified by double-effect reasoning simply because it has a good effect as well as a bad effect. For example, in the case of a tubal ectopic pregnancy, the awareness that nonintervention will result in the death of both mother and child does not mean that *any* intervention can be justified that produces, as a good and desired effect, the continuance of the mother's life, with the death of the unborn child being regarded as an undesired, foreseen though not intended side effect. Whether a life-threatening tubal pregnancy has been resolved ethically depends not on the number of lives saved by medical intervention but on the concrete action performed. William May's moral analysis of managing ectopic pregnancies[17] concludes that the surgical procedure of salpingectomy and the method of expectant management would appear to be ethically acceptable,[18] whereas the use of the chemical methotrexate (MTX) or

---

15. William E. May, "Unjust Laws and Catholic Citizens: Opposition, Cooperation and Toleration," *Homiletic and Pastoral Review* (Nov. 1995): 12.

16. Finnis, "Unjust Laws in a Democratic Society," 601.

17. William E. May, "The Management of Ectopic Pregnancies: A Moral Analysis," in *The Fetal Tissue Issue: Medical and Ethical Aspects,* ed. Peter J. Cataldo and Albert S. Moraczewski, O.P. (Braintree, Mass.: Pope John Center, 1994), 121–47.

18. A salpingectomy is the removal of the entire fallopian tube, the removal being

the surgical procedure of salpingostomy would not be.[19] In his discussion of the procedure of salpingostomy, May notes that "the crucial issue is to identify correctly the moral object of the act, of one's choice."[20] He not only underlines the crucial need to identify the moral object of *any* action but also reveals that reputable philosophers are not immune to identifying the moral object incorrectly. May notes that in earlier drafts of his paper he himself had defended the procedure of salpingostomy, a procedure he had regarded as defensible in accordance with Germain Grisez's and Joseph Boyle's argument that to save the mother's life the performance of a fetal craniotomy could be regarded, on the basis of *intention,* as an *indirect* abortion.[21] May came to accept that his

---

necessary when rupture has occurred or is about to occur. Any child implanted within the tube would be removed with it and, unless some other means of life support could be given, would die. (A partial salpingectomy and reconnection of the ends would also be ethically acceptable.) "Expectant management" consists of monitoring the pregnancy without intervention. Medical evidence suggests that a majority of tubal pregnancies end naturally by spontaneous miscarriage without intervention. With careful monitoring it will be clear if any later medical interventions are required.

19. Methotrexate attacks the outer layer of cells (the trophoblast) produced by the developing unborn child. Once these cells are destroyed the unborn child dies and is aborted. A salpingostomy is an incision in the fallopian tube at the point where the child has implanted. The child would be removed (resulting in death) and the damage caused by the incision repaired.

20. May, "Management of Ectopic Pregnancies," 134.

21. See Germain Grisez, *Abortion: The Myths, the Realities, and the Arguments* (New York: Corpus Books, 1970), 340–41; also Grisez, *Living a Christian Life,* 502–3; Joseph Boyle, "Double-Effect and a Certain Type of Embryotomy," *Irish Theological Quarterly* 44 (1977): 303–8. Finnis's support for fetal craniotomy is expressed in the article co-authored with Grisez and Boyle, "'Direct' and 'Indirect.'" They write: "[D]irect killing of the unborn, even to save the life of the mother, is always wrong. We regard this as a truth of faith. Our position is that a doctor could do a craniotomy, even one involving emptying the baby's skull, without intending to kill the baby—that is, without the craniotomy being a direct killing" (27). Their view is worth comparing with that of Joseph Lombardi, who admits that his intuitive view (also held, he suggests, by many others) is that a craniotomy procedure is justified when the mother's life is in danger. However he concludes that it is "dubious . . . that the intuition [of the rightness of a craniotomy] can be rationalized in a way that is consistent with an absolute prohibition of the direct causation of death." Joseph Lombardi, "Obstetrical Dilemmas and the Principle of Double Effect," *American Journal of Jurisprudence* 37 (1992): 211. See also Kevin L. Flannery, S.J., "What Is Included as a Means to an End?" *Gregorianum* 74, no.

argument (and, by implication, the Grisez-Boyle reasoning he had adopted) was flawed.[22] Other writers come to opposing conclusions as to whether ectopic pregnancies can be resolved by the administration of MTX, the question of whether the death of the embryo arising from such an act is a direct or indirect effect of the action playing a key part in their arguments.[23] Moreover, whether an action is viewed as "direct" or "indirect" is frequently considered with respect to an intention-focused (what I shall refer to as an "intentional") analysis.[24]

Insofar as the "direct-indirect" factor—viewed in terms of intention—is at the heart of Finnis's argument with respect to the moral goodness or otherwise of a legislator's voting for an unjust law restricting abortion, it is very relevant to consider other disputed questions, such as the management of life-threatening pregnancies. Does an intentional analysis fail to resolve correctly these disputed questions? Grisez acknowledges that he has "revised" and even "reformed" the principle of double effect[25] in such a way that some acts previously considered evil (such as fetal craniotomy) can, in his view, be judged good.[26] In order to establish that the action of voting for unjust restric-

---

3 (1993): 499–513. In addition to highlighting key shortcomings in the Grisez-Boyle account of double-effect reasoning, Flannery refers to the nineteenth-century responses from the Holy Office, confirmed by Pope Leo XIII, which give a negative judgment on the moral permissibility of craniotomy procedures.

22. May, "Management of Ectopic Pregnancies." About half of his paper examines whether the salpingostomy procedure is licit. See 133–45.

23. See the two papers by Christopher Kaczor and Gerald Gleeson, expressing opposing views, both entitled "Is the 'Medical Management' of Ectopic Pregnancy by the Administration of Methotrexate Morally Acceptable?" in Gormally, *Issues for a Catholic Bioethic*, 353–70.

24. Christopher Kaczor (see previous note) writes: "The word 'direct' . . . refers to the intention of an agent. . . . Hence, one's account of intention determines whether or not a given act resulting in death should be accounted as 'direct' or 'indirect' killing" (ibid., 353–54).

25. Grisez, *Abortion: The Myths, the Realities*, 340.

26. See Germain Grisez, "Towards a Consistent Natural-Law Ethics of Killing," *American Journal of Jurisprudence* 15 (1970): 64–96. Grisez says here that he has rejected "radical revisions" of the principle of double effect but has "proposed a clarification that will allow a limited extension of its power to justify acts hitherto regarded as evil" (91). Joseph Boyle acknowledges his contribution to Grisez's version of double-effect reasoning and admits that it "does lead to certain practical conclusions at variance with

tive legislation has not been judged good (on the basis of faulty double-effect reasoning) when it should in fact be judged evil, a more precise analysis of this legislative act must be performed.

First, however, I shall consider some implications of Finnis's "intentional" analysis as applied to the question of voting for restrictive legislation. I am not suggesting that a determination of the morality of actions can neglect a consideration of intentions or the consequences of actions. My objection, however, to the prevalent thinking on this question is that there is an excessive focus on these two dimensions when considering the goodness of the action of voting for restrictive legislation. Although Finnis's argument does not focus explicitly on the consequences, it is precisely the consequences—the lives saved—that are uppermost in the thoughts of many who support restrictive legislation, and it is with respect to the consequences that the intentions are formed. It is therefore relevant to consider in more detail some shortcomings with analyses that focus excessively, when judging the goodness of legislative votes, on the intention and the consequences.

Intentions and Consequences

An "Intentional" Analysis

In the text quoted above (at the beginning of the section on "Material Cooperation and Side Effects"), John Finnis considers the action of a legislator enacting a bill of the form "Abortion is permissible up to 16 weeks" (which I shall label "bill X") when the previous legislation had permitted abortion up to 24 weeks. The concrete legislation for which a legislator is voting is crucial to any meaningful deliberation about what a legislator is doing when casting his vote, and the illustration that Finnis provides, although satisfactory in some respects, is open to the criticism that it does not truly correspond to the complexity of actual legislative proposals. An obvious problem with it is that it does not make clear that abortions after 16 weeks would actually be prohibited. My ac-

---

those of the tradition"; see Boyle, "The Principle of Double Effect: Good Actions Entangled in Evil," in *Moral Theology Today: Certitudes and Doubts,* ed. Donald McCarthy (St. Louis, Mich.: Pope John Center, 1984), 254–55.

ceptance of this form of bill as an illustration of the sort of measure under consideration depends upon an understanding that bill X is to be regarded as *a precise statement* of the legislation proposed in an imaginary situation (and that it would, in fact, prohibit abortions after 16 weeks). If the illustration cannot be regarded as a precise statement of legislation it serves little purpose.

Arguing that a vote for bill X constitutes an act of providing legislative protection to unborn children after 16 weeks, Finnis says that it is possible to support this bill "precisely as a proposal to extend legal protection to the life of unborn children after the 16th week."[27] Of course, this action involves *an intention* to protect those children, but is Finnis saying in his statement that "extend[ing] legal protection to the life of unborn children after the 16th week" is precisely what is being done *in the action* of voting, or *as a consequence* of the action? The distinction is similar to that which must be made when considering the goodness of treatments of ectopic pregnancies, in which one must establish whether the mother is the subject of a legitimate medical procedure (i.e., a good action) that has as an unintended consequence a fatal effect on the embryo (i.e., a bad side effect), or whether the embryo is the subject of a direct lethal assault (i.e., a bad action) that has a good consequence for the mother (i.e., an intended good end achieved by a bad means). In particular, one must be wary of describing actions misleadingly—for example, by describing a direct lethal assault on the embryo as an action of "saving the life of the mother," when in fact "saving the life of the mother" is a consequence of the action and not the action itself. Bearing this in mind, it is clear that when he describes the act of voting for bill X as "support[ing] such a proposal precisely as a proposal to extend legal protection to the life of unborn children after the 16th week," Finnis is in fact describing *the consequence* of the action and not the action itself. He says that the continuation of abortion before 16 weeks is a "side-effect" of this act, but by claiming this he has in fact turned double-effect reasoning on its head. Whereas double-effect reasoning properly starts with an identification of *an action* as good, and then determines whether a bad effect of that action can be accepted if it

---

27. Finnis, "Unjust Laws in a Democratic Society," 601.

is unintended, Finnis's reasoning seems to start with the identification of a good intended effect and a subsequent determination that any action leading to that good intended effect (and not intending any associated bad effect) can be judged to be good. The double-effect principle is improperly applied in this instance of voting for legislation. Furthermore, a more general tendency to view the act of enacting legislation in terms of intentions and side effects is, though increasingly common, fundamentally misplaced.

A bioethicist friend of mine who agrees with Finnis's argument for supporting restrictive abortion legislation, claiming that "all acts are to do with intentions and side-effects," has responded to my concerns about this question by asking me to consider an instance of lawmaking that does not deal with an issue like abortion. Surely, my friend says, legislators often encounter omnibus legislation that covers a range of subjects, some aspects of which they agree with and others with which they disagree. In choosing to support the legislation, do they not intend to support only the parts with which they agree and not those parts with which they disagree? For example, in a comprehensive budget bill a legislator who has campaigned against funding for a leisure complex in order to provide greater funds for education or the health service may find that contrary to his wishes the leisure complex is to be allocated funding, the health service will get the amount for which he campaigned, and the education system will receive a high proportion of what he hoped (though less because of the funding for the leisure complex). If the legislator votes against the budget bill because he disagrees with funding a leisure complex and because not enough funding is being given to education, the beneficiaries of the health service and education system will lose out, and on this basis (so it is argued) he votes for the measure, *intending* to support those aspects of the budget with which he agrees and not intending to fund the leisure complex, which he considers a frivolous waste of tax payers' money.[28]

28. I preferred, in the text above, to provide an illustration (that was based, as indicated on one suggested to me) of how an "intentional" analysis might be applied to the act of voting for legislation in an ordinary context. The illustration is consistent with Finnis's writings: "Reflection on the case of paying one's taxes can assist in showing also that a legislator may support an omnibus budget bill for the financing of the whole or a

Although it is possible to see why one might characterize the act of voting in this way so that the intention is regarded as the ultimate determinant of what a legislator does in the act of voting, this view reveals a misconception of what is truly involved in a legislative vote. In voting to enact the bill, each legislator votes to enact *every aspect* of it. Even if some legislators have argued strenuously against providing funding for the leisure complex, they cannot excuse their vote for the bill on the grounds that funding for the leisure complex was a "side effect" of their action. Assuming that the bill is not intrinsically unjust, a legislator's consideration of whether it serves the common good to enact it involves taking into account the circumstances, among which are the consequences of not enacting the legislation. This legislation is on a *political* matter (i.e., it is part of the *ius civile* of human law, and not something that can be characterized as a *moral* matter, i.e., an aspect of the *ius gentium*).[29] On such political matters compromises can legitimately be made, and a legislator's act of supporting the bill is justified as a legitimate political compromise, not on the basis of an inappropriate and faulty intentional analysis. In other words, when voting for legislation on what are properly acknowledged as political matters, legislators need not agree with every aspect of the legislation for which they vote and thus in fact support. Provided that the legislation itself is not contrary to the moral law, and that voting to enact it can be judged to serve the common good, legislators can support the measure as just legislation.

If, however, the legislation contains a component that is contrary to the moral law—a situation that may occur if the legislation is solely concerned with abortion, or if abortion is just one component of an om-

---

large and mixed part of public expenditure, and may give this support without intending or cooperating formally in any wrongful act, even when the bill contains some clauses authorizing gravely immoral expenditures. The decent legislator should do what he reasonably can to amend the budget by eliminating the immoral expenditures, and to make public his rejection and denunciation of the immoral expenditures. But in a final vote, where his options have narrowed to supporting or (in effect) opposing the whole Budget, support for the general bill can be intended only to fund good causes and merely accept as a side-effect (material cooperation) the use of public money for funding immoral activities." See "Unjust Laws in a Democratic Society," 603.

29. Cf. *ST* I-II, q. 95, a. 2; q. 95, a. 4. See Chapter 3.

nibus law the rest of which is entirely ethical and positive and worthy of support—this immoral component renders the legislation in its entirety unjust, just as a purported statement of fact containing one hundred parts is in its entirety untrue if one of its parts is untrue. As Aquinas observed: "For a thing to be evil one single defect suffices, whereas for it to be good simply, it is not enough for it to be good in one point only, it must be good in every respect."[30]

The fallacy of claiming that legislators, on the basis of intention, vote only for the part(s) of a bill they "intend" to support—even though the matter on which they are voting is the whole bill—is comparable to the fallacy of any claim that, on the basis of intention, someone giving evidence may only "intend" to confirm part(s) of a statement—even though the matter on which they are giving evidence is an entire statement. Suppose, for instance, that I were presented with the following statement about myself in a court of law: "Colin Harte is the son of John and Bridie Harte, lives in Scotland, and is the author of *Changing Unjust Laws Justly*." I live in England and have never lived in Scotland. If asked to confirm its veracity I would be obliged to say that the statement is not true, irrespective of whether the error about my place of residence were of any significance. I would be telling a lie if I said it were true, and I could not claim, if I did say that it was a true statement that, in saying this, my intention was to confirm the veracity of the other parts of the statement. Clear statements of fact, like clear legislative proposals, have a precise meaning irrespective of the intentions of those who are affirming their veracity or voting for their enactment.

In due course I shall argue why a legislative vote to enact an intrinsically unjust law is a bad means of achieving one's end. My focus on the chosen means to the end requires an analysis of the object of the act of voting, but it would be mistaken to think that the only problem with Finnis's analysis is one of means. The means chosen is that of "providing legislative protection for some unborn children" in order to achieve the end of "saving some lives." The end is often characterized as that of "saving lives" but one must recognize that it is more specifically that of "saving *some* lives." Although it may seem axiomatic that an intention

---

30. *ST* I-II, q. 20, a. 2.

to "save *some* lives" is a good intention, in the context of legislative acts this needs more careful thought.

Individual actions are necessarily limited. An individual doctor can treat only a limited number of patients; an individual teacher can teach only a limited number of pupils; an individual rescuer attempting to save lives in a house fire may be able to save only a limited number of people. But the enactment of legislation is not an action of this order. A legislator's action is not the type performed by an individual that is inevitably restricted in its scope, but one that must take into account the common good, i.e., *the good of each and all* within the state. The common good is, as John Paul II notes, "the good of all and *of each individual,*"[31] a good that it is impossible to further unless the right to life of all the unborn is defended.[32] When the subject matter of legislation concerns the right to life and the protection of unborn children, the good end to be intended is that of saving *all* unborn children. The act of voting to enact legislation to protect *some* unborn children clearly does not require an intention to save *all* unborn children; indeed, some (abortion-favoring) legislators will be supporting restrictive legislation precisely because they believe abortion should be prohibited, say, after 16 weeks but permitted before 16 weeks. Clearly they do not intend to save the lives of all the unborn. Furthermore, if the objective purpose/intent of the legislation were both to protect some unborn children and not to protect others, a pro-life legislator could not justify voting for this measure on the grounds that he intended to protect *all* unborn children, because the specific action of voting for the measure would involve only an intention of protecting *some* unborn children. It does not follow that a choice to vote for a law prohibiting some abortions is good because one would have voted for a law to prohibit all abortions had one been given the opportunity.

A "Consequential" Analysis

Some philosophers have cited the consequences of voting as a determinant of the goodness of a legislator's act of voting for unjust restric-

31. John Paul II, Encyclical Letter, *Sollicitudo rei socialis* (1987), n. 38.
32. "It is impossible to further the common good without acknowledging and defending the right to life" (*EV* 101).

tive legislation. In discussions I have encountered the argument that the evil of a law permitting abortion is not the law as such but the abortions that are the consequence of the law. Therefore, it is argued, if the consequence of voting for restrictive legislation is a reduction in the number of abortions, the act of voting for the legislation can be judged to be good. Some of those who have expressed such an argument are by no means philosophical consequentialists. I regard their view, however, as a "consequential" argument because it focuses excessively on the consequences of the act of voting, failing to recognize that some acts of voting to enact legislation can be judged immoral per se, irrespective of possible good consequences and irrespective of the legislator's intention.

It may be helpful to clarify the issue at the heart of this chapter and indeed at the heart of this book. This issue is not whether, given the prospect of two alternative abortion laws—one permitting more abortions than the other—an onlooker might wish that the law permitting more abortions not be enacted (just as, if one hears that there are injuries and fatalities in a train crash, and members of one's family were on board, one might wish that they are not among the fatalities).[33] Rather, the issue is *whether a legislator can licitly vote to enact* an intrinsically unjust law permitting fewer abortions. A legislator considering how to vote when faced with legislation that is not intrinsically unjust (e.g., on matters relevant to transport, taxation, the health service, education, etc.) necessarily considers the consequences of enacting the proposed legislation. However, if—for reasons I shall explain in due course—it is never licit to vote to enact an intrinsically unjust law, the consequences of enacting the legislation are not a relevant factor once the legislation has been judged to be intrinsically unjust. The illicitness

---

33. The point I am making here is a precise one. When faced with the knowledge that one of two possible options will be enacted as law—both options being intrinsically unjust but one having more extensive evil consequences than the other—a morally upright person may well wish that the option with the more extensive evil consequences *not be enacted;* however, insofar as he recognizes that the other option is also evil (some may refer to it as a "lesser evil") he cannot wish that this option *be enacted.* Such wishes are, of course, to be distinguished from the intentional component of a moral action.

of the act of voting for an intrinsically unjust abortion law does not depend at all on the consequences of its enactment, and it is not relevant whether the unjust law is "restrictive" (with the consequence that fewer abortions will be performed) or "more liberal" (with the consequence that more abortions will be performed). Accordingly, a legislator performs a moral evil in voting for an intrinsically unjust abortion law even if he is in a minority and the bill is not enacted, or even if the bill is enacted but no abortions are subsequently performed because women and doctors reject abortion. The unacceptability of the act of voting for intrinsically unjust legislation is not determined by a consideration of the consequences.

Because the "consequential" argument maintains that the evil of an abortion law is not the law itself but the abortions that are the consequence of that law, it necessarily implies that *no law* can be identified as evil "as such." Of course, one might claim that a law's goodness or justness depends on intention, but this would require a consideration of individual legislators' subjective intentions—the notion of the objective intent of law being necessarily abandoned if no law can be judged evil "as such"—and would mean that one and the same law could be judged subjectively to be "good" or subjectively "evil."

Characterizing a law as good or evil on account of the consequences of its enactment also poses problems. Is one to judge in an *absolute* sense, with respect to the consequences of its enactment, the goodness of a law? If so, then one could argue that all restrictive abortion legislation is, in fact, evil because it continues to permit or tolerate some abortions, and abortions could occur as a consequence of this legislation (even though, had it not been enacted, these abortions as well as others could have been performed as a consequence of the previous legislation). Or is it *relative,* the goodness or evil of a law depending on whether the consequences will be more evil or less evil than if the law were not enacted? If a relative consideration of the consequences suffices (as proponents of the "consequential" view seem to suggest), then in a country that prohibited all abortions, a proposed law stating "Abortion is permissible up to 8 weeks" would be judged an evil law. In another country, where abortions were permitted up to 24 weeks, a proposed law stating that "abortion is permissible up to 16 weeks" would be judged a good law. Maybe this does or maybe this does not reflect what the "consequentialists" really believe, but it is consistent with their argument, and I trust that the implausibility of such a view is obvious.

The "consequential" argument suggests not only that no *law* can be judged evil "as such" but that no *legislative vote* can be judged morally evil "as such"; its evil or goodness would depend on the consequences. This would seem to mean that in a country that prohibited all abortions, a legislator who supported the enactment of a bill permitting abortions would not be guilty of moral evil *unless* (i) the bill were enacted, *and* (ii) abortions were performed as a result of its enactment. The "consequential" position is, however, more complex than this, because if, in a country that had hitherto prohibited all abortions, a pro-life legislator were voting for a bill to be enacted that introduced permission for abortions, and abortions were in fact performed, he would not be performing moral evil in voting for the law *if* he had voted for it in order to prevent the enactment of a law that would have permitted even more abortions.[34] If a legislator voted in favor of an abortion bill that failed to get majority support, there would be no evil consequence of abortion and so it would seem (according to this "consequential" argument) that his vote would not have been an evil act. If the bill were enacted but no abortions performed (because, say, women instinctively rejected abortion or doctors refused to participate in them), the lack of evil consequences would similarly indicate that the legislator had not performed a moral evil. If the goodness or evil of a legislative vote is determined by the consequences, one could envisage other instances in which a legislator would seem justified in voting for more permissive

---

34. John Finnis maintains that such a vote is approved by John Paul II: "In *Evangelium Vitae* (1995) sec. 73 you find two statements ... (ii) a Catholic elected legislator whose absolute personal opposition to procured abortion is well known can, in a legislative vote decisive for the passage of a bill, licitly give his or her support to a bill for a law which permits abortion but less permissively than the existing law or than a bill which will otherwise be passed and become law." Finnis, "Catholic Church and Public Policy Debates," 268. Anthony Fisher, O.P., takes a similar view in "Some Problems of Conscience in Bio-lawmaking," in Gormally, *Culture of Life—Culture of Death*, 209–10.

abortion legislation that he knew would be resoundingly defeated, if, by his association with the legislators with whom he voted, he was able to get their much needed support, say, for an anti-euthanasia bill that was much more closely contested and that those other legislators might otherwise not have supported. Such an illustration cannot be dismissed uncritically as not to the point; rather, it gets to the heart of the question of what legislators qua legislators can and cannot do. Is the goodness of a legislator's action dependent solely on its end, or is there a means to that end that qualifies it as good or bad?

Veritatis Splendor, n. 78, on the Moral Object

Intention or Object?

I have argued that in much recent discussion of this question priority has been given to the role of intention and to the consequences of enacting restrictive legislation, and that a proper consideration of the means to the end has been overlooked. The anticipated riposte to this claim is that John Paul II's teaching in *VS* 78 about the moral "object" is, as John Finnis has indicated,[35] the philosophical justification for the view against which I am arguing.

Before looking at the teaching of *VS* 78 it is necessary to note that Finnis's moral theory is based on an understanding of the role of "intention" that goes beyond the more restricted use of the term in what is commonly presented as St. Thomas Aquinas's thought, or in recent teachings including *Veritatis splendor* and the *Catechism of the Catholic Church*. Finnis's focus on the role of "intention" is, arguably, a possible cause of confusion in philosophical discourse on this or other questions. For example, his claim that "The one fact which cannot but settle what kind of act, morally speaking, a human act is, is the intention with which what is done is done"[36] appears to be rejected by John Paul II's

---

35. In "Unjust Laws in a Democratic Society," Finnis cites the relevance of *VS* 78 in a footnote (601n13). Elsewhere, he considers the question of voting for restrictive abortion legislation as a particular illustration of what he perceives to be the teaching of *VS* 78; see "Catholic Church and Public Policy Debates," 267–68.

36. John Finnis, "Intention and Side-Effects," in *Liability and Responsibility: Essays in Law and Morals,* ed. R. G. Frey and Christopher W. Morris (Cambridge: Cambridge University Press, 1991), 41.

teaching that "The morality of the human act depends primarily and fundamentally on the 'object' rationally chosen by the deliberate will. . . . The reason why a good intention is not itself sufficient, but a correct choice of actions is also needed, is that the human act depends on its object" (*VS* 78).

I am not suggesting that Finnis's and the pope's statements are irreconcilable, although they would necessarily be if each writer ascribed the same meaning to the term "intention." The perceived discrepancy between the two views is based on the possibility of interchanging the terms "object" and "intention" in ways that, I suggest, may obscure what precisely is meant in a variety of situations when these terms are used.

Finnis notes, not without justification, that the term "object" has not always been used with satisfying clarity in the tradition.[37] Although he recognizes that there are legitimate and more specialized vocabularies (typically regarded as Thomist) that reserve "intention" for the willing of the end and "choice" (traditionally linked to "object") for the willing of the means to that end, nevertheless he argues that other Thomist teachings indicate that the terminology distinguishing means and ends need not be so specifically differentiated.[38] He argues that the "object" of an act can refer to both the end and means of a chosen proposal.[39] Furthermore, he refers to "intention" as including "all that is chosen whether as end or as means,"[40] a view for which he also finds support in Aquinas's teachings[41] and which in turn enables him to argue that the determinant of moral action lies in the intention with

---

37. John Finnis, "The Act of the Person," in *Persona, Verita e Morale* (Rome: Citta Nuova Editrice, 1987), 174.

38. Ibid.

39. "In choosing to act to bring about some state of affairs as a means, whatever one thus envisages doing and bringing about as that means, together with whatever state of affairs one envisages as the end to which that means is a means, together constitute the 'object of the act' so chosen" (ibid., 174). In a footnote Finnis cites Aquinas in support of his view: "Finis, inquantum est res quaedam, est aliud voluntatis objectum quam id quod est ad finem, sed inquantum est ratio volendi id quod est ad finem est *unum et idem objectum*" (*ST* I-II, q. 12, a. 4, ad 2).

40. Finnis, "Intention and Side-Effects," 41.

41. See John Finnis, "Object and Intention: Moral Judgments According to

which what is done is done.[42] Finnis acknowledges (with Grisez and Boyle) that he does not use the terms "object" and "intention" with the same specific meaning as that attributed to them in *Veritatis splendor*,[43] and an awareness of the blurring of the distinction between "object" and "intention" is relevant when considering what precisely Finnis and followers of his theory mean when they refer to the teaching of *VS* 78.

Given that *VS* 78 is cited in the argument of some who support restrictive abortion legislation, and by me in opposition to such votes, let us consider what it teaches:

> *The morality of the human act depends primarily and fundamentally on the "object" rationally chosen by the deliberate will,* as is borne out by the insightful analysis, still valid today, made by Saint Thomas.[44] In order to be able to grasp the object of an act which specifies that act morally, it is therefore necessary to place oneself *in the perspective of the acting person.* The object of the act of willing is in fact a freely chosen kind of behaviour. To the extent that it is in conformity with the order of reason, it is the cause of the goodness of the will; it perfects us morally, and disposes us to recognize our ultimate end in the perfect good, primordial love. By the object of a given moral act, then, one cannot mean a process or an event of the merely physical order, to be assessed on the basis of its ability to bring about a given state of affairs in the outside world. Rather, that object is the proximate end of a deliberate decision which determines the act of willing on the part of the acting person. Consequently, as the *Catechism of the Catholic Church* teaches, "there are certain specific kinds of behaviour that are always wrong to choose, because choosing them involves a disorder of the will, that is, a moral evil."[45] And Saint Thomas observes that "it often happens that man acts with a good intention, but without spiritual gain, because he lacks a good will. Let us say that someone robs in order to feed the poor: in this case, even though the intention is good, the uprightness of the will is lacking. Consequently, no evil done with a good intention can

---

Aquinas," *Thomist* 55 (1991): 20. Finnis cites Aquinas: "Si . . . sub intentione comprehendatur non solum intentio finis sed voluntas operis, sic verum est, in bono et in malo, quod quantum aliquis intendit tantum facit" (*De Malo,* 2, 2 ad 8).

42. This refers to the quotation given above from "Intention and Side-Effects," 41.
43. Finnis, Grisez, and Boyle, "'Direct' and 'Indirect,'" 17.
44. A footnote (n. 126) is inserted in the passage referring to the *ST* I-II, q. 18, a. 6.
45. A footnote (n. 127) in the passage gives a reference to the *CCC,* n. 1761.

be excused. 'There are those who say: And why not do evil that good may come? Their condemnation is just' (*Rom* 3:8)."

The reason why a good intention is not itself sufficient, but a correct choice of actions is also needed, is that the human act depends on its object, whether that object is *capable or not of being ordered* to God, to the One who "alone is good," and thus brings about the perfection of the person. An act is therefore good if its object is in conformity with the good of the person with respect for the goods morally relevant for him. (*VS* 78)

Placing Oneself in the Perspective of the Acting Person

Leaving aside for the moment the first sentence of the passage, one notes that to grasp the object of an act one must "place oneself *in the perspective of the acting person.*" On this account it is argued that the goodness of a legislator's vote for bill X permitting abortion up to 16 weeks depends on how the acting person considers his vote. Is it an "abortion-favoring" kind of vote or an "abortion-restricting" kind of vote? It is claimed that if pro-life legislators are voting in a country that prohibits all abortions they should not vote for bill X, because in such a context it would be regarded as "abortion favoring," although if the country already had a more liberal law in force (or if a more liberal law would otherwise be enacted) the act of voting for it could be regarded as "abortion restricting." One might think that, irrespective of whether the vote was regarded as "abortion favoring" or "abortion restricting," the enactment of a specific law is the outcome of the votes cast, and all legislators voting for it are performing the same physical action of voting for the specific law. Is this relevant? Some interpretations of *VS* 78 would suggest this is not relevant, drawing attention to the part noting that the object of an act is grasped by placing oneself in the perspective of the acting person and that "by the object of a given moral act . . . one cannot mean *a process or an event of the merely physical order.*"

A Priority for "Intention" Not the "Physical Act"?

The rejection of moral actions considered as "physical acts" and the recognition of the need to place oneself in the perspective of the acting person seem, to some philosophers, to indicate the key role of intention in moral action. Thus Anthony Fisher, O.P., writes: "Intentionality is at stake because if the politician's goal is liberalisation of the abortion regime that is an immoral object; but if their goal is tightening up that regime, or reducing a proposed liberalisation of it, thereby saving some babies, then their object here is not immoral but the means may or may not be."[46]

The clear distinction, found in *VS* 78, between the terms "object" and "intention" becomes blurred in Fisher's analysis of the act of voting for legislation like bill X. There are, in fact, two distinct ends of the action of voting for any abortion legislation: (i) the end (the proximate end) viewed in terms of the legislation one votes to enact (the end *Veritatis splendor* would regard as the "object"), and (ii) the end (the further end) viewed in terms of the practical consequences of that legislation being enacted (the end *Veritatis splendor* would regard as the "intention"). Fisher's remarks about the "liberalisation of the abortion regime" and "tightening up that regime" refer, albeit only very loosely, to a proximate end (object); his remark, "thereby saving some babies," refers to a further end (intention). In his analysis Fisher has not shown why an "intention" to save *some* babies should—*in this legislative context*—be regarded as a good intention (a point considered above in the section "An Intentional Analysis"). Furthermore, even if it could be judged to be a good intention, he has given no explanation as to why voting for the restrictive legislation can be chosen as a good means to this end. He is thus begging the question. A false assumption has been made that because "abortion favoring" is "bad," it must follow that anything that is "abortion restricting" is to be considered its opposite and therefore "good." The true opposite of "abortion favoring," however, is not that which "restricts" (i.e., limits) abortion but that which opposes (i.e., prohibits) all abortions. Fisher's acceptance of choices (objects) with a view to ends (intentions) seems to be predicated on an uncritical account of what a legislator is both intending and choosing as a means to achieve those intended ends.

The blurring of the distinction between the terms "object" and "in-

---

46. Anthony Fisher, O.P., "On the Duties of a Catholic Politician with Respect to Abortion Law Reform, with Particular Reference to *Evangelium Vitae* 73," (1998), viewed at http://www.priestsforlife.org/articles/imperflefisher.html.

tention" is particularly evident in the last part of Fisher's statement. In the context of voting for legislation, the object of one's act refers precisely to that which is enacted as a means to a particular end and it is anomalous to say that the object may be "not immoral" but that "the means may or may not be." If he is querying whether the means to the end is or is not moral, Fisher clearly has not established that the object of his chosen act of voting for restrictive abortion legislation is moral.

I do not wish to criticize per se the theory or theories developed by Grisez, Finnis, and Boyle that focus on intentionality, especially as there are valid reasons for not viewing "object" and "intention" as mutually exclusive terms.[47] Indeed, if every action is a human (moral) action precisely because its object is chosen by the rational will for a particular (proximate) end, then every action can legitimately be regarded as an "intentional act."[48] It seems, however, that a particular danger of an analysis that focuses on intention lies in its potential for an excessive subjectivity that overlooks the precise structure of one's acts. Finnis, as noted earlier, justifies voting for bill X as a "proposal to extend legal protection to the life of unborn children after the 16th week." Given that bill X states precisely that "abortion is permissible up to 16 weeks," Finnis leaves himself open to the charge that he is simply redescribing his action and in fact distorting its structural content. At any rate he has not shown that the legislator is choosing a good "object."

The Interior and Exterior Act

I suggest that a correct understanding of the "object" of the act of voting for restrictive abortion legislation, as well as a correct understanding of the passage generally, requires a careful consideration of the first sentence of *VS* 78, which explicitly refers to Aquinas's teaching in *Summa Theologiae* I-II, q. 18, a. 6, a teaching that states: "Now in a voluntary act, there is a twofold act, viz., the interior act of the will, and

---

47. See Martin Rhonheimer, "Intentional Actions and the Meaning of Object: A Reply to Richard McCormick," in *Veritatis Splendor and the Renewal of Moral Theology*, ed. J. A. DiNoia, O.P., and Romanus Cessario, O.P. (Princeton: Scepter Publishers/Our Sunday Visitor, 1999), 245. I have also noted earlier that Finnis's choice of terminology is legitimate and supported by strong arguments.

48. Ibid., 244–49.

the exterior act; and each of these acts has its object. The end is properly the object of the interior act of the will, while the object of the exterior action is that on which the action is brought to bear." A consideration of the moral act in its two components—the interior act of the will and the external act, which "considered morally are one act"[49]—does not appear to feature in the argument of those who believe a legislator may vote for restrictive abortion legislation. This may have much to do with the influence of Grisez's writings on moral action, which specifically question the clarity and coherence of Aquinas's teaching on this point: "I do not claim to reproduce Thomas' thought precisely on 'object of the act,' since I do not think his distinction between the exterior act and the act of the will is altogether clear or coherent."[50]

By his stated confirmation of the contemporary validity of Aquinas's distinction between the interior and exterior act, John Paul II indicates the relevance of considering the properties of "exterior" acts, i.e., the structural or material components that constitute part of the moral act. Some contemporary writers have no objection to using the traditional terminology that views the object of the act in terms of the *finis operis,* as distinct from the *finis operantis,* the object chosen (the *finis operis*) referring to the structure and purpose of the willed action.[51] Grisez, however, argues that the terminology of the *finis operis* "probably is best avoided" as it may suggest that the natural teleology of behavior, considered by itself, is morally significant,[52] the locus of moral significance residing, rather, in the acting person's choices or will or intentions and not in an act's physical dimensions. I accept that Grisez does have a point and I am not embracing the view he rejects, commonly regarded as "physicalism," which claims that "the moral good or

---

49. *ST* I-II, q. 20, a. 3.

50. Grisez, *Christian Moral Principles,* 247.

51. See, for example, Peter Bristow, *The Moral Dignity of Man* (Dublin: Four Courts Press, 1997), 38. See also Martin Rhonheimer, *Natural Law and Practical Reason* (New York: Fordham University Press, 2000), 91–93. He notes, rightly, that the terminology of *finis operis* and *finis operantis* should be used with caution, and that "the *finis operis* is always a *finis operantis*" (432). The *finis operis* is however distinct from the *finis operantis.*

52. Grisez, *Christian Moral Principles,* 247.

evil of an action can be determined merely by its physical features."⁵³ For example, the act of dropping a bomb on a specific target during a war may, for one agent, be a good action of blowing up a munitions factory, the killing of innocent civilians by the bomb being unintended *(praeter intentionem);* or the identical physical act may for another agent be performed to kill the civilians, their deaths being considered a means of demoralizing the enemy. This illustration could be presented as supporting the view that the agent's intention is the morally decisive part of moral action, and that physical actions cannot themselves be reliably judged in terms of their structure and purpose. It also helps, however, to introduce a more pertinent analysis.

Acts in Conformity with Reason

The illustration of the bombers performing physically identical though morally different actions is presented by Steven Jensen.[54] He rejects the view that the moral goodness or evil of an action can be determined by its physical features (a view he characterizes as "extreme physicalism") but argues for a position of "moderate physicalism," a stance he considers consistent with Aquinas's teaching. Identical physical actions should not be distinguished, he suggests, by reference to the agent's "intention" (as Finnis, Grisez, et al. argue) but by how they are conceived by the agent prior to their performance.[55] For Jensen, as for Aquinas, the goodness of the exterior action depends on its being conceived according to reason.[56] This view is consistent with the teaching of *VS* 78 that the willed object must be "in conformity with the order of reason." Other writers use different terminology that, even if it includes an "intentional" component, seems to be consistent with this. For example, Martin Rhonheimer regards the moral object as the *finis operis* or, equivalently, the "basic intentional content" of a concrete action,[57] this being the agent's proximate goal (or end), "the goal he pur-

---

53. This is the definition proposed by Steven J. Jensen in his article "A Defense of Physicalism," *Thomist* 61 (1997): 377.

54. See previous note.

55. Ibid., 399.

56. Ibid.; Aquinas, *De Malo,* q. 2, a. 3; *ST* I-II, q. 20, a. 1.

57. Martin Rhonheimer, "Intrinsically Evil Acts and the Moral Viewpoint: Clarify-

sues independently of the *further* goals he may pursue by choosing this concrete action."[58] He draws a parallel between the objects of human action and the precepts of natural law, the bond between them being reason, each being *"aliquid a ratione constitutum"*[59] and springing from an *"ordinatio rationis."*[60]

Given that the natural law prohibiting all abortions is in accordance with the order of reason, a positive law stating "All abortions are prohibited" can similarly be judged to be in accordance with both the natural law and the order of reason. Bill X, if enacted as Act X, stating "Abortion is permissible up to 16 weeks" would constitute a law that contradicts the natural law and thus not be in accordance with the order of reason. Opponents of my view may concede this point but claim that this does not affect the rationality or the reasonableness of *the act of voting* to enact bill X, the goodness (so they claim) of the moral action of voting for particular legislation not being identifiable with the physical matter of the legislation.

Identifying Different Purposes (Objects) of Physically Similar Actions

Those who suggest that the reasonableness of voting for legislation is not dependent precisely on the reasonableness of the legislation may seem to have a point, given that the notion of *finis operis* (the object) should not be reduced to a consideration of acts seen solely in terms of their structural or physical properties, as is shown by the earlier illustration of the bomber. Thus John Paul II rightly says that "by the object of a given moral act, then, one cannot mean a process or an event of the merely physical order." (*VS* 78). William May, with reference to this sentence, says that John Paul II "makes it a point to show that the 'object' specifying a human act is not the act considered in its materiality,"[61] but in this remark he appears to be overlooking the nuance in the

---

ing a Central Teaching of Veritatis Splendor," in DiNoia and Cessario, *Veritatis Splendor and the Renewal of Moral Theology,* 182, 187.

58. Ibid.

59. Cf. *ST* I-II, q. 84, a. 1.

60. *ST* I-II, q. 90, a. 4. See Rhonheimer, "Intrinsically Evil Acts and the Moral Viewpoint," 184.

61. William E. May, "Theologians and Theologies in the Encyclical [*Veritatis Splendor*]," *Anthropotes* (1994): 55.

pope's teaching that the object is not a process or event *merely (tantum)* of the physical order.⁶² In other words, the physical order itself is not to be overlooked, but in itself it is not sufficient for specifying the moral object. Thus the act of a woman regularly taking an estrogen pill and engaging in sexual intercourse with her husband may or may not be immoral, depending on whether, in taking the pill, the *finis operis* of her act (the object, or purpose) is contraceptive or whether she has a pathological condition for which a regimen of estrogen is medically indicated, the temporary sterility also caused by it being a side effect of what is chosen for a morally good purpose.⁶³ The principal factor when considering the moral goodness of the actions of two women taking an estrogen pill lies in whether the action is chosen by the acting person in accordance with reason. Is a woman taking an estrogen pill the subject of a genuine medical application (an act in accordance with reason), or is she acting in order to make herself infertile so that she can engage in sexual intercourse without the prospect of pregnancy (an act which is not in accordance with reason)? The morality of such actions is, indeed, grasped by placing oneself in the perspective of the acting person.

62. "Ergo nefas est accipere, velut obiectum definiti actus moralis, processum vel eventum ordinis tantum physici" (*VS* 78). It should be noted that *VS* 78 expresses a general principle applicable to all moral acts. The passage is relevant to showing not only how some acts can be good even though they might appear in their materiality to be bad, but also to showing how some acts that might appear in their materiality good can in fact be bad. For example, greeting a friend with a customary kiss would, considered in its materiality, normally be regarded as good, but when Judas kissed Jesus his act had the object of betrayal. May's remarks, though lacking the nuance found in *VS* 78, are appropriate when applied to this sort of act.

63. This illustration does not compare exactly with that of the bomber insofar as there are differences, when considering the act in its materiality, between a woman *with* and a woman *without* a medical condition. The two women not only possess distinct physical characteristics on this account, but the effects of the action are not identical insofar as a medical condition is in one case affected by the treatment. Although I think the view is rightly rejected that the moral good or evil of an action can be determined merely by its physical features, nevertheless the physical features of actions do have their own intelligibility, and a closer consideration of acts in their physical dimension sometimes enables one to make distinctions, relevant for judging the goodness or evil of actions, that are not dependent on the acting person's conception of his or her action. If the estrogen pill had an abortifacient property, this would introduce other considerations, and for the purposes of this illustration I am assuming that this is not a factor.

But some actions, if they are *freely chosen* (this condition of their being freely chosen ensuring that one is not considering acts of the merely physical order), can be rejected as immoral acts when considered with respect to their materiality.[64] Homosexual acts, or heterosexual acts between unmarried couples, can be rejected as immoral chosen acts, not necessarily because of what is intended by such actions but because the willed choice of such acts does not spring from the order of reason; such acts, considered simply as willed physical acts, have an intelligibility that can be judged to be contrary to reason and, equivalently, a violation of the natural law. There may, of course, be some very good ends of such actions (such as increased friendship and trust, bodily comfort, and even, as a result of heterosexual acts, having children created in God's image) but the acts cannot be justified on the basis that the agent intends only these good ends (with the other bad ends being accepted as mere "side effects"), because this sort of act can be rejected as unacceptable merely by a consideration of its object. If "the human act depends on its object, whether that object is capable or not of being ordered to God" (*VS* 78) and if reason (or, equivalently, the natural law) reveals that sexual activity outside of marriage is not "capable of being ordered to God," then any freely chosen homosexual or other nonmarital sexual acts can be judged immoral with respect to their object.

Is, then, the act of voting for unjust restrictive legislation comparable to taking an estrogen pill (i.e., can different purposes—objects—be specified for outwardly similar behaviors, some of which may be morally acceptable and others not?), or like engaging in a nonmarital

---

64. Cf. Aquinas: "nor have exterior acts any measure of morality, save in so far as they are voluntary" (*ST* I-II, q. 18, a. 6). This is stated in the article referred to in the first sentence of *VS* 78 and indicates that some commentators may be reading too much into the teaching of *VS* 78 that "it is necessary to place oneself in the perspective of the acting person" and the following sentence that "the object of the act of willing is in fact a freely chosen kind of behaviour." *VS* 78 is consistent with Aquinas's teaching in highlighting the fact that moral actions are moral precisely because they are voluntary (willed, chosen) acts, and that the determination of the morality of an action requires an understanding of that action from the perspective of the acting person (i.e., what is chosen/willed) and not simply what physical action is observed. *VS* 78 later acknowledges that some physical acts ("kinds of behaviour") "are always wrong to choose, because choosing them involves a disorder of the will, that is, moral evil."

sexual act (an act that can always be rejected as contrary to reason, incapable of being ordered to God, and morally evil by virtue of its object)? The focus of our inquiry must be that of identifying the specific purpose or purposes of legislative votes and seeing whether they conform with "the order of reason" and are "capable or not of being ordered to God." In other words, what exactly is a lawmaker doing when voting for legislation?

An Analysis of Voting

What precisely are legislators doing when they vote? Let us start with John Finnis's consideration of this question:

> The meaning and content of the relevant choices and actions of legislators is conditioned by the procedural context. Consider an example. Suppose that, at stage B in a legislative process, the only legislators who can move a reconsideration of a proposal are those who voted *for* that proposal at stage A in the process. In such a context, it may sometimes be the case that the only way in which a legislator can defeat a proposal at the decisive stage B is by voting *for* it at the preliminary stage A. In such a situation a vote for the proposal at stage A could be an effective way of preventing the proposal becoming law. This example shows that a general, universally applicable or *per se* specification of a legislator's responsibilities cannot be adequately stated in terms of "voting." Rather, the morally relevant matter for choice and moral judgment is: *helping to make a proposal part of the law* (or helping to retain an existing part of the law against proposals for change).[65]

I agree with Finnis's view that a per se specification of a legislator's responsibilities cannot be adequately stated in terms of "voting," but it does not follow from this that the morally relevant matter is whether one's vote is based on "helping to make a proposal part of the law." The illustration Finnis provides does not, in fact, correspond with the reality of voting situations—if it is ever the case, it would certainly be an extremely rare exception to usual legislative processes for legislators to be able to move a reconsideration at stage B only if they had voted *for* a

---

65. Finnis, "Unjust Laws in a Democratic Society," 599–600.

proposal at stage A—so I shall modify it a little to make it consistent both with what tends to happen in reality and with the sort of procedural considerations Finnis seems to be concerned about. In so doing, I hope to reveal that a particular flaw in Finnis's analysis lies in what he is referring to as the "proposal" that he wants to make part of the law. He seems to be considering the action of voting for legislation at stage A ("proposal A," which the legislator does not want to be enacted as law), in order to participate in amending it at a committee stage (stage B, at which "proposal B" and other additional amending proposals may be considered), so that by stage C it may be acceptable ("proposal C," which he does want to be enacted as law), or at least, even if it is still unacceptable, more restrictive in terms of its evil consequences than was the original proposal. Finnis justifies voting for the legislation at stage A on the grounds that he is "helping to make a proposal part of the law."[66] But at that stage, which proposal would Finnis claim his legislator is helping to make a part of the law? Proposal A, the concrete proposal in existence, which is the subject matter of the vote? Proposal B, a proposal that does not yet exist and might never exist, but that might at a later stage amend the original proposal (or, as in the unusual case suggested by Finnis, might prevent the original proposal becoming law)? Or proposal C, the proposal that Finnis's legislator may or may not judge to be acceptable (if proposal A is amended by proposal B) but which, like proposal B, also does not yet exist and which might never exist? Indeed, Finnis's argument could be widened to justify a legislator's vote for proposals A, B, and C when in fact he does not truly favor any of them but chooses to support them as a means of hastening the prospects of another proposal that might have a greater chance of being considered—possibly many months or years in the future—if proposal C is enacted. And whichever "proposal" the legislator might in fact have in mind when voting, Finnis's analysis provides no clue as to what is required for his vote to be judged morally good or bad.

One needs to step back from Finnis's unsatisfactory formula of

66. Though Finnis says that the morally relevant matter is "helping to make a proposal part of the law," his illustration involves the rare, and possibly nonexistent, scenario of voting *for* a proposal (at stage A) in order (at stage B) to prevent its becoming part of the law.

"helping to make a proposal part of the law" and reconsider what precisely legislators do when they vote; this requires an analysis of *the purpose* of voting for legislation at stages A, B, and C. Legislative procedures may, of course, vary in different legislatures, but I will assume that we are dealing with a system, common to most legislatures, in which a legislative proposal is initially presented to the legislature (stage A), considered in greater detail, and possibly amended in a committee and by the full legislature (stage B), and presented again finally to the full legislature to determine whether the proposal that emerges from the committee and amending stages is acceptable for enactment as law (stage C).

Let us start at stage C, which we are regarding in this discussion as the final vote for legislation. I can identify one and only one purpose of voting in favor of legislation at this stage, and this is precisely to enact as law the legislative proposal that is presented. Essential to any deliberation and judgment as to whether a legislator may vote for a bill at this stage is an understanding of what law is. If a legislator does not know what constitutes law, or if he is presented at this stage with a bill that does not fulfill the requirements of law (assuming there are requirements), then he cannot reliably perform a good action in voting for it.

At stage A, the purpose of the vote is entirely different. A legislator who votes "for" the bill at this stage is not voting to enact this proposal (proposal A) as law but is merely voting to accept it as a basis from which to proceed, knowing that the bill will be subject to further debate, amendments, and votes before any judgment as to whether it should be enacted as law. In view of the possibility of supporting amendments at subsequent stages, it could be legitimate to vote for a bill at stage A that did not at this stage fulfill the requirements of law, even though the same bill could not be supported when voted upon for enactment as law at stage C. The purpose of voting at each of these stages differs; in other words, the two actions—of voting at stage A and stage C—have different objects. By equating these specifically different actions in terms of "helping to make a proposal part of the law," Finnis fails to identify the objects of specifically different acts and thus fails to identify what precisely is being done.

The question raised at the end of the previous section was whether there are different purposes for legislative votes. Although I have identified different purposes for voting at stages A and C, the focus of our enquiry concerns votes to enact laws, and so we are concerned specifically with stage-C votes. There would appear to be one and only one purpose of voting for a bill at this stage, and this is to declare, partly on the basis of the legislator's own prudential judgment: (i) that the bill fulfills the criteria of law; legislators cannot claim to be acting in accordance with reason if they are willing to accept as law that which is not law; *and* (ii) that the bill's enactment, at the particular moment in time, serves the common good; the enactment of law serves a public function, and must be considered expedient (i.e., suitable). Law cannot be reasonably enacted if either of these two conditions is absent.

One can compare voting for a bill with the act of speech. Just as the different stages of legislation enable one to identify more than one purpose of voting for a bill, similarly one can identify more than one purpose of speech. One may, for example, be performing vocal exercises, telling humorous stories or jokes, engaging in drama, or communicating facts. The requirement of "truth telling" does not apply with every form of speech, as clearly there is no expectation that what is said in the course of vocal exercises, joking, and drama be factually true. However, in "communicative speech" truth telling is a requirement, and if it were not, the assumptions underpinning social communications would crumble and no one's word would be considered reliable. When engaging, then, in "communicative speech," two conditions must be met: (i) what is said must be true; *and* (ii) the communicator must judge that it is expedient (suitable) to say whatever is said. So, voting to enact a bill as law can be compared with communicative speech, but there is a further specification. The comparison with communicative speech is not that of "simple" communicative speech, but that of the sort of solemn public speech as is made under oath in a court of law. Voting to enact a law and truth telling under oath are both public and serious responsibilities.

Focusing on "Law"

The first judgment to be made when deciding how to vote at stage C focuses on "law," and the question of voting for restrictive abortion legislation must always be considered in the proper context of its being a legislative act. Chapters 2 and 3 have already dealt with some of the relevant jurisprudential aspects of this question, notably highlighting the concept of an "intrinsically unjust" law. Chapters 7 and 8 will deal with key legislative matters and outline a wide range of measures relevant to abortion, indicating which are and which are not intrinsically unjust.

The key question is: *what is law?* Aquinas's definition, accepted in the previous chapter, is that law is "nothing else than an ordinance of reason [*rationis ordinatio*] for the common good, made by him who has care of the community, and promulgated";[67] law is "nothing else but a dictate of practical reason [*dictamen practicae rationis*] emanating from the ruler who governs a perfect community."[68] John Finnis objects to the common translation of *dictamen* by "dictate," claiming, "it is unsound, in so far as 'dictate' suggests arbitrariness and even abuse of power."[69] Although the term "dictate" is widely used,[70] Finnis raises a legitimate concern that it might be misunderstood. However, the term Aquinas uses expresses a central character of law: law must be understood with respect to what it "dictates"—or, if one prefers, with respect to what it "decrees" or "states" or "commands" or "specifies" or "prescribes," etc.

According to Aquinas, then, law is *that which is decreed* (whether verbally or, in the case of parliamentary laws, in legislative texts), this decree being otherwise described as an "ordinance of reason" *(rationis ordinatio)* or a "dictate of practical reasoning" *(dictamen practicae rationis)*. So, in considering the justness of any legislation it is not only rele-

---

67. "definitio legis, quae nihil est aliud quam quaedam rationis ordinatio ad bonum commune, ab eo qui curam communitatis habet, promulgata." *ST* I-II, q. 90, a. 4.
68. "nihil est aliud lex quam quoddam dictamen practicae rationis 'in principe' qui gubernat aliquam communitatem perfectam." *ST* I-II, q. 91, a. 1.
69. John Finnis, *Aquinas,* 256.
70. For example, *normas edere* is translated as "*dictate* norms" in *EV* 71.

vant to consider what precisely is decreed; it is a basic requirement. This has nothing to do with taking a "legalistic" approach to lawmaking but is rather an obviously necessary component of any legislative judgment.[71]

Let us consider legislation on a different matter. A law stating, "Cars more than five years old may not be driven on public roads," cannot, in itself, be judged to be just or unjust. One can at least say that the law is not intrinsically unjust. In itself this sort of law cannot be judged to be contrary to reason, though whether it is, in fact, in accordance with reason depends on other—circumstantial (i.e., extrinsic)—facts. These would include whether cars more than five years old are safe, whether they emit more noxious substances into the environment after five years, whether the economy (and thus people in society) would benefit from the production of more new cars, whether poorer people would be unfairly disadvantaged by such a law, etc. Because a measure of this type does not in itself violate the natural law, and is not in itself contrary to reason (i.e., it is not intrinsically unjust), legislators may freely deliberate whether, in the light of the concrete situation, it is in fact just, and furthermore whether it serves the common good to enact it as law.

By contrast, a law stating "Abortion is permissible up to 16 weeks," considered in itself, is clearly contrary to the natural law, which states that abortion is never permissible and is always to be prohibited and, equivalently, is in itself contrary to reason. It is intrinsically unjust and it is accordingly impossible for a favorable "just" verdict to be given as a result of a consideration of circumstantial factors. I have indicated above that supporters of restrictive abortion legislation may be willing to acknowledge that it is intrinsically unjust but unwilling to accept that this means a legislator acts unethically in voting for it.

71. "Legalism," says Kevin L. Flannery, S.J., "signifies a conforming of oneself to the legal, whether doing so leads to human fulfillment or not," and he notes rightly that the natural law "is by definition the way to human fulfillment." See Flannery, *Acts amid Precepts* (Edinburgh: T. & T. Clark, 2001), 188. If a human law itself violates the natural law, then it is, self-evidently, not the way to human fulfillment and cannot reasonably be chosen as a way to it. A clear and proper assessment of human laws, and a rejection of those that can be identified as intrinsically unjust and contrary to the natural law, has nothing to do with "legalism."

Can one argue, then, that there is a need to distinguish between the intrinsic unjustness of a law and the goodness or badness of the moral action of voting to enact a bill as law? Bearing in mind the previous analysis showing that there is only one purpose of voting to enact any bill, i.e., that the bill on which one is voting be enacted as law, I shall provide two responses to the question.

First, if the particular sort of action (voting to enact legislation) is judged to have only one purpose, it must be determined whether the performance of that sort of action in a particular instance satisfies the criteria that have been established for the proper performance of that sort of action. If my criteria are correct, then one must consider first, prior to enacting a bill as law, whether in fact it is capable of being enacted *as law*. If it is intrinsically unjust and contrary to reason and "not a law" (as Aquinas and the tradition have clearly taught),[72] then one is performing an "impossible action" if one attempts to enact "not a law" as "law"; such an action is a contradiction in itself and in the realm of the absurd.[73]

Second, the act of enacting a law is a collective act. If a majority of legislators express in a vote their support for a bill to become law, then the act of support for the enactment by an individual legislator becomes not simply his or her individual act but the act (or Act) of the legislature. The Act of the legislature is, in essence, the collectivization of the individual acts of the majority of the legislators. So, if the would-be Act is intrinsically unjust and contrary to reason, and not capable of being ordered to God's law, which prohibits all abortions, then the act of voting for the Act must also be judged to be intrinsically unjust, not (as *VS*

---

72. The traditional view is expressed by John Paul II, who quotes Aquinas extensively: "the clear teaching of Saint Thomas Aquinas, who writes that 'human law is a law inasmuch as it is in conformity with right reason and thus derives from the eternal law. But when a law is contrary to reason, it is called an unjust law; but in this case it ceases to be a law and becomes instead an act of violence' [*ST* I-II, q. 93, a. 3, ad 2]. And again: 'Every law made by man can be called a law insofar as it derives from the natural law. But if it is somehow opposed to the natural law, then it is not really a law but rather a corruption of the law' [*ST* I-II, q. 95, a. 2]." *EV* 72.

73. See Tadeusz Styczeń, S.D.S., "Le Leggi Contro la Vita: Analisi Etico-Culturale," in Trujillo, Herranz, and Sgreccia, *"Evangelium Vitae" and Law,* 218; also Styczeń, "Ethics as the Theory of Natural Law," 217.

78 teaches it must be) "in conformity with the order of reason" and not "capable . . . of being ordered to God" (*VS* 78). One cannot separate, in its essence, the legislator's act (of support for the law, expressed in a vote) from the legislature's Act, which actualizes that for which the legislator voted. What precisely is involved in voting is clear when the term "legislature's Act" is acknowledged as having a twofold meaning that encompasses (i) its being a *noun* (i.e., that which is written), and also (ii) its being a *verb* (i.e., what the legislature does), the activity of this Act remaining constant for the duration of the legislation (i.e., as long as the Act is "in force"). I conclude, therefore, that it is a contradiction to claim that it can be a good act to vote for a bad Act because there are not two essentially distinct acts.

This chapter has demonstrated that arguments based on the principles of material cooperation in evil or the double effect to justify votes for (unjust) restrictive abortion legislation are wide of the mark. Far from challenging my argument, the teaching on the moral object by John Paul II in *Veritatis splendor* has been cited in defense of my view. In particular, I have argued that if a legislature's Act can be identified as intrinsically unjust, likewise the act of a legislator voting to enact it must be identified as intrinsically unjust. In other words, the key objection to voting for intrinsically unjust restrictive abortion legislation is that such votes are among the category of intrinsically evil (unjust) acts that "are not capable of being ordered to God and to the good of the person" and which can never be transformed "into an act 'subjectively' good or defensible as a choice" (*VS* 81).

5. A "SPECIAL CASE" CONSIDERATION

In the previous chapter I argued that the identification of a law as intrinsically unjust is sufficient to judge that the act of voting for it is intrinsically unjust and never an ethically good choice. When discussing this point I have encountered the claim that the acceptance of this argument does not end discussion on the question of voting for intrinsically unjust restrictive legislation. For example, Martin Rhonheimer has argued in correspondence with me:

> Of course, normally the act of voting to enact legislation has the purpose of enacting precisely this law, and provided this law is an unjust law, the act of voting for it, i.e., the act of enacting it, is an unjust act. But we precisely are not talking about this normal case of lawmaking.
>
> Notice that every act of lawmaking is an act of political prudence, a political act. Laws are rules which shape the behaviour of citizens and the society as a whole. The relevance of law consists in this shaping power. So, normally by enacting laws I precisely want the kind of shaping the law provides. But in our case this is not so. Here, voting for an abortion law has not the "one and specific purpose" to enact an abortion law, but to prevent the enacting or existence of some other, less restrictive law. This is a different act of political prudence. It is a political move that is licit precisely under the condition that the opposition to abortion of the one so voting is publicly known. That is, the move must be known as one which is performed in the context of an anti-abortion politics.
>
> You must argue against this point and not simply repeat your thesis that any act of voting for an, as such, unjust law is an unjust act. What you have to show is that my argument is not sound. For this purpose you have to show that my distinction between the "normal case" and the "special case" is wrong.[1]

---

1. E-mail correspondence of 13 Nov. 2000. I am grateful to Father Martin Rhonheimer for permitting me to quote from his correspondence.

A "special case"? I assumed by this that Rhonheimer meant an exception to the "normal case" could be applied in this instance, so that a legislator could vote for an intrinsically unjust law. But if such an exception could be made in this instance, why could not "special cases" be identified as exceptions to other "normal cases"? Could one not identify, perhaps, a special case in which one might tell an untruth (say, to protect a professional secret), or might kill an innocent person (say, to prevent several other people being killed)? Of course, it would be easier to justify such a "special case" if one described one's action as "keeping a professional secret" or "saving lives"—just as Rhonheimer described the legislative action, not as "enact[ing] an abortion law," but rather as "prevent[ing] the enacting or existence of some other, less restrictive law." I challenged Rhonheimer on this point and learned that this was not what he meant: "My 'special' case is not meant to be an exception from a 'general rule,' but the very 'special case' considered in *Evangelium vitae* 73 itself."[2]

But does *EV* 73 regard this as a "special case"? I readily acknowledge that John Paul II raises the question whether a legislator can cast a positive vote "in cases where a legislative vote would be decisive for the passage of a more restrictive law, aimed at limiting the number of authorized abortions, in place of a more permissive law already passed or ready to be voted on"—but he does not teach that a legislator can cast such a vote,[3] and furthermore no other magisterial text has ever taught

---

2. Martin Rhonheimer to author, 14 Nov. 2000, e-mail.

3. Much of the confusion about the teaching of *EV* 73, as I shall explain in Chapter 9, has arisen because the pope's description of the "problem of conscience" under discussion has been cited as the resolution to that problem. It has been assumed that the very framing of the problem of conscience (which is essentially a question: "Can legislators in certain circumstances vote for restrictive abortion legislation?") requires that it be answered in the affirmative. In *Humanae vitae* (HV) Pope Paul VI asked whether "the principle of totality" provided a basis for justifying contraception: "Could it not be admitted . . . that procreative finality applies to the totality of married life rather than to each single act?" (*HV* 3). No thoughtful reader would jump to the conclusion that the framing of this question implied that contraception was justified, and furthermore that it was justified with respect to "the principle of totality," but many readers of *EV* 73 have jumped to a similarly unwarranted conclusion with respect to voting for restrictive abortion legislation.

that view. As I shall demonstrate in Chapter 9, the argument I am promoting in this book is entirely consistent with what is taught in *EV* 73 and with John Paul II's public statements on this question since the encyclical was published. If voting for restrictive legislation is rightly regarded as a "special case," the teaching of *EV* 73 cannot be cited as establishing that it is one. And the onus must be on those who believe that it is a "special case" to establish that it is, rather than on me to establish that it is not.

If voting for unjust restrictive legislation is to be regarded as a "special case," on what account is it so regarded? A pro-life legislator voting for legislation of the form "Abortion is permissible up to 16 weeks" (bill X) is indisputably performing the same physical action as a pro-abortion legislator who is voting for it precisely because he supports abortion no later than but nevertheless up to 16 weeks and whose action would not be regarded as morally good.[4] In the previous chapter I acknowledged that some acts, though they appear to be physically identical, can be judged to be morally good in some instances and morally bad in others. Rhonheimer would appear to be suggesting that a pro-life legislator's action of voting for bill X is one such action, and that it can be judged morally good because it is "known as one which is performed in the context of an anti-abortion politics."

The Concept of "Anti-Abortion Politics"

An "anti-abortion politics"? The pro-life movement is rightly engaged with politicians and legislators to promote the right to life as a matter of public policy, but this is not an activity which should be regarded as "anti-abortion politics." On the contrary, the establishment of fundamental moral principles, at the forefront of which is the right to

---

4. As I noted in Chapter 4, John Finnis claims that a pro-life legislator's action of voting for restrictive legislation can be justified as permissible material cooperation in evil, insofar as he *does not* (according to Finnis's analysis) *intend* to permit those abortions which are in fact permitted by the restrictive legislation. A ("less extreme") pro-abortion legislator who votes for the same restrictive legislation and who *does intend* to permit all or even *some* of those abortions, would (according to Finnis's analysis) be cooperating *formally* in evil.

life of all members of society, is a necessary precondition for the exercise of "politics." Rhonheimer has himself observed that the right to life has a "pre-political character."[5] Applying the teaching of the Second Vatican Council that "political authority ... must be exercised within the limits of the moral order,"[6] John Paul II reminded legislators that the "transcendent and inviolable personal dignity in every human being, even the poorest and smallest ... is *the foundation* for working out the political and juridical decisions indispensable for the future of civilization."[7]

In Chapters 3 and 4 I referred to Aquinas's distinction, when considering human law, between the *ius gentium* and the *ius civile*,[8] the latter referring to matters correctly identified as "political," i.e., those matters which do not violate the natural moral law and which can be chosen from a wide range of legitimate options. On account of the range of legitimate options from which one can choose when considering "political" matters, compromises can and sometimes should be made when enacting this sort of legislation. Abortion legislation, however, being a "moral" matter *(ius gentium)* is of a different order, human law being unable to authorize that which contradicts the moral law. It is not legitimate to consider as possible options for public policy (i.e., to regard as "political" options) any that permit or tolerate the deliberate killing of any unborn child, whether as a matter of principle (i.e., a pro-abortion ethic) or as a choice of compromise (i.e., "anti-abortion politics"), and thus Rhonheimer's notion of "anti-abortion politics" is misconceived. The only valid kind of "anti-abortion politics" is one that, by upholding without compromise in legislation the right to life of every unborn child, is in conformity with the moral law. This would, at least, be correct action, even though to characterize it as "politics" would be inappropriate because the establishment of a legal right to life is a condition prior to politics. Aquinas's teaching on the "absoluteness"

5. Rhonheimer, "Fundamental Rights, Moral Law," 176.
6. Vatican Council II, *Gaudium et spes,* n. 74.
7. John Paul II, Address to Participants in the Second European Meeting of Politicians and Legislators (23 Oct. 1998), n. 3, reproduced in *Familia et Vita* 3, no. 3 (1998): 169–72.
8. *ST* I-II, q. 95, a. 2; q. 95, a. 4.

of the moral is also shown in his remarks on justice when he notes that positive justice (or positive law, *ius positivum*) cannot be contrary to natural justice (or natural law, *ius naturale*). He teaches:

> The human will can, by common agreement, make a thing to be just provided that it be not, of itself, contrary to natural justice [*naturalem iustitiam*] and it is in such matters that positive right [*ius positivum*] has its place. . . . If however, a thing is, of itself, contrary to natural right [*ius naturale*] the human will cannot make it just, for instance, by decreeing that it is lawful to steal or to commit adultery. Hence it is written: "Woe to them that make wicked laws" (Isaiah 10:1).[9]

The political is necessarily subordinate to the moral[10] and it is not, as Rhonheimer suggests, an "act of political prudence" to promote and support an intrinsically unjust restrictive measure, but rather an act of moral compromise inconsistent with true morality.[11] Rhonheimer notes that "laws are rules which shape the behaviour of citizens and the society as a whole. The relevance of law consists in this shaping power." By voting for unjust restrictive legislation a legislator's action contributes to the shaping of the behavior of citizens and society so that some abortions are regarded as unacceptable, the implication being that other abortions—specifically those of the more vulnerable of the unborn, i.e., those who are younger, disabled, conceived after rape or incest, etc.—are regarded as (more) acceptable. This objective "shap-

---

9. *ST* II-II, q. 57, a. 2, ad 2.

10. "The subordination of politics to ethics is absolute and even infinite, being based on the subordination of ends. . . . The end of politics is nothing in comparison with the end of ethics." Jacques Maritain, *The Things That Are Not Caesar's* (originally published in French as *Primauté du spirituel*) (London: Sheed and Ward, 1930), 2–3.

11. The Church rightly encourages Catholics to be engaged in public affairs, but this encouragement is not unconditional. Thus John XXIII encouraged Catholics to be involved in economic and social activities (i.e., in political matters) and to collaborate with non-Catholics: "In such circumstances they must, of course, bear themselves as Catholics and do nothing to compromise religion and morality." *Mater et Magistra* (London: CTS, 1961), n. 239, p. 60; see also *Pacem in terris* (London: CTS, 1963), part 5, p. 57. Writing to the German bishops on the question of issuing abortion counseling certificates, John Paul II says: "The unconditional commitment to every unborn life, to which the Church feels bound from the very beginning, permits no ambiguity or compromise" (Letter to German Bishops, 3 June 1999, n. 3).

ing" of society is not avoided by legislators' declarations of personal opposition to the compromise policy that they are, in fact, supporting and by means of which they are, in fact, shaping society. Furthermore, by voting in favor of such unjust restrictive legislation—which objectively constitutes a compromise on a moral matter—pro-life legislators would be shaping society to accept that it is within the competence of a legislature to enact this sort of legislation,[12] and possibly indicating that their votes are being made taking into account the democratic will, an action that distorts (or reveals an ignorance concerning) the concept of democracy. Democracy does not mean that laws governing society should be based purely on the will of the people, but that the will of the people should prevail on *political* matters, it being understood that the political is subordinate to the moral.[13]

Rhonheimer's suggestion that voting for unjust restrictive legislation is a licit move "precisely under the condition that the opposition to abortion of the one so voting is publicly known" is clearly based on John Paul II's sentence in *EV* 73 that says that "an elected official, whose absolute personal opposition to procured abortion was well known, could licitly support proposals aimed at limiting the harm done by [a pro-abortion] law." In subsequent chapters I shall demonstrate that there are indeed some legislative measures to limit the harm done by an abortion law that, being not intrinsically unjust, can be licitly supported. Rhonheimer's qualification that the goodness of a vote for unjust restrictive legislation depends upon the legislator being pro-life and being known to be pro-life (a qualification that is based, I maintain, on a misinterpretation of the teaching of *EV* 73), is noteworthy, and merits careful consideration.

On the one hand, the qualification that only those legislators can

---

12. By contrast John Paul II reaffirms the earlier instruction given by the CDF in *Donum Vitae* (1987), part 3, that "in no sphere of life can the civil law take the place of conscience or dictate norms concerning those things which are outside its competence" (*EV* 71).

13. On democracy John Paul II teaches: "Only respect for life can be the foundation and guarantee of the most precious and essential goods of society, such as democracy and peace. There can be no true democracy without a recognition of *every* person's dignity and without respect for his or her rights" (*EV* 101) (emphasis added).

vote for restrictive legislation who are publicly known as being pro-life might seem to support the argument (presented by John Finnis and others) that votes for restrictive legislation can be justified as material cooperation in evil. On the other, the qualification poses a difficulty which also needs to be addressed.

Finnis argues that a pro-life legislator's vote for a proposal such as "Abortion is permitted up to 16 weeks [and prohibited thereafter]" (when the previous limit was higher) would not be *formal* cooperation in the continued permission for abortion up to 16 weeks, but that it would be *material* cooperation, which (according to Finnis's argument) could be regarded as a side effect of a good act of voting to prohibit abortions after 16 weeks.[14] According to Finnis, a pro-life legislator's vote for such legislation can be judged morally acceptable because although the legislator would be voting (as Finnis admits) "for a law which permits abortion" he would not be voting to permit "precisely to permit" the pre-16-week abortions, but rather, as it were, voting to permit them precisely to prohibit those after 16 weeks.[15] By contrast, a legislator who is not pro-life but is opposed to late abortions might, though he would be acting in a way behaviorally no different from that of the pro-life legislator, be casting his vote precisely to stop abortion after 16 weeks while also in fact cooperating formally in the evil of permitting, precisely to permit, abortions prior to 16 weeks. Indeed, even if a legislator did not support permission for all the abortions allowed up to 16 weeks but willed that only some of those abortions be permitted (say, those up to 10 or 12 weeks, or those carried out up to 16 weeks

---

14. John Finnis, "Catholic Church and Public Policy Debates," 269.

15. Finnis says: "The always illicit vote is for a law *as permitting,* precisely *to* permit, abortion. This is always illicit, even if one is personally opposed to abortion and is voting for it only to keep one's seat and prevent euthanasia or genocide laws, or only to equalize the position of the poor and the rich. The kind of vote which . . . [*EV* 73, as interpreted by Finnis] judges can be licit has as its object not: *to permit* abortions now illegal, but rather: *to prohibit* abortions now legal or imminently likely otherwise to become legal. (Say: the existing law or the threatened alternative bill says abortion is lawful up to 24 weeks, while the law or bill for which the Catholic legislator is voting says abortion is lawful up to 16 weeks.) Even though it is a vote for a law which does permit abortion, it is chosen by this legislator as a vote for a law which restricts abortion." Ibid., 268–69.

for eugenic but not social reasons), there would still be some element of formal cooperation in evil in voting for the measure.

If, contrary to the analysis of *EV* 73 that I shall present in Chapter 9, John Paul II were to agree with Finnis and Rhonheimer that pro-life legislators can vote for restrictive abortion legislation, and in particular if this could be based on an analysis that such votes constitute licit material cooperation in evil, there is still a problem for their argument. For even if the votes of (publicly acknowledged) pro-life legislators for restrictive legislation could be judged to be licit material cooperation in evil and hence justified, the votes of other ("less extreme" but still abortion-favoring) legislators voting for the same legislation would still not be justified; these legislators would be doing evil. If the ("less extreme") abortion-favoring legislators are doing evil—as Finnis and Rhonheimer indicate—it would seem that they should refrain from voting for restrictive legislation, and that pro-life legislators and campaigners should not lobby them to vote for it because this would be an incitement to do evil. In reality, the success of restrictive legislation depends on collaboration between pro-life and ("less extreme") pro-abortion legislators, and experience shows that pressure to encourage the latter to support the legislation is normally required. If, as the analysis indicates, this constitutes pressure to do evil, applying such pressure would seem not to be legitimately undertaken and the prospects of the enactment of restrictive legislation would normally be greatly reduced, if not negligible. Whether or not legislators publicly known as being pro-life could licitly vote for restrictive legislation would seem to be an academic point of little practical relevance if the legislation has little chance of success without the support of "evil-doing" abortion-favoring legislators, whose assistance—so it would seem—should not be solicited.

It might be objected that according to the principles of "counseling the lesser evil" pro-lifers could urge "less extreme" pro-abortion legislators to vote for the unjust restrictive legislation. It is questionable whether the principles (on which, historically, theological opinion has varied)[16] apply at all to this question but even if they do, there remains

16. For an overview of treatments on the question of counseling the lesser evil from the sixteenth to mid-twentieth centuries, see E. T. Hannigan, S.J., "Is It Ever Lawful to Advise the Lesser Evil?" *Gregorianum* 30 (1949): 104–29.

the further question of what precisely pro-lifers could do to steer pro-abortion legislators toward the "lesser evil": would it be acceptable to urge them publicly, or to encourage them privately, or just to manipulate them indirectly into supporting "lesser-evil" restrictive legislation?[17] However, even if it is possible in some ways, according to the principles of "counseling the lesser evil," to "steer" pro-abortion legislators toward supporting restrictive legislation, this should not be confused with the question of whether pro-life legislators themselves can licitly vote for such legislation. As will be seen in Chapter 6, many commentators regard it as axiomatic that the "lesser-evil" considerations apply to the votes of pro-life and pro-abortion legislators alike. And, as Chapter 4 argued, the "cooperation" argument—whence this consideration of "counseling the lesser evil" has arisen—is to be rejected in itself, and not merely on account of some further difficulties arising from it.

17. "Counseling the lesser evil" tends to refer to private situations, not to evils like abortion that are a matter of public policy. If a regime killed many Jewish or black people, I doubt if many would suggest that those who opposed the killing should "counsel the lesser evil" and urge support for a new policy of killing a smaller number. (And even fewer would suggest it could be legitimate for those who believe all killing is wrong *to vote for* the "lesser evil" policy.) Some evils, like killing Jews, black people, and unborn children must be opposed unambiguously and without compromise. In my view it would be illicit for pro-lifers to urge or request *directly* support for (unjust) "lesser-evil" legislation, but they could "steer" pro-abortion legislators toward supporting it *indirectly*. It would be legitimate for pro-lifers to say to their elected representatives: "Our position is clear. We are opposed to all abortions and we believe that laws allowing or in any way admitting the principle of abortion are intrinsically unjust and unsupportable. It is not enough to restrict abortion: the right to life of all should be protected. We stick to our principles. But what about you? You claim to be concerned about the number of abortions—but what are you doing to reduce the number? You claim that abortion is about responsibility and choices—what, then, are you doing to ensure that parents can fulfill their responsibilities so that their girls who are minors do not have abortions without parental consent? Or what are you doing to ensure that women are given full information about abortion and its alternatives so they can make an informed choice? Or what are you doing to ensure that medical personnel are not discriminated against because of their choice not to be involved with abortion?" Pro-lifers need not object if pro-abortion legislators decide to support (unjust) "lesser-evil" legislation—whether or not they have indirectly "steered" them to do so. But they should not thank them for supporting it—rather, they should express their dissatisfaction until they enact fully protective laws.

Why, then, should John Paul II have included the qualification that legislators voting for "proposals aimed at limiting the harm done by [an abortion] law" (proposals that, according to my analysis, are just—like those to be presented in Chapter 7—and quite unlike the kind of intrinsically unjust proposal restricting abortion to *x* weeks) be known to be absolutely opposed to procured abortion? One answer is that legislative procedures are often complex and that without a public statement of their pro-life stance the reasons for pro-life legislators' votes for just proposals could be misunderstood. This point will become clearer when the complexities of legislation are discussed in Chapters 7 and 8. Moreover, given that the primary objective of human law is to protect life, with the foundations of human society being radically undermined when laws fail to do this, one might assume that the actual or prospective undermining of society by legislation that fails to protect each human life automatically requires from morally upright legislators a public declaration in favor of the right to life. The concept of "anti-abortion politics" is flawed because being against abortion (and other offenses against human life) is not a political option; on the contrary, it is foundational for the true exercise of politics.

"Corrupted" Systems and Oath Swearing

It may be objected that what makes this a "special case" is that morally upright pro-life legislators are not in a position to act in accordance with what they acknowledge to be true politics, true democracy, true law, true justice. The legislative system in which they are trying to do good has become corrupted, and they are doing their best in unusual and difficult circumstances.

I will consider this point first by means of an analogy. In the previous chapter I compared the act of voting to enact laws with truth telling,[18] further specifying that I was not referring to simple truth telling in private speech but to the kind of public truth telling made un-

---

18. Aquinas makes a similar comparison: "Just as an assertion is a dictate of reason asserting something, so is a law a dictate of reason commanding something." *ST* I-II, q. 92, a. 2, c. This is not to say that laws and assertions are identical but that there are certain similarities between making (just) laws and making (true) assertions.

der oath. Consider, then, a situation in which a witness is called to testify in a court of law during a murder trial. The witness has 100 percent moral certainty of the innocence of the accused, having been with him at a considerable distance from the murder scene at the time of the crime. However, he knows that the accused harbored much hatred against the murdered man, and that he had expressed not only a wish that he be killed but also an intent to kill him shortly before the murder. The witness knows that his true evidence would be both helpful and detrimental to the accused, but believes it is his duty to tell the truth and trust that a fair presentation of all the evidence during the trial will result in a just acquittal. Before giving evidence, however, the witness becomes aware of a conspiracy involving the police and the prosecution lawyers, who seem to have a good chance of gaining a conviction by providing false evidence. In other words, the situation is that of a corrupted court system.

Like other witnesses, the witness in this hypothetical case takes an oath to tell the truth before he gives his testimony. But what should he do? Should he tell the truth, knowing that in association with the corrupted evidence it will undermine the defendant's case and almost certainly lead to an unjust verdict of guilty? Or should he tell some untruths—e.g., deny that the accused hated and intended to kill the victim—in the hope that this might increase the chances of obtaining a just not-guilty verdict? In the "normal case," the witness, being a morally upright person, would want to tell the truth and nothing but the truth; but could this not be regarded as a "special case" in which the responsibility of the witness is to achieve justice for the defendant—the pursuit of justice being the reason why witnesses are required to testify under oath—rather than to provide a true testimony that will fail to achieve justice because of the corruption in the system? I think it would be commonly accepted that, unless he judged it better to refrain from giving any evidence, the obligation of the witness would be to do that which is required of a witness, i.e., to uphold his oath to tell the truth; he would not be responsible for the evil of a false conviction, the responsibility for this falling on those whose actions corrupted the system. Similarly, the duty of legislators lies in doing the duty that befalls them as legislators, i.e., to enact just laws.

It should not be forgotten that the performance of the legislative office, like other public offices, is also normally preceded by the swearing of an oath. Insofar as the principles of lawmaking—like those of truth telling—are informed by reason, the goodness or otherwise of legislators' actions is not determined by whether or not they have sworn an oath. Taking an oath, however, is a solemn act, and anyone taking one should know precisely what the oath entails and what constitutes its violation. Some—perhaps many—civil authorities may be illegitimate, and Catholic and other upright legislators may, as the *Catechism of the Catholic Church* teaches, be unable to take the required oath, even if this precludes their functioning as legislators or as holders of other offices.[19] The discussion about legislators voting for restrictive legislation is predicated, therefore, on the assumption that we are talking about legislatures where upright (Catholic, pro-life, etc.) men and women are not prevented from being legislators on account of a prior necessity to swear an oath that cannot licitly be sworn.

In the United States, federal and state legislators, as well as judges, state governors, and the president swear an oath of office that, among other things, obliges them to uphold the Constitution of the United States. The presidential oath, laid down in Article II, Section I, Clause 8 of the U.S. Constitution, reads:

> I do solemnly swear (or affirm) that I will faithfully execute the Office of President of the United States, and will to the best of my Ability, preserve, protect and defend the Constitution of the United States.

The current oath for Members of Congress is:

---

19. The *CCC* teaches: "The holiness of the divine name demands that we neither use it for trivial matters, nor take an oath which on the basis of the circumstances could be interpreted as approval of an authority unjustly requiring it. When an oath is required by illegitimate civil authorities, it may be refused. It must be refused when it is required for purposes contrary to the dignity of persons or to ecclesial communion" (n. 2155). This section includes a cross-reference to *CCC* 1903, which states: "Authority is exercised legitimately only when it seeks the common good of the group concerned and if it employs morally licit means to attain it. If rulers were to enact unjust laws or take measures contrary to the moral order, such arrangements would not be binding in conscience. In such a case 'authority breaks down completely and results in shameful abuse' (John XXIII, *Pacem in terris,* n. 51)."

I do solemnly swear (or affirm) that I will support and defend the Constitution of the United States against all enemies, foreign and domestic; that I will bear true faith and allegiance to the same; that I take this obligation freely, without any mental reservation or purpose of evasion; and that I will well and faithfully discharge the duties of the office on which I am about to enter: So help me God.

If they were obliged to regard the Constitution as interpreted by the Supreme Court in the 1973 *Roe v. Wade* ruling, then morally upright pro-life men and women would surely be unable to swear such a solemn oath and would be effectively excluded from such public offices. How could they swear an oath to "preserve, protect and defend" or "support and defend . . . without any mental reservation" a Constitution that, according to the 1973 judgments, grants women a right to abort the most vulnerable and defenseless members of human society?

To the extent that morally upright legislators are able to swear such a solemn oath, it can surely only be on the grounds that they regard the 1973 Supreme Court ruling to be contrary to the Constitution itself, and that in swearing their oath they are defending the "right to life" affirmed by the Constitution: "No person shall be . . . deprived of life, liberty, or property, without due process of law" (Amendment V), "nor shall any state deprive any person of life, liberty, or property, without due process of law; nor deny to any person within its jurisdiction the equal protection of the laws" (Amendment XIV). If the 1973 rulings are regarded as an aberration, then legislators could licitly swear to uphold the Constitution, which, properly understood, does affirm the "right to life" of the unborn.

If pro-lifers cannot licitly swear a solemn oath to uphold a corrupt, abortion-favoring constitution, but are justified in swearing the oath to uphold the U.S. Constitution only insofar as they regard it as affirming the "right to life" of all, including the unborn, this has serious implications for whether, as legislators, judges, governors or the president, they can give their consent to a restrictive abortion law that, by tolerating or permitting some abortions, fails to uphold the right to life of all.

The point I am making can be illustrated by Robert George's consideration of the converse position. He discusses the view of Cass Sunstein, who believes that the U.S. Constitution does—and should—permit abortion, but that the Supreme Court should not have overturned anti-abortion laws in 1973. Sunstein argues:

> The Court would have done far better to proceed slowly and incrementally, and on grounds that could have gathered wider social agreement and thus fractured society much less severely. The Court might have ruled that abortions could not be prohibited in cases of rape or incest, or that the law at issue in Roe was invalid even if some abortion restrictions might be acceptable. Such narrow grounds would have allowed democratic processes to proceed with a degree of independence—and perhaps to find their own creative solutions acceptable to many sides.[20]

In his response George comments on the unprincipled pragmatism expressed by Sunstein and draws attention to the relevance of justices having sworn an oath to uphold the Constitution:

> The pragmatism evident in this passage will likely strike many of Sunstein's readers as unprincipled. Critics will say that fidelity to constitutional principle surely requires justices who genuinely believe that most or all laws restricting abortion violate the Constitution to invalidate such laws. Moreover, the critics will observe, Justices have sworn an oath to uphold the Constitution; do they not violate that oath in declining, for extraconstitutional reasons, to strike down laws that they believe to be unconstitutional?[21]

George's argument against Sunstein should similarly apply to pro-life judges—as well as to legislators and those with executive power—who swear an oath to uphold the Constitution, believing it to be properly understood as defending the right to life of all. My point here is not simply to note that changes in the law that "proceed slowly and incrementally" to restrict abortion and protect the unborn would similarly be "pragmatic" and "unprincipled" but—crucially—that support for any legal change that requires the toleration or permission of any offense against life would constitute a violation of their solemn oath.

Morally upright legislators can licitly take an oath, provided that

---

20. Cass Sunstein, *Legal Reasoning and Political Conflict* (Oxford: Oxford University Press, 1996), 180–81, cited in Robert P. George, *In Defence of Natural Law* (Oxford: Clarendon Press, 1999), 327.

21. Ibid.

the oath does not require them to uphold a system that in its essence is contrary to the dignity of persons or to ecclesial communion.[22] In other words, *the system* must be lawful (i.e., not constituted in such a way that it violates natural or divine law), and the implication of the legislative oath—whether or not it is formally stated—is that legislators are undertaking to act in accordance with the lawful requirements of a lawful (i.e., properly constituted) system: legislators are undertaking to legislate according to law. In the same way that the oath of witnesses in a court of law refers to acting in accordance with truth, likewise the oath of legislators normally specifies—or it is implied—that they undertake to act in accordance with law. In this connection the teaching of John Paul II must be borne in mind:

> Now "a State ruled by law" implies first of all *recognition of and respect for human rights,* foremost among which is the right to life.... "It is a question of inherent universal and inviolable rights. No one, no individual, no authority, no State, can change—let alone eliminate—them because such rights find their source in God himself" (*Christifideles Laici,* n. 38). Therefore the Church points out that democracy demands respect for these rights, but this respect *represents at the same time the limits of democracy.*[23]

If, within a corrupted lawmaking system, morally upright men and women can licitly assume the office of legislator, it is incumbent upon them to fulfill the obligations of that office by voting to enact only just laws. This requires the recognition of the right to life in law of all unborn children. It is an especially solemn duty for legislators to honor their obligations if they have sworn a legislator's oath. Witnesses in a court of law must abide by what is good and true even if their actions do not have the desired good consequences, and the same applies to legislators.

The objection presented at the beginning of this section is, in fact, false. Legislators are always in a position to act in accordance with what they acknowledge to be true politics, true democracy, true law, true jus-

---

22. See note 19, above.

23. John Paul II, Address to Bishops of Portugal's Lisbon and Evora Provinces, 27 Nov. 1992, n. 3, reproduced in *L'Osservatore Romano* (English weekly edition, 16 Dec. 1992).

tice; they are never required or entitled to vote for injustice any more than a witness is required or entitled to give false evidence in a court of law. It is undeniable that, if they are in a minority, pro-life legislators may not always succeed in enacting what is good and true. Their votes for justice and refusal to support injustice will nevertheless be a necessary and important witness to the essential values upon which legislation should be based.

The Context of the Restrictive Law

Martin Rhonheimer suggested that in the "special case" of restrictive legislation, a pro-life legislator's action is not so much that of voting for the (unjust) restrictive law, but that of "prevent[ing] the enacting or existence of some other, less restrictive law." In saying this he fails to recognize that the prevention of the enacting or existence of another less restrictive law is achieved precisely *by means of* the enactment of the unjust law that is more restrictive. Voting *for* the (unjust) more restrictive law is precisely what legislators are doing, and it is not a "special case" consideration but the reality of all legislative enactments that this inevitably prevents the enactment or existence of some other law.

A similar argument is that, given the context of the "special case" we are considering, pro-life legislators should not be regarded as voting for the unjust restrictive law itself but rather as voting for the change in the law that they are effecting. One variation of the argument runs as follows: the change in the law provides protection for some unborn children; granting protection is just; therefore, the change in the law is just. Those who support this line of thinking might point to John Finnis's analysis that describes legislators voting to restrict abortion from 24 to 16 weeks as "making a just change in the law."[24]

Like Rhonheimer's argument, this is also misleading. Every enactment—whether it be an entirely new law or an amendment to a previous law or a repeal of law—necessarily brings about a "change in the law." The means to any such change, however, is the proposal that is enacted, and it is the justness of the proposal itself—*the means* to the

---

24. John Finnis, "Unjust Laws in a Democratic Society," 601.

change—that must be the first consideration. In fact, although he speaks in one place of "making a just change in the law" (as he believes it to be), elsewhere Finnis describes the same action (of supporting the "16-week" proposal) in terms of what it properly is: "a vote for a law which does permit abortion."[25] The vote for the law brings about a change in the (wider) law, and the object of the vote must be considered primarily in terms of the law that is actually being enacted.

The main argument of this book stands or falls on whether the restrictive legislation under consideration is in fact unjust. Unlike Rhonheimer, who acknowledges that the restrictive law in question is unjust, many of those who believe it is defensible to vote for restrictive legislation have tended to avoid acknowledging its unjustness; they have preferred to describe it as "imperfect." Others who are equally convinced that it can be supported have rightly criticized the term "imperfect" law as being not only inadequate but misleading.[26] In an article published in *L'Osservatore Romano,* Angel Rodríguez Luño defends votes for restrictive legislation,[27] and in an interview accompanying the article he rejects use of the term "imperfect law," confirming that restrictive laws—even if called "imperfect"—are properly identified as unjust: "I have never used the expression, which I consider unclear, of imperfect laws in my article. *Evangelium Vitae* does not use that expression either. . . . I clarify that the laws that some call imperfect are, as results from my response to the first question, simply unjust, more or less unjust, but unjust nevertheless. They are not morally acceptable under any condition."[28]

Luño goes on to say: "What one tries to judge is not a law, but the

---

25. Finnis, "Catholic Church and Public Policy Debates," 269.

26. See, for example, Livio Melina, "La Cooperacion en Acciones Moralmente Malas Contra la Vida Humana," in *Commentario Interdisciplinar a la "Evangelium Vitae,"* ed. Ramon Lucas Lucas (Madrid: Biblioteca de Autores Cristianos, 1996), 479n26: "esta formulación [una ley 'imperfecta'] que juzgo no sólo insuficiente, sino también desviante."

27. Angel Rodríguez Luño, "*Evangelium Vitae* 73: The Catholic Lawmaker and the Problem of a Seriously Unjust Law," *L'Osservatore Romano,* English edition 38 (18 Sept. 2002): 3–5.

28. Angel Rodríguez Luño, interview with Zenit, viewed at http://www.zenit.org/english/visualizza.phtml?sid=25920 (3 October 2002).

real meaning—the moral object—of the action of voting in some concrete circumstances."[29] By focusing on the moral object of the action of voting in some concrete circumstances, Luño's argument would appear to be the same as Rhonheimer's, the objection to which I have already noted: the object of the action of voting to enact *any* legislation is precisely that of enacting that legislation; all enactments inevitably result in a "change in the law" and prevent the enacting or existence of a different law. Luño and Rhonheimer are simply re-describing the legislator's action and have not explained why, in some circumstances, voting for restrictive legislation should be regarded as a "special case" such that a legislator's action of voting can be said to have a different moral object from that of voting to enact that which is (objectively) the subject matter of an enactment vote.

Other defenders of votes for restrictive legislation focus not, as Luño does, on the "real meaning of the action" of voting, but on what they regard as the "real meaning" of the restrictive law itself. John J. Rock, S.J., suggests that there is a distinction between the "literal meaning" of the restrictive law, and its "real meaning," claiming: "According to its literal meaning, the law allows certain abortions; according to its real meaning, it would reduce the number of abortions allowed up to that time."[30] Although the "real meaning" of a law requires an understanding of law that is not always apparent by the surface meaning of the words used in its formulation, it would seem that Rock is advancing a view that the "real meaning" of a law can be the opposite of what it actually specifies. The following illustration of a change in a law on speed limits indicates some relevant considerations.

Consider a country that, having set a maximum legal speed limit for motor vehicles of 40 miles per hour (mph), lowers that limit to 30 mph. The change could be brought about either by a repeal of the old law and the introduction of a new law establishing a limit of 30 mph, or by amending the original law in a variety of ways, for example, by substituting the figure "30" for the previous figure of "40." The new law

---

29. Ibid.
30. John J. Rock, S.J., "*Evangelium Vitae:* Some Highlights," *Linacre Quarterly* 64 (Feb. 1997): 13.

could specify: (a) "Motor vehicles are prohibited from traveling at speeds in excess of 30 mph," or (b) "Motor vehicles are permitted to travel at speeds not in excess of 30 mph," or (c) "The speed limit for motor vehicles is 30 mph," or it could be worded in a variety of other ways. The law would be the same not only in its practical effect but also in its essence, no matter which of these forms it took.

Prohibiting motor vehicles from traveling at speeds in excess of 30 mph—as law (a) specifies—may "literally" involve a prohibition, but the real meaning of the law is that it contains both a prohibition (from traveling more than 30 mph) and a permission (to travel up to 30 mph). Similarly, law (b) involves both a permission and a prohibition. And law (c), which refers to neither permission nor prohibition, similarly contains both, because this is the *real meaning* of the concept of a speed limit. The real meaning of voting for any of these laws is that all legislators would be both permitting and prohibiting, and it would be entirely false to say that the "real meaning" of any individual legislator's vote could involve just a prohibition (without a permission) or a permission (without a prohibition). It would similarly be false to say that legislators were voting solely for the change in the law (i.e., reducing the limit from 40 to 30 mph) but not voting for the 30 mph speed limit itself (i.e., voting for the permission to travel up to 30 mph and the prohibition on traveling more than 30 mph). If this is accepted—as it should be—with respect to laws reducing a speed limit, it should also be accepted with respect to laws reducing abortion time limits (or with respect to laws that similarly protect some unborn children but not others). Irrespective of their wording (though in some instances the wording might make explicit what is involved), the real meaning of laws that reduce abortion time limits is that legislators are supporting *both* a prohibition *and* a permission (or intention). Returning to Finnis's illustration, legislators voting for a law that lowers the limit from 24 to 16 weeks are voting neither for "the change in the law" nor "to prevent the existence of a less restrictive law" but for the law itself, which contains both a permission and a prohibition. And it is *this law*—for which they are voting—that is unjust.

A Different Kind of "Special Case"

The title of Charles Rice's book *No Exception: A Pro-Life Imperative*[31] suggests that his view is similar to the one being advanced in this book. He expresses the view that

> Only an uncompromising, no-exception approach, that refuses to support or vote for legal toleration of the intentional killing of innocent human beings, can offer the educational potential to restore reverence for the sanctity of life of every age and condition. When the murder of the innocent is at issue, the only "pro-life" position is to insist without compromise that the murder be forbidden in every case.[32]

Rice rightly rejects the unsound argument that a duty to save whatever lives we can justifies votes for incrementally restrictive abortion legislation,[33] and he expresses the view that the pro-life movement "created to defend a right as inalienable will lose credibility and effectiveness, at least over the long run, by conceding exceptions to that 'inalienable' right."

Having argued for "an uncompromising, no-exception approach" it is therefore surprising to see Rice accept a compromise. He explains:

> It would be unjust to reproach those who do their best to achieve total protection for the unborn and then reluctantly support or vote for legislation that provides exceptions to that protection. There is a difference, however, between the pro-life advocate who fights the good fight, is beaten down and then, under protest, takes what he can get and the one who himself takes the initiative in promoting, as an "incremental" strategy, laws that allow abortion. Sometimes, pro-lifers and legislators convince themselves that an authentically pro-life law cannot be enacted; consequently, they propose compromises that validate the anti-life position by implicitly defining the lives of some unborn children as negotiable. "If we can support exceptions at the bitter end," they ask, "why can't we propose them in the first place if we honestly believe they are inevitable?" One answer is

---

31. Charles Rice, *No Exception: A Pro-Life Imperative* (Notre Dame: Tyholland Press, 1990). See also Rice, *The Winning Side* (Mishawaka, Ind.: St. Brendan's Institute, 1999).
32. Rice, *No Exception,* 88.
33. Ibid., 86.

that, in practical terms, that tactic is not only a predictable loser but also a contributor to the dominance of the anti-life ethic. Every time a pro-lifer proposes a law that would tolerate the execution of some unborn children, his pro-life rhetoric is drowned out by the loud and clear message of his action, that he concedes that the law can validly tolerate the intentional killing of innocent human beings. The incremental approach should be rejected not as immoral but as counterproductive.[34]

Rice seems to be presenting a different kind of "special case" scenario according to which a pro-life legislator cannot *propose* legislation containing a compromise but can support the compromise legislation provided that the support is reluctantly given at the final stage of the passage of legislation that originally sought to protect all the unborn without compromise. I shall argue that there is a fundamental problem with Rice's proposal. Even aside from the fundamental problem, however, it seems that in accepting such a proposal Rice is contradicting his own argument. He makes the point that "every time a pro-lifer proposes a law that would tolerate the execution of some unborn children, his pro-life rhetoric is drowned out by the loud and clear message of his actions, that he concedes that the law can validly tolerate the intentional killing of innocent human beings." But substitute "proposes" for "votes to enact" and exactly the same applies: by the act of voting to enact such a law pro-life legislators would be similarly conceding that the law can validly tolerate the intentional killing of innocent human beings. Rice's acceptance of a last-stage vote for compromise legislation, accepted reluctantly, is also inconsistent with his statement that "We should introduce no-compromise bills, fight for them and vote against anything less. Surely we will lose at first, but we are losing now through our own acquiescence. When we lose we should come back and fight again and again without compromise."[35]

Although Rice's "no-exceptions" theory of legislative voting can be criticized for being internally inconsistent, the more fundamental problem with it is that it fails to address the moral question of what constitutes a good or a bad legislative vote. In Chapter 4 I drew atten-

34. Rice, *Winning Side*, 236–37. An almost identical view is expressed in *No Exception*, 84–85.
35. Rice, *No Exception*, 110.

tion to the need to focus on the object of a legislator's action, and I noted that the object or purpose of voting for a bill differs according to the stage of the legislation's passage. Accordingly, at the first stage, a legislator would normally be not voting to enact as law the bill that has been presented to the legislature, but merely deciding whether or not to accept it as a suitable basis for further deliberation, knowing that the bill may be subject to many amendments, additions, and deletions before further votes determining whether it will be enacted or rejected.

Rice inverts the order of importance of legislative votes, maintaining that pro-life legislators must support nothing other than a "no-exceptions" bill from the outset, while being able to support at the final stage a bill—an intrinsically unjust bill—with exceptions. On the contrary, in the previous chapter I showed that *at the first vote* pro-life legislators faced with a bill containing exceptions could vote for it if they believed there was a possibility of passing amendments during its passage so that the exceptions were removed and the bill were rendered just. If the bill remained unjust when presented for the final vote, pro-life legislators could not support it.

Supporting a "no-exceptions" bill at the first vote does not, of itself—i.e., when the purpose of the first vote is understood for what it objectively is—constitute a witness to the right to life of all the unborn. Thus "less extreme" pro-abortion legislators might support a first-stage vote for a bill prohibiting all abortions with a view to then supporting amendments allowing exceptions. Their vote for the bill when initially presented would not be a witness to the right to life of all the unborn—not because they do not *intend* it to be but because objectively this is not what the vote of any legislator would be. Legislators provide a witness to what they believe is legally acceptable when they vote at the final stage—i.e., at the stage that determines what is to be accepted as law.

Rice concludes the long passage, quoted above, with the statement that "the incremental approach should be rejected not as immoral but as counterproductive." It remains unclear why his argument that it is counterproductive *to propose* incremental legislation (i.e., intrinsically unjust abortion legislation containing exclusions) should not also apply *to supporting* incremental legislation, however reluctantly, at the crucial final stage. More important, however, is his omission of any analysis of the goodness or badness of legislative votes (bearing in mind the different purposes of votes at the different stages of a bill's passage), and, crucially, of the object of voting for a bill at its final stage when legislators are voting to enact a bill as law. Such an analysis reveals a distinctly *moral* and not solely *practical* problem with voting for (intrinsically unjust) incrementally restrictive legislation.

A Return to the "Object"

The moral goodness or badness of voting for unjust restrictive legislation depends principally on the "object" of the chosen act, and I have referred to the determination of the object in terms of establishing the purpose(s) or proximate end(s)of the act. It is at the level of the "object," not "intention," that this question must be principally considered, the meaning I am ascribing to these terms being that given in *Veritatis splendor,* not alternative meanings that others—however justified their use of the terms may be—might prefer. If the action of a pro-life legislator doing what appears to be voting to enact unjust restrictive legislation can in fact be judged to have a different object from that of *actually* voting to enact unjust restrictive legislation, then it can be said to have a different purpose, and it is only by establishing a different—and licit—purpose that (what appears to be) votes for unjust restrictive legislation could be justified. Thus, as shown in the illustration provided in Chapter 4, the act of *what appears to be* the taking of a "contraceptive pill" is not *an actual act* of taking a "contraceptive pill" if the pill is taken for a bona fide medical purpose by someone with a medical condition that could be treated by it. This point can be considered by means of a different illustration: the *Catechism of the Catholic Church* restates the traditional teaching that "masturbation is an intrinsically and gravely disordered action"[36] and lists it as one of the "sins gravely contrary to chastity."[37] A certain sort of physical activity is involved in masturbation, but is the willed physical activity necessarily what is condemned as masturbation? Martin Rhonheimer suggests that the physi-

36. *CCC* 2352.
37. *CCC* 2396.

cal activity, if performed to get semen for fertility analysis (an activity sometimes described as "medically indicated masturbation"),[38] is a different and morally permissible action with respect to its object; what *appears to be* masturbation is not, in his view, *actually* masturbation as traditionally condemned by the Church.[39] I am not convinced that Rhonheimer's view is correct, but the rightness or wrongness of his view is not relevant to my present remarks.[40] The point is that his argumentation in which medically indicated masturbation is distinguished by its "object" or purpose from condemned masturbation, even though it is the same "physical act," is on the right lines and pertinent to a consideration of the present question.

I have been trying to show that although a "physicalist" account of moral action (i.e., one that holds that the moral good or evil of an action can be determined merely by its physical features) is rightly rejected, nevertheless all concrete actions have structures that can be intelligibly accounted for.[41] The nature of some physical acts (e.g., homosexual

---

38. See Ronald Lawler, Joseph Boyle, and William E. May, *Catholic Sexual Ethics* (Huntington, Ind.: Our Sunday Visitor, 1996), 192.

39. Rhonheimer, "Intentional Actions and the Meaning of Object," 254. He bases his argument on the definition of masturbation in the *Catechism of the Catholic Church*: "By masturbation is to be understood the deliberate stimulation of the genital organs in order to derive sexual pleasure" (*CCC* 2352), and argues that masturbation in order to provide semen for analysis has a specifically different object from that of masturbation in order to derive sexual pleasure.

40. Aside from philosophical queries there is the factor that this point has already been addressed with some degree of authority. Although there do not appear to have been pronouncements on this subject during recent pontificates, Pius XII confirmed twice a directive from the Holy Office of 2 August 1929 that masturbation was not licit even to obtain sperm for medical examination (Pius XII: Address to Delegates at the Twenty-sixth Congress of Urology, 8 Oct. 1953; Address to the Second World Congress on Fertility and Sterility, 19 May 1956).

41. Cf. Kevin L. Flannery, S.J., "Practical Reason and Concrete Acts," in *Natural Law and Moral Inquiry,* ed. Robert P. George (Washington, D.C.: Georgetown University Press, 1998), 107–34. Flannery notes that the "the exterior [act] has its own intelligibility and even primacy. Even if it is true that an act of adultery is dependent on an interior act of the will for its very existence, the exterior act of the will is for something—that is, for something that might be signified in human moral discourse and as such excludes not being that thing" (119).

acts) is such that they can never be ordered to reason; anyone freely choosing to engage in such acts lacks an upright will and acts immorally. Whether or not the physical act of taking an estrogen (contraceptive) pill or the physical act associated with masturbation may in some instances be performed with a good will depends on whether those actions in those specific instances are for a purpose that can be judged to be in accordance with reason. The physical act of voting to enact intrinsically unjust restrictive abortion legislation also has an intelligibility such that it would appear never to be "in conformity with the order of reason" and thus must always be an immoral act.

If this account of voting is incorrect, what other "purpose" of voting for an intrinsically unjust restrictive measure can be identified, so that a pro-life legislator's act of voting to enact it can be established as being of a different order from that of a "less extreme" pro-abortion legislator who is performing the identical physical act of voting to enact it (whose act, as shown above, must be judged to be immoral)? I have been unable to identify a different purpose and I maintain that this is precisely because the act of a pro-life legislator voting for intrinsically unjust restrictive legislation is not of a different order from that of a pro-abortion legislator voting for the same legislation. The purpose of voting to enact the bill "Abortion is permissible up to 16 weeks" remains constant irrespective of whether all abortions were previously prohibited, or permitted, say, up to 10 weeks or 24 weeks or 32 weeks; the purpose of voting to enact the bill remains constant irrespective of whether a legislator is performing the act in accordance with a (misconceived) "anti-abortion politics" or in accordance with a "pro-abortion politics"; the purpose remains constant and it is precisely to establish *hic et nunc* a legal limit of 16 weeks. The fact that some legislators may vote for such a measure in accordance with an "anti-abortion politics" or a "pro-abortion politics" is a factor relevant on the level of "intention" (or "motive")[42] and not on the level of the "object" of the action.

---

42. Whether there is in fact a distinction in this instance between an "intention" and a "motive" may depend on one's chosen definitions of these concepts. See G. E. M. Anscombe, *Intention* (Oxford: Basil Blackwell, 1958), 18–21.

Form and Matter

Having rejected the "special case" objection, I shall conclude my argument that voting to enact any intrinsically unjust legislation is an intrinsically unjust/evil action by returning to the long passage quoted in the previous chapter from *Veritatis splendor*, n. 78 (*"The morality of the human act depends primarily and fundamentally on the 'object' rationally chosen"*). The teaching of St. Thomas Aquinas, explicitly confirmed as "still valid today" in the first sentence of *VS* 78, refers to "the interior act of the will and the exterior act."[43] Aquinas teaches that "the end is properly the object of the interior act of the will, while the object of the exterior action is that on which the action is brought to bear."[44] Aquinas develops his point:

> Now that which is on the part of the will is as form in relation to that which is on the part of the exterior act, because the will uses the members to act as its instruments; nor have exterior acts any measure of morality, save in so far as they are voluntary. Consequently, the species of a human act is considered formally with regard to the end, but materially with regard to the object of the exterior act. Hence the Philosopher says that *he who steals that he may commit adultery is, strictly speaking, more adulterer than thief.*[45]

The concluding remarks do not mean, of course, that the theft is bad solely on account of the adultery. In the next article Aquinas clarifies this, saying: "we say that he that commits theft for the sake of adultery is guilty of a twofold malice in one action."[46] And the converse point is made in *VS* 78, showing that a single malice in the action is sufficient for the action to be judged, in its totality, evil:

> And Saint Thomas observes that "it often happens that man acts with a good intention, but without spiritual gain, because he lacks a good will. Let us say that someone robs in order to feed the poor: in this case, even though the intention is good, the uprightness of the will is lacking. Consequently, no evil done with a good intention can be excused." (*VS* 78)

---

43. *ST* I-II, q. 18, a. 6.
45. Ibid.
44. Ibid.
46. *ST* I-II, q. 18, a. 7.

The action of a pro-life legislator who, on the basis of a misconceived notion of "anti-abortion politics," votes to enact an (intrinsically unjust) restrictive abortion law is like a thief who steals in order to give the proceeds to the poor.[47] A ("less extreme") pro-abortion legislator voting for the same legislation is like a thief who steals in order to commit adultery. The latter is rightly regarded as *cooperating formally in the evil of abortion,* and he may, perhaps, be judged more harshly on account of his support for abortion than on account of his bad lawmaking activities. The "formal" end of the pro-life legislator's action may have been to "save some lives," but the means chosen to do this cannot be dismissed as a "material" and irrelevant factor, any more than stealing can be dismissed as a "material" and irrelevant part of one's "formal" action of helping the poor. In voting for (intrinsically unjust) restrictive abortion legislation, pro-life and pro-abortion legislators are both responsible for choosing a bad legislative act(ion) though their intentions (or motives) differ. Each is freely choosing an action that involves a disorder of the will, that is, a moral evil; an action that is not in conformity with the order of reason; an action that is not capable of being ordered to God. By the standards of *VS* 78, *any legislator* voting to enact (intrinsically unjust) restrictive abortion legislation must be judged to be performing an action that, with respect to its object, is immoral.

47. One might ask how this is like the actions of a thief. To whom has justice been denied? The *CCC* teaches that "Justice is the moral virtue that consists in the constant and firm will to give their due to God and neighbour" (n. 1807). A vote for unjust restrictive abortion legislation fails to give what is due both to God and to those unborn children excluded from the legislation. Indeed, because restrictive legislation in most cases excludes the most vulnerable, the legislator can in a sense be said to be stealing from the poorest to help the less poor.

6. AVOIDING ETHICAL INCONSISTENCIES

A judgment as to the moral goodness of voting for restrictive legislation requires the sort of analysis given in Chapter 4. A faulty analysis, or a failure to undertake such an analysis, may lead to the adoption of some unsatisfactory arguments in favor of restrictive abortion legislation. In this chapter I shall address arguments referring to the lesser evil, "the principle of totality," and "the law of gradualness." I shall argue that the acceptance of any of these arguments as a justification for voting to enact (unjust) restrictive legislation is inconsistent with the Church's teaching on the proper application of the principles with respect to the different question of contraceptive intercourse.

The Lesser Evil

Chapter 2 explained the reasons for maintaining that a law denying the inviolable right to life of any innocent human being lacks the goodness proper to law, such that it is not good: it is bad, unjust, or evil. A law tolerating (or permitting or obligating) abortion until, say, the 24th week of pregnancy can be regarded as an "evil law." A law tolerating (or permitting or obligating) abortion until, say, the 16th week of pregnancy can also be regarded as an "evil law," although, when considered in relation to the former type of law, it tends to be viewed as a "lesser evil." My analysis, in Chapter 9, of the teaching of *Evangelium vitae* 73 will show that John Paul II does not permit legislators to vote for unjust restrictive legislation. Some of those who take a different view, however, maintain that the principle of the lesser evil is a justification for such votes and that the teaching of *EV* 73 (as they understand it) is based on this principle.[1]

---

1. With respect to the teaching of *EV* 73, Theo Mayer-Maly writes: "This state-

"Doing" and "Tolerating" the Lesser Evil

Within moral-theological teaching there is a legitimate consideration of the "lesser evil." It has, however, a specific application, and the identification of a lesser evil does not in itself provide a justification for performing a chosen action. Thus the identification of contraceptive sexual intercourse as a lesser evil in relation to another evil does not (as Paul VI teaches in *Humanae vitae*) provide a justification for its practice. The tradition, restated in *Humanae vitae,* notably makes the distinction between "*doing* a lesser evil" and "*tolerating* a lesser evil," rejecting the former and approving (in some cases) the latter.

Doing (a lesser) evil refers to the performance of a chosen act that should not be performed;[2] it is active. "Doing a lesser evil" is not morally distinguishable from "doing evil" and can never be sanctioned. St. Paul's teaching that one cannot do evil as a means to achieving good (cf. Rom. 3:8) has been constantly taught and is specifically reaffirmed by John Paul II in *Veritatis splendor.*[3] *Tolerating* (a lesser) evil refers to a decision not to confront directly the evil actions of others (sometimes at the price of personal suffering), or to the acceptance of the experience of suffering; it is passive.[4] The principle of toleration can perhaps be

---

ment follows the tradition of the moral-theological teaching of the *malum minus,* the lesser evil." See his "Il Diritto alla Vita e la Trasmissione della Vita," in Trujillo, Herranz, and Sgreccia, *"Evangelium Vitae" and Law,* 82. Robert P. George writes: "Can one legitimately judge, as a matter of prudence, that the imperfect, though more protective, proposal is a 'lesser evil'? Here [in *EV* 73] the Pope says yes." See his "Gospel of Life." Given that John Paul II makes no specific reference to the "lesser evil," George's remarks constitute not only a misinterpretation but also an incorrect statement of the teaching of *EV* 73.

2. John Finnis defines "doing evil" as "choosing an *act* that should not be chosen, making a *choice* that should not be made." See his *Fundamentals of Ethics* (Oxford: Clarendon Press, 1983), 112. Finnis's frequent focus on what is "chosen" (the choice) as opposed to what is "done" (the act) leads, I suggest, to a difficulty when determining whether some acts are intrinsically evil, a point that is relevant to the question at the heart of this book. A notable critique of his view is provided by Janet E. Smith, "Natural Law: Does It Evaluate Choices or Acts?" *American Journal of Jurisprudence* 36 (1991): 177–201.

3. Cf. *VS* 79, the heading for which is: "'Intrinsic evil': it is not licit to do evil that good may come of it (cf. Rom 3:8)."

4. The active-passive distinction that I am making should not be understood in too broad a sense, and some qualifications are called for. "Doing evil" can also apply to

better understood as the principle of *"non impedire,"*[5] whereby one neither wills nor promotes the evil nor directly opposes it, but rather accepts its existence, just as God allows the existence of evil that he neither wills nor promotes but that he does not impede. An example of tolerating the lesser evil is given by Leo XIII when he teaches that a workman, though he has a right to a just wage, may legitimately choose to work for a wage lower than justice rightly demands and accept the concomitant hardships, rather than refuse to be employed under such conditions and face "a worse evil" of even greater hardship and poverty for himself and his family.[6] In accepting such employment conditions the worker himself is not *doing* any evil, but is rather *experiencing evil* because his unjust employer is not providing his workers with a just wage. The worker can legitimately tolerate the (lesser) evil he experiences of not receiving a sufficient wage.

The distinction I am making between tolerating and doing (a lesser) evil, noting the licitness of the former attitude and the illicitness of the latter, is clearly stated in *Humanae vitae*. Teaching that one cannot validly argue that a lesser evil is to be preferred to a greater one in order to justify deliberately contraceptive sexual intercourse, Paul VI makes the distinction: "Though it is true that sometimes it is lawful to tolerate a lesser moral evil [malum morale *tolerare*] in order to avoid a greater or in order to promote a greater good, it is never lawful, even for the gravest reasons, to do evil [*facere* mala] that good may come of it."[7]

Assuming, then, that a law tolerating (or permitting, or obligating) abortion to 16 weeks is a "lesser evil" in relation to a law tolerating (or

---

some so-called "passive" actions. For example, someone who has a responsibility for a vulnerable person and who purposefully omits to provide necessary nourishment or treatment can be said to be "doing evil." Also, although I am describing the experience of suffering as "passive," I am not suggesting that suffering should be identified with an attitude of passivity. Given the Christian understanding of the salvific value of suffering, the opposite is the case: suffering experienced by an individual can be transformed into a life-giving activity in union with Christ's salvific suffering. See John Paul II, Apostolic Letter, *Salvifici doloris* (1984), n. 30.

5. See note 42 to Chapter 2, above.

6. Leo XIII, Encyclical letter, *Rerum novarum* (1891), n. 34, in Catholic Truth Society (1991) edition.

7. *HV* 14. This teaching was reaffirmed by John Paul II in *VS* 80.

permitting, or obligating) abortion to 24 weeks, can legislators vote for this law on the basis of the principle of the lesser evil? In other words, by voting for this law, are they doing or tolerating (a lesser) evil?

George Woodall considers some instances of "*tolerating* the lesser evil" and, with reference to the teaching of *EV* 73, says: "John Paul II's teaching on voting for a less harmful piece of legislation is another example." Noting that "if there is no strict obligation to act, toleration may be justified," Woodall explains how "tolerating the lesser evil" applies, in his view, to restrictive abortion legislation:

> When there is a positive act of commending, drafting or voting for legislation with the view that a lesser evil will be tolerated in order either that a greater evil already operative will be restricted or that a greater evil already determined upon and morally certain to occur will be prevented, given the known opposition of those involved to what is (to be) practised and their will only to save those who will be protected if the lesser evil is effected, toleration may be justified.[8]

The main problem with Woodall's remarks is that they fail to acknowledge that there is a strict obligation for laws to protect human life, and thus a corresponding strict obligation for lawmakers to reject legislation that, by tolerating, permitting, or obligating abortion, falls short of what is required to protect any life. It is not clear whether Woodall acknowledges that a vote for a law *permitting* or *obligating* fewer abortions than an alternative that will remain or become law if the restrictive law is rejected does not constitute toleration. However, even if he were focusing specifically on laws that *tolerate* abortion, the mere fact that legislators might tolerate abortion as a "lesser evil" through their support for a "lesser evil" law, is not sufficient for their action to be good. Woodall himself acknowledges that toleration of evil may be justified only if there is no strict obligation to resist such toleration. And as Chapter 2 argued, laws can neither tolerate nor permit nor obligate abortion. An unjustified toleration of evil—failing to do what should be done—is, in fact, *doing* evil by omission.

8. George Woodall, "The Use of the Condom to Prevent the Transmission of HIV," *Medicina e Morale* 3 (1998): 570.

Forced to Choose the Lesser Evil?

But surely, one might say, there are times when one's choices are so limited that evil is present in whichever choice is made, and in such instances is it not better to choose the lesser evil? Of course, if this point is legitimate, it might appear to apply in the case of a woman who feels "forced" to resort to the evil of contraception as a lesser evil, compared with the evil of the breakup of her marriage (and the possible absence for her children of their father) if she is unwilling to engage in contraceptive intercourse. Germain Grisez presents such a "forced choice" scenario with respect to legislative decisions on abortion:

> There are, of course, cases in which there is literally no choice but that between two evils. For example, if a legislative body has directed a committee to consider various proposals for relaxing existing abortion laws and to report one of them, a member of that committee may be forced to vote on which of the proposals should be considered. In such a situation, there is obviously no compromise in preferring the less unjust alternative.[9]

Leaving aside the abortion legislation scenario let us consider an appropriate illustration, provided by Bartholomew Kiely, S.J., of a "forced choice" in which one might legitimately make a decision based on lesser evil reasoning:

> In situations of forced choice between courses of action, each of which involves some evil, and when even with the best of efforts one can find no further possibility, one chooses the course of action involving the lesser evil. Thus, if an airplane must crash in either a densely-populated or a thinly-populated area, with no chance of crashing in an unpopulated area, then one should choose to crash in the thinly-populated area.[10]

Kiely's pilot does make a reasonable choice to direct the plane toward the thinly populated area, and this is a valid illustration of the application of the principle of "the lesser of two evils." It is not, however (and Kiely does not suggest that it is), an illustration of *doing* the lesser evil. A moral action is one that is *chosen,* and the pilot has not chosen to

---

9. Grisez, *Abortion: The Myths, the Realities,* 459.

10. Bartholomew Kiely, S.J., "The Impracticality of Proportionalism," *Gregorianum* 66, no. 4 (1985): 660.

crash the plane. The laws of mechanical malfunction and gravity have determined that the plane is going to crash, and the pilot is merely trying to limit the evil consequences of the plane's crashing. The pilot is not responsible for doing any evil and cannot therefore be said to be *doing* the lesser evil. Janet Smith provides a similar illustration, saying that if a car's brakes suddenly fail the driver may legitimately choose to steer the car to avoid five pedestrians on his right, even if in so doing, he is likely to hit a single pedestrian on his left:

> Clearly one should make the choice that results in the "lesser evil" of risking the life of the one pedestrian rather than risking the life of the five. *But obviously no moral evil has been done;* one is not choosing to kill the one pedestrian; one is choosing to avoid killing the five. Nor is one choosing the death of the one pedestrian as a means of saving the life of the five, for the death of the one is a consequence of one's choice to avoid killing the five, not a means to one's end.[11]

Smith recognizes rightly that the principle of the lesser evil "does not refer to *doing* evil so that good may come of it, but to *tolerating* evil in order to promote a greater good."[12]

Some proponents of the case for legislation to restrict abortion, such as Joseph Joblin, S.J., who speaks of the "inescapable choice which legislators must make between two evils,"[13] present the issue as though the situation were comparable to the examples given by Kiely and Smith. But are legislators really faced with an inescapable, or necessary, or forced choice similar to those experienced by pilots or car drivers about to crash? Joblin presents the issue as though legislators have to choose either (i) an (existing) abortion law permitting many abortions, or (ii) a proposed law permitting fewer abortions. (This is also the sort of example that Grisez presents.) Although one can see why the situation seems to approximate the decisions faced in Kiely's and Smith's illustrations, these are not, in fact, the two options with which legislators are faced. The presentation of a bill tolerating abortion up to 16 weeks,

---

11. Smith, *Humanae Vitae: A Generation Later,* 95. Emphasis added.
12. Ibid., 94.
13. Joseph Joblin, "I Cattolici Nella Società Pluralista: Attualità del Problema," in Joblin and Tremblay, *I Cattolici Nella Società Pluralista,* 7.

thereby replacing legislation tolerating abortion up to 24 weeks, does not require legislators to choose *either* a 16-week *or* a 24-week limit. It presents them with three possible choices: (a) to vote for the bill tolerating abortion up to 16 weeks, or (b) to vote against the bill tolerating abortion up to 16 weeks, or (c) to abstain from voting. If pro-life legislators judge (correctly in my view) that they cannot vote for the bill tolerating abortion up to 16 weeks, they can justly vote against it or abstain from voting. Although a consequence of their action may be that the previous legislation tolerating abortion up to 24 weeks remains in force, abstaining or voting against a 16-week-limit bill does not constitute a vote in favor of the existing 24-week-limit law.

The key difference between the situation of voting for the 16-week limit and the illustrations provided by Kiely and Smith is that the pilot and driver were unable to avoid crashing. The legislators, however, can choose from the options—two of which are legitimate and one of which is illegitimate—that confront them. By voting against the bill or by abstaining they are supporting neither the previous law (the "greater evil") nor the proposed law (the "lesser evil"). They are, in fact, *avoiding* evil. If they could do good and vote for a law that prohibited *all* abortions they would do so, but they are not culpable for being in a position of being unable to do good, a point to which John Paul II refers in *Veritatis splendor:* "It is always possible that man, as the result of coercion or other circumstances, can be hindered from doing certain good actions; but he can never be hindered from not doing certain actions, especially if he is prepared to die rather than do evil."[14]

The fundamental principle of the moral law is that good is to be done and pursued and evil is to be avoided.[15] The positive aspect of this precept—doing good actions—is *conditional* on the opportunities present at a given time; the negative aspect—avoiding evil actions—is *unconditional*. Legislators can and must always avoid doing evil; they cannot freely choose *to do* the (lesser) evil of voting to enact an unjust (albeit more restrictive) abortion law. By voting, in the illustration above, to enact a 16-week upper-limit bill, legislators are choosing to do the

---

14. *VS* 52.
15. *ST* I-II, q. 94, a. 2.

(lesser) evil of enacting an intrinsically unjust law. Legislators voting against the bill are not doing evil but are rather impeding the (lesser) evil of the enactment of an intrinsically unjust law. Legislators abstaining from voting in this instance are also not doing evil; but they are *not impeding* the (lesser) evil of the enactment of the intrinsically unjust law. It is precisely this abstention from voting (i.e., from acting)—the non-impeding of (a lesser) evil—that, in the context of legislative votes on abortion, constitutes *toleration of the lesser evil*.

Archbishop Bertone's Consideration of the Lesser Evil

The view of Archbishop Tarcisio Bertone, S.D.B., expressed while he was secretary of the Congregation for the Doctrine of the Faith, merits particular attention. He maintains not only that *EV* 73 permits legislators to vote for (unjust) restrictive abortion legislation,[16] but that "lesser evil" considerations are relevant to the question: "the participation of lay Christians in the drafting of 'imperfect laws' necessarily conjures up a kind of compromise with evil, as expressed in the traditional expression 'choice of the lesser evil.'"[17]

In the conclusion of his treatment on the responsibility of legislators when faced with "imperfect laws," Archbishop Bertone suggests three possible attitudes. The first is "prophetic resistance," Bertone saying that when some fundamental values are undermined by laws this attitude may be justified "if a lay Christian prefers to opt for the value placed in question by the law rather than opt for the lesser evil."[18] However, Bertone suggests that a second attitude of "collaboration" is also legitimate:

---

16. Tarcisio Bertone, S.D.B., "Catholics and Pluralist Society: 'Imperfect laws' and the Responsibility of Legislators," in Correa and Sgreccia, *Evangelium Vitae: Five Years of Confrontation,* 206–22. Archbishop Bertone's paper is a personal view and does not constitute an official interpretation of the teaching of *EV* 73 by the CDF. The personal character of the paper is indicated by the frequent use of the expression "it seems to me" when Bertone describes the sorts of measures he thinks legislators could support in the light of the teaching of *EV* 73. See, for example, 214, 215, and 217.

17. Ibid., 217–18.

18. Ibid., 218.

> A less radical attitude, or one of greater collaboration, is permitted by the Church if it is possible to promote a lesser evil than that proposed by the law. We may remark here that it is not the evil as such that is at issue here, *but the good, more specifically the good necessary to defuse or reduce the evil that the evil in question may produce.* In Christianity it is never permitted to do evil or use evil means to produce a good end; nonetheless, each value, by the very fact that it belongs to what is good or what is true, asks to be respected. This attitude, that aims at what is good, within a situation characterized by what is evil, may be difficult to understand for those not directly involved in the political experience and unfamiliar with its very complex ramifications. Just for this reason, this choice of what is good, in a situation characterized by what is evil, must be *publicly explained* by those who take such a decision on grounds of conscience.[19]

Third, Bertone considers the attitude of "tolerance."

> The third attitude is the tolerance of the evil expressed through an unjust law. Such tolerance can only be possible if resistance to the evil would involve a yet greater evil. Here too, the object taken into consideration by the act of tolerance, is not the evil as such, but the good necessary to impede a greater evil.[20]

Bertone acknowledges the point I have been making that one can never *do* evil: "In Christianity it is never permitted to do evil or use evil means to produce a good end." His remarks about the third attitude of tolerance also seem to indicate that he is viewing tolerance, in accordance with the way I have described it above, in terms of inaction or nonconfrontation with evil, i.e., as the principle of *"non-impedire."* Yet he suggests that it is possible to collaborate "to promote a lesser evil than that proposed by [a previous] law." So, what does he mean by *promoting* a lesser evil? Unlike the inaction or nonconfrontation that constitutes tolerance (or toleration), a specific action is involved in the very notion of promoting anything. Although Bertone states that one cannot "*do* evil" (a statement that in the context would also seem to encompass "*doing* a lesser evil"), this principle seems to be contradicted by his remarks about "promoting" a lesser evil, the "promoting" in question be-

---

19. Ibid., 219.
20. Ibid.

ing such aspects of the legislative process as the drafting of legislative measures, or voting to enact such measures.

Bertone's remarks call for careful analysis. With respect to "promot[ing] a lesser evil than that proposed by the law" he emphasizes that "it is not the evil as such that is at issue here, but the good, more specifically the good necessary to defuse or reduce the evil that the evil in question may produce." What does he mean by that? At the heart of the problem seems to be a possible confusion as to which "evil" we are considering. Is it the evil of *abortion?* Or the evil of *a law*—an intrinsically unjust law—that permits abortion? If one focuses on the evil of abortion, without a consideration of (or perhaps an incorrect judgment concerning) the goodness or badness of a law to restrict abortion, it is possible that one might think that a legislator was voting for a good law (i.e., doing good) which resulted in the "lesser evil" of fewer abortions. If this is what Bertone has in mind he may have escaped the charge of saying that legislators can willfully "do evil" or "use evil means to produce a good end." But he may still have incorrectly judged not to be evil what is in fact evil.

Let us consider legislation that overcomes the charge of being in itself unjust (i.e., evil) and that might result in the good of fewer abortions. I have in mind the kind of legislation (which will be discussed more fully in Chapter 7) stating such things as "Public money [e.g., money raised by taxes] cannot be used to fund abortions." Perhaps this sort of legislation would fall within the category of measures proposed by Bertone to "promote a lesser evil." Those who could afford to pay for an abortion would still be able to obtain one if abortions were not legally prohibited, but it is likely that the "lesser evil" of fewer abortions would be a consequence of a law which prevented women getting financial assistance.

We should be attentive to the subject matter of the legislation, which, contrary to what one might think, is not in fact *abortion,* the permissibility of which is not affected by this legislation. Rather, its subject matter is *public funding,* and an absolute prohibition of public funding for abortion is entirely just (albeit somewhat irregular given that law should properly prohibit all abortions so the question of public funding should not normally arise). The public-funding legislation suggested above, then, can be judged to be good and can be expected to have as a consequence the "lesser evil" of fewer abortions. But by voting for it, are pro-life legislators in fact "promoting a lesser evil"? Are they not, rather, promoting a "good" (ensuring that public money is not spent on facilitating intrinsically immoral actions) with a view to a further good end (that babies, whose deaths would be otherwise facilitated, will not be killed). Because the good end might be registered statistically in terms of fewer abortions, one might view the consequences as effecting a "lesser evil" in comparison with what might have been the case prior to its enactment. But is this really saying anything pertinent about "lesser evils"? All actions have consequences, and what might be regarded on one scale as achieving a "greater good" can, on another, be rated as achieving a "lesser evil." The relevant moral analysis is not, in fact, whether this sort of legislation results in the "lesser evil" of fewer abortions; what counts, rather, is whether the action giving rise to the consequences is good or evil. (One notes that although the legislation might achieve the good end—or "lesser evil"—of fewer abortions, it might alternatively have no impact at all on the abortion rate and be regarded merely as an inconvenience to women who would in any case manage to self-fund or get assistance from another source to obtain an abortion; in terms of its effect on abortion it might not produce a "lesser evil" at all.) All things considered, a legislator voting for this sort of *just* legislation could be judged to be performing a good act, the goodness of the act being in no way determined by the "lesser-evil" principle. If this were the sort of legislation that Archbishop Bertone had in mind, my disagreement with him would be merely that his explanation for a justified moral action is unsatisfactory. The problem with his argument, however, lies at a deeper level.

The illustration I have given of just legislation that might be viewed (albeit inappropriately) as achieving a "lesser evil" (in terms of the number of abortions performed) has as its subject matter the use of public funds. Abortion is not the subject matter, and this sort of public-funding legislation, which is legitimately restricted to a consideration of whether specified activities may or may not receive public funding, in no way permits or tolerates abortions; such public-funding legislation is separate from other legislation permitting or tolerating abortion. (This point, developed in Chapter 7, may not be immediately comprehended, but is crucial to an understanding of why this sort of legislation, which might *prevent* abortion, can be just, whereas other legislation, which *restricts* abortion, is unjust.) By contrast, the sort of legislation Archbishop Bertone is considering in terms of the "lesser evil" does have abortion for its subject matter. His "lesser-evil" arguments must be understood within the context of his view that "it would be morally licit to become promoters of a new law on abortion that is more restrictive than the one in force, *but that legalizes or depenalizes some cases of abortion.*"[21] In other words, he is considering the licitness of supporting, for example, legislation of the form "Abortion is tolerated [or permitted] up to 16 weeks" as a replacement for legislation stating "Abortion is tolerated [or permitted] up to 24 weeks." Let us consider his remarks in the light of this sort of scenario.

As I have already indicated, a particular question must be answered. If a legislator votes for the measure "Abortion is tolerated up to 16 weeks," which "lesser evil" is he "promoting"? Is it the "lesser evil" in terms of the evil of *abortion?* Or is it the "lesser evil" in terms of *the law* about abortion? I suggested above that Bertone's remarks, though inappropriate, were less objectionable if he had in mind the lesser evil with reference to the practice of abortion. He might then think that a legislator supporting this measure was seeking the good represented by fewer abortions (otherwise labeled a "lesser evil") rather than the evil itself. However, even if, contrary to my view, Bertone is correct to suggest this, one factor remains, as Bertone himself acknowledges: "it is never permitted to do evil or use evil means to produce a good end."[22] The good end would appear to be that of preventing some abortions (a good end that might also be regarded, it seems, as the "lesser evil"), and the means to that end involves, precisely, the law for which the legislator is voting. So the crucial question is whether the means to that end— the act of voting for a specific law—can be judged to be a good action.

Chapter 2 showed that laws can justly *tolerate* (without permitting) some moral evils; thus a law may tolerate some immoral behavior, such

---

21. Ibid., 215. Emphasis added.
22. Ibid., 219.

as sexual acts between unmarried consenting adults. Consider, then, the actions of a morally upright legislator in a society that has a (just) law tolerating immoral sexual behavior between unmarried adults aged 21 years or older. (The law is of the form "It is a criminal offense for anyone under the age of 21 to engage in nonmarital sexual intercourse.") Changes in that society's sexual mores have led to the introduction of a bill that would tolerate sexual behavior for those aged 14 years or older. An alternative option specifying 18 years is also proposed. Although the morally upright legislator would prefer the current legislation's 21-years-of-age specification, he is willing to support a bill to lower the age to 18 if this prevents the option of 14 years from being enacted. He may think that changing the law to 18 years is undesirable because it might result in more immoral sexual behavior among teenagers, but that a further reduction to 14 would probably lead to even more immoral behavior and that this option will be passed unless he and other like-minded legislators concede to the 18-years option. I maintain that the legislator can justly vote for the 18-years option and that he could do so arguing that this law would "tolerate a lesser evil" than the 14-years option. However, *the law itself would not be evil,* and accordingly the morally upright legislator voting for it would not be doing evil but would be voting for a legitimate law that would tolerate evil. If, however, the 18-years option *permitted* sexual behavior outside marriage (e.g., the law was of the form "Those over the age of 18 have a right to engage in consensual sexual intercourse irrespective of their marital status"), the law itself would contradict the natural/moral law and be unjust and "not a law." In this situation legislators would not be dealing with the (just) legal toleration of an evil but with the enactment of a legal evil. A legislator could not claim that the act of voting for a law *permitting* sexual acts outside of marriage for those over the age of 18, as a means of preventing the enactment of a law permitting such acts for those over 14, constituted "toleration of a lesser evil" because the action involves the choice to vote for what can be judged to be, in itself, a "legal evil."

Let us return, then, to Archbishop Bertone's acknowledgment that "it is never permitted to do evil or use evil means to produce a good end." Is he not overlooking the fact that by voting for legislation which, though "more restrictive ... legalizes or depenalizes some cases of abortion,"[23] he is, in fact, using evil means—a "legal evil"—to produce a good end? Richard McCormick, S.J., readily acknowledges that in "choosing the lesser evil" in such a context one is making a choice in favor of a "legal evil."[24] One would assume that in deliberations on the application of the "lesser evil" Bertone would tend not to see eye to eye with McCormick's argumentation, an observation that makes their apparent agreement on this point quite remarkable. If restrictive abortion legislation can be identified as "evil" (a point generally conceded by those who refer to the act of voting for the "lesser evil"), a legislator voting for it is clearly "using evil means" to produce the good end of fewer abortions. This in itself seems to counter Bertone's acceptance of voting for such legislation. The analysis in Chapter 4 of the moral act of voting for legislation revealed that the act of voting to enact any intrinsically unjust legislation (such as a law tolerating abortion) must be judged to be unethical, and that a legislator choosing to vote to enact any intrinsically unjust restrictive abortion legislation must be judged to be doing evil.

Archbishop Bertone's support for restrictive abortion legislation, with respect to "lesser-evil" arguments, contradicts the principles he acknowledges. Furthermore, he seems to be losing sight of the distinction between what is "aimed at" (the legal protection of, at least, some unborn children) and what is "chosen" (an unjust law to achieve that protection). In his section on "collaboration," quoted above, he refers to the attitude "which aims at what is good" and incorrectly identifies this with "a choice of what is good." Certainly, the legislator is *aiming at* the good of protecting some unborn children (a "good" that might be regarded as a "lesser evil" because it is only a partial good, protecting only *some* lives in a legislative context that calls for the legal protection of

---

23. Ibid., 215.

24. "In designing present legislation we are confronted at the present time with a choice of two legal evils. No choice is going to be very satisfactory, because the underlying conditions for truly good legislation are lacking. What is to be done when one is dealing with evils? Clearly the lesser evil should be chosen while attempts are made to alter the circumstances that allow only such a destructive choice." Richard McCormick, S.J., "Notes on Moral Theology," 357–58.

all). But what is *chosen* is the legislation that (irrespective of some good consequences) is not good but "unjust" and "evil." Bertone has thus made a fundamental error in his judgment of the goodness of the choice. Applied to the problem of conscience considered in *Humanae vitae,* Bertone's remarks could be cited to justify the "lesser evil" of contraception, a couple claiming that their action was "aiming at" the good of the unity of their marriage and family life (which might be threatened by noncontraceptive intercourse) and that their "choice" should be identified in terms of what is "aimed at" rather than the concrete actions that bring about what is "aimed at."

It is appropriate to note now a point that will be clearer when the complexities of legislation are considered in the following chapters. In a codified legislative system it may be possible to repeal one or more articles of an abortion law, while other articles remain unaffected. The act of repealing such articles would be like repealing one or more Abortion Acts in a UK-type legislature while other Acts allowing more restricted abortion remain unaffected. It would not correspond to the enactment of amendment bills restricting abortion (as the following chapter shows). It can be justified to vote for a proposal to repeal an article in a codified system, or to repeal an Act in a UK-type system, the consequence being that fewer categories of abortion are legally tolerated or permitted. This scenario, however, does not correspond with arguments about "choosing a lesser evil": (a) because *the proposal to repeal* the article or Act—Proposal X—is not in itself evil, so voting for it does not involve a choice for evil let alone a lesser evil; and (b) because although a consequence of voting for Proposal X may be that fewer abortions are performed (a "lesser evil"), *voting for X does not involve a choice for that "lesser evil."* One is not choosing the "lesser evil" of fewer abortions; rather, one is choosing to repeal the article or Act to stop the abortions that would be otherwise tolerated or permitted by the article or Act. Voting for X concerns X, not other articles or Acts independent of X.

The previous paragraph acknowledges that it is possible to cast some votes licitly for proposals that in themselves do not restrict abortion to certain categories (and so are not unjust), but that have *as a consequence* that some abortions, previously allowed, are prohibited. Not only are arguments based on the "lesser evil" irrelevant to the justification of such votes, but this is clearly not the sort of scenario Archbishop Bertone has in mind. Rather, he indicates the conditions according to which "it seems to me that it would be morally licit for Catholics to become promoters of a new law on abortion that is more restrictive than the one in force, but that *legalizes or depenalizes some cases of abortion.*"[25] In other words, his remarks are concerned with voting for a "legal evil," and, as my analysis has shown, a vote for a "legal evil" is always a morally bad or "evil" act. Once a chosen action—whether it be that of contraceptive sexual intercourse or that of voting for an intrinsically unjust law—is identified as "evil," a further specification of it as a "greater evil" or "lesser evil" adds nothing to the determination that it is an unworthy and immoral choice.

Supporting the Lesser Evil in Situations of Particular Gravity?

But is it not, perhaps, legitimate to choose to do the lesser evil in particularly grave situations, not least when the inestimable good of human life is at stake, and when the consequences of one's vote may make the difference between life and death for hundreds, thousands, or possibly even hundreds of thousands of unborn children every year? Consider, for example, the situation confronting pro-life Polish legislators in the early 1990s when they sought to prohibit the 200,000 or so abortions performed annually. Unable to prohibit all abortions, they had the opportunity of voting to enact legislation that would prohibit about 199,000 abortions; the legislation would affirm the "right to life" yet (somewhat incongruously) abortion would not be prohibited if pregnancy constituted a danger to the life of the mother, or presented a serious danger to the health of the mother, or if pregnancy resulted from a criminal act (i.e., rape), or if the unborn child would be born with a serious and permanent disability. In fact, the legislation—supported by many pro-life legislators and enacted in 1993 with the consent of President Lech Wałęsa—unjustly denied some unborn children the right to life, and is intrinsically unjust.[26] Some might think it per-

25. Bertone, "Catholics and Pluralist Society," 215. Emphasis added.
26. The Polish text of "The Family Planning, Protection of the Human Conceptus, and the Conditions for the Permissibility of Termination of Pregnancy Act," 7 Jan.

verse not to vote in favor of such legislation, given its far-reaching consequences in terms of saving lives, thus contributing profoundly to the lives of families, communities, and even the nation as a whole. Perhaps those who objected to the actions of these pro-life legislators would be accused, in a manner not dissimilar to the hearers of Caiaphas—whose words are sometimes cited as illustrative of favoring the lesser evil[27]—of not grasping the gravity of the situation, and of failing to see that it is better for a limited number of babies to be aborted than for the multitude of Poland's unborn children to be denied legal protection (cf. John 11:49).

It is worth returning to the passage, quoted above, in which Paul VI made the distinction between "doing" and "tolerating" a lesser evil, taking note of the remarks (not quoted above) that follow it. An awareness of the most far-reaching consequences of one's action (or inaction) does not justify *doing* evil, even if it is judged to be a "lesser evil":

> Though it is true that sometimes it is lawful to tolerate a lesser moral evil in order to avoid a greater or in order to promote a greater good, *it is never licit, even for the gravest reasons, to do evil that good may come of it* (cf., Rom. 3:8)—in other words, to intend positively [*in id voluntatem conferre*] something which intrinsically contradicts the moral order, and which must therefore be judged unworthy of man, *even though the intention [quamvis eo consilio fiat] is to protect or promote the welfare of an individual, of a family or of society in general.*[28]

This teaching, explicitly re-affirmed by John Paul II in *Veritatis splendor,* n. 80, took into account that the gravity of particular situations—such as that of Poland in 1992–93—still does not justify "doing a lesser evil."

The Principle of Totality

Humanae vitae considered whether "the so-called principle of totality" could be applied to justify deliberately contraceptive intercourse.

1993, is in *Dziennik Ustaw Rzeczypospolitej Polskiej* 17 (Warszawa, 1 March 1993): 429–31.

27. See Lysaght, "Lesser Evil," 7.

28. *HV* 14. Emphasis added.

"Could it be admitted" Paul VI asked, "that procreative finality applies to the totality of married life rather than to each single act?"[29] Although "the principle of totality" has not been invoked by name (at least not in print) to justify voting for restrictive abortion legislation, an argument based on this principle has been advanced. Could not a vote in favor of restrictive legislation be justified, it is suggested, if it is known that the overall orientation of the legislator is in favor of life, particular votes for (admittedly, unjust) restrictive legislation being justified as part of a strategy that in its totality seeks the right to life of all the unborn?

Applied properly in medical ethics, the principle of totality provides a justification for such actions as the excision of a bodily organ or member, something that would ordinarily be regarded as illicit mutilation, if this were required for the good of the whole body. Pius XII teaches that an individual organ or member of the human body "can be sacrificed if it puts the whole organism in danger, a danger which cannot in any other way be averted";[30] this subordination in cases of conflict of a particular organ to the body as a whole is founded on what he calls "the principle of totality."[31] The principle does not apply merely to the removal of diseased parts of the body but even to healthy parts that, if not removed, could harm other parts.[32] Pius XII cautions against erroneous applications of the principle even when it is used in the limited context of somatic matters,[33] and moreover the completeness of the principle when correctly applied is open to question.[34]

Let us consider, first, the way in which "the principle of totality"

29. *HV* 3.

30. Pius XII, Address to the Italian Medical-Biological Union of St. Luke, 12 Nov. 1944, in *The Human Body* (papal teachings selected and arranged by the monks of Solesmes) (Boston: St. Paul Editions, 1960), 55.

31. Pius XII, Address to the Delegates at the Twenty-sixth Congress of Urology, 278.

32. Ibid.

33. Ibid., 278–79. In particular he rejects an appeal to "the principle of totality" to justify sterilization procedures, even if the sterilization is performed because future pregnancies might jeopardize the woman's health.

34. Although the principle of totality may be cited as justification for removing an organ for the overall good of the body, the possibility of removing a healthy organ from one person in order to donate it to another poses the question whether the principle of

was invoked to justify contraceptive intercourse. The majority report of what came to be regarded as the "Papal Birth Control Commission" argued, prior to the publication of *Humanae vitae,* that the use of contraceptives within marriage should be approved: "The morality of sexual acts between married people takes its meaning first of all and specifically from the ordering of their actions in a fruitful married life, that is, one which is practiced with responsible, generous and prudent parenthood. It does not then depend on the direct fecundity of each and every particular act."[35] The report's argument that one must bear in mind the totality of the fruitfulness of a married couple's life was countered by Paul VI's teaching that it was not valid to argue "that such [contraceptive] intercourse would merge with the normal relations of past and future to form a single entity";[36] his principal concern was that the full "meaning" of *each act* of sexual intercourse, with respect to its unitive and procreative dimensions, be always respected,[37] a key point at which he diverged from the view of "meaning" presented by the majority report as quoted above. Failure to respect the unitive and procreative meaning or signification of each sexual act constitutes a falsification of the sexual act. John Paul II later described it as "a falsification of the inner truth of conjugal love,"[38] or, as it may be expressed simply, "a lie."[39]

Voting for restrictive abortion laws involves some different considerations, but "the principle of totality" would appear to apply to it in a similar way. The teaching of *EV* 73 clearly permits legislators to vote for some sorts of "proposals aimed at limiting the harm done by" an abortion law; furthermore, the encyclical gives permission to vote for

---

totality suffices as a philosophical tool. See George V. Lobo, S.J., *Guide to Christian Living* (Westminster, Md.: Christian Classics, 1991), 353.

35. The Majority Report of the Papal Commission for the Study of Problems of the Family, Population and Birth Rate, established by John XXIII and reappointed by Paul VI, quoted by Ralph McInerny, "*Humanae Vitae* and the Principle of Totality," in *Why Humanae Vitae Was Right: A Reader,* ed. Janet E. Smith (San Francisco: Ignatius Press, 1993), 329–341, at 334.

36. *HV* 14.

37. *HV* 12.

38. John Paul II, Apostolic Exhortation, *Familiaris consortio* (1981), n. 32.

39. See Smith, *Why Humanae Vitae Was Right,* 17.

such "proposals" only to those legislators "whose absolute personal opposition to procured abortion was well known."[40] The teaching appears to justify the view of some commentators that voting for a law to restrict abortion—even if it is an unjust law that permits abortions (albeit fewer abortions)—is licit provided that it is "one which is performed in the context of an anti-abortion politics," a point that was discussed in Chapter 5. In other words, it is argued that the goodness of the action can be determined by considering the action in its overall context and "the principle of totality" would appear to be invoked, in all but name, to justify the action.

Let us return to the teaching of *Humanae vitae*. Janet Smith identifies as its "most controversial line" the statement that "*each* conjugal act [must] remain ordained in itself to the procreating of human life" (*HV* 11).[41] She notes, "If the word 'each' did not appear in this phrase, the document would be rendered relatively innocuous. Many accept the connection between sexual intercourse and procreation but fail to see why each act of sexual intercourse must remain ordained to procreation."[42] If *each* act of sexual intercourse must be properly ordained, can the same be said for each act of voting for legislation? Does, for example, the view that "where the laws are just (and expedient) authorities serve their communities well; where they are unjust (or inexpedient), they serve their communities badly"[43] mean that *each* law must be just and expedient, and that, as I have argued, the properties of both (legal) justness and (social) expedience must be present with *each act* of voting for legislation? I have highlighted the fact that any law tolerating, permitting, or obligating abortion must be judged to be intrinsical-

---

40. The quotations in this sentence are from *EV* 73.

41. This is Smith's own translation of the Latin: "Verumtamen Ecclesia, dum homines commonet de observandis praeceptis legis naturalis, quam constanti sua doctrina interpretatur, id docet necessarium esse, ut quilibet matrimonii usus ad vitam humanam procreandam per se destinatus permaneat" (*HV* 11). The English translation on the Vatican's web site reads: "The Church, nevertheless, in urging men to the observance of the precepts of the natural law, which it interprets by its constant doctrine, teaches that each and every marital act must of necessity retain its intrinsic relationship to the procreation of human life."

42. Smith, *Why Humanae Vitae Was Right*, 327.

43. Robert P. George, "Natural Law and Positive Law," 327.

ly unjust (Chapters 2 and 3) and argued that it is always unethical to vote for an intrinsically unjust law (Chapter 4). The argument that a legislator's vote for (unjust) restrictive legislation must be judged in the overall "context of an anti-abortion politics" cannot be sustained (Chapter 5) and would appear to be as illegitimate as an attempt to justify a single act of contraceptive intercourse by appealing to the overall context of a fruitful marriage. The preceding chapters have highlighted justness as an essential property of law. If the goodness of the act of voting for any law depends principally on the justness of the law for which one is voting, it would seem that a single act of voting for unjust restrictive legislation would be a falsification of the true meaning of the act of voting for legislation; i.e., it would be, like the act of contraceptive intercourse, "a lie."

The Law of Gradualness

Living a Christian life is rightly regarded as a journey, a process of gradual development toward a perfection that is never fully achieved in this life. We sin and fail and need to be "continually converted" to God. As we grow in perfection we realize how far away we are, in fact, from perfection and that we never cease needing to be continually converted to God, living *"in statu conversionis."*[44] This gradual growth toward holiness can be regarded as a "law of gradual growth" or a "law of gradualness."[45] Because of the imperfection of our wills there can be an inconsistency between what we acknowledge to be the norm to be lived and how we act, not least perhaps in sexual matters. Bartholomew Kiely, S.J., identifies how "the law of gradualness" is acknowledged, for example, in the *Catechism*'s teaching on homosexuality: "Homosexual persons are called to chastity. By the virtues of self-mastery . . . by prayer and sacramental grace, they can and should gradually and resolutely approach Christian perfection."[46] In his eluci-

---

44. John Paul II, Encyclical Letter, *Dives in misericordia* (1980), n. 13. This Latin phrase is not translated in the Vatican's English version.

45. Bartholomew Kiely, S.J., "Formation in Chastity: the Need and the Requirements," in Gormally, *Issues for a Catholic Bioethic,* 146.

46. *CCC,* n. 2359; Kiely, "Formation in Chastity," 146–47.

dation of the teaching of *Humanae vitae* John Paul II acknowledged that "man . . . knows, loves and accomplishes moral good by stages of growth" and that married people are called upon to "progress unceasingly in their moral life," a step-by-step advance that he referred to as "the law of gradualness."[47] The "law" would appear to apply mainly in the pastoral context of encouragement to those who fail to live up to the standards of the moral law,[48] and so its extension to the question of voting for abortion legislation seems, at first glance, somewhat surprising.

It must be admitted that supporters of restrictive abortion legislation do not appeal, by name, to "the law of gradualness" to justify their arguments, and arguments related to the "law" are expressed in different ways. For example, Pedro Rodriguez suggests that voting for restrictive laws could be regarded as a cooperation in the redemptive work (which would occur gradually) of healing society. The factor of "cooperation in evil" present in supporting a law that is not in itself acceptable could be transformed, he suggests, into a "cooperation in healing" *(cooperatio ad sanationem)*.[49] M. Cathleen Kaveny argues that (what she claims to be) a Thomistic approach to human (civil) law justifies an incremental approach toward gaining legal protection for the unborn. She maintains that, according to St. Thomas Aquinas, "the central function of law is pedagogical: to lead persons to a state of virtue"[50] and that law should be formulated "that will *gradually* lead persons to virtue."[51] Kaveny seems to be suggesting that restrictive legislation, which in the course of time might gradually lead to even more

---

47. John Paul II, *Familiaris consortio*, n. 34.

48. Its particular applicability to a pastoral context is demonstrated by its being labeled "the pastoral 'law of gradualness'" in the document from the Pontifical Council for the Family, *Vademecum for Confessors Concerning Some Aspects of the Morality of Conjugal Life* (1997), n. 9.

49. Pedro Rodriguez, "Pastori e Laici: Distinzione dei Loro Ruoli nella Dottrina Sociale della Chiesa," in Joblin and Tremblay, *I Cattolici e la Società Pluralista*, 196–97.

50. M. Cathleen Kaveny, "The Limits of Ordinary Virtue: The Limits of the Criminal Law in Implementing *Evangelium Vitae*," in *Choosing Life: A Dialogue on Evangelium Vitae*, ed. Kevin Wm. Wildes, S.J., and Alan C. Mitchell (Washington, D.C.: Georgetown University Press, 1997), 142.

51. Kaveny, "Towards a Thomistic Perspective on Abortion," 391.

restrictive legislation, is an illustration of the way Aquinas envisages people being gradually led to virtue by law.

Aquinas appears to lend support to Kaveny's view in his statement that "the purpose of human law is to lead men to virtue, not suddenly, but gradually."[52] However, one citation taken out of context does not seem to be a sufficient basis for constructing a theory, and other writers advance the view that Aquinas teaches that the purpose of human law is not to promote individual virtue but to establish temporal peacefulness in society.[53] In support of their view they quote Aquinas: "For the purpose of human law is the temporal tranquility of society, a purpose which the law attains by coercively prohibiting external acts to the extent that they are evils which can disturb the peaceful condition of society. It is instead the concern of divine law to lead men to eternal happiness."[54] Whether the primary focus of human law is to promote individual virtue or temporal peacefulness is not my concern here.[55] But even if Kaveny were right to focus on the law's capacity to inculcate virtue, would she be right to think that voting for restrictive abortion legislation accords with Aquinas's view of promoting virtue (gradually) through law? We come back to the question considered in depth in

52. *ST* I-II, q. 96, a. 2, ad 2.

53. See, for example, John Finnis, "Public Good: The Specifically Political Common Good in Aquinas," in George, *Natural Law and Moral Inquiry,* 174–209; Rhonheimer, "Fundamental Rights, Moral Law," 135–83.

54. *ST* I-II, q. 98, a. 1.

55. It seems to me that Kaveny's view is clearly opposed by the teaching of *Evangelium vitae:* "The real purpose of civil law is to guarantee an ordered social coexistence in true justice, so that all may 'lead a quiet and reasonable life, godly and respectful in every way' (1 Tim 2:2). Precisely for this reason, civil law must ensure that all members of society enjoy respect for certain fundamental rights which innately belong to the person, rights which *every positive law* must recognize and guarantee. First and fundamental among these is the inviolable right to life of *every* innocent human being" (*EV* 71, emphasis added). In a response to Kaveny's paper, Kevin P. Quinn, S.J., questions whether she is "deconstructing *Evangelium Vitae* in search of an alternative moral theory, one that would play better in pluralistic America," and he asks whether Kaveny's paper should be viewed as a synopsis of the encyclical she thinks John Paul II should have written. See Quinn, "Whose Virtue? Which Morality? The Limits of Law as a Teacher of Virtue—A Comment on Cathleen Kaveny," in Wildes and Mitchell, *Choosing Life: A Dialogue on Evangelium Vitae,* 154.

Chapter 3 about the essence of law, and recall Cardinal Ratzinger's expression of concern that "the very concept of law is losing its precise definition,"[56] that the problem at the heart of lawmaking is one of *"recta ratio"* and that "this right reason must try to discern what is just—the essence of law."[57] The essential property of law is justness.

As Kaveny acknowledges, in the quote from Aquinas with which she begins her paper considering the connection between the limits of ordinary virtue and the limits of the criminal law: "Law should be virtuous, just, possible to nature."[58] If law should be just, then one encounters an obstacle in attempting to promote virtue *gradually* by means of a "law" that is unjust. One can attempt, with respect to law, to inculcate the virtues gradually, by refraining from the enactment of laws requiring the exercise of the virtues. Hence human law need not *require* the practice of religion, or acts of faith, hope and charity, or total patience, continence, kindness, etc. However, a law that contradicts the moral law by authorizing, permitting, or tolerating specific acts that seriously undermine the well-being of others—e.g., murder, theft and such things[59]—must be judged to be unjust. The moral law prohibits all abortions; restrictive abortion legislation that specifically permits some abortions, or tolerates them by failing to grant legal protection to some categories of unborn children, must be judged to be unjust. Kaveny's suggestion that Aquinas's teaching on promoting virtue could be applied to restrictive abortion legislation is implausible because it would require the enactment of legislation that, being unjust, violates what Aquinas (and, apparently, Kaveny herself) acknowledges to be an essential property of law.

Returning to John Paul II's consideration of "the law of gradualness" with respect to the question of contraception, we find a noteworthy distinction: "Married people . . . cannot however look on the law as

---

56. Joseph Cardinal Ratzinger, "Contemporary Crisis of Law."

57. Ibid.

58. *ST* I-II, q. 95, a. 3, ob. 1. Aquinas considers and rejects the objections to Isidore of Seville's description of positive law: "Law should be virtuous, just, possible to nature," etc. Aquinas distinguishes between that which is "virtuous" (i.e., "it fosters religion") and that which is "just" (i.e., in accord with "the order of reason").

59. Cf. *ST* I-II, q. 96, a. 2.

merely an ideal to be achieved in the future. . . . And so what is known as the "law of gradualness" or step-by-step advance cannot be identified with "gradualness of the law" as if there were different degrees or forms of precept in God's law for different individuals and situations."[60] Recalling the pastoral application of "the law of gradualness," the distinction John Paul II is making would seem to be as follows. Someone who is finding difficulty in observing the moral law should not be encouraged to aim for a standard that falls short of the moral law, and then progressively to aim for higher and higher standards until he or she attains the standard of the moral law. For example, a priest hearing the confession of a penitent who has committed the same sinful act five times each month for the past two years should not suggest that the penitent aim at committing that sinful act just four times in the coming month, three times the following month, and so on until (perhaps) he or she avoids this act completely. If a priest gave such advice he would be undermining the requirements of the moral law and suggesting that there was a "gradualness of the law," or as John Paul II describes it, "different degrees or forms of precept in God's law for different individuals and situations." Rather, a priest should commend the efforts a penitent has made to turn away from sin, even though there may still be instances of failure, and encourage him or her constantly to a full observance of the moral law.

If the distinction between "the law of gradualness" and "the gradualness of the law" applies to acts (such as contraceptive or homosexual acts as already mentioned) with respect to which, because of the weakness of the flesh, the moral law may be particularly hard to observe, the relevance of the distinction when considering abortion legislation is even more apparent. If the moral law says that "all direct abortion is prohibited," and if a human law permitting or tolerating any abortion constitutes an unjust law that violates the moral law, then the act of voting for a law that prohibits some but not other abortions is an act that violates the moral law. The act of voting for such legislation cannot be justified with reference to "the law of gradualness" because (as is evident) the law itself no longer conforms to the moral norm and has be-

60. John Paul II, *Familiaris consortio*, n. 34.

come "gradualized." Voting for restrictive abortion legislation manifestly requires embracing the unacceptable notion of "the gradualness of the law."

This chapter has attempted to demonstrate that the application of arguments based on the lesser evil, the principle of totality, and the law of gradualness to the question of contraceptive sexual intercourse is similar to their application to the question of voting for restrictive abortion legislation. It is inconsistent to reject the arguments with respect to the former question, but to accept them with respect to the latter.

In the Introduction I noted the inadequate simplicity of the argument comparing support for restrictive legislation with the act of trying to save lives in a fire or similar emergency situation. Other arguments, notably the "lesser-evil" argument, can be challenged not only for being inconsistent. For the purpose of discussing the argument in this chapter I did not question the common assumption that a law permitting a small number of abortions is a "lesser evil" in relation to a law permitting a larger number. But can it really be regarded as a "lesser evil"? If a single human being can be said to have an infinite or incommensurable or incomparable or inestimable or priceless or sacred value,[61] then the evil of the direct act of killing even a single human being must surely be an unquantifiable evil such that it cannot be rated as a "lesser evil" in relation to the killing of a greater number. Similarly, a law permitting a few abortions—or even one abortion—cannot be rated as a "lesser evil" in relation to a law permitting more abortions. Francesco Compagnoni, O.P., would appear to interpret *EV* 73 as teaching that a legislator can vote for the sort of restrictive legislation suggested by Arch-

---

61. These different expressions of value are frequently found in the teachings of the magisterium. In *Evangelium vitae* the expressions used include that of "incomparable [*incomparabilis*] value" (*EV* 2); "sacred [*sacrum*] value" (*EV* 2); "priceless [*inaestimabile*] value" (*EV* 25); "incomparable [*immense,* also meaning incommensurate or infinite] worth" (*EV* 96). John Paul II has spoken of "the inestimable [or infinite/incommensurate] value of the person" *(immensae "valoris" personae)* in his Apostolic Exhortation, *Pastores Dabo Vobis,* n. 9. Our understanding of the value of human beings is informed by our faith: "With the eyes of faith we can see with particular clarity the infinite value [*nieskończona wartość*] of every human being" (John Paul II, Homily at Kalisz, Poland, 4 June 1997).

bishop Bertone and many others. He has, however, a noteworthy perspective because he says that one cannot invoke "lesser-evil" reasoning when one is referring to human persons, each of whom has, in Christian (and, as he notes, in Kantian) thinking, an "incomparable value." He thus views a legislator's act of voting for restrictive legislation in terms of favoring the "lesser good."[62] My purpose here is not to defend Compagnoni's "lesser-good" reasoning, which, insofar as it may overlook a judgment concerning the justness or unjustness or the legislation being considered, is open to objections similar to those I have made against Archbishop Bertone's view. Rather, I am drawing attention not only to the inadequacy of the "lesser-evil" argument but to the possibility that the identification of restrictive abortion laws as a "lesser evil" is fundamentally flawed.

62. Francesco Compagnoni, O.P., "La Responsabilità dei Politici nella *Evangelium Vitae*," in *Scienza Medicina Etica 13: Evangelium Vitae e Bioetica: Un Approccio Interdisciplinare* (Milan: Vita e Pensiero, Pubblicazione dell'Università Cattolica, 1996), 109.

PART IV

LEGISLATIVE MATTERS

7. IDENTIFYING JUST AND UNJUST PROPOSALS

I have argued that laws tolerating, permitting, or obligating abortion are intrinsically unjust, and that it is an intrinsically unjust (evil) act to vote to enact an intrinsically unjust law: a good intention of saving the lives of some unborn children does not affect the intrinsic unjustness of the legislative act of voting to enact an intrinsically unjust Act. In a situation where all abortions are legally prohibited it is normally not difficult to identify proposed legislation as either obligating or permitting or tolerating abortion and hence as being intrinsically unjust and unworthy of support. Where, however, there is already an abortion law, it may sometimes be unclear whether legislative proposals regarded as improving the situation are in fact just or (intrinsically) unjust.

Part of the problem when discussing the question of changing abortion legislation is that simplified illustrations of laws are frequently used. For example, in previous chapters I have discussed attempts to lower the abortion time limit from 24 to 16 weeks, using proposals suggested by John Finnis that are of the form: "Abortion is lawful up to 16 weeks" and "Abortion is permissible up to 16 weeks."[1] Although such illustrations serve a purpose (and, like Finnis, I have used them myself to discuss some general points), they do not always represent adequately the complexities of the legislation being considered. Instead of saying that abortion "is lawful up to" or "permitted up to" 16 weeks, would it make a difference if the legislation said abortion is "not lawful after" or "prohibited after" 16 weeks? Could this be, as some have contended, consistent with the moral law that does indeed prohibit abortion after

1. John Finnis, "Unjust Laws in a Democratic Society," 600–601; "Catholic Church and Public Policy Debates," 268–69.

16 weeks? Some writers who are generally sympathetic to the argument of this book have suggested that the wording is crucial to whether a proposal can be accepted, and that the justness of a law to reduce the abortion limit to 16 weeks would depend on its wording.² Though I ac-

> 2. See, for example, Bernard Sadler, *Legislating for Life: A Commentary on* Evangelium Vitae *73* (Sydney: Newman Graduate Education, 2003), 5; Damian P. Fedoryka, "Thoughts towards a Clarification of Evangelium vitae #73," in Joseph W. Koterski, S.J., ed., *Life and Learning* 12 (Proceedings of the Twelfth University Faculty for Life Conference at Ave Maria Law School 2002) (Washington, D.C.: University Faculty for Life, 2003), 311–32; Michael Baker, "*Evangelium Vitae* 73 and the Supreme Principle of Morals" (2003), viewed at http://www.superflumina.org/ev73suprempr_final.html (12 Dec. 2003). These writers are to be generally commended for rejecting as unethical votes for intrinsically unjust restrictive legislation, but I disagree with their view that it is legitimate to vote for proposals that appear solely to prohibit some abortions. Their view is most clearly expressed by Michael Baker:
>
>> Assume that existing legislation allows a woman to abort her unborn child up to twenty weeks of pregnancy. The state of the society is such that it is not possible to obtain a majority of votes in the parliament for any proposal to outlaw abortion completely. A bill is proposed to amend the law so as to reduce the period to sixteen weeks. It is likely to gain a majority of votes. Our lawmaker's absolute personal opposition to procured abortion is well known. Can he vote for it?
>> The answer depends on the words in which the amending bill is expressed.
>> If the amending bill was to say—*No woman who undergoes an abortion is guilty of an offence unless her pregnancy is proved to have exceeded sixteen weeks and no doctor who performs an abortion is guilty of an offence unless the pregnancy of the woman on whom he performs the abortion is proved to have exceeded sixteen weeks*—he could *not* licitly vote for it. Why not? Because the words in this formulation state explicitly that some abortion is lawful. What abortion? Abortion which takes place prior to sixteen weeks of pregnancy.
>> However, if the amending bill was to say—*Notwithstanding the other provisions of this Act, a woman whose pregnancy is proved to have exceeded sixteen weeks and who undergoes an abortion is guilty of an offence and a doctor who performs an abortion on a woman whose pregnancy is proved to have exceeded 16 weeks is guilty of an offence*—the lawmaker could licitly vote in favour of it. Why? Because there are no words in this formulation which state that any abortion is lawful. It asserts that *some* abortion will be prosecuted, namely, abortion occurring after sixteen weeks of pregnancy. It is an improvement on the status quo which allows abortion to twenty weeks of pregnancy. If it is silent on the evils of other abortion that cannot be laid at the feet of our lawmaker.
>
> In my view, Baker (like Sadler and Fedoryka) overlooks what precisely is involved in the legal "toleration" of offenses against life and the intrinsic unjustness of such propos-

cept that one cannot overlook its precise wording, I have already explained—in Chapter 5, when considering the "real meaning" of various formulations that could be enacted to lower a speed limit—that the meaning of a legislative proposal sometimes requires an understanding of law that goes beyond a "literal" reading. This can be especially important when considering proposals that (unjustly) "tolerate," even if they do not specifically "permit," offenses against human life.

In this chapter I shall begin to consider in more depth (though still at a simplified level) some of the features of abortion legislation. In so doing I shall draw attention to the need to understand the sorts of concrete measures that are represented by simplified illustrations of laws. Arguments about legislation based solely on simplified illustrations of legislation may be unreliable; rather, if illustrations are to be employed they must be understood with respect to the sort of concrete legislation to which they correspond.

Concrete legislation is frequently complex, but some basic considerations about law should be kept in mind. The "law" on any matter is a constituent part of "Law" (i.e., the totality of law) and in itself may consist of several constituent parts, each of which must be considered as a legal entity. Thus, "the law" on abortion is one part of "the Law," and "the abortion law" may consist of one or more laws (established perhaps by a constitution and/or statute(s) and/or judicial judgment(s), or a combination thereof) and within each such constituent part (i.e., each law) there may be various prohibitions, tolerations, permissions, or obligations (i.e., different laws). The constituent parts of law must be respected and treated as distinct legal entities. The examination of abortion laws presented in this chapter will show the need to be attentive to the different aspects of law within the totality of a country's abortion law.

As we shall see, abortion laws typically contain two distinct types of law. In highlighting the distinct types, one sees that there are some legislative proposals, relevant to abortion, that can be judged not to be intrinsically unjust. In the next chapter there will be a more detailed con-

---

als. I contend that there is no reasonable basis for introducing a cut-off point of 16 weeks in legislation dealing with abortion, and that the introduction of such a point in each of Baker's proposals is arbitrary and unjust.

sideration of some of the complex arrangements of voting for legislative proposals, especially votes that arise during the passage of a bill. My premise being that any proposal obligating, permitting, or tolerating abortion is intrinsically unjust and unworthy of support, I am now concerned primarily with identifying what sorts of concrete legislative proposals are in fact intrinsically unjust. A judgment that a proposal is not intrinsically unjust does not mean that in any concrete instance it is in fact just and should be supported. A consideration of the circumstances (including consequences and side effects) must be made in order to judge whether a proposal that is not intrinsically unjust is in a concrete instance just or unjust.

Primary and Secondary Aspects of Abortion Laws

Before considering an illustration of an abortion law, some observations should be made about abortion laws generally, notably that two distinct types of law can be distinguished. The first type refers to the victims whose direct killing is either obligated or permitted or tolerated; the law might say that abortion is required or can be chosen if the child has been conceived after rape, has a disabling condition, is simply unwanted, is a possible threat to the mother's health or life, is a certain number of weeks old, etc. Notwithstanding the different meaning associated with the term in a general legislative context, I refer to this as *the primary abortion legislation,* and insofar as it would obligate or permit or tolerate the destruction of even one human being whose right to life should always be safeguarded by law, it must be regarded as intrinsically unjust and never acceptable.

If the direct abortion of any unborn child is obligated or permitted or tolerated, one must consider how that "primary legislation" is to be practically implemented. Can abortions be performed anywhere or only in specified places? Can anyone perform them? Are any particular procedures to be approved or prohibited? How will they be funded? What degree of information, if any, must women receive before having an abortion? Can hospitals, doctors, nurses, or others whose assistance might be required decline to be involved in abortions? These and various other practical questions dealing with the implementation of the primary legislation can be regarded as *the secondary legislation.*

The Subject Matter of Legislation

Although some legislation that affects whether a greater or lesser number of abortions will be performed is rightly regarded as "abortion legislation," this label is sometimes used inappropriately. There is a need to distinguish whether abortion itself is the subject matter of legislation (and thus label it "abortion legislation") or whether its subject matter is in fact something different. For example, legislation that makes adoption harder (or easier) might increase (or decrease) the number of abortions, but it cannot be regarded in itself as "abortion legislation" or "anti-abortion legislation." The subject matter of the legislation is "adoption," though the legislation might have an impact on abortion rates. Whether "secondary legislation" can be judged to be just or unjust, and hence worthy or unworthy of support, depends principally on whether its subject matter refers to "abortion" or to something else.

Among the "secondary legislation" matters mentioned above was the question of who would perform abortions. Granted that secondary abortion legislation is a consequence of the obligation, permission, or toleration of abortions for some or all pregnant women (i.e., it is a consequence of primary abortion legislation), what sort of legislation might govern who performs abortions? Legislation stating "Abortions can be performed only by qualified medical practitioners" is predicated on the lawfulness of abortion,[3] it being impossible to enact this sort of law in a situation where legal protection is granted to all the unborn. Being predicated on an intrinsically unjust law that either obligates, permits, or tolerates abortion, it must be judged in itself to be unjust, i.e., it is intrinsically unjust. Even if pro-life legislators felt inclined to support the legislation as a means of preventing more abortions or of preventing greater injury to women as a result of undergoing abortions

---

3. To avoid the need for clumsy qualifications, I shall use the term "lawful" to refer to any law obligating or permitting or tolerating abortion. I acknowledge that an objection could be made that a law *tolerating* abortion does not make abortion "lawful." However, because the distinction between laws permitting and laws tolerating abortion (see Chapter 2) is not normally acknowledged, abortion is commonly regarded as "lawful" in countries where the law may properly be said to tolerate abortion, and here I am similarly using the term simply to mean "not legally prohibited."

at the hands of unqualified personnel, the legislation itself could not be licitly supported because it would be intrinsically unjust.

Legislation stating "Doctors have a right not to participate in abortion procedures" has as its subject matter the "rights of doctors" and not abortion, even though abortion is mentioned. Given that doctors do have a right in the natural moral order not to participate in abortion procedures, this legislation is entirely just, irrespective of whether other legislation does or does not obligate, permit, or tolerate any abortions, and whether under any other legislation there is a prohibition or permission or toleration of doctors' performing abortions. The subject matter is not "abortion" insofar as the legislation does not in itself or by implication support any abortion. If, however, the legislation stated "Doctors have a right to decide *whether or not to be involved* in abortion procedures," the legislation would be clearly predicated on the lawfulness of at least some abortions; it would not be possible to grant doctors a right to decide to be involved unless the law on abortion failed to prohibit all abortions, and was thus intrinsically unjust. In practical terms pro-life doctors, and the pro-life movement generally, might find that it made little if any difference whether the legislation stated "Doctors have a right not to participate in abortion procedures" or "Doctors have a right to decide whether or not to be involved in abortion procedures." However, the two pieces of legislation are essentially different, the latter being predicated on the licitness of abortion and the former on the right of doctors not to perform an act that can never be licitly performed.

Compromise

One might ask whether legislation stating "Doctors have a right not to be involved in abortion procedures" is a compromise. Should not the law state: "Doctors have no right to be involved in abortion" or, more precisely, "Doctors are prohibited from involvement in abortion procedures"? And indeed, one might object that the law refers only to doctors, and not to nurses or other medical or administrative personnel who might find themselves caught up in a situation where abortions are performed. I would answer that the question should not focus on whether legislation is or is not a compromise but on whether or not it is just. It is by no means unethical to compromise in legislation, provided that the compromise is just; indeed it may sometimes be unethical *not* to compromise.[4] Regrettably, all too often the notion of compromise has been highlighted without a consideration of whether one is referring to a just or an unjust compromise. Not all compromises are to be censured, and those that are should be censured not so much because they are a "compromise" but because they are unjust and thus unethical.[5]

Furthermore, just because it does not achieve as much as might have been otherwise desirable, it does not mean that legislation should be regarded as a "compromise" or, more relevantly, as "unjust." Indisputably, legislation stating "Doctors are prohibited from involvement in abortion procedures" achieves more than legislation stating "Doctors have a right not to be involved in abortion procedures." The question is not, however, whether a better law could be enacted but whether a particular law under consideration is or is not unacceptable on account of intrinsic unjustness. These two illustrations of laws have "doctors" as their subject matter, not "abortion." Neither law discriminates unjustly

---

4. See Cardinal Joseph Ratzinger, *Church, Ecumenism and Politics* (Slough: St. Paul Publications, 1988), 149. When voting on political matters (i.e., *ius civile*) compromise is not only legitimate but it can sometimes be unethical *not* to compromise. However, compromise on *moral* matters such as abortion (i.e., *ius gentium*) is unethical. See also CDF, *On the Participation of Catholics in Political Life* (2002): "When political activity comes up against moral principles that do not admit of exception, compromise or derogation, the Catholic commitment becomes more evident and laden with responsibility. In the face of *fundamental and inalienable ethical demands,* Christians must recognize that what is at stake is the essence of the moral law, which concerns the integral good of the human person. This is the case with laws concerning *abortion* and *euthanasia*. . . . Such laws must defend the basic right to life from conception to natural death," n. 4.

5. In other words, compromise is legitimate—and indeed can be morally obligated—in many instances, but it is unacceptable when it goes against whatever is good, true, just, or ethical. Even if the choice to support a bill to give doctors a legal right not to participate in abortions were viewed as a compromise (e.g., if this proposal was being accepted only because there was no chance of getting support for a bill to prohibit the participation of doctors, or no chance of getting support for a bill that would also give a legal right to nurses, administrative personnel, and others), the proper identification of the subject matter of the legislation would show that it did not constitute compromise in an *abortion* law.

between born and unborn human beings, or between some categories of the unborn; the laws, rather, are restricted to a consideration of whether doctors are granted a right not to do *x* or are prohibited from doing *x*. Insofar as it is legitimate to grant doctors a right not to do what they have a legitimate entitlement not to do, or to prohibit doctors from doing something that they can be legitimately prohibited from doing, neither of these laws is intrinsically unjust.

A Typical Abortion Act

Moving away from an illustration of a law that merely states "Abortion is lawful up to 16 weeks," I now present a model of a "Typical Abortion Act," introduced in a state where a previous law, the "Protection of Human Life Act 18__" gave full protection to all human beings, born and unborn. This Typical Abortion Act is necessarily less complex than the United Kingdom's Abortion Act 1967 (see Appendix B) or similar legislation enacted in other countries. It contains, nevertheless, the main features of such actual legislation.

Typical Abortion Act 19__
An Act to amend and clarify the law relating to the termination of pregnancy

BE IT ENACTED:

1. Abortion shall not be a punishable crime under the criminal law if it is:

(a) Performed before the end of the 24th week of pregnancy, at the request of or with the consent of the pregnant woman, with or without a medical reason;

(b) Performed before the end of the 30th week of pregnancy, at the request of or with the consent of the pregnant woman, if tests indicate that the fetus, if born, is likely to be disabled;

(c) Performed at any stage of the pregnancy, at the request of or with the consent of the pregnant woman, if there are reasonable grounds for believing that the pregnancy resulted from a criminal act.

2. Abortions designated by clause 1 cannot be performed outside publicly funded hospitals or private premises specifically licensed by local authorities to perform abortions.

3. Doctors have a right not to participate in abortion procedures if they have any moral or religious objections.

4. Local health authorities may determine whether any woman in their area who is in receipt of state benefits, and who incurs expenses in having an abortion in private licensed premises, may reclaim expenses incurred.

5. The Protection of Human Life Act 18__ is amended in accordance with the provisions of clause 1.

Although this Typical Abortion Act is presented as a single law, it deals with six distinct points of law. Three of these (clause 1) refer to circumstances in which it will not be a punishable crime for a woman to have an abortion, i.e., the primary abortion legislation. The three other points (clauses 2–4) deal with where those abortions will be performed, the rights of doctors not to be involved, and a financial matter, i.e., the secondary legislation.

This is clearly an abortion law typical of the sorts of law found in many countries, yet it neither obligates nor permits any abortions. Rather, it can be said to *tolerate* abortion, even though in specifying the sorts of circumstances in which abortion may be tolerated the law does appear to be lending considerable weight to the acceptability of those abortions to which it refers. In denying the due protection of the law to some categories of human beings the law is unjust and, more specifically, intrinsically unjust.

The identification of just one clause as being intrinsically unjust is sufficient to render the Typical Abortion Act in its entirety intrinsically unjust.[6] This does not mean, however, that no parts of the Act, considered individually, are just. For example, clause 3, referring to the rights of doctors, is entirely just. Although this clause is incorporated within the Abortion Act, and although its inclusion is relevant (as secondary

6. "For a thing to be evil one single defect suffices, whereas for it to be good simply, it is not enough for it to be good in one point only, it must be good in every respect." *ST* I-II, q. 20, a. 2.

legislation) to the general law on abortion, nevertheless its subject matter is doctors and their rights. If this clause had not been incorporated within the Typical Abortion Act, morally upright legislators could licitly have voted to enact it as part of a "Rights of Doctors Act." The recognition that some of the constituent parts of an intrinsically unjust law can be judged, when considered individually, to be just, is the key to making just changes to the law in ways favorable to the pro-life cause.

What could a morally upright pro-life legislator do, in the imaginary state in which the Typical Abortion Act has been enacted? It is entirely just to vote for a bill to repeal the Act, but let us assume that most legislators are unwilling to support a vote for repeal. After some time it emerges that many legislators are willing to amend the Typical Abortion Act slightly to lower the time limit for the abortions referred to in clause 1(a) from the 24th to the 16th week.

At this point it can be seen why simple illustrations like "Abortion is lawful up to 16 weeks" and "Abortion is permissible up to 16 weeks" do not represent adequately the complex legislative reality, because the Typical Abortion Act's reference to abortions up to 24 weeks does not say that they are either "lawful" or "permissible." Although legislation that made abortion "lawful" or "permissible" up to 16 weeks could be introduced (and readily rejected as intrinsically unjust), the sort of legislation more likely to be introduced would be markedly different, and the reason why it would also be intrinsically unjust may not be so obvious.

Amendment Bills

Primary Legislation Bills

A likely way of changing the law to reduce the limit from 24 to 16 weeks would be by means of an amendment bill:

TYPICAL ABORTION (AMENDMENT) BILL X
A Bill to amend section 1 of the Typical Abortion Act 19__

BE IT ENACTED:

In clause 1(a) of the Typical Abortion Act 19__, the word "24th" shall be substituted by "16th."

At the moment we are concerned not with various procedural or amendment votes that occur during the passage of legislation (such votes being considered in the following chapter), but solely with a legislator's final vote to enact legislation. As I have argued, whether a legislator can licitly vote for this amendment bill to be enacted as law depends primarily on a judgment as to the justness or unjustness of the bill.

Is this amendment bill, then, just or (intrinsically) unjust? At first glance it may seem that the amendment bill is just: it may seem that the amendment bill, considered in itself, neither obligates, permits, nor tolerates abortion because it makes no mention of obligating, permitting, or tolerating abortion. If this is the case, what, one must ask, does the bill do? What is the meaning or, as one might say, the intent of the legislation? The answer to this involves the recognition that one cannot determine the meaning or intent of the amendment bill without considering the Typical Abortion Act to which the bill refers. The amendment bill's reference to "24th" and "16th" is meaningless unless one understands it in relation to the Typical Abortion Act.

Our task, moreover, is not simply to discern the meaning or intent of the amendment bill but also—indeed primarily—its justness. The words of the amendment bill, taken in themselves, do not help one to discern its justness any more than they reveal its meaning or intent. The justness of the amendment bill is determined similarly by considering it with respect to the law it is amending.

In the first place, the meaning or intent of the amendment bill, understood in relation to the Typical Abortion Act that it amends, is that it shall not be unlawful for an abortion to be performed if requested by any pregnant woman before the end of the 16th week of pregnancy. Insofar as this constitutes the legal toleration of abortion until the end of the 16th week of pregnancy, the amendment bill must be judged intrinsically unjust. However, it would be a mistake to think that this is the only meaning or intent of the amendment bill.

An amendment bill to a previous Act essentially "opens up" for reconsideration the whole of that previous Act. If the amendment bill does not refer to some aspects of that Act, this means that the legislature is content (at that moment in time) not to alter the provisions of those clauses to which it does not refer. The legislature could have freely chosen to introduce a bill to repeal the whole of the Typical Abortion Act, or a bill to delete clauses 1, 2, 4, and 5, both sorts of bill having a meaning or intent that was consistent with a pro-life position. Given that the legislature's free choice has been to exclude from consideration all of the Typical Abortion Act apart from one part of one clause, the meaning or intent of the amendment bill is that all those parts of the typical abortion law *not* amended by the bill remain in force. In other words, the meaning or intent of voting for the amendment bill is *that the Typical Abortion Act should remain in force as it is but with an amendment,* the amendment in this case being that instead of abortions on request being tolerated up to the end of the 24th week, they will be tolerated up to the end of the 16th.

Similarly, the justness of the amendment bill can be understood only with reference to the Act that it amends. The question is not whether a reduction from 24 to 16 weeks is just, or even whether it is just for abortions performed at the request of the woman up to the end of the 16th week to be treated as "not unlawful." Rather, the question is whether the amendment bill itself is just or unjust, and this is discerned by a consideration of whether the Typical Abortion Act *as amended* by the amendment bill is just or unjust. Legislatures frequently encounter amendment bills on a wide variety of measures and, insofar as these are political matters *(ius civile)* that are not intrinsically unjust, voting for such legislation does not normally involve such complex considerations. However, voting to enact any amendment bill is governed by a particular principle: the amendment bill must be judged to be just, and the justness of the amendment bill is determined by a judgment as to the justness of the original Act or Acts to which it refers *as amended* by the amendment bill.

The principle just stated can be considered again by means of a different amendment bill. Suppose that instead of introducing Amendment Bill X legislators had thought that they could prohibit all abortions for which "request" alone was regarded as a justification. Thinking that there was no prospect of getting sufficient support to prohibit abortion after rape/incest or in cases of fetal disability, they nevertheless think it is possible to prohibit the abortions represented by clause 1(a) of the Typical Abortion Act and a bill is introduced:

Typical Abortion (Amendment) Bill Y
A Bill to amend section 1 of the Typical Abortion Act 19__

BE IT ENACTED:

Delete clause 1(a) of the Typical Abortion Act 19__.

What, then, are legislators doing if they vote for this bill? It might seem that they are not supporting any abortions because the text of the bill does not refer to the obligation, permission or toleration of any abortions. Rather, one notes that clause 1(a) of the Typical Abortion Act constitutes toleration of some abortions, and that in deleting clause 1(a) the unjust toleration of those abortions will be ended. It might seem that legislators voting for the bill are merely prohibiting some abortions and in no way supporting any other abortions.

The key question, as shown by our previous consideration of Amendment Bill X, is whether Amendment Bill Y is just or (intrinsically) unjust, and, as I argued, its justness is determined by a judgment as to the justness of the Act to which it refers *as amended* by the amendment bill. The amendment bill is inextricably linked to the Act to which it refers: in determining the justness of Amendment Bill Y one cannot limit one's attention solely to clause 1, or even solely to clause 1(a). One must, rather, take into account the whole of the Act of which clause 1 is part. The meaning and intent of Amendment Bill Y is determined by considering it in relation to the whole of the Typical Abortion Act, and the justness of the bill is determined by a consideration of whether the Act, *as amended,* is just or unjust. Because the amended Act would still tolerate other abortions (after rape/incest, or if the child would be born disabled) it would still be unjust, and the bill to amend the Act in such a way must be judged to be intrinsically unjust.

In the first chapter, I argued that there were some practical problems, viewed in relation to the virtue of solidarity, encountered in supporting legislation that prohibited some abortions but not others. The reason a legislator cannot licitly vote for Amendment Bills X or Y is not, however, that the bills do not protect all of the unborn, but rather that they are judged in themselves unjust, the act of voting for them also being thus intrinsically unjust. The reason the legislation cannot be supported is not simply that some abortions would be prohibited and others not prohibited, but that the legislation fails to fulfill the requirements of good law. The following chapter will note instances in which legislative proposals could be supported even though they result in the prohibition of some abortions but not others, and I think a simple illustration is also called for here.

Consider a country in which all abortions were prohibited and a law (Act A) were passed, stating, "Abortion is not a criminal offence if performed after a pregnancy arising from a criminal act, or if performed on a pregnant woman whose child is likely to be born disabled." The next year another law (Act B) is passed, stating, "Abortion is not a criminal offense if performed at the request of the pregnant woman." Some time afterward legislators have the opportunity to vote to repeal Act B. If they repeal it, Act A will nevertheless remain in force. At this point I am not concerned with the question of whether it would be prudent or consistent with the demands of solidarity to engage in a protracted public campaign that focused solely on repealing Act B. I am merely asking whether the act of voting to repeal Act B is just or unjust. My response is that, unlike an amendment bill—the meaning, intent, and justness of which is inextricably bound up with the Act or Acts to which it refers—a bill that simply repeals an intrinsically unjust Act (like Act B) is not itself intrinsically unjust,[7] this judgment being in no way affected by an awareness that other intrinsically unjust Acts (like Act A) may remain in force even after the repealing bill is enacted. Similarly, in some legal systems, notably codified systems, it may be possible and even just to repeal some parts of an abortion law even if other unjust parts remain in force. However, in a UK-

---

7. The repeal of an intrinsically unjust Act could lead to a situation where there is "no law" on abortion, with many more abortions being tolerated than if the intrinsically unjust Act (which prohibits some abortions while allowing others) remained in place. In such an instance it would be imprudent and contrary to reason (i.e., unjust) for pro-life legislators to vote to repeal the intrinsically unjust Act. The repealing Act would be unjust in the light of the circumstances, but not intrinsically unjust. Pro-abortion legislators might choose to repeal the Act because they think that to have "no law" on abortion would give women greater access to abortion. In this instance, their act of voting for the repealing Act would be intrinsically unjust, even though the unjustness of the repealing Act itself would be circumstantial, not intrinsic.

type system of law (a system that serves as a model for many other legislatures), a vote for an amendment bill (even if it specifies only that a part of another law be deleted) involves entirely different considerations. Whether it is a just act to vote for the amendment bill depends on a consideration of the justness of the Act to which the bill refers, *as amended* by the bill.

Secondary Legislation Bills

Amendment Bills X and Y, above, have dealt with the primary abortion legislation. Are different considerations introduced when dealing with secondary legislation? Under the terms of the Typical Abortion Act it would not be a criminal offense for the specified abortions to be performed in publicly funded hospitals, and local authorities have the power to decide whether to assist women to pay for abortions in private facilities. If abortions were not available in publicly funded hospitals and if financial assistance were not given, this would not only signal that abortion is not as publicly acceptable as other procedures for which there would be public funding, but might even prevent some women having abortions. An amendment bill is accordingly introduced:

TYPICAL ABORTION (AMENDMENT) BILL Z
A Bill to amend the Typical Abortion Act 19__

BE IT ENACTED:

1. In clause 2 of the Typical Abortion Act 19__, delete the words "in publicly funded hospitals or."
2. Delete clause 4.

Whether or not this bill can be licitly supported involves the same sorts of considerations made with respect to Amendment Bills X and Y. The relevant question is not whether it is right to stop public funds paying for abortion, but whether the legislative proposal is just, and (as in the previous instances) this judgment is made by considering whether the Typical Abortion Act as amended by Amendment Bill Z is just? Because the Act as amended by Bill Z would still be intrinsically unjust, Amendment Bill Z itself must be intrinsically unjust.

In short, if an amendment bill is introduced in an attempt to change an Act that is intrinsically unjust, the justness of that amendment bill is determined by judging the justness of the Act or Acts to which it refers, as amended by the amendment bill. If the Act as amended remains intrinsically unjust, then the amendment bill is intrinsically unjust. Pro-life legislators encounter an ethical difficulty when they attempt, with respect to both the primary and secondary legislation, to amend an abortion Act by means of an amendment bill.

Introducing Freestanding Legislation

If amendment bills pose a problem, an alternative would be to introduce freestanding legislation that does not constitute an amendment bill. Assuming that a country's abortion law is governed solely by the Typical Abortion Act, let us consider freestanding legislation with respect, first, to the primary legislation and, then, to the secondary legislation.

Primary Legislation

Instead of introducing Amendment Bill X, it would be possible to introduce freestanding legislation, as follows, to prohibit abortions after 16 weeks, performed solely on the grounds of "request":

ABORTION LIMITATION (WEEKS) BILL
A Bill to prohibit abortions after a specified period

BE IT ENACTED:

1. It shall be a crime punishable by [. . .] for an abortion to be performed on any pregnant woman, on the grounds of simple request, after the end of the 16th week of pregnancy.

2. This Act takes precedence over any previous legislation.

The Typical Abortion Act would still be in force if the Abortion Limitation (weeks) Bill were enacted, although clause 1(a) would (necessarily) be amended as a result of this legislation. Even though it was crucial when considering the justness of voting for Amendment Bills X, Y, and Z, above, the fact that the Typical Abortion Act would remain in force or that it would be amended is not, in my view, a relevant concern (as I shall explain when dealing with secondary legislation, below).

One might think that the Abortion Limitation (Weeks) Bill in itself is unobjectionable insofar as it is does not specifically say that abortions are "lawful" or even that they are "not unlawful" up to the end of the 16th week of pregnancy, and the legislation itself does not comment on the lawfulness (or unlawfulness) of abortions performed for reasons other than "request": i.e., those deemed unlawful in the Typical Abortion Act with respect to the fetus being disabled or pregnancy occurring after a criminal act.[8] If abortions other than those referred to in the bill were already unlawful, this bill could be regarded as ensuring that full protection is given to the unborn and not as tolerating abortion. Could one argue, then, that this bill is not *intrinsically* unjust? Might one argue that the justness of such a bill depends on the circumstances? If it does depend on the circumstances, I would argue that in the (imaginary) situation in which the Typical Abortion Act is in force this bill would still be unjust, constituting a law that tolerates abortion. In such a situation the Abortion Limitation Bill would be rightly seen, as indicated by its subtitle, as nothing other than a bill to limit abortion: it prohibits some abortions but not others, i.e., it tolerates some abortions.

Two points are noteworthy. The first is that if all other abortions were previously unlawful except those to be made unlawful by the abortion limitation bill, the obvious requirement would be for legislation to establish that *all* abortions are unlawful, not legislation referring to abortions after 16 weeks. The second is that the Abortion Limitation Bill can be judged to be unjust not only in the imaginary situation we are considering but in *any* situation, i.e., it is intrinsically unjust. This is because the specification of the unlawfulness of abortion after the 16th week of pregnancy is entirely arbitrary. It makes a distinction between abortions before and after 16 weeks when there is no justification for such a distinction. Sometimes distinctions can be justified. For exam-

---

8. I do not propose to focus on other objections to the bill, based on interpretation. For example, the bill if enacted might allow women to have abortions for reasons other than that of "simple request" (say, for fetal disability or after a criminal act) at any time after 16 weeks, even extending the period specified for such abortions in the Typical Abortion Act.

ple, even though killing after birth is no more justified than killing before birth, legislation specifying a penalty for a particular crime of killing a newborn child (while making no reference to the lawfulness of killing an unborn child or older infants or adults) need not be viewed as legislation tolerating other offenses. Compared with unborn children or older infants, a newborn child has different needs and social relationships, and legislation to take into account particular categories of children with different needs is neither arbitrary nor intrinsically unjust.

In short, the Abortion Limitation Bill must be judged to be intrinsically unjust, and not unjust simply with respect to circumstances. Bills that focus on restricting some categories of abortion but not others are, similarly, intrinsically unjust.[9]

Secondary Legislation

The Typical Abortion (Amendment) Bill Z, aimed at preventing women from having assistance from public funds to abort, was judged to be intrinsically unjust. Instead of the amendment bill, freestanding legislation could have been introduced:

Public Funding Bill
A Bill to prohibit public funds from being used to pay for abortions

BE IT ENACTED:

1. It shall be unlawful for public funds to be used to finance abortions.

2. Previous legislation affected by this Act will be amended accordingly.

---

9. The key point is the focus (or subject matter) of the legislation. It is possible to focus legislation on something other than abortion, e.g., on the rights of women or the rights of disabled people, and to include within that legislation a proposal which prevents discrimination before birth. This might ensure that abortion is prohibited specifically on the grounds of fetal disability or gender. This sort of legislation, having different subject matter—the rights of women or the rights of disabled people—is distinguishable from legislation that has "abortion" as its subject matter. The enactment of such legislation, however, need not mean that it is illegal to abort disabled or female fetuses; it may merely mean that gender or disability could not be cited as the grounds

This legislation does not prohibit any abortions, and though it may affect women seeking an abortion, it is not legislation on abortion as such. Rather, it deals with a matter of public funding. The legislation is anomalous, given that in a state in which all abortions were prohibited, it would be unnecessary. However, in itself, it is unobjectionable. If the legislation had said that public funding for abortion were unlawful except in cases x, y, or z, then it would have (at least) tolerated public funding of abortion in such instances and would be intrinsically unjust. At this point I am not dealing with the question whether, in a concrete instance, it would be prudent for a pro-life legislator to support such legislation, let alone whether it would be prudent to mount a prolonged campaign for it, but simply whether it is the sort of legislation that in itself can be regarded as objectionable. Being not intrinsically unjust it is not, in itself, objectionable.

If the Public Funding Bill were enacted, clauses 2 and 4 of the Typical Abortion Act would be amended. Various other Acts—for example, to do with public funding, hospitals, local government, health care provision, etc.—might also be amended. When drafted, a bill would normally refer to the legislation affected by it. It seems to me that even if the amendment to the Typical Abortion Act had been explicitly stated, this would not have affected the justness of voting for this Public Funding Bill. This is because the amendment of the Typical Abortion Act would be an indirect effect of the direct act of voting directly *for* the ban on public funding of abortions; references in the Public Funding Bill to changes in other acts are necessary changes that result from what the bill itself does, and are more descriptive than prescriptive. By contrast, attempts to prohibit public funding by means of the Typical Abortion (Amendment) Bill Z, presented earlier, involve the *direct amendment* of the Typical Abortion Act. References in Amendment Bill Z to the changes in the Act are prescriptive, not merely descriptive: they are the basis for changes to that Act.

Let us consider another example of freestanding legislation. The Typical Abortion Act included a clause giving doctors the right not to participate in abortion procedures, but this does not refer to nurses. A

---

for abortion. If abortions were still allowed "on request," the mere request would be sufficient for a woman to abort a disabled or female fetus.

Rights of Nurses Bill could be introduced to ensure that nurses similarly had a right not to participate in abortions.

Rights of Nurses Bill
A Bill to grant nurses the right to dissociate themselves from procedures with respect to which they have moral or religious objections

BE IT ENACTED:

1. Nurses have the right to refuse to participate in any procedure with respect to which they have an ethical or religious objection.
2. Previous legislation affected by this Act will be amended accordingly.

It is legitimate to have legislation focusing solely on the rights or duties of nurses, and the justness or unjustness of the legislation is not affected by the fact that it does not refer to doctors or nonmedical administrative personnel whose rights might also need to be safeguarded. The legislation does not refer to abortion, though abortion could be included as the sort of matter covered by the legislation. Other matters covered would be such procedures as blood transfusions, which would be a matter of concern for nurses who were Jehovah's Witnesses.

The Rights of Nurses Bill does not in itself grant protection to any unborn child. If enough nurses exercised their right not to be engaged in abortions, however, the lives of some unborn children might be saved as a result of the practical difficulty of obtaining an abortion. Granting nurses (or doctors or others) the right not to participate in such activities can also help to promote a pro-life culture within the health care profession that in turn may extend to society more generally.

In the following chapter I shall show that in addition to supporting freestanding legislation that affects the secondary legislation, legislators may support similar secondary legislation proposals introduced during the passage of abortion legislation. The relevant question when judging the suitability of legislative proposals (introduced either during the passage of a bill or as freestanding legislation) is not whether they will restrict or might prevent abortion, but whether they are just. I shall now consider in broad terms relevant considerations of justness in a wide range of legislative proposals. Even if a legislative proposal is not intrinsically unjust, the reasonableness—justness—of supporting it in a concrete situation depends upon a consideration of the circumstances and possible side effects. Voting for legislation does involve a consideration of side effects of one's votes—but the sort of consideration I propose differs from that proposed by John Finnis and others, which was considered and rejected in Chapter 4.

A Range of Legislative Proposals

The range of legislative proposals introduced to prohibit or prevent some abortions, or to contribute toward a pro-life culture, can be categorized as follows:

i. Proposals to prohibit certain categories of abortion.
ii. Proposals to prohibit certain procedures.
iii. Proposals specifying certain conditions to be met before an abortion is provided.
iv. Proposals prohibiting abortion for certain categories of women.
v. Proposals referring to locations where abortions can be provided.
vi. Proposals referring to funding.
vii. Proposals referring to forced abortion.
viii. Proposals referring to non-involvement in abortion on grounds of conscience.
ix. Proposals referring to registering abortions.

I shall consider the sorts of legislative proposals that might be considered within each of these groups. Although I accept generally that some proposals can be justly supported, whether they could in fact be supported in a concrete instance would depend wholly on how the proposal was presented and whether it was, in fact, just.

i. Proposals to Prohibit Certain Categories of Abortion

Abortions are commonly categorized according to the age of the unborn child (or the length of the pregnancy) measured in days, weeks, or trimesters, and/or the "grounds" under which the abortions are being performed: as a matter of "request"; for reasons of financial hardship or social deprivation; after rape; if the child is disabled, etc. In previous chapters I have argued that because the protection of each human life is a fundamental requirement of any system of human law, any law obligating, permitting, or tolerating the deliberate destruction of a human being must be judged to be intrinsically unjust. A law that permits some abortions is clearly intrinsically unjust even if the same law prohibits other abortions. Furthermore, I have shown that a law that appears merely to prohibit a category of abortion without appearing to refer to other abortions is also intrinsically unjust.

Any law specifying that some—but not all—categories of abortion are prohibited is intrinsically unjust because it makes an arbitrary distinction between groups of unborn children.[10] Some may contend this is not so and provide an illustration to prove their point. Imagine a country, they might say, where all abortions are legally prohibited, but where female fetuses are aborted (illegally) because males have a higher social status. In this situation might it be legitimate to support legislation prohibiting the abortion of female fetuses? A similar illustration—except that it deals with female infanticide[11]—has been given by Anthony Fisher, O.P.,[12] and there are several objections to it. If all abortion (or all homicide) is prohibited, to prevent females being aborted (or killed after birth) does not require the enactment of new legislation but the enforcement of the existing legislation. If the existing legislation is not enforced there is no reason to believe that new legislation will be enforced. This is not to say that legislators cannot enact legislation reinforcing the prohibition of *all* abortion (or infanticide). And they could even stipulate that offenses against females are an additional offense, in the same way that crimes against individuals motivated by racial or religious prejudice can be subject to additional penalties.

10. I am not referring here to legislation to repeal an Act or to abrogate articles of law in a codified system. As I indicated above, in the section on amendment bills, such repealing/abrogating legislation does not in itself make a distinction between categories of unborn children. Rather, it repeals intrinsically unjust legislation that makes this sort of illegitimate distinction.

11. Bills dealing with the prohibition of the infanticide of newborn girls or the abortion of female fetuses involve identical considerations.

12. Fisher, "Some Problems of Conscience," 195.

I have emphasized that the key point is the subject matter of the legislation and, insofar as abortion is the subject matter, the only just law is necessarily one prohibiting all abortions. If the subject matter were "the rights of women" (such subject matter being justified because there are differences between men and women and it is not arbitrary for a law to be enacted at a particular time focusing on the needs that apply to one gender though not the other), it would be legitimate to include a measure ensuring that their rights were also protected before birth.

Similarly, a bill referring to "the rights of disabled people" might, among other things, prohibit screening tests performed in order to detect disability with a view to abortion, or even specifically prohibit the abortion of disabled babies. One has to be attentive to what is actually proposed. It would be unsatisfactory to support a measure simply saying that disability was not an acceptable grounds for abortion, because if abortion were available on other grounds—notably, simply at the mother's request—disabled babies could still be aborted by citing one of those different grounds.

If the subject matter of the legislation is abortion, then the prohibition of some—but not all—abortions entails supporting an intrinsically unjust law that tolerates some abortions. Voting for such legislation is unethical irrespective of who is included within and who is excluded from the legislation.

ii. Proposals to Prohibit Certain Procedures

Because late-term abortions are commonly regarded with less approval than earlier ones it may be easier to gain support for legislation prohibiting abortion after, say, 24 or 30 weeks than it would be to prohibit earlier abortions, but such legislation, being intrinsically unjust (as I have argued), could not be licitly supported. Would I, then, refrain from supporting legislation to prohibit the practice known as "partial birth abortion" (PBA), a clearly objectionable practice of killing the child during the passage of birth before he or she has been completely removed from his or her mother's womb?

My answer is that PBA legislation involves a different consideration from one prohibiting abortions after a particular time limit. The legislation prohibits *a procedure*. It grants no rights to unborn children of any particular gestational age, nor does it deny any rights to others. Just as legislators could legitimately choose, if there were just reasons, to prohibit other procedures—such as kidney or heart/lung transplant operations—similarly they could legitimately choose to prohibit the unjust procedure of PBA. The fact that other unjust procedures are not affected by the legislation does not affect the justness of the legislation prohibiting PBA, provided that it does not authorize any other unjust procedure and cannot be judged to be unjust for some other reason. Legislation prohibiting prostaglandin abortions—i.e., legislation prohibiting the *procedure* of abortion involving prostaglandin—could be supported for the same reason. Similarly, chemical abortions induced by the "abortion pill" RU486 could be prohibited by legislation that prohibits the manufacture and/or the administration to pregnant women of RU486, in the same way that the manufacture and/or the administration to pregnant women of the drug thalidomide could be justly prohibited.

Such legislation *does not make an illicit distinction of persons,* protecting some in a situation that calls for the protection of all, because, in itself, the legislation does not make any distinction of persons. It does not, in itself, protect any (category of) unborn child, and the enactment of such legislation would (regrettably) not prevent unborn children being aborted by other methods. The prohibition of partial-birth, prostaglandin, or RU486 abortions does not, in itself, grant protection to any unborn children, but there may be good consequences of prohibiting those procedures in terms of promoting a more critical public attitude toward abortion that may in turn result in saving lives.

Similarly, even if there is legislation permitting or tolerating abortion, it is legitimate to support legislation prohibiting *the procedures* of IVF, or embryo research, or embryonic cloning or embryonic stem cell research, etc. Likewise, it would be legitimate to support legislation opposing euthanasia even if the legislation does not at the same time address abortion, or to support just anti-abortion legislation in a country where euthanasia remains legal. One needs to be attentive to the precise subject matter of the legislation.[13]

13. Anthony Fisher, O.P., refers to a hypothetical situation in a fictional "African Union" in which a pro-life legislator is attempting to prohibit cloning. Fisher speaks of opposition to the legislator's bill from a group declaring "that they cannot support any

iii. *Proposals Specifying Certain Conditions to Be Met Before an Abortion Is Provided*

If it is not possible to prohibit abortions, it may be possible to specify that some conditions be met before they can be procured. Among such conditions are that more than one doctor approve the abortion, that there be a "cooling-off period" between requesting the abortion and its being carried out, that counseling be provided beforehand, that certain information about the development of the unborn child and the abortion procedure be presented so that the woman can give informed consent, etc. Other conditions might be that the father of the unborn child consent, or at least does not object, and in the case of a minor that she have parental consent.

Pro-lifers might think that such proposals might help to dissuade women from having an abortion, or draw attention to the fact that abortion is not a simple procedure to be undertaken lightly. Even many people in favor of abortion might think that these sorts of conditions are reasonable. There may be some negative consequences of these sorts of proposals (e.g., the informed consent provision might reinforce a view that abortion is only objectionable if undertaken without full consent), but the first consideration when judging whether to support such proposals is not the consequences—good or bad—but whether the proposals themselves are just.

The problem with this sort of proposal generally is that it is predicated on the lawfulness of abortion and refers solely to the question of abortion. To enact a law saying, e.g., that women must have counseling or give informed consent before having an abortion implies acceptance of abortion *provided that* it follows counseling and informed consent. The same applies to the other conditions I have listed, and it seems that any legislation that refers specifically to abortion when establishing such conditions must be judged to be intrinsically unjust.

If such conditions are regarded as favorable to the pro-life cause,

---

bill which does not at least go for a complete ban on all artificial reproduction, sex education in schools, and the public dissemination of the theory of evolution" (ibid., 195–96). Fisher is, of course, caricaturing the view he is opposing. It can be seen, however, from what I have said above that my view cannot be regarded as comparable to that of the African pro-life legislator in Fisher's hypothetical situation.

then their establishment in legislation must be done without focusing on abortion. Thus legislation requiring parental consent before a minor has *any* medical treatment or surgery should ensure that no minor has an abortion (or even a tooth extraction) without her parents' approval. Such legislation, not referring to abortion, would be just and could be supported even though it would not help to protect the lives of unborn children whose mothers were minors and who gained parental consent for abortion. Similarly, if a cooling-off period, counseling, and informed consent were regarded as requirements before *any* non-emergency surgery, then these conditions would apply to a woman wanting an abortion (provided that abortion was not regarded as emergency surgery).

It seems that one could not justly enact in law some of the conditions, notably the condition specifying that more than one doctor approve the abortion. Of course, it is possible that a law be enacted requiring that more than one doctor approve *any* medical treatment or surgery, but this does not seem to be a reasonable proposal. One could also not justly enact legislation saying that a woman could have an abortion *provided that* the child's father did not object, because this implies that abortion is licit provided that the condition is met. It would also not be possible to grant the father a legal right to veto an abortion. Naturally, one has enormous sympathy for a desperate father facing the awful prospect of having his child aborted. However, any law giving a legal right *to veto* an act presupposes that the act is licit provided that the veto is not declared.[14] Perhaps it would be possible to enact legislation granting fathers an equal say when making decisions on serious matters concerning their children, but there could be complex consequences of such legislation, and its applicability to abortion might be subject to unfavorable legal interpretations and court judgments.

---

14. The question of the rights of fathers arose in the UK Parliament. As part of his Infant Life (Preservation) and Paternal Rights Bill 1987, Peter Bruinvels, MP, sought to introduce an amendment to the Abortion Act 1967, in which the words would be added: "that the father of the unborn child has been consulted about the mother's intention to terminate the pregnancy and that, where he is the mother's husband, his consent as to the termination has been obtained." The bill did not have the support of SPUC and the other main pro-life groups, and it did not gain the support of Parliament.

iv. *Proposals Prohibiting Abortion for Certain Categories of Women*

Women can be grouped into different categories according to their age, wealth or poverty, their religious, social, or cultural background, their nationality, their possession of a disability, whether they are citizens of a country, permanent residents, or temporary visitors, etc. Granted that it is unethical to *permit* or *obligate* abortion for any category of women, is it possible to justly prohibit any category from having abortions without this implying that abortion is *tolerated* for other categories of women?

It is necessary to return to the question of the subject matter of the legislation and whether its particular focus is reasonable and just, or arbitrary and unjust. Most legislation does not, in itself, restrict its focus to particular categories of women. For example, legislation does not prohibit poorer women from doing x or y; rather their lack of money prevents them having the means to do it. If legislation prohibited a woman (or man) from doing something good (and generally acknowledged to be good) because of her (or his) religious, cultural, or social background, this would be regarded as unjust discrimination. If however, a woman (or man) were given a legal right to refrain from doing something contrary to her (or his) religious or moral convictions (a right that was not also extended to others) this would not necessarily be unjust. A "right *not* to do x" implies that one could choose to do x if one wanted, and this is not the sort of right we would be legislating for in the abortion context (unless we were in a state that obligated abortion).[15] If it were licit to prohibit abortion for a category (or categories) of women, it would have to be established that it was legitimate for the legislation to be restricted to that category of women.

Could one, for example, support legislation specifically prohibiting abortion for poor women, or for rich women, or for disabled women, or for able-bodied women? Unless there is a general context in which some things can be justly prohibited for some categories of women but

---

15. A man or woman could, on account of their religion, be given a legal right not to work on days recognized as holy days by their religion. A law could justly exempt male Sikhs from the law, applicable to others, of wearing crash helmets on motorcycles, on account of their wearing turbans.

not for others, it would appear to be arbitrary and unjust to prohibit some abortions in this way. In particular, one would have good reason to view askance legislation that prohibited rich or able-bodied women from having an abortion, especially as this might appear to signify a social policy favoring abortion for poor and disabled women.

There is one category of women who could legitimately be treated differently from others, and this would be not on account of their being women but because they were not citizens or did not have residential status in a country. Because the laws in their own countries (or part of their country) may prohibit abortion or greatly restrict it, some women may want to travel to another country (or part of their country) where abortion is more readily available. If it is not unjust to deny (nonresident) men or women from other countries (or areas) access to legitimate services ordinarily enjoyed by resident men or women, one could argue that it is not unjust to deny them access to abortion services. For example, if a law can be enacted justly prohibiting the sale of such things as houses or cars to people visiting the country (even though residents may legitimately buy them), or prohibiting those with nonresidential status from working in the country (even though residents may legitimately work), or prohibiting nonresidents from going to certain places or attending certain functions (even though residents may legitimately go or attend), then it would appear not to be unjust to enact legislation specifying that nonresident women are prohibited from having abortions while visiting the country. The legislation would focus not on abortion but on the entitlements of nonresident visitors, and insofar as it would be focusing specifically and legitimately on nonresident visitors as its subject matter, it could not be said to tolerate any other abortions because its subject matter would be "nonresident visitors" and not "abortion."

Whether it is ethical to support legislation depends on its justness and not simply on whether it might be practically effective in preventing women from having an abortion. It would, for example, be possible to greatly restrict the number of nonresident women having abortions by imposing conditions, like requiring that their personal doctor in their home country be notified before or after any abortion is performed. Such legislation might deter many women from having an abortion out of fear that the abortion would appear on their medical records, but it could not be justly enacted, as it would indicate that an abortion could be obtained *provided that* the specified conditions were fulfilled.[16]

v. Proposals Referring to Locations Where Abortions Can Be Performed

If a country permits (some) abortions, the question arises where these permitted abortions may be performed. Although it would be unjust to say where abortions may be performed, it is a different matter to say where they *may not* be. For example, in the UK Abortion Act 1967 a clause states, "This Act does not extend to Northern Ireland," thereby excluding that area of the UK from the Act's abortion-favoring provisions.

If it is legitimate to exclude a region of a country from the provisions of legislation generally, then it would appear to be legitimate to make some areas abortion-free zones. For example, if legislation were being formulated regulating licenses for nightclubs or the erection of sports arenas, it would not be unjust to heed serious concerns expressed in a particular area of the country—say, Dorset—and to introduce a clause to the legislation stating, "This Act does not apply to Dorset." Similarly, the Abortion Act 1967 could have had a clause in it saying that its provisions did not apply to Dorset, and it would be legitimate to introduce subsequent legislation particular to Dorset, specifying merely that within the geographical area of Dorset abortion is prohibited.

This sort of proposal is not comparable to primary abortion legislation proposals prohibiting particular categories of abortion, say, abortions performed simply because the child was unwanted, or abortions after 16 weeks. The primary legislation proposals to restrict abortion

---

16. The Abortion (Treatment of Non-Resident Women) Bill 1987 was introduced by a pro-life legislator, Edward Leigh, MP, in the UK Parliament. It was intrinsically unjust because it accepted the principle that abortions could be obtained *provided that* the doctors of nonresident women were notified of the abortion. The bill specifically stated that notification was not required for women who were British citizens or who had been resident in the United Kingdom for at least twenty weeks prior to seeking an abortion.

make *a distinction of persons:* certain unborn babies are favored more than others on account of particular characteristics: e.g., they have reached a certain age, they are not disabled or not conceived after rape, etc. If abortion is prohibited in Northern Ireland or in Dorset, an illicit distinction of persons has not been made; rather, there is a licit distinction based on geographical territory.

It would also be legitimate to grant regional or local authorities or health authorities responsibility for abortion-related matters by means of just legislation of the form: "Authorities [X or Y or Z] are entitled not to provide abortion services in facilities for which they are responsible." However, one could not justly support legislation, even if it had the same practical effect, that gave such authorities license to provide abortion services, e.g.: "Authorities [X or Y or Z] are entitled to determine *whether or not* abortion services be provided in facilities for which they are responsible."

A legislator could justly vote for a proposal stating: "Authorities [X or Y or Z] are entitled to regulate matters relating to pregnancy and childbirth." This proposal may *be interpreted* as referring to the provision of abortion (and it would thus enable health authorities to permit, prohibit or regulate abortion), but it does not *necessarily* have anything to do with abortion; abortion is not mentioned and it would be reasonable to support this proposal irrespective of the law on abortion. If the law generally does not prohibit abortion, the enactment of this just proposal would enable the authorities affected by it to introduce measures hindering access to abortion.

If, as I have argued, it is legitimate to prohibit abortions within a particular geographical territory, other restrictions based on location could be similarly supported. Just legislation could be supported prohibiting abortions in public hospitals, or in private hospitals, or in military or Catholic hospitals. Such legislation would neither grant nor deny the right to life of any unborn child, but would have as its subject matter the services provided by public or military or Catholic hospitals, etc. Legislation need not specifically prohibit abortions in order to be just. For example, one could justly support proposals stating: "No hospital is obliged to provide [abortion or other] services that its governing body deem ethically objectionable," or "Each hospital's governing body has the right to decide which services are provided by the hospital." This would ensure that no hospital was obliged to provide abortion (or other objectionable services) contrary to the principles of its governing body, but it would not prohibit other hospitals from providing abortion if this were otherwise a legal option. Legislators could not, however, support a proposal—even though it would have the same practical effect—specifying: "Each hospital's governing body has the right to decide whether or not abortion and other services are provided by the hospital."

vi. Proposals Referring to Funding

The state is not obliged to pay, with funds raised by taxation or other means, for everything that it permits or tolerates. It can prohibit public funds from being used to finance projects even though it is not illegal for those projects to be developed by private funds. Within a medical context it could prohibit public funding of various procedures (or their performance on premises funded by public money) on the grounds that they are too expensive, or controversial, or too uncertain of success, etc.

Legislators could not support a proposal stating, "Abortions must be funded privately and not from public money raised by taxes," because this authorizes privately funded abortions. If the subject matter of the legislation were "the use of public funds," a proposal specifying "Abortions may not be financed by public money" would be just and worthy of support. Because the legislation legitimately restricts its attention to "the use of public funds," the possibility that privately funded abortions may (or may not) be legal does not affect its justness. Legislation prohibiting funding, however, only for certain categories of abortions, such as social abortions, would be intrinsically unjust, as it makes an illicit distinction of persons.

In some countries access to health care services depends upon one's own health care insurance plans. Just legislation could prohibit health care insurers from funding abortions or grant them a right to determine which services they are willing to insure, enabling them to refrain from supporting abortion.

vii. Proposals Referring to Forced Abortion

Women have neither a right to become pregnant nor a right to an abortion if they become pregnant. No one, however, has the right to deliberately end a woman's pregnancy prematurely, and women thus have the natural right not to be forced to have an abortion.

Legislation may licitly protect women (or men) from being forced to undertake something that, were it freely chosen, could be legitimately undertaken. For example, legislation can prohibit forced marriage. Similarly, insofar as the subject matter of legislation is that of not being forced to do something that one should not be forced to do, it would be legitimate to support a proposal specifying, "It is unlawful for a woman to be forced to have an abortion." A legislator could not justly support a proposal specifying that "it is unlawful for an abortion to take place unless the woman has freely given informed consent," as this is predicated on abortion's being licit *provided that* the condition of informed consent is given.

viii. Proposals Referring to Non-involvement in Abortion on Grounds on Conscience

In the earlier part of this chapter I devoted considerable attention to this question. It is legitimate for the subject matter of legislation to focus in a limited way on the rights of doctors and/or nurses and/or others involved in health care provision, and so legislation could justly specify such things as: "Doctors [and/or nurses and/or health care workers] have a right not to be involved in [abortion or] any procedure with respect to which they have a religious or ethical objection." Just as a woman has a natural right not to be forced to have an abortion, those involved in providing health care services have a natural right not to be forced to provide services that are properly identified as contrary to their professional ethic. In addition to their natural right *not to be forced* to participate in unethical activities, there is a duty *not to choose* to be engaged in them, this duty of not choosing being distinguishable from the right not to be forced. One could not licitly support a proposal stating that "doctors [and/or nurses and/or health care workers] have *a right to be involved or not to be involved* in abortion procedures," because this includes support for a right to be involved—which contradicts their duty not to be involved—and is intrinsically unjust.

ix. Proposals Referring to Registering Abortions

Many countries regard abortion as a medical procedure that, like other medical procedures, would be automatically registered. Registration of abortion would help to record the number of abortions and various other statistics, such as the age of the mother, the geographical location, the "grounds" under which abortions are performed, etc., and it might be helpful to those opposing abortion to have this information. The value of having abortions registered as a means of acknowledging the lives of unborn children rejected by the society that facilitated their deaths is also not to be underestimated.

If a country does not automatically register medical procedures, would it be licit to vote for a proposal to register abortions? Such a proposal might be of the form, "All abortions [approved by law] must be registered, with a record of the age of the mother, her place of residence, her marital status, the stage of the pregnancy, and the reason for the procedure." Although the information gained by the enactment of this proposal might be useful, there would appear to be a problem in voting for this actual proposal if (as would ordinarily be the case) it were predicated on abortion itself being licit. The validity of proposing that such records be made would not ordinarily be separated from the premise that abortion is a licit procedure for which a record may be licitly made. Of course, legislation can legitimately require the recording of identified crimes—murders, thefts, even illegal abortions, etc.—but in such instances they are recorded, appropriately, as crimes. Support for legislation requiring the recording of identified *criminal* abortions does not pose a problem, especially as their recording would be made as part of the process of attempting to bring those responsible for them to justice. However, supporting a legislative proposal to register legal abortions implicates legislators in the intrinsically unjust legislation that governs those abortions. In a sense, a proposal that legal abortions be registered would be similar to proposals requiring such things as counseling or a cooling-off period before abortion: i.e., it would be a condition for the performance of the abortion. If statistics about abortions are not automatically registered, a just proposal to provide them would have to be broader, specifying, for example, that "all medical procedures must be registered, with a record of the ages of the patients undergoing the procedures, their place of residence, their marital status, and the reason for the procedure."

The UK Abortion Act 1967 supports abortion if there is "substantial risk" of a "seriously handicapped" child being born. There have been reports, however, of doctors aborting children with minor disabilities, such as cleft palate or cleft lip, which can be easily corrected. Objecting to this as an "abuse" of the law, pro-life legislators introduced a proposal, which only narrowly failed to become law, which would have required the nature of the disability to be specified when abortions were performed on grounds of disability.[17]

Legislation requiring the nature of the disability to be recorded poses the same problem, as stated above, for the registering of abortions generally: i.e., it is predicated on the intrinsically unjust legislation allowing abortions, and is therefore also intrinsically unjust.

A Consideration of Side Effects

All actions have consequences, and these may include some that, even if they are foreseen, are unintended and in no way included within the aims or goals of the acting person. Possible unintended consequences—side effects—must be borne in mind before voting for legislation in a concrete instance. A proper understanding of side effects in legislative voting should, however, be distinguished from the sort critiqued in Chapter 4, and I shall contrast the two now.

A Correct Understanding of Side Effects

The principle underpinning the theory of legislative voting advanced in this book is that it is always unethical to vote for a legislative proposal that is intrinsically unjust. The possibility of good consequences, such as the saving of lives or gains in support for the pro-life

17. The proposal was introduced during the committee stage of the bill that was subsequently enacted as the Human Fertilisation and Embryology Act 1990. The proposal was defeated by just one vote.

movement, does not justify voting for legislation that is intrinsically unjust. It does not follow, however, that one must always vote to enact legislation judged not to be intrinsically unjust. In a concrete instance there may be bad, albeit unintended, consequences of enacting such legislation and one must be attentive to these side effects before any legislative vote.

The previous section, listing a range of legislative proposals, identified many that could be formulated in such a way that they would not be intrinsically unjust: e.g., proposals to prohibit the procedures of IVF, stem cell research, chemical abortions like RU486, prostaglandin abortions, partial birth abortions; proposals to prohibit abortions in particular geographical locations or in particular medical premises; proposals to prohibit forced abortions; proposals to curb certain types of funding for abortions; proposals to grant doctors and others the right not to be involved in abortion, etc. Whether or not such proposals should be supported in a concrete instance would depend on a consideration of the circumstances and the anticipated consequences of supporting them. For example, before voting for legislation prohibiting prostaglandin abortions or chemical abortions one would need to be attentive to such things as the general law on abortion, what proportion of abortions were performed by these means, and whether the enactment of a prohibition would help to prevent those abortions from taking place or merely entail that they were performed by a different method. In particular, there would be a need to consider such things as whether the proposal would unhelpfully imply that pro-life concerns lay not with abortion per se but with those particular methods of abortion. Protracted campaigns often accompany legislation, and attentiveness to such side effects must be borne in mind before deciding whether to embark upon them.

One must be attentive to similar side effects when considering other legislation. Would support for a law prohibiting public funding of abortion contribute to the view that abortion was justified provided that it was paid for privately? Or would legislation to prohibit forced abortions, or to prohibit overseas funding for countries like China, in which women are forcibly aborted, have a seriously bad side effect of contributing to the view that abortion is objectionable only when forced upon a woman? The sort of legislation being discussed is not intrinsically unjust, but whether it is suitable to enact it requires a consideration of the side effects resulting from the particular circumstances, i.e., extrinsic factors.

In one country, a consideration of extrinsic factors and possible side effects might lead to a judgment not only that legislation to prohibit forced abortions was not intrinsically unjust but that its enactment was desirable and would be generally beneficial. In another country, the same considerations might lead to a judgment that the same legislation, though not intrinsically unjust, would be detrimental to the pro-life cause generally as it would undermine opposition to voluntary abortions. A side effect of enacting such legislation could be judged to be so damaging (when considered in proportion to the good sought by the legislation itself) that it would be unreasonable—in that place, and at that time—to vote for the legislation. In other words, when considered extrinsically, the legislation is not justified: extrinsic considerations, and an awareness of side effects, can lead to a judgment that it would be unreasonable—unjust—to vote for the legislation. Though it is not *intrinsically* unjust, the legislation could be judged to be *extrinsically unjust*, and accordingly should not be supported.

In brief, a judgment that legislation is intrinsically unjust is sufficient for legislators to know that they *cannot* vote ethically to enact it. It does not mean that they *should* vote for legislation provided that it is not intrinsically unjust. If negative side effects are identified and judged to be out of proportion to the good sought by the legislation itself, then it would be unreasonable—unjust—to vote for the legislation. On account of the circumstances, the legislation can be judged unreasonable or unjust. Legislators can vote only for just legislation, and cannot therefore support proposals that are judged to be either intrinsically or extrinsically unjust.

A Mistaken Understanding of Side Effects

A consideration of side effects has been central to some of the arguments favoring votes for (intrinsically unjust) restrictive legislation. John Finnis says that if abortion is legal up to, say, 24 weeks, a pro-life legislator could vote to grant legal protection to some unborn children by supporting a proposal of the form "Abortion is permissible up to 16 weeks."[18] He argues that the continued permission of abortion up to 16 weeks can be accepted—given that it is not (in his analysis) "intended" by the pro-life legislator—as "a bad side-effect."[19]

Finnis outlines some other bad side effects and says that it is about the fairness of accepting all these types of bad side effect that one must judge when deliberating whether to vote for the 16-week law to save unborn children between 16 and 24 weeks. The side effects he outlines are: (a) the bad effects on one's feelings and dispositions of voting for a law (which, as Finnis acknowledges, "does in fact permit abortion up to 16 weeks"), in concert with other legislators who positively support the legality of those abortions; (b) the danger that the "cooperation" of pro-life legislators with those who positively support the abortion legislation might lead to "formal cooperation" in some other morally bad project; (c) the comfort likely to be drawn "from the principal wrongdoer from one's cooperation, understood by the wrongdoer as endorsement of the wrongdoing"; (d) the scandal to third parties who might understand one's "cooperation" to be identical to that of the pro-abortion legislator; (e) the resentment of victims of the wrongdoing; (f) the impairing of one's witness to the moral truth.[20]

I have already argued, in Chapter 4, that voting to enact law may be regarded as a "collaborative" act, but it is not the sort of "cooperation" matter that Finnis suggests. Each legislator voting for Finnis's "16 week" proposal is expressing his or her will to enact it, and the actual enactment depends upon whether those expressing their will to enact it are in the majority group. Because their votes are separate, individual acts, the act of voting by one legislator in no way contributes to the act of voting by any other legislator. In what are, properly speaking, "cooperation" problems, there is a "principal wrongdoer" whose wrongdoing is assisted by the actions of others (whose actions may indeed be good). But when voting for legislation, there is no principal wrongdoer, whose action (i.e., the expression of his or her will that legislation be enacted) is assisted by any other voting legislator. Some of the "side ef-

18. John Finnis, "Unjust Laws in a Democratic Society," 601.
19. Ibid.
20. John Finnis, "Catholic Church and Public Policy Debates," 270–71.

fects" Finnis mentions would apply in genuine instances of material cooperation, but are beside the point in this instance as we are not dealing with a true cooperation matter. There are various problems with some of the other conditions he mentions. For example, who are "the victims of the wrong doing" who might feel resentment? It presumably cannot be the unborn children who are aborted. Is Finnis referring to those excluded from the protection of the law—such as those who are disabled or conceived after rape—who, if born, might feel resentment that their right to life was overlooked and that they have been treated as inferior to other human beings whose rights are guaranteed? If one is to take into account such side effects, how does one quantify them in relation to the supposed "good" of voting for the restrictive legislation? It should be observed that when concrete legislation has been introduced in the UK and other countries such side effects have been readily discounted in favor of the supposed "good" of restrictive legislation.

The goodness of the moral object of voting for legislation cannot be dissociated from the goodness of the legislation itself: whether the legislation is good or bad—just or unjust—is the first consideration. In concluding his remarks about side effects, Finnis indicates that his argument to support the enactment of restrictive legislation does not regard this as of any account:

> All the bad side effects which I have just listed as that third set are of particular importance in reflecting on the engagement of the Church itself, through its leaders and representatives, notably the bishops. For the mission of the Church is precisely to bear witness to the truth, particularly the moral truths at stake in Jesus' summons to repent and live a life worthy of the Lord. It is one thing for a legislator to vote for the law [i.e., a law specifying "Abortion is permissible up to 16 weeks" if the previous limit was 24 weeks], quite another for Catholic bishops to be heard as saying that such a law is acceptable.[21]

Finnis's statement appears to imply, unsatisfactorily, that the Church's witness to the truth is the witness of its bishops, and that the witness of Catholic legislators and others is, perhaps, less demanding.[22]

---

21. Ibid., 271.

22. As the Second Vatican Council teaches, the mission of bearing witness to the truth is the task not solely of bishops but the duty, according to their circumstances, of

Finnis's statement is, however, illuminating insofar as he appears to acknowledge that the law for which legislators would be voting to restrict abortion to 16 weeks is not acceptable. If the law is acceptable, why should not Catholic bishops say it is?[23] And if the law is not ac-

---

all the Church's members. See *Lumen gentium*, n. 17; *Ad gentes*, n. 23. Martin Kriele makes a similar point to Finnis's when he suggests that though a legislator may compromise in voting for restrictive legislation, *the Church* cannot be willing to compromise. See Kriele, "Influsso della Legislazione sulla Coscienza dei Cittadini," in Joblin and Tremblay, *I Cattolici e la Società Pluralista*, 97. My response to Finnis and Kriele is the same. The Church comprises all her members, including those who are legislators. If "the Church" cannot compromise, legislators who are part of the Church cannot compromise. It cannot be argued that because those in holy orders ought not generally to be engaged in secular matters (cf., *Lumen gentium*, n. 31) bishops should not comment on voting for restrictive legislation, and that this is a wholly secular matter which is proper and particular to the laity. Certainly those in holy orders should not normally be engaged in secular (political) matters—for example, indicating which political party should be favored in an election, or giving directives to Catholics when legislation on political *(ius civile)* matters are being decided—because these are matters on which Catholics (and others) should be free to make choices from a range of legitimate (i.e., acceptable) options. If, however, some options are not legitimate (i.e., not acceptable), bishops have a right and a duty to guide those making decisions so that only legitimate (acceptable) options are considered and chosen.

23. An objection has been made that I am not taking into account that saying that something is "acceptable" has different meanings in different contexts. The objector has suggested that normally one could not rightly say, "please cut off my hands" or "please use a condom," but that one could rightly say such things—because they would have a different meaning—in the context of being threatened with having one's arms cut off or with rape. Thus it has been suggested that Finnis's remarks would be like saying: "it would be one thing to ask for your hands, instead of your arms, to be cut off, and quite another for anyone to say that having your hands cut off was acceptable." My reply to the objection is that this is a false comparison, applicable only if we were considering the legitimacy of encouraging "moderate" pro-abortion legislators to vote for a "lesser-evil" abortion law when they were inclined to vote for a "greater evil." The issue that concerns us, however, is whether *pro-life legislators* themselves (who are not victims acting under duress) can legitimately vote for the same "lesser evil." Given that support for restrictive legislation normally involves pro-life legislators in collaborating with pro-abortion legislators, a fitting analogy would be one that considered whether a morally upright person could freely choose to collaborate with evil-doers in cutting off a hostage's hands rather than refrain from collaboration and let the hostage endure the "greater evil" of having not just his hands but his arms cut off by the evil-doers acting alone. If it were judged—as I believe it would be rightly judged—that it would be illic-

ceptable—as Finnis seems to be acknowledging—then it is a contradiction for legislators to vote for it, because a vote to enact any law constitutes a judgment that, "yes, this is acceptable." A sound ethical theory of legislative voting must avoid such an inconsistency, and practical decisions as to what may be supported to further the pro-life cause depend crucially on identifying whether specific legislative proposals are (i) intrinsically unjust (and thus fundamentally unacceptable), or (ii) unjust, but not intrinsically unjust (i.e., not acceptable in a particular instance in view of the circumstances), or (iii) just (and therefore acceptable). The acceptability—justness—of the proposal is the primary consideration.

---

it to collaborate in cutting off the hostage's hands, this judgment should be similarly applied to the analogous situation of voting for restrictive legislation.

8. VOTING OPPORTUNITIES

Legislative voting involves more than voting at the final stage for a bill to be enacted as law. Legislators are faced with complex considerations, not only with respect to the justness of of a bill when it is presented for enactment but also with respect to the appropriateness of supporting a bill in its entirety at an early stage of its passage, or of supporting particular proposals, considered individually, as a bill makes progress and is examined in greater detail.

In order to discuss the range of legislative voting opportunities I shall consider a simplified system that corresponds to the systems of many legislatures. In some countries, notably those with a codified system of law, there may be some other opportunities. Although such opportunities are not considered directly here, the relevant principles are discernible from the examples I shall give. In some countries, such as the United States, the scope for legislation may be restricted on account of a judgment from the judiciary claiming constitutional support for abortion, or on account of indisputable (i.e., explicit, written) constitutional support. Irrespective of such restrictions the principle that legislators can enact only just legislation is to be upheld.

In the simplified system I am proposing, I shall discuss the relevant considerations affecting votes at three different stages during the passage of legislation:

Stage A: The initial vote to decide whether a bill, presented to the legislature, is to be accepted as a basis for legislation and considered further.

Stage B: This consists of votes on individual parts of the bill, and a range of votes affecting the bill in a variety of ways may be encountered at this stage. It may be that only some of the legislators, forming a committee, are able to vote at this stage.

Stage C: A vote to decide whether the bill, possibly amended at stage B, should become law, i.e., whether the bill fulfills the criteria of law (notably, justness) and its enactment is suitable at that time and place. A stage-C vote has this meaning even if the agreement of another legislative chamber or of a head of state is required before a bill is actually enacted as law.

I shall present a range of bills and amendments that could be introduced over a period of time and shall indicate how it seems to me that pro-life legislators could rightly vote. Judgments that legislators *cannot* vote for some proposals (i.e., a bill at stages A or C, or amendments at stage B) mean that it would be wrong, in principle, for them to do so. Judgments that legislators *could* vote for some proposals do not imply that they *should* vote for them in every instance. In a concrete situation legislators would have to consider not only the legislation but also the circumstances and the side effects of voting, as described at the end of the previous chapter.

The following discussion does not focus precisely on the type of legislation that should be *proposed by* pro-life legislators, but rather on how they should or could vote when faced with legislation proposed by others. It assumes that the pro-life legislators have become members of the legislature some years after the enactment of abortion legislation. We begin by situating ourselves in 1980, in an imaginary legislature in an imaginary country that allows abortion under the Abortion Act 1970. This Act corresponds to the "Typical Abortion Act" presented in the previous chapter:

Abortion Act 1970
An Act to amend and clarify the law relating to the termination of pregnancy

BE IT ENACTED:

1. Abortion shall not be a punishable crime under the criminal law if it is:

(a) Performed before the end of the 24th week of pregnancy, at the request of or with the consent of the pregnant woman, with or without a medical reason;

(b) Performed before the end of the 30th week of pregnancy, at the request of or with the consent of the pregnant woman, if tests indicate that the fetus, if born, is likely to be disabled;

(c) Performed at any stage of the pregnancy, at the request of or with the consent of the pregnant woman, if there are reasonable grounds for believing that the pregnancy resulted from a criminal act.

2. Abortions designated by clause 1 cannot be performed outside publicly funded hospitals or private premises specifically licensed by local authorities to perform abortions.

3. Doctors have a right not to participate in abortion procedures if they have any moral or religious objections.

4. Local health authorities may determine whether any woman in their area who is in receipt of state benefits, and who incurs expenses in having an abortion in private licensed premises, may reclaim expenses incurred.

5. The Protection of Human Life Act 1860 is amended in accordance with the provisions of clause 1.

6. This Act may be cited as the Abortion Act 1970.

The Unborn Children (Protection) Bill of 1980

As a result of elections, the composition of the legislature in 1980 has changed dramatically from what it was ten years before, and a pro-life legislator introduces a bill to prohibit all abortions.

UNBORN CHILDREN (PROTECTION) BILL 1980
A Bill to protect unborn children from abortion

BE IT ENACTED:

1. The Abortion Act 1970 is repealed.

2. The unborn child is recognized as a living human being from the time of conception/fertilization, is accorded the full dignity and status of a human being, and is entitled to the same legal protection before as after birth.

3. It is unlawful for a doctor or any other person to participate or in any way to assist in an abortion. Anyone convicted of participation or assistance in an abortion will face the range of punishments established for the crime of homicide.

4. This Act may be cited as the Unborn Children (Protection) Act 1980.

Stage A

[Vote 1]

Comment: A vote in favor of the bill at this first stage would be justified. The bill is an excellent basis for promoting a just law. In voting for it individual legislators need not necessarily agree with all its provisions. For example, some pro-life legislators may have concerns about the justness or appropriateness of specifying the same punishment for abortion as for homicide generally. A legislator voting for the bill at this stage is not voting to enact it as law but to accept it as a basis from which to proceed, and the possibility exists of its being amended at a later stage.

[The bill proceeds after a majority vote for it.]

Stage B

Amendment 1

In clause 3, after each of the two occurrences of the words "an abortion," insert the words: ". . . unless the abortion is considered beneficial to the pregnant woman's physical or mental health."

[Vote 2]

Comment: This amendment provides an exception to the unlawfulness of abortion. Irrespective of who proposed the amendment, and irrespective of whether it would be interpreted in a narrow way or more liberally to allow abortion for virtually any reason, legislators could not licitly support the proposal. It would seem appropriate to vote against the amendment.

Amendment 2

Insert a new clause: "Those who participate in or in any way assist an abortion, where pregnancy is reasonably believed to be the consequence of a criminal assault on the pregnant woman, will not be guilty of any offence under the law."

[Vote 3]

Comment: In deciding whether they should vote for this amendment legislators should not be influenced by whether the amendment was introduced by a legislator who thinks that, as a matter of principle, abortion should be an option for those who become pregnant as a result of a criminal assault, or by whether it was introduced by a legislator who thinks that such abortions are unethical, but that the bill as a whole has no chance of being enacted unless this amendment were accepted. Similarly, the justness of voting for the amendment does not depend on the voting legislator's ethical or pragmatic stance. The relevant consideration is whether the amendment is just: is it just to withhold legal protection from those unborn children conceived (or thought to be conceived) as a result of a criminal assault? In line with the consistent argument of this book, this must be answered in the negative. The amendment is unjust and it would therefore be unjust to support it, irrespective of one's motives or the consequences of not voting for it.

Amendment 3

Insert a new clause: "Those who participate in or in any way assist an abortion, undertaken to prevent a woman giving birth to a severely disabled child, will not be guilty of any offence under the law."

[Vote 4]

Comment: Voting for this amendment would be unjust for the same reasons already given for amendments 1 and 2. Pro-life legislators could not vote for the amendment and argue that the law was not precisely "supporting" abortion of severely disabled unborn children, any more than they could argue that the Abortion Act 1970 was possibly acceptable because it does not precisely "support" abortion. The amendment (and any law that contained it) is intrinsically unjust for failing to provide the protection that should be accorded to severely disabled children who are positively excluded from protection by this amendment.

Amendment 4

Amend clause 3, replacing "the range of punishments established for the crime of homicide" with "a punishment up to a maximum sentence of eight years in prison."

[Vote 5]

Comment: Specific punishments for particular offenses are not established as an absolute principle but can be determined in the light of various social, cultural, or political considerations. It is legitimate for the punishment for abortion, like that for other crimes, to vary in different jurisdictions. One could argue that the punishment for abortion should be the same as that for killing someone after birth. John Finnis, for example, in saying "what the law [on abortion] should be" says that because the unborn are human beings with the rights of persons from conception, a consistent defense of those rights requires that there should be no difference of principle between abortion and other forms of homicide: "Full and equal protection of the state's laws against homicide should be accepted as extended to the unborn. There should be no special law prohibiting abortion."[1] The possible inconsistency between what Finnis says the law "should be" and his willingness to support laws that fall short of this is not my concern at the moment. The relevant question is whether it necessarily follows that the punishment for abortion must be the same as the punishment for other killings. On this point I am undecided.[2] It would seem to be reasonable to argue that the punishment for abortion should be the same as the punishment for killing someone after birth. However, it would also seem to be reasonable to argue that all killings need not have an identical punishment, and that the main concern should be whether the specified punishment is a sufficient deterrent for the law to be accepted as one providing appropriate protection to those whose lives might otherwise be at risk. If the amendment specifying a maximum penalty of eight years in prison were intrinsically unjust, then this amendment (and any bill containing it) could not be licitly supported. If intrinsic unjustness is

---

1. Finnis, "Legal Status of the Unborn Baby," 8.

2. I am also undecided as to who, precisely, must be punished. It seems reasonable to punish those who perform, assist in, or facilitate an abortion. I am undecided whether women undergoing an abortion should also be liable for prosecution and punishment. This may be required if the law is to give adequate protection to the unborn, in which case it seems reasonable to take into account, when establishing the punishment, the emotional and psychological pressures that might lead some desperate women to abort. Such pressures are recognized by the lower punishments specified in the laws on infanticide (by the mother) in some countries.

not established, legislators would be free to decide whether or not to support the amendment, taking into account the range of circumstantial factors such as the advantages or disadvantages generally of the considered penalty being accepted as law, as well as the prospects of the bill's enactment after the decision made at this amendment stage.

Stage C

[Vote 6]

Following the votes for each amendment at stage B, the bill presented at stage C is different from that of stage A. The result of the votes is that amendments 1 and 4 are defeated and amendments 2 and 3 accepted. The bill, as presented for its final vote, is as follows:

UNBORN CHILDREN (PROTECTION) BILL 1980
A Bill to protect unborn children from abortion

BE IT ENACTED:

1. The Abortion Act 1970 is repealed.

2. The unborn child is recognized as a living human being from the time of conception/fertilization, is accorded the full dignity and status of a human being, and is entitled to the same legal protection before as after birth.

3. It is unlawful for a doctor or any other person to participate or in any way to assist in an abortion. Anyone convicted of participation or assistance in an abortion will face the range of punishments established for the crime of homicide.

4. Those who participate in or in any way assist an abortion, to prevent a woman giving birth to a severely disabled child, or where pregnancy is reasonably believed to be the consequence of a criminal assault on the pregnant woman, will not be guilty of any offence under the law.

5. This Act may be cited as the Unborn Children (Protection) Act 1980.

Comment: The vote at this stage constitutes approval for the bill's becoming law. The legislation would achieve some good things, namely the repeal of the Abortion Act 1970, and protection for most unborn children. However, it would be an intrinsically unjust law, as it specifically fails to provide protection for those unborn children excluded by clause 4. Pro-life legislators could not justify voting for the law by claiming that they were voting solely to enact the "good" parts of it, because their vote constitutes an act of voting to enact the whole of the law, a law that is intrinsically unjust and therefore can never be licitly supported.

It cannot be argued that pro-life legislators have already demonstrated their commitment to all the unborn by voting for the bill at stage A, because a stage-A vote does not objectively demonstrate such a commitment. After all, those legislators who voted for the stage-B amendments and supported the bill at stage C only because those amendments were included (i.e., they believe—as a matter of principle—that the law should allow abortions in the specified instances) would probably also have supported it at stage A. Nor can it be argued that pro-life legislators may support the bill at this stage if they have demonstrated their opposition at stage B to the amendments that now constitute clause 4. The object of the act of voting at stage C is not affected by what has been supported or opposed at other stages.

Morally upright (pro-life) legislators would be acting unethically if they voted to enact this intrinsically unjust law. Normally they would be obliged to vote against such legislation. However, the situation is that if this legislation is not enacted another intrinsically unjust law, the Abortion Act 1970, allowing more abortions, will remain in force. It would be legitimate to tolerate the enactment of the more restrictive 1980 legislation by not voting against it, i.e., by abstaining from voting, in accordance with the principle of toleration *(non impedire)* discussed in Chapter 2. Legislators could not, however, vote in favor of the bill. Because the bill is intrinsically unjust, the consequences of voting or not voting for it do not affect the judgment that it is unethical to vote for its enactment.

Although pro-abortion legislators might vote against the 1980 bill precisely because they support the Abortion Act 1970 (which the bill will repeal), pro-life legislators voting against the 1980 bill would not be responsible for the continuation of the Abortion Act 1970. A vote against the 1980 bill or an abstention does not, in itself, constitute a vote of support for the Abortion Act 1970 but is rather an action demonstrating that the 1980 bill itself is not supported.

Result of final vote: By a narrow minority the bill is defeated. Abortion is still allowed under the terms of the Abortion Act 1970.

The Unborn Children (Protection) Bill of 1982

Having gauged the opinion of all the members of the legislature, one of the supporters of the final version of the Unborn Children (Protection) Bill of 1980 realizes that several of those who had abstained from voting or who had voted against the bill would be willing to support it if it were reintroduced, and that there is a good chance that the bill would be enacted. This legislator therefore decides to reintroduce the bill as the Unborn Children (Protection) Bill of 1982:

UNBORN CHILDREN (PROTECTION) BILL 1982
A Bill to protect unborn children from abortion

BE IT ENACTED:

1. The Abortion Act 1970 is repealed.

2. The unborn child is recognized as a living human being from the time of conception/fertilization, is accorded the full dignity and status of a human being, and is entitled to the same legal protection before as after birth.

3. It is unlawful for a doctor or any other person to participate or in any way to assist in an abortion. Anyone convicted of participation or assistance in an abortion will face the range of punishments established for the crime of homicide.

4. Those who participate in or in any way assist an abortion, to prevent a woman giving birth to a severely disabled child, or where pregnancy is reasonably believed to be the consequence of a criminal assault on the pregnant woman, will not be guilty of any offence under the law.

5. This Act may be cited as the Unborn Children (Protection) Act 1982.

Stage A

[Vote 7]

Comment: It will be observed that, apart from the year, this 1982 bill is identical to the 1980 bill when it was presented at stage C. Although legislators could not justly support that 1980 bill at stage C, they could support it now at stage A. In voting for the bill at stage A they are not voting to enact *this bill* as law but to accept it as a basis from which a just and acceptable law may eventually emerge. Even if pro-life legislators who voted against or abstained at stage C in 1980 thought there was little prospect of gaining sufficient support for amendments to render the bill just, nevertheless they could licitly support the bill at this stage if they intended to do everything possible to render it just. They might think that the very introduction of the bill would be profitable to the pro-life cause in opening up the issue and giving them the opportunity to promote pro-life opposition to all abortions.

When judging how to vote, legislators must be attentive to legislative procedures. For example, if the longer title of the bill stated not "a Bill to protect unborn children from abortion," but "a Bill to repeal the 1970 Abortion Act and to prohibit abortion unless there is an indication of fetal disability or criminal assault," it might be the case that legislators would be unable, because of the legislative procedures, to table an amendment to clause 4. If this were the case, pro-life legislators could not vote for the bill at stage A because there would be no possibility of its being an acceptable basis for formulating just law.

Although a vote in support of the bill could be justified, pro-life legislators could also be justified in deciding to vote against the bill, or in abstaining. It might be thought that instead of helping to promote a pro-life view, the passage of the bill would in fact help to reinforce a mentality in favor of abortion for disabled babies or after criminal assaults. Because the reason for one's vote is not always obvious, it would be appropriate for all pro-life legislators to express publicly their total opposition to all abortion to avoid the possibility of confusion or scandal as a result of their votes.

[The bill proceeds after a majority vote for it.]

Stage B

Amendment 1

Delete clause 4.

[Vote 8]

Comment: By voting in favor of this amendment, the clause allowing abortion in certain instances would be removed. Given that this clause has no rightful place in any legislation, pro-life legislators would be justified in voting in favor of the amendment. Irrespective of how pro-life legislators voted at stage A, they would be entitled to vote in favor of this amendment. Given that the bill would be just if clause 4 were removed, it would seem inappropriate to vote against the amendment or to abstain.

Stage C

[Vote 9]

Amendment 1 was defeated, as were other amendment votes (which do not need to be detailed), and the bill at stage C is identical to the bill at stage A.

Comment: Although pro-life legislators could have licitly voted for the bill at stage A, they could not licitly vote for it at stage C, just as they could not licitly vote for the 1980 bill at stage C. Votes for the same bill at stages A and C have different objects.

Result of final vote: A narrow majority votes in favor of the bill and it is enacted as the Unborn Children (Protection) Act 1982. The Abortion Act 1970 is repealed and abortion is a punishable crime unless undertaken to prevent a woman's giving birth to a disabled child or unless pregnancy is reasonably believed to be the result of a criminal assault.

Comment: It is likely that, compared with the Abortion Act 1970, there would be a great reduction in abortions under the Unborn Children (Protection) Act. Nevertheless the new Act is intrinsically unjust. Those who voted for its enactment at stage C would be responsible for enacting an intrinsically unjust law that allowed some abortions. (Indeed, the new Act would allow some abortions that were not previously allowed. Whereas the 1970 Act allowed abortion in cases of disability up to the end of the 30th week of pregnancy, the 1982 Act specifies no time limit, so abortion in cases of disability could be allowed up until birth. Even if the 1982 Act had maintained the same 30th-week limit, it would still have been intrinsically unjust.) Those who voted against the 1982 Act would not be responsible for the abortions it allows, nor would they have been responsible, if the Act had not been passed, for the abortions taking place under the previous law. Those pro-life legislators who voted in favor of the bill at stage A but not in favor at stage C would have contributed to the bill's enactment. However, their action at stage A—undertaken for a good purpose and with no bad intention—would have been a good action that others took advantage of for a bad purpose. It could be said that those pro-life legislators voting at stage A had cooperated materially (and licitly) in the evil act (performed by others) of the subsequent enactment of the intrinsically unjust abortion law.

The Abortion Bill of 1986

After four years of "restrictive" abortion legislation, and after an election in which many pro-life legislators lose their places in the legislature, a bill is introduced to provide greater access to abortion.

Abortion Bill 1986
A Bill to provide greater access to abortion

BE IT ENACTED:

1. The Unborn Children (Protection) Act 1982 is repealed.
2. A woman has a right to abortion up to the 20th week of pregnancy if, in the judgment of one doctor, this would be beneficial to her physical or mental health.
3. A woman has a right to abortion up to the 26th week of pregnancy if there is evidence that the fetus is likely to be born with a serious disability.
4. Abortions may be performed only by qualified medical practitioners and only in publicly funded or publicly registered health facilities.

5. Any person found guilty of performing an abortion not authorized by this Act will receive a prison sentence of up to six months
6. This Act may be cited as the Abortion Act 1986.

Stage A

[Vote 10]

Comment: This bill clearly does not provide a suitable basis for a just law, and pro-life legislators could not justly vote for it. It would seem appropriate to vote against it and not to abstain. A vote against the bill does not constitute a vote in favor of the intrinsically unjust Unborn Children (Protection) Act 1982, which will remain in force if this bill is defeated.

[The bill proceeds after a majority vote for it.]

Stage B

Amendment 1
Amend clause 2, replacing "20th week" with "26th week."

[Vote 11]

Comment: Pro-life legislators cannot support this amendment and it seems appropriate to vote against it. Some legislators may vote against the amendment precisely because they support clause 2 as it stands. However, by voting against the amendment pro-life legislators are not expressing support for an unamended clause 2, but, rather, their withholding of support for the amendment itself.

Pro-life legislators would recognize the impossibility of amending the bill sufficiently so that it would be just and worthy of support by stage C. Even if they are resolved to vote against the bill in its entirety at stage C, this does not absolve them of their responsibility of exercising just votes, such as voting against this amendment, at stage B.

[The amendment is defeated.]

Amendment 2
Amend clause 2, replacing "20th week" with "16th week."

[Vote 12]

Comment: This amendment has been considered only because amendment 1 was defeated. One would expect those legislators who actually thought the law should allow abortion up to 26 weeks to have proposed and supported amendment 1. Similarly amendment 2 might be proposed and supported by "less extreme" abortion supporters who believe that the law should allow abortion no later than 16 weeks. It is possible, however, that amendment 2 was proposed by a pro-life legislator who was resolved to vote against the bill at stage C and who, as a matter of principle, was opposed to all abortions. This pro-life legislator might think that he and other pro-life colleagues should unite with "less extreme" abortion supporters in order to restrict the scope of abortion allowed under the law if this bill is enacted.

Pro-life legislators might have good motives in voting for the amendment, but it would be unjust for them to do so. A judgment as to the goodness of one's vote for the amendment does not depend on who introduced it, or the legislators' individual motives or views on abortion. A vote in favor of this amendment has an objective meaning that, considered individually, this is a proposal that can be licitly supported. In supporting the amendment at this stage, legislators should be considering whether the amendment, considered individually, fulfills the requirements of good law, to be included in a bill for enactment. Considered individually, this amendment is incapable of being good law, and so legislators cannot vote licitly in favor of it. Whether they should vote against it or abstain from voting would be a matter of prudential judgment.

Amendment 3

Delete clause 2.

[Vote 13]

Comment: Clause 2, supporting abortion up to 20 weeks if it is judged by a doctor to be beneficial to a woman's physical or mental health, is entirely unjust and no law should include such a proposal. Pro-life legislators could licitly vote for the amendment, even if they voted against the bill in its entirety at stages A and C. A vote in favor of this amendment does not constitute support for any other clause of the bill; this vote is concerned only with deleting unjust clause 2.

Amendment 4

Delete clause 3.

[Vote 14]

Comment: Clause 3 supports abortion up to 26 weeks if the fetus is likely to be born with a serious disability. Pro-life legislators could licitly support this amendment in the same way that they could licitly have supported amendment 3.

Amendment 5

Insert a new clause: "Women who have a right to abortion under the law must receive counseling from a center independent of the abortion provider, and be given full information about the development of the unborn child and the abortion procedure."

[Vote 15]

Comment: A pro-life legislator who thought that counseling might help to deter women from having abortions that would be allowed if this bill were enacted could have proposed this amendment. Alternatively, it could have been proposed by an abortion-favoring legislator who either wanted to demonstrate support for properly informed free choice on abortion or thought the bill's chances of success would be greater with this amendment. The judgment as to how a pro-life legislator should vote is not, however, dependent on who proposed the amendment or the reasons for its proposal. The first consideration is whether the proposal itself is just. This amendment is predicated on the acceptance of a right to abortion, and essentially it establishes a condition on the exercise of that right. It is, therefore, intrinsically unjust and it cannot be licitly supported. Legislators can make a prudential judgment as to whether they vote against the amendment or abstain from voting.

Amendment 6

Insert a new clause: "Medical practitioners have a right not to be involved in abortion procedures."

[Vote 16]

Comment: This sort of amendment was discussed in some detail in Chapter 7. Like other amendments it can be considered in isolation and a vote in favor of it does not constitute support for any other part of the bill. Medical practitioners have a moral right not to be involved in abortion and it is legitimate to support human law that accords with the moral law. Legislators could justly support the amendment.

Amendment 7

In clause 4 delete the words: "publicly funded or."

[Vote 17]

Comment: Clause 4 reads: "Abortions may be performed only by qualified medical practitioners and only in publicly funded or publicly registered health facilities." Legislators voting in favor of amendment 7 are voting solely that the words "publicly funded or" be deleted. It is possible for other amendments to focus on other parts of the clause, e.g., to delete the words "only by qualified medical practitioners and" or "public registered health facilities" or "or publicly registered," or to add something to the clause. This possibility helps one to understand why, when voting simply to delete the three words mentioned in amendment 7, legislators cannot be said to be voting in favor of the wording "Abortions may be performed only by qualified medical practitioners and only in publicly registered health facilities." If amendment 7 were passed and the rest of the clause remained unchanged and subsequently enacted, then the law would not specifically authorize abortions in publicly funded facilities. Equally, however, it would not prohibit them. It would seem that the relevant authorities would be free to decide whether the publicly funded health facilities for which they had responsibility did or did not provide abortions. It is legitimate, at this stage, to vote to remove an unjust part from a bill, when one's vote is concerned solely with the removal of that unjust part, i.e., when the vote does not objectively constitute support for other parts of the bill. Pro-life legislators could justly support this amendment.

Amendment 8
Insert a new clause: "This Act does not apply to region X."

[Vote 18]

Comment: In the previous chapter I explained why pro-life legislators could vote for this sort of proposal. By supporting this amendment pro-life legislators are not indicating their support for the Act in any other region (as they would if the amendment had stated, "This Act applies in regions W, Y, and Z, but not in region X"). The justness of voting for the amendment is not determined by whether its sponsor supports or opposes abortion. The proposal is not intrinsically unjust, but whether it would in fact be just (i.e., reasonable) to support it at any particular time or place would depend on a consideration of the intended and unintended (though possibly foreseen) consequences of it being accepted. It may, for example, be the case that much opposition to the bill comes from legislators from region X and that a good chance of the bill's being defeated at the final stage will be lost if this amendment is accepted.[3]

Stage C

[Vote 19]

Following the votes for each amendment at stage B, the bill presented at stage C is different from that of stage A. The result of the votes is that amendments 1, 2, 3, and 4 were defeated, and amendments 5, 6, 7, and 8 were accepted. The bill, as presented for its final vote, is as follows:

---

3. The UK Abortion Act 1967 includes a clause that reads, "This Act does not extend to Northern Ireland." A report in the *Guardian* (17 Aug. 1999) claimed that "the province [of Northern Ireland] was excluded from the Act because resistance would have hindered or even prevented the passing of the Act."

Abortion Bill 1986
A Bill to provide greater access to abortion

BE IT ENACTED:

1. The Unborn Children (Protection) Act 1982 is repealed.

2. A woman has a right to abortion up to the 20th week of pregnancy if, in the judgment of one doctor, this would be beneficial to her physical or mental health.

3. A woman has a right to abortion up to the 26th week of pregnancy if there is evidence that the fetus is likely to be born with a serious disability.

4. Abortions may be performed only by qualified medical practitioners and only in publicly registered health facilities.

5. Women who have a right to abortion under the law must receive counseling from a center independent of the abortion provider, and be given full information about the development of the unborn child and the abortion procedure.

6. Medical practitioners have a right not to be involved in abortion procedures.

7. Any person found guilty of performing an abortion not authorized by this Act will receive a prison sentence of up to six months

8. This Act does not apply to region X.

9. This Act may be cited as the Abortion Act 1986.

Comment: The bill is clearly unjust and cannot be supported. A vote against it would be definitely justified. Though some legislators might vote against the bill because they, in principle, support the existing abortion law—the Unborn Children (Protection) Act 1982—a vote against the bill at stage C does not constitute a vote in support of the (intrinsically unjust, though more restrictive) 1982 Act; it constitutes rejection of the 1986 bill.

Result of final vote: A majority votes in favor of the bill and it is enacted as the Abortion Act 1986. The Unborn Children (Protection) Act 1982 is repealed and women have a right to abortion subject to the conditions of the 1986 Act.

Comment: Pro-life legislators who voted against the bill at stages A and C and who gave no support to any unjust amendments have not acted unethically. Not only have they avoided evil but they have performed good actions by casting just votes. The votes of pro-life legislators have also made a positive difference to the bill. Just votes at stage B (e.g., voting against amendment 1 and for amendment 7) ensured that the bill did not include even more abortion-favoring provisions, and other just votes (e.g., supporting amendments 6 and 8) introduced some positive additions to the bill. Although it was not ethical for pro-life legislators to support amendment 5 which introduced the new clause 5, they could have tolerated it by not voting against the amendment.

The Abortion (Amendment) Bill of 1992

Six years after the enactment of the Abortion Act 1986, there is a concern among the public and legislators alike that abortions are being obtained too easily. It is commonly recognized that by saying abortion would be beneficial to her mental health under clause 2 of the Abortion Act 1986, any woman can obtain an abortion. A legislator who objects to this easy access to abortion introduces a bill to remove clause 2 from the 1986 Act.

ABORTION (AMENDMENT) BILL 1992
A Bill to amend the Abortion Act 1986 in order to prohibit abortions performed for the physical or mental health of the pregnant woman

BE IT ENACTED:

1. Remove clause 2 of the Abortion Act 1986.
2. This Act may be cited as the Abortion (Amendment) Act 1992 and the principal Act and this Act may be cited together as the Abortion Acts 1986 and 1992.

Stage A

[Vote 20]

Comment: As it stands the bill does not satisfy the criteria for being enacted as law, but this is not what is being decided at this stage. The relevant question is whether it is an acceptable basis from which to begin the process that may result in the enactment of just law. The longer title of the bill describes its purpose of prohibiting abortions performed for the physical or mental health of the pregnant woman. If this meant that legislators would be unable to propose and vote for amendments, say, to remove clause 3 of the Abortion Act 1986, then this would remove the possibility of changing the bill so that it could become just and suitable for enactment. In this case, pro-life legislators could not vote for the bill at stage A. Whether they should vote against the bill or abstain would be a matter of prudential judgment. If there were a possibility of amending the bill so that it could become just and suitable as law, then pro-life legislators could decide, taking into account the circumstances and using their prudential judgment, whether it would be better to vote for or against or to abstain at this stage.

Result of stage-A vote: A majority opposes the bill and it makes no further progress. The law on abortion is still governed by the Abortion Act 1986.

Comment: Let us assume that this bill had progressed through the legislature, and that the same bill was being voted upon at stage C. It is worth comparing a vote for the bill at stage C with vote 13, above, which occurred at stage B of the 1986 legislation. At vote 13, pro-life legislators could licitly vote for the clause of the bill to be deleted because at stage B the different parts of a bill can be considered in isolation. In voting for the enactment of the 1992 bill legislators would not be voting to delete a clause from a bill (which is not yet law) but voting for a bill *to amend a law*. Some consequences of removing the clause from the Abortion Act 1986 might be good, even very good. However, the key question would not be whether there might be some good consequences but whether it would be a good act to vote for the bill amending the intrinsically unjust 1986 law. As I argued in the previous chapter, the justness of an amendment bill is determined by considering the justness of the original act as amended. This 1992 bill would constitute intrinsically unjust legislation that could not be licitly supported.

The Abortion (Amendment) Bill of 1995

After nearly ten years of easy access to abortion, there is general acceptance of the Abortion Act 1986. Some supporters of abortion, however, object to the requirement that women must receive counseling prior to obtaining an abortion. They maintain that counseling should be available for those who want it but that it should not be a legal requirement. In particular, they claim that counseling can inflict mental suffering on some women before they have abortions, and that in some areas women are unable to have abortions as early as they would wish because of the counseling requirement. A bill sponsored by a pro-abortion legislator is introduced to amend the 1986 Act so that counseling will not be a legal requirement.

ABORTION (AMENDMENT) BILL 1995
A Bill to amend the Abortion Act 1986 to remove some restrictions to abortion

BE IT ENACTED:

1. Remove clause 5 of the Abortion Act 1986.

2. This Act may be cited as the Abortion (Amendment) Act of 1995 and the principal Act and this Act may be cited together as the Abortion Acts 1986 and 1995.

Stage A

[Vote 21]

Comment: The general purpose of the bill, as indicated by the longer title, is to increase access to abortions. It seems highly unlikely, if not impossible, for this bill to be amended so that it could become just legislation. However, even if there were the technical possibility that the bill could be amended in such a way that a just law prohibiting all abortions was achieved, such a bill would not ordinarily be regarded as a suitable basis from which to achieve just legislation.

The particular purpose of the bill is to amend the Abortion Act by removing clause 5. This specifies that before having an abortion women must receive counseling and full information about the development of unborn children and the abortion procedure. Clause 5 was inserted into the 1986 Act at vote 15 (stage B), above. Because the clause, considered individually, is predicated on an acceptance of abortion and is thus intrinsically unjust, pro-life legislators could not licitly vote for it at vote 15. This does not mean, however, that they must now support the bill to remove it. If, as may well be the case, the advantages of its remaining within the intrinsically unjust Abortion Act 1986 are greater than any disadvantages, then pro-life legislators, provided that their votes are just, can choose whatever best serves the pro-life cause.

The amendment bill at stage A can be judged an unsuitable basis for legislation and pro-life legislators can therefore vote justly against the bill. Voting against the bill does not constitute support for clause 5, let alone support for an unamended Abortion Act 1986. It merely signifies that legislators do not accept the bill as a satisfactory basis from which to develop a just and suitable law. Voting "against" at stage A is a vote against the bill, not a vote for clause 5.

[The bill proceeds after a majority votes for it.]

Stage B

Amendment 1

In clause 4 of the Abortion Act 1986 remove the words "and only in publicly registered health facilities."

[Vote 22]

Comment: Clause 4 of the Abortion Act 1986 states, "Abortions may be performed only by qualified medical practitioners and only in publicly registered health facilities." If amendment 1 is accepted and the bill subsequently enacted, then the law would not specify where abortions must be performed. Qualified medical practitioners could perform abortions anywhere. Because abortions would be subject to less regulation, women might find access to them easier and possibly cheaper, and this might result in more abortions being performed. It is also possible that the situation would involve greater risks to the life or health of women undergoing abortions.

All things considered, it would seem appropriate to vote against the amendment. In so doing pro-life legislators would not be voting wholly or partly *for* clause 4 of the Act itself (i.e., legislators would not be voting that abortions be performed only in publicly registered health facilities), but rather voting *against* an acceptance of the amendment as part of the amendment bill.

Amendment 2

Insert a new clause: "Women are entitled to abortions free of charge. Private facilities can charge the relevant government health authority for any abortion services they provide."

[Vote 23]

Comment: Pro-life legislators should vote against the amendment, which, if enacted, might encourage more abortions. Government health authorities would have to pay for abortions with public money (e.g., money raised by taxes) and it is legitimate to try to prevent public money being spent on immoral projects. By voting against the amendment, pro-life legislators are not suggesting that abortion is acceptable provided that it is paid for privately.

Stage C

[Vote 24]

Following the votes for each amendment at stage B, the bill presented at stage C is different from that at stage A. Amendment 2 was defeated, but amendment 1 was passed. The bill, as presented for its final vote, reads as follows:

ABORTION (AMENDMENT) BILL 1995
A Bill to amend the Abortion Act 1986 to remove some restrictions to abortion

BE IT ENACTED:

1. Remove clause 5 of the Abortion Act 1986.

2. In clause 4 of the Abortion Act 1986 remove the words "and only in publicly registered health facilities."

3. This Act may be cited as the Abortion (Amendment) Act 1995 and the principal Act and this Act may be cited together as the Abortion Acts 1986 and 1995.

Comment: The bill is clearly unjust and cannot be supported. There would seem to be no justification for not voting against it. A vote against the Abortion (Amendment) Bill does not signify approval for the unamended Abortion Act 1986.

Result of final vote: A majority votes in favor of the bill and it is enacted as the Abortion (Amendment) Act 1995. Abortion is now legal in accordance with the Abortion Act 1986, as amended by the Abortion (Amendment) Act 1995. The law on abortion is as follows:

THE ABORTION ACT 1986
AS AMENDED BY THE ABORTION (AMENDMENT) ACT 1995

BE IT ENACTED:

1. The Unborn Children (Protection) Act 1982 is repealed.
2. A woman has a right to abortion up to the 20th week of pregnancy if, in the judgment of one doctor, this would be beneficial to her physical or mental health.
3. A woman has a right to abortion up to the 26th week of pregnancy if there is evidence that the fetus is likely to be born with a serious disability.
4. Abortions may be performed only by qualified medical practitioners.
5. Medical practitioners have a right not to be involved in abortion procedures.
6. Any person found guilty of performing an abortion not authorized by this Act will receive a prison sentence of up to six months.
7. This Act does not apply to region X.
8. The Abortion Act 1986 and the Abortion (Amendment) Act 1995 may be cited together as the Abortion Acts 1986 and 1995.

Comment: The passing of the Abortion (Amendment) Act 1995 has not changed the categories of unborn children who may be aborted. However, the 1995 Act has made access to abortion easier, because counseling is no longer required and abortions can be performed anywhere. This may result in more abortions.

The Human Embryo (Protection) Bill of 2000

The development of technologies like *in vitro* fertilization (IVF) has become a matter of concern for many legislators. They believe that human procreation should not be dissociated from the marital act and are particularly aware of the vulnerability of embryos created *in vitro*. For each baby born as a result of IVF, many embryos are created and destroyed. The legal status of embryos created by IVF is unclear, and destructive research is conducted upon some of them, which is another matter of grave concern. A bill is introduced to prohibit the creation of embryos outside a woman's body, thereby protecting some embryos from harm.

HUMAN EMBRYO (PROTECTION) BILL 2000
A Bill to prevent the creation of human embryos outside a woman's body

BE IT ENACTED:

1. No person is authorized to:
   (a) procure the fertilization of a human ovum *in vitro* (that is to say, outside a woman's body), or
   (b) to have in his or her possession a human embryo produced by *in vitro* fertilization.

2. Any person who contravenes clause 1 shall be guilty of an offence and shall be liable, on conviction, to imprisonment for a term of up to five years.

3. This Act may be cited as the Human Embryo (Protection) Act 2000.

Stage A

[Vote 25]

Comment: Although it is called the Human Embryo (Protection) Bill, the bill does not, in fact, grant protection to the class of human beings that can be called embryos (i.e., human beings in the first eight weeks of life). This bill does not affect the provisions of the Abortion Acts 1986 and 1995, which allow pregnant women to abort unborn children (including embryos) up to the 20th or 26th week of pregnancy.

The bill does not, in fact, give protection to a class of human beings but prohibits a particular action that refers only to a particular class of human beings. Although it is unjust to support abortion legislation that makes arbitrary distinctions of persons (e.g., by permitting abortion up to x weeks, or by prohibiting abortion after x weeks), it is not unjust to prohibit *particular actions* (e.g., the prescription or distribution of pills like RU486 that would be used for abortion, or the procedure of partial birth abortion, etc.). The fact that, if this bill is enacted, other embryos may still be vulnerable, say, to the "morning after pill" or other abortions, does not affect the justness of supporting this bill.

This bill prohibits actions that can be legitimately prohibited and if presented in this form at stage C it could be supported as just legislation. Pro-life legislators could justly vote for the bill at stage A as a suitable basis from which to begin the process toward enacting law.

[The bill proceeds after a majority votes for it.]

Stage B

Amendment 1

Add to the end of clause 1, ". . . unless the embryo is being produced or has been produced for the purpose of enabling a specified woman to bear a child by means of embryo insertion, and has not been and will not be used for any other purpose."

[Vote 26]

Comment: This amendment would create an exception to the general prohibition of creating or possessing embryos outside a woman's body, authorizing embryos to be created and kept if they will be then inserted into a woman so she can bear a child. Such actions are contrary to the moral law, and legislation "authorizing" this would be intrinsically unjust, just as legislation "authorizing" or "permitting" (and not simply "tolerating") such acts as adultery or prostitution is intrinsically unjust. The amendment could not be supported and it would seem appropriate to vote against it.

Stage C

[Vote 27]

Amendment 1 is passed. Other amendments were considered and defeated. The bill, as presented for its final vote, reads as follows:

HUMAN EMBRYO (PROTECTION) BILL 2000
A Bill to prevent the creation of human embryos outside a woman's body

BE IT ENACTED:

1. No person is authorized to:

    (a) procure the fertilization of a human ovum *in vitro* (that is to say, outside a woman's body), or

    (b) to have in his or her possession a human embryo produced by *in vitro* fertilization, unless the embryo is being produced or has been produced for the purpose of enabling a specified woman to bear a child by means of embryo insertion, and has not been and will not be used for any other purpose.

2. Any person who contravenes clause 1 shall be guilty of an offence and shall be liable, on conviction, to imprisonment for a term of up to five years.

3. This Act may be cited as the Human Embryo (Protection) Act 2000.

Comment: Because Amendment 1 was passed at stage B, the bill has been significantly changed. The bill at stage C would provide embryos with some protection (e.g., it would be illegal to experiment on embryos created by IVF), but it also now authorizes the creation of embryos by IVF provided that they will be transferred to the body of a specified woman for whom they were created. This authorization is contrary to the moral law that prohibits the deliberate separation of the unitive and procreative meanings of the conjugal act.

If no legislation were passed there would be no law prohibiting IVF, irrespective of whether it were performed with a view to pregnancy and birth or to create embryos for the purpose of research. Some pro-life legislators might think that this legislation, which would at least prohibit destructive research, is better than the existing "no law" situation. However, because the bill specifically authorizes IVF if performed to produce a pregnancy, it is intrinsically unjust.[4] It would be unethical to enact this bill as a means of prohibiting destructive research. Pro-life legislators could not vote justly in favor of the bill at stage C.

Result of final vote: A majority votes in favor of the bill and it is enacted as the Human Embryo (Protection) Act 2000. Before its enactment there was no law on embryo experimentation and IVF for pregnancy. Neither action was specifically authorized, but because they were not prohibited doctors and scientists were able to act without legal restraint. The Human Embryo (Protection) Act 2000 prohibits some actions that may have been formerly practiced. The action that has not been prohibited (IVF for pregnancy) is now not simply "tolerated" by law but specifically authorized. The good act performed at stage A of supporting the bill did not have the intended good consequence of its leading to a just law. Pro-life legislators who voted against the bill at stage C are not responsible for the enactment of the intrinsically unjust law. Other legislators have abused the pro-life legislators' good act of voting for the bill at stage A, and this act can be regarded as (permissible) material cooperation in the enactment of the intrinsically unjust law.

One notes that the enactment of the bill in its final form (or its enactment if it had remained unchanged from stage A) does not affect the practical implementation of the Abortion Acts.[5]

4. The bill I have presented is similar to the Unborn Children (Protection) Bill promoted in 1984 in the UK Parliament by Enoch Powell, MP, to prohibit human embryo experiments. The bill was widely supported by pro-life organizations and the Catholic Church in the UK. The Powell Bill attempted to prohibit IVF unless it were *authorized* by the secretary of state solely for the purpose of childbearing: "The Secretary of State's authority shall be given expressly for the purpose of enabling a specified woman to bear a child by means of embryo insertion, and not for any other purpose" (clause 2[a]). The Powell Bill must be judged intrinsically unjust because it included authorization for IVF. If the Powell Bill and my hypothetical Human Embryo (Protection) Bill 2000 had prohibited embryo experimentation, and only *tolerated* (i.e., not permitted or authorized) IVF, would this have meant it was *not* intrinsically unjust and that it could (taking into account the circumstances) have been justly supported? On this point I am undecided.

5. This sort of bill shows how, to some extent, pro-life matters can be considered

Voting Opportunities: A Summary

Having considered a range of bills that could be introduced and a variety of votes encountered during the passage of a bill, the following points can be made in summary:

1. The key vote is the final vote at stage C. Because this is a vote to decide whether a bill will be enacted as law, a judgment must be made, first of all, as to whether it is just and thus qualifies to be enacted as law. If a bill is intrinsically unjust because it tolerates, permits, or obligates any offense against life, like abortion, it is *unethical to vote for it* at stage C, irrespective of the legislators' motives or intentions, or a consideration of the circumstances and consequences of voting for it.

The circumstances and anticipated consequences can never make it licit to vote to enact (i.e., to vote "for") an intrinsically unjust law. They should, however, be considered before deciding whether to vote against such a law or to abstain from voting. If the proposed law would enable more abortions to be performed (see, for example, votes 19 and 24) it would be appropriate always to vote against it. If, however, the proposed law, though intrinsically unjust and not worthy of support itself, would have some good consequences if enacted, pro-life legislators could decide whether the pro-life cause was better served by voting against the law or by abstaining from voting (see vote 9).

2. At stage C, legislators cannot vote for a bill to be enacted as law if it is unjust. A vote at stage A, however, constitutes merely a judgment that the bill can be judged to be a suitable basis from which to proceed to make law. Pro-life legislators can vote licitly for a bill, at stage A, that does not at that stage fulfill the requirements of justness (see vote 7), but cannot vote licitly for an identically worded bill at stage C, the stage at which justness is a primary requirement (see vote 9).

3. At stage B parts of the bill are considered individually, and pro-life legislators can participate in votes at this stage even though any bill expected to come to a final vote for enactment is likely to be intrinsically unjust. In such cases, legislators should vote at stage B according to the following guidelines:

---

individually. In a similar way legislation to prohibit euthanasia could be supported, even if other legislation supported abortion. Support for anti-euthanasia legislation would in no way signify support for any separate abortion legislation.

(a) Legislators should normally vote against any amendment that introduces or extends a pro-abortion measure (see vote 11). Because the amendments do not constitute just and valid law, it would be unethical to vote for them. A consideration of the circumstances (for example, whether the amendment's inclusion in the bill might increase the prospects of defeating the bill at stage C) might, exceptionally, reveal good reasons for pro-life legislators to abstain from voting.

(b) Legislators should normally vote for amendments that delete an unjust part of the bill (see votes 13, 14 and 17). A consideration of the circumstances (notably those that might increase the chances of an unjust bill's being defeated at stage C) might, exceptionally, justify voting against the amendment or abstaining from voting.

(c) Legislators should normally vote for any amendment that, considered apart from other parts of the bill, can be judged to constitute just and valid law (see votes 16 and 18). A consideration of the circumstances (notably those that might increase the chances of an unjust bill's being defeated at stage C) might, exceptionally, justify voting against the amendment or abstaining from voting.

(d) Legislators can abstain from voting when faced with an amendment that is unjust in itself but could be advantageous for the pro-life cause (see votes 12 and 15). It would be unethical to vote in favor of such an amendment. Voting against could also be justified.

4. During stage B it is legitimate to vote for an amendment to delete part of the bill, especially if the part deleted is intrinsically unjust because it favors abortion in some way. During stage B parts of the bill can be considered individually and a vote on an amendment to delete a part of the bill concerns only the part considered for deletion (see vote 14). It is a very different situation when legislators are faced with a bill (notably at the stage C vote) to amend an existing Act, in which the amendment bill aims to amend *the whole* Act by deleting part of it (see the second "comment" after vote 20). Legislators must take into account not simply the part of the Act that is being deleted by the amendment bill but the whole Act of which the section being deleted is merely a part. One must consider, prior to casting a vote, the justness of the existing Act as amended by the amendment bill. If, having been amended by an amendment bill, an Abortion Act continues to obligate,

permit, or tolerate any abortions, then the amendment bill—which must always be judged with respect to the Act that it is amending—is intrinsically unjust.

5. Pro-life legislators can support legislation only if it is consistent with the moral law, i.e., is consistent with right reason, or just. Their responsibility is greater than simply withholding support from unjust legislation. They also have a responsibility to promote just legislation, whether this be to prohibit justly and without exceptions particular unethical actions (see votes 1 and 25) or to promote some other just proposals that contribute to the "culture of life" so that abortions, even if not prohibited, are less easily obtained (see votes 16, 17, and 18).

The enactment of just legislation is a desirable consequence of one's just votes, but ethical behavior does not guarantee "success," and legislators' actions are no less good if they are unable to gain majority support for the enactment of just legislation. By comparison, the legal prohibition of some abortions achieved by the means of supporting intrinsically unjust restrictive legislation seems attractive as it provides some semblance of "success." Legislators are not called, however, to "success" (whether it be real or illusory) but to be good legislators, faithful to the requirements of their office of lawmaking.

PART V

MAGISTERIAL TEACHING AND A CONCLUSION

9. *EVANGELIUM VITAE*

No magisterial text issued prior to 1995 by or with the approval of the Holy See can be cited as teaching that legislators can vote for restrictive abortion legislation. On this point there seems to be unanimous agreement. The correctness or otherwise of the widespread belief that the Holy See now teaches that such votes are permissible depends upon what is meant by a particular passage in one section (n. 73) of Pope John Paul II's 1995 encyclical letter *Evangelium vitae* (*EV* 73). Another section, *EV* 90, is also cited as a subsidiary text. In this chapter I shall argue that what many people believe has been taught has not in fact been taught.

Reading *Evangelium vitae,* nn. 73 and 90, in Context

The two disputed sections, *EV* 73 and 90, being part of a larger text, must be understood, of course, within the context of previous magisterial teachings and of the encyclical as a whole. It is not legitimate to interpret these sections in such a way that they conflict with other parts of the encyclical or with other authoritative teachings. In particular, *EV* 73 is part of a treatise discussing the relationship between the moral law and civil law (*EV* 68–74: *"'We must obey God rather than men' (Acts 5.29): civil law and moral law"*). Some of the teaching of *Evangelium vitae* on the relationship between the moral law and civil law, in line with traditional teaching, has already been mentioned in earlier chapters, especially Chapter 2. I do not intend to repeat here the relevant teaching, which notes the distinction between laws "permitting" and "tolerating" moral evils, but I shall draw attention to just a few points.

EV 71 emphasizes "a need to recover the *basic elements of a vision of the relationship between civil law and moral law.*" This is followed by two significant sentences: "Certainly the purpose of civil law [*legis civilis of-*

ficium] is different from and more limited in scope than that of the moral law. But in no sphere of life can the civil law ... dictate norms concerning things which are outside its competence." Within these two short sentences *EV* 71 raises three important points regarding: (i) the purpose of law; (ii) the competence of law; and (iii) law being that which "dictates norms."

First, it is noted that the role of civil law is more limited in scope than that of the moral law and so it does not need to prohibit everything that is immoral. However, it notes that there is *a purpose* of civil law. For St. Thomas Aquinas, the purpose is "the temporal tranquility of society, a purpose which the law attains by coercively prohibiting external acts to the extent that they are evils which can disturb the peaceful condition of society."[1] In line with this, *EV* 71 states: "the real purpose of civil law is to guarantee an ordered social coexistence in true justice, so that all may 'lead a quiet and peaceable life, godly and respectful in every way' (1 Tim 2:2)." The text continues immediately, "Precisely for this reason, civil law must ensure that all members of society enjoy respect for certain fundamental rights which innately belong to the person, *rights which every positive law must recognize and guarantee*. First and fundamental among these is the inviolable right to life of every innocent human being."[2] Any legislation, supported as "restrictive legislation," that tolerates or permits some abortions fails to recognize and guarantee the innate and inviolable right to life that *every positive law must recognize and guarantee*. Were *EV* 73 to support votes for such restrictive legislation, it would be contradicting the pope's teaching at *EV* 71.

Second, *EV* 71 notes that some things are *outside the competence* of the civil law and accordingly beyond the competence of civil legislators. At a minimum, civil law cannot rightly violate the natural law or natural rights. A law permitting or tolerating even one abortion violates the natural right to life and is outside the competence of legislators. John Paul II teaches that it is "urgently necessary" to "rediscover those essential and innate human and moral values ... which no individual, no

---

1. *ST* I-II, q. 98, a. 1.
2. *EV* 71. Emphasis added.

majority and no State can ever create, modify or destroy, but must only acknowledge, respect and promote."[3] One must assume that these remarks also apply to pro-life legislators who, motivated by a desire to save *some* lives, are prohibited from "modifying" something—notably the right to life for all—which must be only acknowledged, respected, and promoted.

Third, contrary to the opinion of those who maintain that the goodness of a law is determined by some good consequences of its enactment, John Paul II restates the traditional view of law: it dictates norms. As Aquinas teaches, "Law is nothing else but a dictate of the practical reason."[4] The goodness of any law is determined, in the first place, not by comparing it with a previous law or with another law that might otherwise be enacted but by whether it is in accordance with the moral law, with right reason. A law that is not in conformity with the moral law, or with right reason, is "an unjust law" and "not really a law." John Paul II's position, expressed in *EV* 72, is wholly that of Aquinas:

> This is the clear teaching of Saint Thomas Aquinas, who writes that "human law is law inasmuch as it is in conformity with right reason and thus derives from the eternal law. But when a law is contrary to reason, it is called an unjust law; but in this case it ceases to be a law and becomes instead an act of violence."[5] And again: "Every law made by man can be called a law insofar as it derives from the natural law. But if it is somehow opposed to the natural law, then it is not really a law but rather a corruption of the law."[6]

---

3. Ibid.

4. *"Nihil est aliud lex quam quoddam dictamen practicae rationis." ST* I-II, q. 91, a. 1. John Finnis objects to the common translation of *dictamen* as "dictate," claiming, "it is unsound, in so far as 'dictate' suggests arbitrariness and even abuse of power"; see his *Aquinas,* 256. Although the term "dictate" is widely used (for example, the official Vatican English text of *EV* 71 translates *normas edere* as "*dictate* norms"), Finnis raises a legitimate concern that the term "dictate" might be misunderstood. However, the point remains that law must be judged primarily in terms of what it "dictates"—or "states," "commands," "specifies," "prescribes," etc.—and not solely in terms of some consequences of its enactment or the motives or intentions of those enacting it.

5. *ST* I-II, q. 93, a. 3, ad 2.

6. *ST* I-II, q. 95, a. 2.

Laws permitting or supporting abortion[7] are condemned as being "radically opposed not only to the good of the individual but also to the common good; as such they are completely lacking in authentic juridical validity."[8] The same condemnation must surely apply to restrictive abortion laws that, irrespective of the motives of those voting for them, permit or support abortion.

Protection of the good of man—and principally of his life itself—is the very *raison d'être* of a system of human law;[9] the right to life has, indeed, "a pre-political character."[10] *Evangelium vitae* does not suggest in any way that legislation on abortion should follow "political" rules, or that legislators should follow public opinion or the views of the majority of legislators in order to protect as many lives as possible. On the contrary, John Paul II criticizes the fact that "in the democratic culture of our time it is commonly held that the legal system of any society should limit itself to taking account of and accepting the convictions of the majority. It should therefore be based solely upon what the majority itself considers moral and actually practices."[11] Legislation on abortion should not be subject to those "democratic" principles—public opinion, or the will of the majority of legislators—which govern legislation on matters that are properly within the competence of civil legislatures. The moral law, not a desire to "restrict abortion as much as seems currently possible," is the true guide for legislators in a democratic assembly contemplating what abortion legislation to support. The "moral" value of democracy, as *EV* 70 teaches, "depends on conformity to the moral law." Further on, the encyclical says, "Only respect for life can be the foundation and guarantee of the most precious and essential goods of society, such as democracy and peace. There can be no true democracy without a recognition of *every person's* dignity and without respect for his or her rights."[12]

---

7. *"Leges igitur quae permittunt euthanasiam abortumque iisque favent"* (*EV* 72). The Vatican translation referring to laws "which authorize or promote abortion" has a slightly different shade of meaning from the Latin text.

8. *EV* 72.

9. See Styczeń, "Le Leggi Contro la Vita," 214.

10. See Rhonheimer, "Fundamental Rights, Moral Law," 176. This point was discussed in Chapter 5.

11. *EV* 69.

12. *EV* 101. Emphasis added.

Restrictive abortion legislation does not respect life itself, but only some lives. Although no unjust legislation is worthy of support, this book has highlighted the unjustness of legislation that excludes from protection some unborn children. By obligating, permitting, or tolerating the abortion of some unborn children, the legislation is intrinsically unjust. Such legislation fails to recognize the dignity of every person and indicates that the "democratic" legislature and society supporting the law is not on a sure foundation. In the Instruction *Donum vitae* (1987), the Congregation for the Doctrine of the Faith (CDF) observed that "when the State does not place its power at the service of *each citizen,* and in particular of *the more vulnerable,* the very foundations of a State based on law are undermined."[13] *Evangelium vitae* is consistent with John Paul II's teaching that failure to respect the right to life undermines the state and the democratic idea. In his earlier encyclical letter *Centesimus annus* (1991), John Paul II teaches that "authentic democracy is possible only in a State ruled by law"[14] and he warns that "a democracy without values easily turns into open or thinly disguised totalitarianism."[15] With reference to this teaching John Paul II addressed the bishops of Portugal:

> Now "a State ruled by law" implies first of all *recognition of and respect for human rights,* foremost among which is the right to life.... "It is a question of inherent, universal and inviolable rights. No one, no individual, no group, no authority, no State, can change—let alone eliminate—them because such rights find their source in God himself" (*Christifideles laici,* n. 38). Therefore the Church points out that democracy demands respect for these rights, but this respect *represents at the same time the limits of democracy.*[16]

---

13. CDF, Instruction *Donum vitae* (Editiones Pauline, Vatican translation, 1987) Part 3, emphasis added. See also Jarosław Merecki and Tadeusz Styczeń, "Denying Equal Legal Protection to Weakest Undermines the State Itself," *L'Osservatore Romano* 44, English weekly edition (1 Nov. 1995): 10.

14. *Centesimus annus,* n. 46.

15. Ibid.

16. John Paul II, Address to Bishops of Portugal's Lisbon and Evora Provinces (27 Nov. 1992, n. 3).

Restrictive abortion legislation, which obligates, permits, or tolerates some abortions, fails to recognize and respect the human right to life of all. In itself, it violates what should be acknowledged as an inviolable right. The pope's teaching is restated in *Evangelium vitae*:

> The value of democracy stands or falls with the values which it embodies and promotes. Of course, values such as the dignity of every human person, respect for inviolable and inalienable human rights ... are certainly fundamental and not to be ignored.[17]

> It is therefore urgently necessary, for the future of society and the development of a sound democracy, to rediscover those essential and innate human and moral values which flow from the very truth of the human being and express and safeguard the dignity of the person: values which no individual, no majority and no State can ever create modify or destroy, but must only acknowledge, respect and promote.[18]

The teaching of *Evangelium vitae* on the question of voting for restrictive legislation must be understood in the wider context of the encyclical's teaching: that civil laws must be in conformity with the natural moral law, that democracy has its limits, and that there are some values—notably the inalienable right to life—"which no individual, no majority and no State can ever create, modify or destroy, but must only acknowledge, respect and promote." The value and dignity of *every* human person, which the encyclical places such emphasis on, is called into question by restrictive legislation excluding some unborn children—even one unborn child—from the protection of the law that is rightly theirs. To hold the view that *EV* 73 authorizes legislators to vote for (unjust) laws obligating or permitting or tolerating abortions in order to restrict abortion, one must either be inattentive to the broader teaching of the encyclical or admit that the encyclical is inconsistent. The following analysis of *EV* 73 (and its subsidiary section *EV* 90) demonstrates that there is no inconsistency and that the teaching of *EV* 73 and 90 is radically different from common interpretations of these sections.

17. *EV* 70.
18. *EV* 71.

Understanding *Evangelium vitae*, n. 73

A "Problem" and a "Solution"

What, then, does *Evangelium vitae* teach with respect to voting for restrictive abortion legislation? The disputed part of *EV* 73 is the final paragraph (73.3), which can be subdivided into three sections: (a) a presentation of the problem that needs to be addressed, (b) an explanation of how the problem has arisen, and (c) the proposed "solution" to this problem. These subdivisions are not specified in the normative Latin text or in the official translations, but their identification—particularly that of (a) the problem and (c) the solution—helps to avoid the sort of confusion and misinterpretation that has arisen. The full, official English translation of *EV* 73.3 reads:

[*(a) The problem*]
A particular problem of conscience can arise in cases where a legislative vote would be decisive for the passage of a more restrictive law, aimed at limiting the number of authorised abortions, in place of a more permissive law already passed or ready to be voted on.

[*(b) Why the problem has arisen*]
Such cases are not infrequent. It is a fact that while in some parts of the world there continue to be campaigns to introduce laws favouring abortion, often supported by powerful international organizations, in other nations—particularly those which have already experienced the bitter fruits of such permissive legislation—there are growing signs of a rethinking in this matter.

[*(c) The solution*]
In a case like the one just mentioned, when it is not possible to overturn or completely abrogate a pro-abortion law, an elected official, whose absolute personal opposition to procured abortion was well known, could licitly support proposals aimed at *limiting the harm* done by such a law and at lessening its negative consequences at the level of general opinion and public morality. This does not in fact represent an illicit cooperation with an unjust law, but rather a legitimate and proper attempt to limit its evil aspects.[19]

---

19. [*The problem*] De conscientia nominatim agitari potest quibusdam forte evenientibus casibus, cum legatorum suffragia necessaria sunt ut strictiori legi faveatur, quae

Our concern lies with what is presented as "the problem" and "the solution" and not with the middle section. The first point to note is that one cannot state "the problem" as though that were "the solution." For example, if someone is asked if 2 + 2 = 5, and responds that the answer is obvious if one uses a calculator, it cannot be said that the person has answered that 2 + 2 = 5: that is the problem that has been posed, not the solution. With respect to the teaching of *EV* 73, however, many reputable commentators have failed to note the distinction between the problem posed and the solution. For example, John Finnis says that in *EV* 73 the following "statement" is found: "a Catholic elected legislator whose absolute personal opposition to procured abortion is well known can, in a legislative vote decisive for the passage of a bill, licitly give his or her support to a bill for a law which permits abortion but less permissively than the existing law or than a bill which will otherwise be passed and become law."[20]

My disagreement with what Finnis says at this point is not based on a difference of interpretation but rather on a recognition that the "statement" to which he refers is not to be found anywhere in the encyclical; it is, rather, his account of what is taught, an account that is flawed because it does not differentiate what is written as "the problem" and what as "the solution." The encyclical indisputably does not state that a legislator can "licitly give his or her support to a bill for a law which permits abortion but less permissively than the existing law or than a bill which will otherwise be passed and become law," as Finnis and some other reputable commentators have claimed.[21] To be precise, it states that "when it is not possible to overturn or completely ab-

---

scilicet circumscribat abortuum lege admissorum numerum pro laxiore lege quae iam viget vel suffragiis probanda . . . [*The solution*] Superiore in casu, quoties vitari antiquarive non potest abortus lex, liquet legatum, qui palam alioquin vulgoque abortui adversetur, suffragari licite posse illis consiliis quae eiusmodi legis *damna minuere velint* et perniciosum effectum extenuare qui sive culturam sive moralitatem publicam respicit. Hac enim agendi ratione officium suum non praestat illicitae vel iniustae legi; potius vero aequus opportunusque inducitur conatus ut eius iniquae cohibeantur species.

20. John Finnis, "Catholic Church and Public Policy Debates," 268.
21. For example, Livio Melina states as the teaching of *EV* 73 what is, in fact, written as "the problem," in his paper "La Cooperacion en Acciones Moralmente," 481.

rogate a pro-abortion law, an elected official ... could licitly support proposals aimed at *limiting the harm* done by such a law and at lessening its negative consequences at the level of general opinion and public morality." (It should be noted that on the two occasions that the CDF has referred to the teaching of *EV* 73, it too has cited the part that I have called "the solution" and not confused this with the part that can be regarded as "the problem.")[22] The question that needs to be addressed is what exactly is meant by this somewhat obscure reference to "proposals aimed at limiting the harm done by such a law." Does this mean that a legislator can support *any* legislative proposal, or are some proposals acceptable and others not?

The Illicitness of Voting for Intrinsically Unjust Legislation

Chapters 2 and 3 drew attention to the concept of an intrinsically unjust law, noting that any law obligating, permitting, or tolerating abortion or any offense against human life is intrinsically unjust. The intrinsic unjustness of voting to enact any intrinsically unjust law was demonstrated in Chapter 4. The concept of intrinsic unjustness in legislation is necessary for a correct understanding of *EV* 73.3, especially as its teaching is prefaced by a one-sentence paragraph (*EV* 73.2) that teaches the very point I have been emphasizing, that it is never licit to vote to enact an intrinsically unjust law: "In the case of an intrinsically unjust law [*de lege ... suapte natura iniqua*] such as a law permitting abortion or euthanasia, it is therefore never licit to obey it [*eidem se accommodare*] or to 'take part in a propaganda campaign in favour of such a law, or vote for it [*latis suffragiis sustinere*].'"

The quotation reproduced at the end of the sentence is from a passage of the CDF's *Declaration on Procured Abortion* (1974), which expresses a similar view:

> "It must in any case be clearly understood that a Christian [*hominem*] can never conform to a law which is in itself immoral [*legi intrinsece inhonestae*], and such is the case of a law which would admit in principle the lice-

---

22. See the *Doctrinal Note on some Questions regarding the Participation of Catholics in Political life* (24 Nov. 2002), n. 4; *Considerations Regarding Proposals to Give Legal Recognition to Unions between Homosexual Persons* (3 June 2003), n. 10.

ity of abortion [*si lex feratur quae principium liceitatis abortus recipiat*]. Nor can a Christian [i.e., *homo*] take part in a propaganda campaign in favour of such a law, or vote for it [*Is praeterea non potest esse particeps alicuius motus publicae opinionis, qui eiusmodi legi faveat, neque potest latis suffragiis sustinere*]." (n. 22)[23]

Authoritative magisterial teachings frequently refer to earlier teachings to show that what is being taught is either a restatement or a development (without contradiction) of what has been previously taught. The quotation within the teaching of *EV* 73.2 can be regarded, therefore, as affirmation of the ongoing validity of the previous teaching. In this instance, the restatement of what the CDF taught (with the approval of Paul VI) in 1974 helps to ensure that the teaching of *EV* 73.2 is not misunderstood by a partial reading of it. In particular, it would be a mistake to think that abortion laws are intrinsically unjust only if they specifically *permit* abortion: *EV* 73.2 refers to laws permitting abortion as *an example* of an intrinsically unjust law,[24] and it would be wrong to think that this example suggested that laws that "obligate" or "tolerate" abortion are not intrinsically unjust because they do not "permit." To understand fully the partial citation in *EV* 73.2 of the 1974 CDF *Declaration*, one must understand the whole of the passage of the earlier document. In the 1974 *Declaration* the magisterium taught that it was illicit to vote for "a law which is in itself immoral," and the new description of "an intrinsically unjust law" (*de lege . . . suapte natura iniqua*) would appear to be an equivalent expression. In the 1974 *Declaration*, the example given of such a law was not (as with *EV* 73.2) "a law permitting abortion or euthanasia" but "a law which would admit in principle the liceity of abortion." The words from the 1974 *Declaration* recalled and confirmed in *EV* 73.2—noting, among other things, that some laws cannot be voted for—are fully understood not only with respect to *EV* 73.2 but also with respect to what they referred to when originally used. The partial citation of n. 22 from the 1974 *Declaration* draws attention to all that is relevant about that citation, including the

23. The normative Latin text, unlike the English translation, does not suggest that the teaching here applies only to Christians. It applies rather to all lawmakers and all who are subject to laws.
24. It refers to a law "*such as* a law permitting."

teaching that a law that would admit in principle the liceity of abortion is intrinsically unjust. This is an important consideration when considering whether it is licit to vote for restrictive legislation or other regulatory matters, e.g., on parental consent or mandatory pre-abortion counseling. In *EV* 73.2 John Paul II confirms the earlier teaching that legislation admitting in principle the liceity of abortion has been judged intrinsically unjust and unsupportable.

If it is never licit to vote for an intrinsically unjust law, then the first consideration when judging the licitness of voting for any abortion legislation is precisely the norm dictated by that legislation. A pro-life legislator's intention (or motive) of saving some lives does not justify voting for a law that—by tolerating, permitting, or obligating some abortions (or by accepting in principle the liceity of abortion)—is intrinsically unjust and hence never worthy of support. Before voting for any proposal a judgment must be made that it is just and hence truly is law.

In Chapters 7 and 8 I described a number of proposals that could be supported—as just proposals—either as separate items of legislation or as proposals introduced during the passage of abortion legislation. In particular, I highlighted the distinction between two sorts of legislation that I identified as primary and secondary legislation. The primary abortion legislation determines which categories of abortion will be obligated, permitted, or tolerated, whereas the secondary legislation is relevant to the implementation of the primary, focusing on such matters as where abortions will be performed, who will perform them, how they will be funded, and so on. Some secondary legislation, such as proposals requiring a cooling-off period before obtaining an abortion, being conditions for obtaining an abortion and clearly predicated on the primary abortion legislation, is intrinsically unjust. (Such proposals admit in principle the liceity of abortion.) Other secondary legislation, e.g., granting doctors a right not to be obliged to perform abortions, or preventing public funding for abortion, is not predicated on abortion being licit, and the legislation can be just.

The "solution" in *EV* 73 says: "When it is not possible to overturn or completely abrogate a pro-abortion law a legislator ... could vote for proposals aimed at limiting the harm done by such a [i.e., abortion] law." It does not say that legislators can vote for a "law" (i.e., an "abortion law" or "restrictive abortion law") that prohibits some categories of abortion while tolerating or permitting or obligating others. And given that such a law would be intrinsically unjust, *EV* 73.3 could hardly permit legislators to vote for such laws without contradicting the preceding paragraph, *EV* 73.2, which teaches that it is never licit to vote for such a law.[25] *EV* 73 teaches that legislators can vote for "proposals" and these are, necessarily, *just* proposals—the sorts of proposal that can be introduced, as I have shown, as separate items of legislation or during the passage of legislation.

The terms "imperfect" law and "imperfectly just" law have been introduced since the late 1980s to describe restrictive abortion legislation.[26] The employment of these terms has obscured the relevance of determining whether the restrictive legislation under consideration is or is not in fact just. If the restrictive legislation obligates, permits, or tolerates any abortions and is therefore intrinsically unjust, the label "imperfectly just" should be rejected as a misnomer. And what does "imperfect" law mean? Some writers suggest that all human laws are necessarily "imperfect." Others may use the term solely for laws that limit a moral evil (irrespective of whether this is achieved by a just or unjust measure); or for any unjust law that violates the moral law; or for a (just) law that does not exactly fulfill the true desires of the legisla-

---

25. Some commentators have claimed that that *EV* 73.3 provides an exception to the rule that legislators cannot vote for an intrinsically unjust law. See Leslie C. Griffin, "*Evangelium Vitae:* Abortion," in Wildes and Mitchell, *Choosing Life: A Dialogue on "Evangelium Vitae,"* 159–73: "Politicians should in most cases not vote for abortion laws.... As a rule, Catholics are never supposed to vote for 'intrinsically unjust' abortion laws. But the encyclical identifies one exception to this rule; the Pope states that in some circumstances Catholic politicians may vote for laws that permit some abortion" (170). If *EV* 73.3 were intended to teach that in some instances it would be justified to vote for an intrinsically unjust law, surely this would have been taken into account before *EV* 73.2 taught so uncompromisingly that it is *never licit* to vote for an intrinsically unjust law.

26. See the section on "the essence of law" in Chapter 3. An early use of this term is found in a document produced by the Catholic Bishops' [of the UK and Ireland] Joint Committee on Bio-Ethical Issues, "Imperfect Laws: Some Guidelines," in *Briefing* 19 (7 July 1989): 298–300.

tor who supported it merely as a political compromise; or for a law that, owing to flaws in its drafting, fails to be as effective as envisaged. Just "secondary" legislation[27]—the enactment of which might reduce the number of abortions—could be called "imperfect" insofar as it would not be necessary if full legal protection were given to all the unborn. The key question is whether legislation is "just" or "unjust," and the introduction of the imprecise term "imperfect" law should be rejected as counterproductive to serious attempts to resolve the complexities of legislating on abortion. Although several commentators have claimed that *EV* 73 authorizes legislators to vote for "imperfect" legislation, I have avoided the use of the term (just as *Evangelium vitae* itself does) and have referred instead to "restrictive" legislation—it being understood that I am focusing on the sort of restrictive legislation that, by obligating, permitting, or tolerating some abortions is intrinsically unjust.

Questions Posed by *Evangelium vitae*, n. 73

The preceding remarks have demonstrated that *EV* 73 has not taught that legislators can vote for (unjust) restrictive abortion legislation. I shall now raise some questions, the responses to which give further grounds for rejecting the view that *EV* 73 teaches that such restrictive legislation can be supported.

(a) *If* EV *73 teaches that restrictive legislation can be supported, what is the purpose of voting for it?*

If one surveys the literature presented by the pro-life movement to justify campaigns for restrictive (or "imperfect" or "incremental") legislation, the main (and often the only) reason given is that it seeks to *save lives*. For example, in a publication stating its "aims, ethics and activities" the Society for the Protection of Unborn Children explained its policy of supporting legislation to stop some abortions (irrespective of whether the legislation permitted or tolerated other abortions): "The

---

27. The way in which the terms "primary" and "secondary" legislation are being used in this discussion (as distinct from the ways these terms may be otherwise understood) was explained in Chapter 7.

principal focus of the pro-life political campaign in Britain is to tighten the current law to stop the practice of abortion on demand: a realistic legislative objective which would save as many unborn lives as possible in as short a time as possible."[28] In the Introduction I mentioned that many believe votes for restrictive legislation are justified because they are undertaken in order to "save lives." It is, therefore, notable that the teaching of *EV* 73 does not even mention this, let alone suggest that voting for unjust legislation is justified by an overriding duty to try to "save lives." Rather, the encyclical provides two reasons for supporting the said "proposals."

First, the proposals are aimed at "limiting the harm done by such a law." The essence of an abortion law is that the right to life of some or all unborn children is denied (i.e., the primary legislation). Just secondary legislation has as its subject other legitimate considerations—the proper allocation of public money, the rights and duties of doctors, legitimate hospital regulations, etc.—and abortion is considered as one object (among several possible objects) in relation to the particular subject. Any primary legislation proposal, such as one that attempts to lower the time limit for abortions, does not have the effect of "limiting the harm done" by a particular abortion law but rather replaces that law with another abortion law. By contrast, a proposal stating that public money may not be used to pay for abortions (or any other just proposal which involves secondary legislation) does not constitute an abortion law, yet it does "limit the harm" done by the primary legislation, which is the essential part of an abortion law. The point is clearer, perhaps, if one considers that one would attempt to "limit the harm" done by a hurricane not by restricting the physical force of the hurricane itself but by secondary measures such as having securer buildings, removing objects from open spaces, taking cover in safe areas, etc. Acting in this way one is limiting not the hurricane but the harm that might otherwise be done by it. Similarly, the "proposals" referred to in *EV* 73 are aimed not at "limiting abortion" (as some commentators have claimed)[29] but at "limiting the harm" of an abortion law. In fact, the

28. SPUC, *Our Aims, Ethics and Activities* (London: SPUC, 1997), 27.
29. For example, John J. Rock, S.J., writes: "John Paul states that an elected official whose absolute personal opposition to abortion is well-known could support proposals

only words emphasized by italics in *EV* 73.3, as if to highlight the point I am making, are "limiting the harm."

Second, the proposals are aimed "at lessening its [the abortion law's] negative consequences at the level of general opinion and public morality." This is not an entirely satisfactory translation of the Latin, which refers not so much to the effect of voting for such proposals on "general opinion" but rather to the "culture" of the society in which these proposals will be enacted.[30] Properly understood, the focus is on how voting for the permitted "proposals" improves the "culture and public morality," and little attention seems to have been paid to what this actually means. The term "culture," which, as the Second Vatican Council teaches, refers to "all those things which go to the refining and developing of man's diverse mental and physical endowments"[31] has many facets, including the institutions (understood either in a physical or social sense) that contribute to society. If, as the Council teaches, there is a duty to respect "the right of every man to human and civil culture in harmony with the dignity of the human person, without distinction of race, sex, nation, religion, or social circumstances,"[32] one cannot appeal to the concept of culture in order to justify voting for a proposal to prohibit some (but not other) abortions because in so doing one will be failing to respect the cultural (and other) rights of those excluded by the law. Furthermore, in view of the fact that the proposal would specifically treat the most vulnerable of the unborn (i.e., younger babies, those conceived after rape or incest, those likely to be born disabled) in a way that further marginalizes their status in society, the culture would be negatively affected by such a measure. By contrast, secondary legislation proposals ensuring that doctors have a right not to participate in abortions, or that public money may not be used to fund

---

aimed at *limiting abortion,* when it is not possible to overturn or completely abrogate a pro-abortion law" (emphasis added). See his *"Evangelium Vitae:* Some Highlights," *Linacre Quarterly* 64 (Feb. 1997): 13.

30. "suffragari licite posse illis consiliis quae eiusmodi legis damna minuere velint et perniciosum effectum extenuare qui sive culturam sive moralitatem publicam respicit" (*EV* 73). The Spanish and Italian texts translate the Latin literally as "cultura."

31. Vatican Council II, *Gaudium et spes,* n. 53.

32. Ibid., n. 60.

abortions, would, within the limited terms of reference of such proposals, uphold with integrity the social or institutional structures to which they refer, thereby contributing positively to both the culture and public morality.

(b) *If EV 73 teaches that restrictive legislation can be supported, does it justify supporting it on the grounds that it is licit "cooperation" in evil?*

Chapter 4 addressed the argument that voting for restrictive abortion legislation can be justified as permissible material cooperation in evil. It is claimed that support for the "material cooperation" argument is to be found in the final sentence of *EV* 73, in which the Pope, referring to voting for the permitted proposals, says, "This does not in fact represent an illicit cooperation with an unjust law, but rather a legitimate and proper attempt to limit its evil aspects." The statement is commonly interpreted as teaching that a legislator who votes for restrictive legislation is making a *licit cooperation* with an unjust law.

John Finnis argues that voting to enact restrictive abortion legislation can be justified as material cooperation in evil and maintains that *EV* 73 supports his argument.

> Sec. 73 of *Evangelium Vitae* concludes with the words: "This does not in fact represent an illicit cooperation with an unjust law, but rather a legitimate and proper attempt to limit its evil aspects." The wording is a little incautious, for the sentence is dealing with two things at once. It is implicitly saying *first* what I have been saying, that such a vote need not be *formal* cooperation in the wicked choice to permit abortion up to 16 weeks.... But the sentence at the end of sec. 73 is also saying, secondly, that the legislator's non-formal but obviously real material cooperation in enacting the new law which does in fact permit abortion up to 16 weeks can be justifiable. The incautiousness in the wording is twofold. On the one hand, the sentence says, not *"can* be" (as I did) but *"does in fact* represent a legitimate and proper attempt" etc. The legitimacy of material cooperation depends upon many factors, not all of which are considered by the paragraph. "Does" should be read as meaning "can be, provided all relevant conditions are fulfilled."[33]

---

33. Finnis, "Catholic Church and Public Policy Debates," 269.

Am I, then, disputing the teaching of *EV* 73, which appears to say that a legislator voting for the sorts of measures I believe cannot be supported is not making "an illicit cooperation with an unjust law"? A problem for those focusing on the "licit cooperation" argument is that they are depending on a translation of *EV* 73 that does not correspond to the normative Latin text, which states: *Hac enim agendi ratione officium suum non praestat illicitae vel iniustae legi.* This translates literally: "Acting in this way [i.e., by voting for the said "proposals"] he or she [the pro-life legislator] does not give his or her office to [i.e., does not support or vote for] an illicit or unjust law."[34] The Latin text, as can be seen, does not mention "cooperation" and makes no reference whatsoever to the principle of permissible material cooperation. The adjective "illicit" is linked not to the legislator's action (or "cooperation") but to "law." A legislator who votes to prohibit some but not all abortions—say, to lower the upper limit from 24 to 16 weeks—by means of an amendment bill or by a measure of the form "Abortion is permitted up to 16 weeks [and prohibited thereafter]"—is voting for an unjust and illicit law. The sort of "proposal" approved in *EV* 73 is clearly not this sort of measure because the text specifies that a legislator voting for the permitted "proposals" would not be voting for an illicit or unjust law.[35]

---

34. The official English translation is: "This does not in fact represent an illicit cooperation with an unjust law."

35. One critic of my view objected that it does not make sense to speak of an "illicit law." If he is correct, this is a criticism of the Latin text and not of my translation, which is consistent with the Latin. However, I do not believe the objection is valid. An illicit law is one that is not permitted, a "law" that is "unlawful." This is an entirely appropriate description of a law that, by violating the moral/divine law, is intrinsically unjust and "not a law" (cf. *EV* 72). It is commonly understood that papal encyclicals are drafted in Italian and later translated into Latin. It is, therefore, interesting that the English translation corresponds with the Italian text ("Così facendo, infatti, non si attua una collaborazione illecita a una legge ingiusta"), and that the texts of other major European languages, including the German, French, Spanish, and Polish, are similar. The authoritative teaching of *EV* 73 is to be found, however, in the Latin text published in the *Acta* and not in the vernacular versions. My interpretation of *EV* 73 is aided by the Latin text, which says that the sort of "proposal" a legislator can support would not be illicit or unjust. It is not, however, undermined by the vernacular translations. If John Paul II had approved the Italian text (and had expected the Latin text to correspond to it), the dispute would focus not on the translation but on its interpretation. It could still be assumed (especially in view of the teaching of *EV* 73.2) that voting for unjust propos-

With respect to the argument claiming that *EV* 73 justifies voting for restrictive legislation as permissible material cooperation, one also notes that this view requires, at least for Finnis, a criticism of the text itself as being "a little incautious." Finnis acknowledges that his argument based on material cooperation is not directly taught in *EV* 73 but that the text is "implicitly saying . . . what I have been saying." The Latin text, however, indicates that neither the English translation nor Finnis's interpretation of it is consistent with what the pope is actually teaching.

(c) If EV *73 teaches that restrictive legislation can be supported, can only pro-life legislators vote for it?*

The "solution" given in *EV* 73 does not state that *all* legislators may vote for the "proposals" to which it refers but specifies merely that *some* legislators—those "whose absolute personal opposition to procured abortion was well known"—may licitly support them. In Chapter 5 I explained why pro-life legislators voting for *just* proposals should express publicly their opposition to all abortions. I acknowledged that the qualification of being publicly opposed to all abortions might appear to support the argument that pro-life legislators could vote for unjust restrictive measures (the argument suggesting that they would be cooperating materially and not formally in the tolerated or permitted abortions). However, I also demonstrated that acceptance of this argument also requires an acknowledgment that those legislators who are not opposed to all abortions *could not vote* for such restrictive legislation without cooperating formally in at least some abortions, and hence, without doing evil. If *EV* 73 is to be regarded as teaching that legislators can vote for (unjust) restrictive measures, it must be regarded as teaching that only those legislators "whose absolute personal opposition to procured abortion was well known" can vote for them, and that others could not as they would be *doing evil*. It would seem that pro-life legislators could not, therefore, encourage those other legislators to support

---

als was illicit, and that in voting for the permitted (just) "proposals" legislators would not be making "an illicit cooperation with an unjust law" precisely because, by voting for just proposals, they would not be cooperating illicitly with an unjust law.

(unjust) restrictive legislation because this would be encouragement to do evil.

The logic of the "material cooperation" argument is that pro-life legislators would be acting ethically in voting for an unjust restrictive law that, in principle, they did not agree with, whereas other (abortion-favoring) legislators would be acting unethically in voting for an unjust restrictive law which, in principle, they did agree with. Even if one believes that it is not unreasonable to accept such logic, one must acknowledge that the prospects of successfully enacting restrictive legislation would be greatly reduced (if not negligible) if only pro-life legislators can licitly vote for it and cannot solicit wider support. One cannot appeal to *EV* 73 to support votes for unjust restrictive legislation without accepting the implications of one's argument.

(d) If EV *73 teaches that restrictive legislation can be supported, does this depend on there being a more permissive law currently in force?*

The "solution" given in *EV* 73 says that a legislator can vote for the permitted proposals "when it is not possible to overturn or completely abrogate a pro-abortion law." Yet again, the English text is not a satisfactory translation of the Latin *quoties vitari antiquarive non potest abortus lex,* which makes it clearer that the two relevant situations, with respect to voting for the permitted "proposals," are those of either (i) being unable to avoid the enactment of an abortion law that has not yet been enacted *(vitari),* or (ii) being unable to overturn or repeal an existing abortion law *(antiquari).* Other translations, such as the Italian *(quando non fosse possibile scongiurare o abrogare)* reveal these two conditions more clearly.[36]

If the term "proposals" refers to unjust restrictive legislation, then *EV* 73 must be understood as teaching that a legislator may vote for a law permitting or tolerating abortion up to 16 weeks *even if the previous law prohibited all abortions,* if he is voting for this in order to prevent a

---

36. The "problem" stated in *EV* 73 refers to casting a legislative vote for a law "in place of a more permissive law already passed or ready to be voted on." Although this quote might appear to provide a more favorable illustration of my point, the teaching of *EV* 73 is to be found, as I demonstrated earlier, in what is stated as the "solution," not the "problem."

law permitting or tolerating even more abortions. John Finnis supports this view, saying that *EV* 73 states that a legislator could "licitly give his or her support to a bill for a law which permits abortion but less permissively [i] than the existing law or [ii] than a bill which will otherwise be passed and become law."[37]

I have argued that *EV* 73.3 must be understood in light of *EV* 73.2, which states that "in the case of an intrinsically unjust law ... it is therefore never licit to ... vote for it." Although I have argued that this statement indicates that it is never licit to vote for any legislation that, in restricting abortion to certain categories, is intrinsically unjust, it must surely apply *at least* to the law that originally tolerates or permits abortion. If it is "never licit" to vote for this original law, and if *EV* 73 also teaches that a "restrictive" law replacing a fully prohibitive law may be supported to prevent the enactment of a law that will otherwise tolerate or permit even more abortions, then *EV* 73 contradicts itself. The whole section would be rendered meaningless.

Evangelium vitae, n. 90

The responsibility of legislators is also addressed in *EV* 90. One section in particular tends to be highlighted:

> [T]he Church encourages political leaders, starting with those who are Christians, not to give in, but to make those choices which, taking into account what is realistically attainable [*ratione habita verarum opportunitatum*], will lead to the re-establishment of a just order [*iustum restituant rerum ordinem*] in the defence and promotion of the value of life. (*EV* 90.4)

Largely on account of an inadequate English translation, *EV* 90 has been understood as teaching that legislators may legitimately choose to

---

37. "The Catholic Church and Public Policy Debates," 268. "In *Evangelium Vitae* (1995) sec. 73 you find two statements: (i) it is never licit to vote for a law permitting abortion, (ii) a Catholic elected legislator whose absolute personal opposition to procured abortion is well known can, in a legislative vote decisive for the passage of a bill, licitly give his or her support to a bill for a law which permits abortion but less permissively than the existing law or than a bill which will otherwise be passed and become law. Are these two statements consistent? Someone may say that they are not. . . . But the objection is, I think, mistaken, and the two statements are consistent."

vote for "realistically attainable" proposals (without a consideration as to their justness or other ethical considerations) that form a stage in the process toward enacting a law that will eventually provide ("lead to") full protection for the unborn.[38] The Latin text, however, is more nuanced: political leaders are encouraged to make choices *quae, ratione habita verarum opportunitatum, iustum restituant rerum ordinem.* The English text focuses on the end result of the choice—i.e., that which may be attained—whereas the Latin indicates not so much what may be "realistically" achieved but what "true opportunity" is offered as the basis of action. The Latin text is concerned with what may be done, not with the *effect* of what may be done. The English text is interpreted as teaching that legislators may vote for a measure restricting, say, abortion from 24 to 16 weeks, if this is all that can be realistically attained in the circumstances. Even though the "true opportunities" presented would require a consideration of the circumstances, the Latin text indicates more clearly that the legislators' choices must be made according to the moral law.[39]

The English translation of *EV* 90 is also faulty in saying that certain choices may be made that "will lead to the re-establishment of a just order." Unlike the English translation, the Latin text does not speak of justness being restored at some point in the future but uses the subjunctive, indicating that justness be achieved in the present in the actual legislative choices that are made: *iustum restituant rerum ordinem.* The English translation lends itself to an interpretation that one can vote for unjust restrictive measures if they are supported as part of a gradual change in the law that *may* eventually—possibly years or decades down

---

38. An analysis of *Evangelium vitae* by Brian V. Johnstone, C.Ss.R., includes a section entitled "Realism." He writes: "The Pope is realistic about what can be done. He urges political leaders in promoting the value of life to aim for what is 'realistically attainable' (90). A politician could support a law limiting the number of abortions when the alternative was an even more permissive law (73)." See "Life in a Culture of Death," in *Priests and People* 9 (Nov. 1995): 413.

39. The Italian text speaks of making choices *tenendo conto delle possibilità concrete;* the Spanish is similar: *teniendo en cuenta las posibilidades concretas.* These translations do not focus on what may be possibly attained; the "concrete possibilities," like "true opportunities," are more easily recognized as those that may be chosen only if they are in accordance with the moral law.

the line—result in a just law that prohibits all abortions. The Latin, however, indicates that justness must be present in the actual proposals (the sorts of proposals proposed in Chapters 7 and 8) that achieve, within their limited objectives, a just order.

EV 90 appears to support votes for unjust restrictive legislation only if one overlooks the Latin text and reads the English text selectively and out of context. Earlier in the same section (*EV* 90.3) John Paul II reiterates the point he has already expressed emphatically: "I repeat once more that a law which violates an innocent person's natural right to life is unjust and, as such, is not valid as law. For this reason I urgently appeal to all political leaders not to pass laws which, by disregarding the dignity of the person, undermine the very fabric of society." It would be inconsistent for the pope to emphasize this and to say just a few sentences later that legislators can vote for unjust restrictive measures that, as such, are "not valid as law" and that, by disregarding the dignity of those excluded (abortion for whom might even be expressly permitted) undermine the fabric of society.

Authoritative Clarifications of *Evangelium vitae,* n. 73

During the nine years since publication of *Evangelium vitae* in March 1995, there have been very few authoritative statements about the teaching of *EV* 73. Prior to *EV* 73 the Holy See had offered no explicit guidance on the disputed question of voting for (unjust) restrictive legislation, so if John Paul II had intended to resolve the issue in *EV* 73, it is quite remarkable that far from explaining the thinking behind the teaching, or even acknowledging that the issue had been resolved, there has been almost complete silence from the Holy See on this question since the encyclical was published. It is especially remarkable as there have been several occasions on which John Paul II might reasonably have drawn attention to the teaching and explained its significance, but nothing pertinent was said.[40] Up to March 2004 there

---

40. For example, the subject was not raised in John Paul II's address to the World Pro-Life Congress organized by the Pontifical Council for the Family (3 Oct. 1995); addressing the Pontifical Academy for Life he mentioned the "problem area" of law but did not refer directly to the teaching of *EV* 73 (20 Nov. 1995); most notably, perhaps, he

have been just four notable authoritative indicators as to how *EV* 73 should be understood.[41]

The first was given by Cardinal Joseph Ratzinger at the first presentation of the encyclical on 30 March 1995, and I quote in full his remarks referring to *EV* 73:

> In this context the Pope touches on another much discussed problem of political morality: how should an elected official who is guided by the norms of biblical faith and the basic human values brought to light by that faith act when he sees the possibility of essentially improving an extremely unjust abortion law, but has no possibility of finding a majority for the total rejection of the direct, voluntary killing of the unborn? In order to remain faithful to the conviction of his own conscience, should he vote against the improved law, which continues to justify an injustice, and become an accomplice of those who seek to give further sanction to the injustice already in existence? But can compromises be made when it is a matter of choosing good and evil? The Pope says in this regard: it is essential that the elected official not allow any doubt to be inferred about his absolute personal opposition to abortion and that this attitude also be stated clearly, publicly and unequivocally. Under these conditions, the official can support proposals aimed at "limiting the harm . . . and lessening the negative consequences" (n. 74 [*sic*]).[42] Of course, he can never vote for injustice to be declared justice.[43]

---

offered no clarification when addressing a Symposium at the Vatican on the specific issue of "*Evangelium vitae* and Law" (24 May 1996); the issue was also avoided in his address at the Vatican to participants in the Second European Meeting of Politicians and Legislators (23 Oct. 1998). John Paul II's address to commemorate the fifth anniversary of *Evangelium vitae* (14 Feb. 2000) alluded in a notable way to the teaching of *EV* 73, as I shall describe in the main text. The teaching was also alluded to in an address to government leaders, Members of Parliament, and politicians (4 Nov. 2000), but there was no clarification on that occasion.

41. I do not include among the four notable authoritative indicators the view expressed by Archbishop Tarcisio Bertone, S.D.B., while he was secretary of the CDF, in his paper, "Catholics and Pluralist Society," 206–22. It is clear from Archbishop Bertone's frequent use of the expression "it seems to me" that he is putting forward a personal view and not an official CDF interpretation of *EV* 73. Chapter 6 critiques some aspects of Bertone's paper.

42. The quotation is actually from *EV* 73.

43. Cardinal Joseph Ratzinger, Presentation of *Evangelium vitae* to Journalists (30 March 1995), *L'Osservatore Romano*, English edition (5 April 1995): 2.

Cardinal Ratzinger poses several questions that seem at first not to be answered directly. Is he suggesting that one cannot remain faithful to the conviction of one's own conscience by voting for a law (even an "improved" law) that continues to justify an injustice? Is he suggesting that this is a matter of choosing good or evil and that a compromise cannot be made? First of all, Ratzinger gives an indirect answer to his questions by simply quoting the passage from *EV* 73 that says that officials can support proposals aimed at "limiting the harm . . . and lessening the negative consequences." The questions receive, however, a direct answer in the one-sentence clarification that follows it and that concludes his remarks on the passage: "Of course, he can never vote for injustice to be declared justice."

What precisely a legislator is voting for depends on the legislative context, as I have argued in earlier chapters. At some stages, and in particular at the final-vote stage, a legislator would be voting precisely that the proposal under consideration become law, and this requires a judgment that the proposal can *be* law, i.e., that it is just. A vote in favor of a proposal's becoming law is at the same time a declaration that it is just.

Ratzinger's significant final-sentence clarification corresponds to what I have presented as a correct translation of the pope's concluding remarks in *EV* 73 *(Hac enim agendi ratione officium suum non praestat illicitae vel iniustae legi),* which teach that in voting for the permitted "proposals" a legislator would not be voting for a law that is illicit or unjust. Both the Latin text of *EV* 73 and the focus of Cardinal Ratzinger's clarification support my contention that a legislator cannot licitly vote for any legislation that is unjust. The fact that Ratzinger's final sentence begins with "of course" indicates that the point he is making should be obvious and readily accepted.

The second noteworthy indicator came nearly five years later, when John Paul II, in a discourse to mark the fifth anniversary of *Evangelium vitae,* alluded to the teaching of *EV* 73, saying: "Do not leave anything undone in the attempt to eliminate legalized crime or at least to limit the harm of such laws, keeping in mind the radical obligation to respect the right to life of every human being from conception to natural death, even if he is the last and least gifted."[44] The reference to

44. John Paul II, Address to Participants at the Sixth General Assembly of the

"limit[ing] the harm of such laws" repeats the language of *EV* 73, but here the pope presents for the first time, in connection with how one should "limit the harm," the important qualification that one must keep in mind the radical obligation to respect the right to life of every human being, even if he is the last and least gifted. Because they are his first—and only—remarks on the *EV* 73 question, John Paul's remarks assume particular significance. In Chapter 1 I demonstrated that any legislation to prohibit some but not all categories of abortion makes an illicit distinction of persons that is compounded by the fact that the weakest—"the last and least"—will always be treated, contrary to all principles of justice, solidarity, and basic human decency, in an unfavorable way. Legislators can hardly keep in mind the radical obligation to respect the right to life of every human being if they are supporting legislation violating the right to life of some human beings, and notably those who may be regarded as "the last and least gifted."

A third authoritative statement about *EV* 73 was made in the *Doctrinal Note on Some Questions Regarding the Participation of Catholics in Political Life,* published by the Congregation for the Doctrine of the Faith (CDF) in January 2003 with John Paul II's approval.[45] Referring to *EV* 73, the *Doctrinal Note,* first of all, simply states the teaching:

> As John Paul II has taught in his Encyclical Letter *Evangelium vitae* regarding the situation in which it is not possible to overturn or completely repeal a law allowing abortion which is already in force or coming up for a vote, "an elected official, whose absolute personal opposition to procured abortion was well known, could licitly support proposals aimed at limiting the harm done by such a law and at lessening its negative consequences at the level of general opinion and public morality." (*EV* 73)[46]

Pontifical Academy for Life, commemorating the Fifth anniversary of *Evangelium vitae* (14 Feb. 2000), n. 4, reproduced in Correa and Sgreccia, *Evangelium Vitae: Five Years of Confrontation with the Society,* 10.

45. The *Doctrinal Note,* published in Jan. 2003 but dated 24 Nov. 2002, was approved by John Paul II on 21 Nov. 2002. According to one commentator, the *Doctrinal Note* "clearly settles the dispute between the pragmatist and total protection camps" in line with the sort of argument I have presented in this book. See Patrick Delaney, "Compromise or Principle?" *Latin Mass Magazine* 12, no. 1 (2003): 77.

46. CDF, *Doctrinal Note on Some Questions Regarding the Participation of Catholics in Political Life,* n. 4.

This restatement of the teaching of *EV* 73 does not advance one's understanding of it. The *Doctrinal Note*'s next sentence, however, does: "In this context, it must be noted also that a well-formed Christian conscience does not permit one to vote for a political program or an individual law which contradicts the fundamental contents of faith and morals." Referring to the context of the teaching of *EV* 73, i.e., the situation in which a legislator is unable to "overturn or completely repeal a law allowing abortion," the CDF's *Doctrinal Note* (approved by John Paul II) highlights that one is not permitted to vote for a law that contradicts the fundamental contents of faith and morals. *Evangelium vitae* itself notes some of the fundamental contents of morality: "Of course, values such as the dignity of every human person, respect for inviolable and inalienable human rights, and the adoption of the 'common good' as the end and criterion regulating political life are certainly fundamental and not to be ignored" (*EV* 70).

When engaged in civil legislation, morality requires fundamentally that no law is supported that obligates, permits, or tolerates the violation of anyone's right to life. The *Doctrinal Note* highlights that the essence of the moral law is at stake when faced with fundamental and inalienable ethical demands, and that some moral principles do not admit of exception or compromise:

> When political activity comes up against moral principles that do not admit of exception, compromise or derogation, the Catholic commitment becomes more evident and laden with responsibility. In the face of fundamental and inalienable ethical demands, Christians must recognize that what is at stake is the essence of the moral law, which concerns the integral good of the human person. This is the case with laws concerning abortion and euthanasia. . . . Such laws must defend the basic right to life from conception to natural death.[47]

The CDF's *Doctrinal Note* clarifies that the situation considered by *EV* 73 is not to be regarded as an exception to the norm prohibiting legislators from voting for laws that violate the right to life. Even if it were being supported with a view to prohibiting some abortions, a law that in itself obligates or permits or tolerates other abortions can be regard-

47. Ibid.

ed as violating the right to life. Such a law is rightly judged to be intrinsically unjust. The *Doctrinal Note* is consistent with Cardinal Ratzinger's remarks when the encyclical was first published, as well as the final sentence of *EV* 73.3, both of which clarify that the "proposals" supported as a means of "limiting the harm" of an abortion law include only those that are just.

A fourth notable reference to *EV* 73 was included in the CDF's *Considerations Regarding Proposals to Give Legal Recognition to Unions between Homosexual Persons,* dated 3 June 2003:

> When legislation in favour of the recognition of homosexual unions is already in force, the Catholic politician must oppose it in the ways that are possible for him and make his opposition known; it is his duty to witness to the truth. If it is not possible to repeal such a law completely, the Catholic politician, recalling the indications contained in the Encyclical Letter *Evangelium vitae,* "could licitly support proposals aimed at limiting the harm done by such a law and at lessening its negative consequences at the level of general opinion and public morality," on condition that his "absolute personal opposition" to such laws was clear and well known and that the danger of scandal was avoided [*EV* 73.3]. This does not mean that a more restrictive law in this area could be considered just or even acceptable; rather, it is a question of the legitimate and dutiful attempt to obtain at least the partial repeal of an unjust law when its total abrogation is not possible at the moment (n. 10).

After citing the teaching of *EV* 73.3 (that legislators can support proposals aimed at limiting the harm, etc.) the CDF comment is: "This does not mean that a restrictive law in this area could be considered just or even acceptable." Is this saying that legislators are allowed to vote for a restrictive law even though it cannot be regarded as just or acceptable? If this were the case, then the CDF would be contradicting what it had previously indicated as its interpretative guidelines for *EV* 73. But this is clearly not what the CDF is saying, and there is no contradiction. The CDF's remarks focus on proposals that (partially) repeal an unjust law: "it is a question of the legitimate and dutiful attempt to obtain at least the partial repeal of an unjust law when its total abrogation is not possible," something that requires a proper understanding of the meaning of repeal. In Chapters 6 and 7 I noted that legislators could justly vote to repeal an unjust law that was part of a larger law on abortion. An unjust and unacceptable law would be in place after the repeal of part of an abortion law, but legislators would be voting solely for the repeal, and not for the unjust and unacceptable law that would remain in force. There may be few opportunities for such (partial) repeal in the legislative systems of countries like the United States and the United Kingdom, but greater opportunities may exist in countries, like Italy, that have codified systems of law (which, understandably, might be regarded as normative for those in Rome deliberating on this question) that more easily allow for simple repeal.

If the CDF's 2003 *Considerations* were to be interpreted as teaching that legislators can vote to restrict abortion by supporting a law that, by its toleration of or permission for even one abortion would be intrinsically unjust, then not only would the document contradict the 2002 *Doctrinal Note,* it would also be internally contradictory. Any document must be internally consistent, and just as any interpretation of *EV* 73 must be rejected that contradicts any other part of the encyclical, so too must interpretations of difficult passages be understood with respect to clearly articulated principles, like the one expressed in the 2003 *Considerations:* "Every humanly-created law is legitimate insofar as it is consistent with the natural moral law, recognized by right reason, and insofar as it respects the inalienable rights of every person" (n. 6). Considered in itself, and with respect to its authoritative clarifications, the concern of *EV* 73 is clearly that of changing unjust abortion laws *justly.*

10. AN OVERVIEW AND CONCLUSION

How is it possible to speak of the dignity of every human being when the killing of the weakest and the most innocent is permitted? In the name of what justice is the most unjust of discriminations practiced: some individuals are held to be deserving of defence and others are denied that dignity?

John Paul II, *Evangelium vitae,* n. 20

If a society is unwilling to recognize the right to life of all the unborn and to prohibit all abortions, it may nevertheless be willing to prohibit *some* abortions—in particular, late abortions and those undertaken for what some regard as insufficiently serious reasons. As Chapter 1 described, unborn children with a mental or physical disability, or conceived after rape or incest, or in the earlier stages of development, or expected to cause serious problems to their mother's health or life, tend to be excluded from restrictive abortion legislation, because society tends to be more approving of abortion for these children. This view is borne out not only by the experience of the pro-life movement in the United Kingdom but also by experiences in other countries. For example, the Polish abortion law, enacted in 1993 with the support of pro-life legislators, prohibited most abortions that had been previously allowed, but it made an exception for unborn children who might be born with a serious and permanent disability, were conceived after rape, or posed a serious danger to their mother's health. And, as the Introduction noted, U.S. state legislatures might be faced with votes for such legislation if *Roe v. Wade* is overturned and responsibility for abortion laws devolves to individual states. The principal problem of restrictive abortion laws is not simply that they fail to protect all unborn children but that "the last and least" are excluded and the principle of solidarity is violated.

Chapter 1 provided a practical demonstration of attempts to restrict abortion in the United Kingdom. Public arguments and the adoption of certain strategies are normally necessary for the successful enactment of legislation on any matter. Chapter 1 demonstrated that the arguments and strategies adopted by pro-life legislators and campaigning organizations in the UK to gain support for restrictive legislative proposals further marginalized "the last and least," who were in any case marginalized by their exclusion from the proposals. It might be objected that the account in Chapter 1 merely demonstrates the pro-life movement's need to be more circumspect in its statements and actions when supporting restrictive legislation. This, however, would be to miss the point that even if pro-life legislators and campaigners were to proclaim unequivocally their opposition to all abortions, their actions of excluding some unborn children from protection would contribute to society's prejudice that such abortions are less, if at all, objectionable. And if the restrictive legislation itself is not consistent with pro-life principles, and is being supported for pragmatic reasons, then it is hardly surprising if those supporting it say and do things, as I described, which are similarly pragmatic and inconsistent with true principles.

With Pope John Paul II we can ask: "How is it possible to speak of the dignity of every human being when the killing of the weakest and the most innocent is permitted [*sinitur*]"? How could legislators and pro-life campaigners in Poland speak of the dignity of every human being while simultaneously supporting the enactment of the purportedly "pro-life" 1993 restrictive law that allows abortion if the unborn child has been conceived after rape or incest, or would be born with a serious and permanent disability, or for other specified reasons? How could British legislators and pro-life campaigners speak of the dignity of every human being while simultaneously supporting the purportedly "pro-life" restrictive legislation introduced by David Alton, MP, described in Chapter 1, which would have allowed abortions generally *up to* 18 weeks, though in some instances, notably if the unborn child were disabled, at a later stage?

With John Paul II, we can also ask: "In the name of what justice is the most unjust of discriminations practiced: some individuals are held to be deserving of defence and others are denied that dignity?" The question of changing abortion laws is, principally, a question of law, at the heart of which is the concept of justice.

Chapter 2 noted that an early (1970) account of the jurisprudential options on abortion claimed that "there are only three ways by which the law can operate with regard to abortion."[1] The law could prohibit all abortions, prohibit no abortions, or settle for a position anywhere in between that prohibited some abortions but not others. This account of the jurisprudential options is regarded as unsatisfactory, principally because it fails to make a distinction between the "permission" (or "authorization," granting as a right, etc.) of abortion, and its "toleration" (or "decriminalization," withdrawal of prohibition, specification that it is an "unpunishable act," etc.). Human law is not required to prohibit every immoral act, and so it is not, for example, required to prohibit some immoral acts like prostitution. However, in "not prohibiting" there is an important distinction between a law that merely "tolerates" and another that specifically "permits" prostitution. Unlike a law "tolerating" it, a law specifically "permitting" prostitution must be judged in every instance to be unjust, i.e., it is *intrinsically* unjust. With respect to abortion or any other offense against life, laws are intrinsically unjust not only if they "permit" abortion but also if they "tolerate" it, because human law must fulfill the primary requirement of protecting human life. Seven ways of legislating on abortion—seven "jurisprudential options"—were identified. Six of these referred to situations in which the law obligated, permitted, or tolerated abortion in some or all instances, and all laws that fall within each of these six options are intrinsically unjust. The seventh option—a law prohibiting all abortions—is just, and should be regarded as a legislative norm.

"In the name of what justice . . . ?" Keeping the focus on the justice (or justness) of human law, the different types of unjustness were described in Chapter 3 with particular focus on the concept of *intrinsic* unjustness. To say that an abortion law is *intrinsically* unjust means that

1. Drinan, "Jurisprudential Options," 161.

its unjustness is a property of the law itself, and not something arising from some legislators' motives or intentions. or the circumstances in which they are voting for the law. This is relevant to the question of voting for restrictive abortion legislation, which, insofar as it obligates, permits or tolerates any abortions must always be judged to be *intrinsically* unjust. Justness or, equivalently, right reason is identified as the essence of law, and one can legitimately ask whether an intrinsically unjust law is properly regarded as "not a law" or even an "anti-law." The argument that it is absurd to vote for "not a law" to be enacted as "law" is certainly defensible. Chapter 3 accepted the view, however, that intrinsically unjust laws have some properties of law, and argued that on this account there are particular objections to voting to enact them.

Just or Unjust?

This book does not argue merely that it is *preferable* not to support "restrictive abortion legislation" but that there is a fundamental moral problem in so doing, precisely because the legislation is intrinsically unjust. The main argument of this book stands or falls on whether such legislation is, in fact, rightly identified as being unjust. Could, for example, Poland's 1993 law, granting legal protection to most unborn children but specifically allowing abortion for those unborn children who truly can be regarded as "the last and least," be anything other than intrinsically unjust? Some supporters of restrictive abortion legislation, like Robert George, Martin Rhonheimer, and Angel Rodríguez Luño, have acknowledged that such legislation is indeed unjust,[2] while many have taken cover under the misleading—and, in my view, mean-

2. George has acknowledged that restrictive abortion legislation—which he believes pro-life legislators may rightly vote for—is objectively (i.e., intrinsically) unjust: "While it can never be fair to will that members of a disfavored class—whether the unborn, the disabled, or members of some racial or religious group—be excluded from legal protections one wills for oneself and those dear to one a legislator or voter is personally responsible for no unfairness to the victims of an objectively unjust law where he supports that law precisely, and only, because the alternative is even less protective of its victims." See George, "Gospel of Life." Chapter 5 discussed arguments presented by Rhonheimer and Luño for restrictive legislation that they both acknowledge to be unjust.

ingless—description of it being "imperfect" legislation.[3] When expressing his disagreement with an article of mine on the question of supporting restrictive abortion legislation,[4] William May—apparently unaware that some supporters of restrictive abortion legislation do in fact acknowledge it to be unjust—confirmed for me the relevance of focusing on the question of the justness of the legislation: "I know of no one who has defended the view that John Paul II taught that a legislator may enact 'unjust' restrictive abortion legislation. Those who disagree with Harte maintain, however, that he *has taught* that 'legislators . . . may vote for *restrictive* abortion legislation.'"[5]

May's remarks seem to indicate that he believes not only that approval to enact "unjust" restrictive abortion legislation has not been given, but that it could not be given. In this case, it is essential—as I have argued—to establish whether the restrictive legislation under consideration is just or unjust. Human laws are either just or unjust: there is no third category of law, such as one describing them as "restrictive" or "imperfect." Luño has recently made the same point:

> From the point of view of political ethics, civil laws are just when they correspond here and now to the common good: laws that oppose the essential content of the common good are unjust or grievously depraved. Just laws are always or almost always perfectible, at least regarding their technical-juridical efficacy and expression. Likewise, unjust laws can be defective in lesser or greater degrees. However, a third category that would fall between just and unjust laws does not exist. . . . The teachings of John Paul II do not support a third ethical category of imperfect laws which would fall between just and unjust laws.[6]

3. As noted in Chapter 5, even some supporters of restrictive legislation have objected to the adoption of the term "imperfect" legislation, saying that it is unclear and misleading.

4. Colin Harte, "Inconsistent Papal Approaches towards Problems of Conscience?" *National Catholic Bioethics Quarterly* 2, no. 1 (2002): 99–122.

5. William E. May, "*Evangelium Vitae* 73 and the Problem of the Lesser Evil," *National Catholic Bioethics Quarterly* 2, no. 4 (2002): 577–79. The part in quotation marks—which I have quoted in full, as it was published—is presented as though May were quoting John Paul II, but John Paul II has never made this statement. For my response to May, see Colin Harte, "*Evangelium Vitae* 73 and Intrinsically Unjust Laws," *National Catholic Bioethics Quarterly* 3, no. 2 (2003): 241–43.

6. Angel Rodríguez Luño, "The Dilemma of Catholic Legislators Faced with

I have argued that legislators voting for any enactment are themselves enacting *law* and the relevant judgment concerns the justness of the proposal they are enacting, not the end state of the general law on abortion after the proposal's enactment. For example, after the enactment of a just proposal to prohibit public funding of abortion, the intrinsically unjust law permitting or tolerating abortions would still exist, but legislators would have voted for the just proposal prohibiting public funding, not for the intrinsically unjust law permitting or tolerating abortion. However, votes for legislative proposals to restrict abortion—such as one to reduce the upper limit for abortions from 24 to 16 weeks—involve support for proposals that both prohibit some abortions and permit (or tolerate) others, and such proposals are intrinsically unjust. If the restrictive abortion legislation being subject to a vote for enactment is (intrinsically) unjust—as George, Rhonheimer, and Luño acknowledge it to be[7]—then legislators cannot licitly vote for it: this has been taught by John Paul II in *EV* 73.2, and I have presented a philosophical defense of this position in Chapters 4 and 5. Arguments such as those that have been presented by John Finnis, based on an action theory involving a consideration of "intentions and side effects" or the principles of material cooperation, do not justify voting for legislation that is intrinsically unjust.

In the Preface I noted that the purpose of this book is not to convince readers of the rightness of my argument but to encourage them to consider it: to reject it if it is unsound and to accept it if it holds. It is therefore right to acknowledge a significant objection made by John

---

Proposals Seeking to Ameliorate Unjust Laws Promoting Artificial Procreation," paper delivered on 21 Feb. 2004 to the Tenth General Assembly of the Pontifical Academy for Life (19–22 Feb. 2004), sec. 1.

7. George, Rhonheimer, and Luño acknowledge the restrictive legislation to be unjust, and even though they use different terminology seem to accept that it is *intrinsically* unjust. George speaks of it as being "objectively" unjust (see note 2). Rhonheimer speaks of "an, as such, unjust law" (see the long passage of his cited at the beginning of Chapter 5). Luño speaks of "a seriously unjust law" and explains what he means by this by referring to the passage by Aquinas, *ST* I-II, q. 94, a. 4, which I also cited in Chapter 3 as foundational for an understanding of intrinsically unjust laws (see Luño, "*Evangelium vitae* 73: The Catholic Lawmaker and the Problem of a Seriously Unjust Law," n. 2).

Finnis during the period of this book's completion: if the argument I have presented possibly has a fundamental flaw, then readers are entitled to be made aware of this. As noted, the main argument of this book stands or falls on whether I am right in judging that restrictive abortion legislation is intrinsically unjust and, in order to highlight the importance of this point, I asked Finnis, as part of a debate undertaken for publication, to clarify whether, in his view, a range of hypothetical legislative proposals presented by me were just or unjust.[8] One of the hypothetical proposals was in substance the Polish law of 1993 (which I have judged to be intrinsically unjust), and Finnis maintained that this, like the other proposals I had presented, was not intrinsically unjust: rather, it was *just*.[9] If Finnis is right on this point, then I would concede that there is not a fundamental moral objection to voting for such restrictive laws, but I do not accept he is right.[10]

Finnis's response to my argument has resulted in a significant adjustment to his own argument, and he acknowledges some important flaws in his previous action-theory analysis, with its focus on "intention and side effect" and cooperation.[11] In his earlier action-theory analysis, critiqued in Chapter 4, Finnis had acknowledged that legislators restricting abortion from 24 weeks by means of a proposal, "Abortion is

---

8. See Colin Harte, "Problems of Principle in Voting for Unjust Legislation," in Watt, *Cooperation, Complicity and Conscience*.

9. Finnis, "Restricting Legalised Abortion," sec. 5.

10. I stand by the argument I have presented that, in view of the natural law's prohibition of all abortions, the 1993 Polish law, and other laws that permit or tolerate abortion—even if restrictive when compared with other laws—are intrinsically unjust. For my response to Finnis's argument, see Colin Harte, "The Opening Up of a Discussion—A Response to John Finnis," in Watt, *Cooperation, Complicity and Conscience*. The volume will also include a further paper from Finnis—replying to my response—which I have not yet seen.

11. See Finnis, "Restricting Legalised Abortion," secs. 6 and 7. On the role of intention, Finnis now says: "In my previous treatments of this whole issue I too failed to analyse it with all the precision that it calls for. As a result, my earlier discussions gave too much prominence to the distinction between intention and side-effect" (sec. 6). His revised opinion, in response to my critique of his argument, is that "there is strictly no need to attend to the question of cooperation in order to answer the question in debate" (sec. 7). See also Harte, "The Opening Up of a Discussion," secs. 1.3 and 1.4., and my critique of Finnis's argument in Chapter 4.

permitted up to 16 weeks [and prohibited thereafter]," were supporting a law that "does in fact permit abortion up to 16 weeks."[12] His revised opinion is based on a new legal analysis that the proposal *does not* in fact permit abortion up to 16 weeks and is thus just. I do not accept Finnis's new legal analysis, but in many respects his new argument effectively confirms what I have been arguing in this book: that the ethics of voting for restrictive legislation depends crucially on whether the legislation is *just*. Finnis's new argument seems to be that I am right in principle to insist that legislators must vote only for just legislation, but that my practical analysis of laws is wrong. However, if he is right in saying that my practical analysis of laws is wrong, then it must be conceded—as Finnis effectively does concede—that the arguments used to justify voting for restrictive legislation by those who believe (as I do) that the legislation is itself unjust are also wrong. Finnis's reconsideration of the issue reveals that supporters of restrictive legislation are far from agreed as to which argument—if any—justifies their position.

This book has, however, focused on the arguments (including those of Finnis himself before the recent revision of his opinion) that have been generally presented and that have consistently acknowledged—sometimes implicitly and other times explicitly—that restrictive abortion legislation is itself *unjust*. I have argued that several mistakes can be made with respect to intrinsically unjust laws. One mistake is to accept that legislators cannot normally vote for an intrinsically unjust law but that intrinsically unjust restrictive abortion legislation is a "special case" that justifies support. Chapter 5 argues against this view. Another mistake, identified in Chapter 6, is to maintain that the adoption of arguments based on "the lesser evil" or "the principle of totality" or "the law of gradualness" justifies voting for intrinsically unjust restrictive abortion legislation. A different mistake, to which attention is given in Chapter 7, consists of accepting the principle that it is never licit to vote for an intrinsically unjust law, but of failing to discern what precisely, in practice, constitutes an intrinsically unjust law. I had not anticipated, however, that anyone would suggest—as Finnis now does—that legislation like Poland's 1993 abortion law is just. (The argument Finnis is

---

12. See Chapter 4, which considers Finnis's argument.

now presenting would also mean that legislation like the Abortion Act 1967, reproduced in Appendix B, would not be intrinsically unjust—i.e., it could be regarded as just—if it had been supported by pro-life legislators in order to prevent an imminent vote for an alternative law that would have allowed more abortions.)[13] Clearly, if any magisterial statement on the issue confirms the opinion (now held, it would appear, by both Finnis and myself) that it is never licit to vote for *unjust* restrictive legislation, it would be necessary for it to clarify what precisely would be unjust and what would be just.

The legislative matters considered in Chapters 7 and 8 attempt to provide a practical guide for those concerned with some of the nuts and bolts of the legislative process. The judgment that it is always unethical to vote for intrinsically unjust legislation does not mean that pro-life legislators are unable to vote for any proposals aimed at "limiting the harm" of abortion laws. Details of (what I believe to be) the types of just proposals that can be supported, not only in votes to enact law but also during the passage of legislation, are provided in these two chapters on legislative matters. Attention is drawn, in particular, to the fact that in addition to the "primary" abortion legislation, which focuses on abortion per se (i.e., the legislation refers to the particular groups of unborn children, if not all, for whom abortion is obligated, permitted, or tolerated), there is a range of "secondary" legislation that might be considered consequent to a law denying any unborn child the right to life. Some secondary legislation is intrinsically unjust because it is predicated on an acceptance of abortion itself, requiring, for example, counseling or a cooling-off period before having an abortion. Secondary legislation need not, however, focus on abortion per se. It may, for example, focus on the rights of doctors or other health care personnel, or the use of public funding or public premises for abortion.

Because its subject matter is not in fact abortion, just secondary legislation should not be regarded as "abortion legislation" or "restrictive abortion legislation," even though a consequence of its enactment may be that access to abortion is prevented and the number of abortions de-

---

13. See Finnis, "Restricting Legalised Abortion," sec. 4, and Harte, "The Opening Up of a Discussion," sec. 1.2.

creases. Accordingly, one can say that it is *never* licit to vote for "restrictive abortion legislation." However, just secondary legislation, for example, legislation prohibiting public funding for abortions, may "prevent abortions," and even though the subject matter of the legislation is not properly speaking "abortion" but "the allocation of public funds" (which in this instance refers to abortion), such legislation might also be regarded—incorrectly, in my view—as "(restrictive) abortion legislation." At times, in order to make allowances for those who might regard proposals like those prohibiting public funding for abortion as "restrictive abortion legislation," I have said that it is never licit to vote for "unjust [or intrinsically unjust] restrictive abortion legislation." Even if there is an element of tautology in qualifying the term "restrictive abortion legislation" with the adjective unjust (or intrinsically unjust), the adjective highlights what this book argues is a primary consideration, i.e., the identification of any legislative proposal as being intrinsically unjust is sufficient in every instance to judge that legislators act unethically if they vote to enact it.

In dealing with the jurisprudential and ethical aspects of the question, support for the thesis promoted in this book has been found in the teaching of the magisterium. Although *EV* 73, stating that legislators "could licitly support proposals aimed at *limiting the harm* done by [an abortion] law," has been widely cited as teaching that legislators can vote for restrictive legislation, Chapter 9 argues that the thesis presented in this book is consistent with what John Paul II has taught.

Witnessing without Compromise to the Value of Each Human Life

An objection has been made to me that, were my view accepted, the pro-life movement in the United Kingdom would be unable to continue the campaigns for legislative success that it has pursued for more than thirty-six years. But what legislative success has there been? Not a single legislative proposal to restrict abortion has been enacted since the passing of the Abortion Act 1967: on the contrary, the abortion time limit for some unborn children has been extended up until birth as the (unintended) result of a campaign undertaken by the pro-life movement to restrict abortion.[14] The argument I have presented would not

14. See Appendix E, which details the changes to the Abortion Act 1967 made by

have prevented any of the true successes that have been achieved by the UK pro-life movement. Moreover, what should we regard as "success"? Compared with attempts in any other country to restrict abortion, Poland's 1993 restrictive abortion law must be regarded as the most "successful"—but surely a law specifying that abortions can be tolerated in some, even if limited, instances does not merit the label "success." I do not doubt that the pro-life legislators who collaborated with their pro-abortion colleagues in enacting that law had good intentions and were reluctant to support the "compromise" they eventually agreed to accept.[15] But the compromise that was made in accepting the unjust restrictive law should be recognized for what it was—a defeat for the pro-life movement. Let us not dress up defeats as "successes." Of course, there are just proposals—such as those I have described—that can be supported, and pro-life legislators should do what they reasonably can to support them. But true legislative "success" for the pro-life movement consists in the enactment of laws that establish the right to life of all. In Poland, pro-lifers may still uphold, as a matter of principle, that the law *should* protect all the unborn, but this seems to be regarded as such a distant ideal—unrealistic and unachievable in the foreseeable future—that the pro-life movement cannot be said to be actively pursuing the objective of protecting all the unborn. Rather, the objective seems to be that of defending the (intrinsically unjust) 1993 law from challenges that might allow more abortions, and the plight of those for whom abortion is allowed under the terms of the 1993 law appears to be largely overlooked. It seems particularly tragic that the principle of solidarity has been violated in the nation that promoted it as foundational for social justice.[16]

---

the Human Fertilisation and Embryology Act 1990. The 1990 Act separated the Infant Life Preservation Act 1929 from the Abortion Act 1967 and as a result no upper time limit was set for some "hard-case" abortions, notably if the unborn child would be "seriously handicapped." Otherwise, the 1990 Act specified that abortions generally could take place up to the end of the 24th week of pregnancy. Some might claim that this restricted abortion but, as I have described in Chapter 1, the previous upper limit was a matter of dispute, and prior to 1990 the association of the Abortion Act with the 1929 Act arguably set a lower limit.

15. The pro-life president of the Polish Senate, Alicja Grześkowiak, spoke of support for the 1993 law as a "compromise" in "Difesa della Famiglia," 76.

16. Though the province of Northern Ireland is part of the United Kingdom, the

The immediate prospects of enacting just protective laws for all the unborn in virtually all countries may seem slim, but this does not mean the pro-life movement should stop its efforts and give up hope. Far from it. The pro-life movement is called to witness to the truth about the dignity and value of all human life, without compromise, and this witness has its own value even if it does not achieve legislative "success." The value of ethical conduct is not dependent on achieving "success"—whether those successes are real or illusory, and no matter how important the matter may be—and Christianity, above all, recognizes this. As Cardinal Ratzinger (though not speaking specifically about abortion) notes:

> And if our Lord himself ends up on the Cross, one sees that God's ways do not lead immediately to measurable successes. This, I think, is really very important. The disciples asked him certain questions: What's going on, why aren't we getting anywhere? And he answered with the parables about the mustard seed, the leaven, and the like, telling them that statistics is not one of God's measurements.[17]

And if the pro-life movement acknowledges the illusory success that restrictive abortion legislation truly represents, this does not mean that it cannot do much good and save many lives—with no compromise to its principles—outside the legislative or judicial arenas. For example, a large number of American pro-life leaders—academics, med-

---

abortion law for the rest of the UK does not apply to the province, and there is a similar violation of the principle of solidarity. It is well documented that disabled unborn children are aborted in public hospitals, but the legality of these abortions is debatable. The pro-life movement in Northern Ireland and the rest of the UK has for many years had a policy of silence about these abortions, fearing that any admission that the abortions take place—let alone any legal challenge—might open up the question of whether abortions should be allowed on wider grounds. It seems that the pro-life movement is willing to concede to a situation that allows abortion for some unborn children—always those who are the most vulnerable—in order to protect the lives of other children. And this concession undermines the very foundations of the pro-life movement, which must be based on a fundamental *and active* concern for the right to life of *each* and *all*.

17. Joseph Cardinal Ratzinger, *Salt of the Earth* (San Francisco: Ignatius, 1997), 15–16. See also Joseph Ratzinger, *Milestones: Memoirs 1927–1977* (San Francisco: Ignatius, 1998), 155: "When you stand on the side of God you do not necessarily stand on the side of success."

ical professionals, religious leaders, ethicists, and cultural observers—signed a 3,700-word statement, *Building a Culture of Life* (2002), in which they framed an approach toward awakening respect for the dignity of each human person in American society. Among other things, the leaders pledged themselves to a program of cultural actions that they believed could bring about "a 50 percent reduction in abortion by 2005." Having listed various steps—which involved no compromise whatsoever to their pro-life principles—the statement noted: "The steps enumerated above do not require one change in existing law."[18]

Let it not be said that this book is an invitation to inaction. On the contrary, I acknowledge fully the enormity and grave importance of the task facing the pro-life movement. I endorse completely such things as the proposed program of cultural actions, recognizing—as the American pro-life leaders surely do themselves—that such programs call for an increase in pro-life activity, not a diminishing. Though the Partial-Birth Abortion Ban Act, which President Bush signed into law in November 2003, may have caught the headlines, the program of cultural actions clearly has potential to generate far more support for the pro-life movement and to provide much greater benefits for those who are vulnerable to anti-life laws and attitudes.[19] And, of course, the pro-life movement must continue to urge the protection of all in the laws—even in the very constitutions—of all countries. A

---

18. The statement and details of many of its signatories—among whom are many who have adopted a position that I have argued against in this book—is reproduced in William L. Saunders and Brian C. Robertson, eds., *Building a Culture of Life Thirty Years after Roe v. Wade* (Washington, D.C.: Family Research Council, 2002), 3–10.

19. As I explained in Chapter 7, it is legitimate to support just legislation to outlaw the procedure of partial-birth abortion. Whether particular legislation like the Partial-Birth Abortion Ban Act 2003 can be supported depends primarily on a judgment that it is not intrinsically unjust, e.g., by admitting in principle the liceity of other abortions (cf. the CDF's *Declaration on Procured Abortion,* n. 22; *EV* 73.2; and the discussion in Chapter 9). Whether, in a concrete situation, legislation that is not intrinsically unjust is in fact just depends on such further considerations as whether it might undermine opposition to earlier abortions or simply lead to abortions being performed anyway by another procedure. Some remarks, relevant to both sets of considerations, were made in the House of Representatives prior to his decision to vote for the Act by Rep. Ron Paul; see http://www.house.gov/paul/congrec/congrec2003/cr060403.htm (4 June 2003).

minimum requirement must be the steady promotion of bills for the sort of just protective law—which in some countries can be enshrined in a country's constitution—that should be foundational for all other lawmaking activities.

I draw to the end by returning to the concern raised in the Introduction, which may have accompanied the reader through this book. If it can be judged that the protection of some can licitly be achieved through (unjust) laws that permit or tolerate the deaths of others, how does this differ from the judgment of Caiaphas that it was better for one man to die than that the whole nation perish (cf. John 11:50)? Caiaphas's judgment—situated at the heart of the drama of Christ's life—is also at the heart of the problem of changing abortion laws. And the question it ultimately obliges us to answer is: what price do we really attach to an individual human life? How firmly do we defend the rights of some—even of one person—if the consequence of doing so may be that lethal harm comes to many others? I submit the opinion of this book to the judgment of the magisterium, with the confidence that—whatever judgment is ultimately given—the shepherds of the Church are shepherds after the heart of the good shepherd who would not abandon the one sheep for the sake of the ninety-nine (cf. Jer. 3:15; Matt. 18:12–14).

This book expresses concerns that need to be addressed by moral philosophers, jurists, legislators, and the pro-life movement generally. In the first place, it highlights a concern about supporting any legislative proposal—even if regarded as "restrictive" in comparison to an existing law or a law that may otherwise be enacted—that tolerates, permits, or obligates even one direct abortion. Such legislation is always arbitrary and unjust. Indeed, as John Paul II teaches, "the height of arbitrariness and injustice is reached when certain people, such as physicians or legislators, arrogate to themselves the power to decide who may live and who may die."[20] Second, to the extent that proposals—not

20. *EV* 66. I have given my own translation of the Latin text: ". . . cum quidam medici vel legum latores de vita morteque decernendi sibi vindicant potestatem." The official English translation ends: ". . . to decide who ought to live and who ought to die," a translation that is not justified in view of either the Latin or the context of John

based on making distinctions between unborn children—can be supported to "limit the harm" of an abortion law (cf. *EV* 73.3), this book emphasizes the need for the justness of these proposals to be established as a precondition of voting to enact them. Though the need for solidarity with all the unborn has been the fundamental concern of this book, it is recognized that solidarity itself, as well as licit decisions with respect to the sort of legislative proposals that might be supported to further the pro-life cause, cannot be found beyond the parameters of what is just.

Paul II's remarks. It makes no difference whether legislators are pro-abortion and deciding who may live and who may die in accordance with their pro-abortion beliefs, or whether they are pro-life and making a pragmatic decision in order to save some lives: the decision as to who may live and who may die is arbitrary and unjust and no legislator has the right to make it.

APPENDICES
BIBLIOGRAPHY
INDEX

APPENDIX A
THE UK ABORTION LAW PRIOR TO THE ABORTION ACT 1967

Offences Against the Person Act 1861

Section 58 established that it was a felony for anyone to intentionally cause a miscarriage, with a maximum penalty on conviction of life imprisonment.

> §58: Every woman, being with child, who, with intent to procure her own miscarriage, shall unlawfully administer to herself any poison or other noxious thing, or shall unlawfully use any instrument or other means whatsoever with the like intent, and whosoever, with intent to procure the miscarriage of any woman, whether she be or be not with child, shall unlawfully administer to her or cause to be taken by her any poison or other noxious thing, or shall unlawfully use any instrument or other means whatsoever with the like intent, shall be guilty of felony, and being convicted thereof shall be liable . . . to be kept in penal servitude for life.

Section 59 established that it was a misdemeanor punishable by imprisonment for anyone to provide the means of procuring a miscarriage, even if the woman was not in fact pregnant.

> §59: Whosoever shall unlawfully supply or procure any poison or other noxious thing, or any instrument or thing whatsoever, knowing that the same is intended to be unlawfully used or employed with intent to procure the miscarriage of any woman, whether she be or be not with child, shall be guilty of a misdemeanor, and being convicted thereof shall be liable . . . to be kept in penal servitude.

Infant Life (Preservation) Act 1929

Whereas born children, and those who were unborn, had the protection of the law, the status of children in the process of being born was uncertain. The Infant Life (Preservation) Act 1929 established the felony of "child destruction" for anyone who intentionally caused the death of "a child capable of being born alive." Twenty-eight weeks of pregnancy was regarded as *prima facie* proof that a child was capable of being born alive. The 1929 Act provides an exception if the act causing the death of a child is performed "in good faith for the purpose only of preserving the life of the mother." It should be noted that the 1929 Act did not apply to unborn children below the age indicated as being capable of being born alive. The 1861 Act continued to prohibit all earlier intentional miscarriages with no exception to preserve the life of the mother.

(1) . . . any person who, with intent to destroy the life of a child capable of being born alive, by any willful act caused a child to die before it has an existence independent of its mother, shall be guilty of felony, to wit, of child destruction, and shall be liable on conviction thereof on indictment to penal servitude for life: Provided that no person shall be found guilty of an offence under this section unless it is proved that the act which caused the death of the child was not done in good faith for the purpose only of preserving the life of the mother.

(2) For the purposes of this Act, evidence that a woman has at any material time been pregnant for a period of twenty-eight weeks or more shall be prima facie proof that she was at the time pregnant of a child capable of being born alive.

Case Law: 'R v Bourne' [1938] 3 All ER 615

A London gynaecologist, Dr Aleck Bourne, performed an abortion on a 14-year-old girl who had apparently been gang-raped by soldiers. He reported the abortion to the police and was charged under section 58 of the Offences Against the Person Act 1861 with performing an illegal abortion. The trial judge, Mr Justice Macnaughten, informed the jury that the exception to save the mother's life provided in the Infant Life (Preservation) Act 1929 should also be read back into the Offences Against the Person Act 1861, and in his direction to the jury he suggested that allowing abortion "for the purpose of preserving the life of the mother" could be interpreted broadly:

> Those words ought to be construed in a reasonable sense, and, if the doctor is of the opinion, on reasonable grounds and with adequate knowledge, that the probable consequence of the continuance of the pregnancy will be to make the woman a physical or mental wreck, the jury are entitled to take the view that the doctor . . . is operating for the purpose of preserving the life of the mother.

Dr Bourne was acquitted. This 1938 case set a precedent and abortions could thereafter take place to prevent a woman becoming "a physical or mental wreck," though what precisely this might cover was not clear.

APPENDIX B
ABORTION ACT 1967

An Act to amend and clarify the law relating to termination of pregnancy by registered medical practitioners. [27th October 1967]

BE IT ENACTED by the Queen's most Excellent Majesty, by and with the advice and consent of the Lords Spiritual and Temporal, and Commons, in this present Parliament assembled, and by the authority of the same, as follows:—

§ 1 Medical Termination of Pregnancy

(1) Subject to the provisions of this section, a person shall not be guilty of an offence under the law relating to abortion when a pregnancy is terminated by a registered medical practitioner if two registered medical practitioners are of the opinion, formed in good faith—

(a) that the continuance of the pregnancy would involve risk to the life of the pregnant woman, or of injury to the physical or mental health of the pregnant woman or any existing children of her family, greater than if the pregnancy were terminated; or

(b) that there is a substantial risk that if the child were born it would suffer from such physical or mental abnormalities as to be seriously handicapped.

(2) In determining whether the continuance of a pregnancy would involve such risk of injury to health as is mentioned in paragraph (a) of subsection (1) of this section, account may be taken of the pregnant woman's actual or reasonably foreseeable environment.

(3) Except as provided by subsection (4) of this section, any treatment for the termination of pregnancy must be carried out in a hospital vested in the Minister of Health or the Secretary of State under the National Health Service Acts, or in a place for the time being approved for the purposes of this section by the said Minister or the Secretary of State.

(4) Subsection (3) of this section, and so much of subsection (1) as relates to the opinion of two registered medical practitioners, shall not apply to the ter-

mination of a pregnancy by a registered medical practitioner in a case where he is of the opinion, formed in good faith, that the termination is immediately necessary to save the life or to prevent grave permanent injury to the physical or mental health of the pregnant woman.

§ 2 Notification

(1) The Minister of Health in respect of England and Wales, and the Secretary of State in respect of Scotland, shall by statutory instrument make regulations to provide—

> (a) for requiring any such opinion as is referred to in section 1 of this Act to be certified by the practitioners or practitioner concerned in such form and at such time as may be prescribed by the regulations, and for requiring the preservation and disposal of certificates made for the purposes of the regulations;
>
> (b) for requiring any registered medical practitioner who terminates a pregnancy to give notice of the termination and such other information relating to the termination as may be so prescribed;
>
> (c) for prohibiting the disclosure, except to such persons or for such purposes as may be so prescribed, of notices given or information furnished pursuant to the regulations.

(2) The information furnished in pursuance of regulations made by virtue of paragraph (b) of subsection (1) of this section shall be notified solely to the Chief Medical Officers of the Ministry of Health and the Scottish Home and Health Department respectively.

(3) Any person who wilfully contravenes or wilfully fails to comply with the requirements of regulations under subsection (1) of this section shall be liable on summary conviction to a fine not exceeding one hundred pounds.

(4) Any statutory instrument made by virtue of this section shall be subject to annulment in pursuance of a resolution of either House of Parliament.

§ 3 Application of Act to visiting forces etc.

(1) In relation to the termination of a pregnancy in a case where the following conditions are satisfied, that is to say—

> (a) the treatment for termination of the pregnancy was carried out in a hospital controlled by the proper authorities of a body to which this section applies; and
>
> (b) the pregnant woman had at the time of the treatment a relevant association with that body; and
>
> (c) the treatment was carried out by a registered medical practitioner or a person who at the time of the treatment was a member of that body

appointed as a medical practitioner for that body by the proper authorities of that body, this Act shall have effect as if any reference in section 1 to a registered medical practitioner and to a hospital vested in a Minister under the National Health Service Acts included respectively a reference to such a person as is mentioned in paragraph (c) of this subsection and to a hospital controlled as aforesaid, and as if section 2 were omitted.

(2) The bodies to which this section applies are any force which is a visiting force within the meaning of any of the provisions of Part I of the Visiting Forces Act 1952 and any headquarters within the meaning of the Schedule to the International Headquarters and Defence Organisations Act 1964; and for the purposes of this section—

(a) a woman shall be treated as having a relevant association at any time with a body to which this section applies if at that time—

(i) in the case of such a force as aforesaid, she had a relevant association within the meaning of the said Part I with the force; and

(ii) in the case of such a headquarters as aforesaid, she was a member of the headquarters or a dependant within the meaning of the Schedule aforesaid of such a member; and

(b) any reference to a member of a body to which this section applies shall be construed—

(i) in the case of such a force as aforesaid, as a reference to a member of or of a civilian component of that force within the meaning of the said Part I; and

(ii) in the case of such a headquarters as aforesaid, as a reference to a member of that headquarters within the meaning of the Schedule aforesaid.

§ 4 Conscientious objection to participation in treatment

(1) Subject to subsection (2) of this section, no person shall be under any duty, whether by contract or by any statutory or other legal requirement, to participate in any treatment authorised by this Act to which he has a conscientious objection:

Provided that in any legal proceedings the burden of proof of conscientious objection shall rest on the person claiming to rely on it.

(2) Nothing in subsection (1) of this section shall affect any duty to participate in treatment which is necessary to save the life or to prevent grave permanent injury to the physical or mental health of a pregnant woman.

(3) In any proceedings before a court in Scotland, a statement on oath by any person to the effect that he has a conscientious objection to participating in any treatment authorized by this Act shall be sufficient evidence for the pur-

pose of discharging the burden of proof imposed upon him by subsection (1) of this section.

§ 5 Supplementary provisions

(1) Nothing in this Act shall affect the provisions of the Infant Life (Preservation) Act 1929 (protecting the life of the viable foetus).

(2) For the purposes of the law relating to abortion, anything done with intent to procure the miscarriage of a woman is unlawfully done unless authorised by section 1 of this Act.

§ 6 Interpretation

In this Act, the following expressions have meanings hereby assigned to them:—

"the law relating to abortion" means sections 58 and 59 of the Offences against the Person Act 1861, and any rule of law relating to the procurement of abortion;

"the National Health Service Acts" means the National Health Service Acts 1946 to 1966 or the National Health Service (Scotland) Acts 1947 to 1966.

§ 7 Short title, commencement and extent

(1) This Act may be cited as the Abortion Act 1967.

(2) This Act shall come into force on the expiration of the period of six months beginning with the date on which it is passed.

(3) This Act does not extend to Northern Ireland.

APPENDIX C
ABORTION (AMENDMENT) BILL

[This bill, presented by David Alton, MP, was published on 16 December 1987. Its first parliamentary debate (its "second reading") was held on 22 January 1988. The pro-life movement in the UK actively supported the bill.]

A BILL TO

Limit the period within pregnancy during which an abortion may be performed, subject to certain exceptions.

BE IT ENACTED by the Queen's most Excellent Majesty, by and with the advice and consent of the Lords Spiritual and Temporal, and Commons, in this present Parliament assembled, and by the authority of the same, as follows:—

§ 1 Time-limit for termination of pregnancy

(1) A woman's pregnancy may be terminated in accordance with section 1 of the Abortion Act 1967 at any time up to the beginning of the 18th week of gestation.

(2) Thereafter, up to the end of the 28th week of gestation, the pregnancy may be terminated by a registered medical practitioner in a public hospital or approved place if, and only if, either—

(a) two registered medical practitioners are of the opinion, formed in good faith, that—

(i) the termination is necessary in order to save the life of the woman, or

(ii) the child is likely to be born dead or with physical abnormalities so serious that its life cannot be independently sustained, or

(b) the practitioner carrying out the termination is of the opinion, formed in good faith, that it is immediately necessary to save the woman's life or to prevent grave permanent injury to her physical health.

(3) Sections 2 to 5 of the Act of 1967 (Secretary of State's power to make regulations; modification for women associated with defence forces from

overseas; saving for right of conscientious objection; saving for Infant Life (Preservation) Act 1929) have effect as if references to that Act and section 1 of it included subsection (2) above.

(4) In subsection (2) above "public hospital" means a hospital vested in the Secretary of State for the purposes of his functions under the enactments relating to the National Health Service, and "approved place" means a place approved by him for the purposes of section 1 of the Act of 1967.

(5) This Act may be cited as the Abortion (Amendment) Act 1987; and—

(a) the Abortion Act 1967 and this Act may be cited together as the Abortion Acts 1967 and 1987;

(b) this Act extends only to England and Wales and Scotland and comes into force on the expiration of two months beginning with the date of its passing.

APPENDIX D
ABORTION (AMENDMENT) BILL

[After being amended during its committee stage, the bill was still actively supported by David Alton, MP, and the pro-life movement inside and outside of Parliament. The amended bill was debated in the House of Commons on 6 May 1988. The bill was filibustered and not put to a vote and it made no further progress.]

A Bill
[As Amended By Standing Committe C]
To

Limit the period within pregnancy during which an abortion may be performed, subject to certain exceptions.

BE IT ENACTED by the Queen's most Excellent Majesty, by and with the advice and consent of the Lords Spiritual and Temporal, and Commons, in this present Parliament assembled, and by the authority of the same, as follows:—

§ 1 Time-limit for termination of pregnancy

(1) A woman's pregnancy may be terminated in accordance with section 1 of the Abortion Act 1967 at any time up to the beginning of the 18th week of gestation.

(2) Thereafter, up to the end of the 28th week of gestation, the pregnancy may be terminated by a registered medical practitioner in a public hospital or on a consultant gynaecologist's recommendation, in an approved place if, and only if, it is certified—

> (a) that the termination is necessary in order to save the woman's life, or
>
> (b) that it is likely that if the child were born it would suffer from severe physical or mental disability (the nature of the disability to be identified in the certificate), or
>
> (c) that the pregnancy appears to be due to an act of rape or incest com-

mitted against the woman at a time when she was under the age of 18, or

(d) that the termination is immediately necessary to save the woman's life or to prevent grave permanent injury to her physical health.

(3) Nothing in subsection (1) or (2) above shall make it unlawful for a woman's pregnancy to be terminated by a medical practitioner in a public hospital or approved place after the end of the 28th week of gestation if the practitioner carrying out the termination is of the opinion, formed in good faith, that it is immediately necessary to save the woman's life or to prevent grave injury to her physical health.

(4) Sections 2 to 5 of the Act of 1967 (Secretary of State's power to make regulations; modification for women associated with defence forces from overseas; saving for right of conscientious objection; saving for Infant Life (Preservation) Act 1929) have effect as if references to that Act and section 1 of it included subsection (2) above.

(5) In subsections (2) and (3) above—

(a) "approved place" means a place approved by the Secretary of State for the purposes of section 1 of the Act of 1967;
(b) "certified" means—

(i) for the purposes of (a), (b) and (c) of the subsection, certified as their opinion by a consultant gynaecologist and one other registered medical practitioner, and
(ii) for those of paragraph (d), certified as his opinion by the practitioner carrying out the termination;

(c) "consultant gynaecologist" means a person employed in the National Health Service and holding an appointment as consultant gynaecologist on the staff of a public hospital; and
(d) "public hospital" means a hospital vested in the Secretary of State for the purposes of his functions under the enactments relating to that service.

(6) This Act may be cited as the Abortion (Amendment) Act 1988; and—

(a) the Abortion Act 1967 and this Act may be cited together as the Abortion Acts 1967 and 1988;
(b) this Act extends only to England and Wales and Scotland and comes into force on the expiration of two months beginning with the date of its passing.

APPENDIX E
HUMAN FERTILISATION AND EMBRYOLOGY ACT 1990

[The Human Fertilisation and Embryology Act was sponsored by the government, which meant that—unlike bills promoted by individual pro-life Members of Parliament—there was little chance of its being filibustered. The pro-life movement had vigorously campaigned for a section to be included about late abortions in order for Parliament to have the opportunity to resolve the issue that had been raised with the Abortion (Amendment) Bill (see Appendices C and D). Section 37 of the 1990 Act, reproduced below, changed the law on late abortions, specifying that most abortions could take place up to the end of the twenty-fourth week of pregnancy but that other abortions, specified as exceptions made to this limit, could now take place up to birth. The possibility of abortion taking place up to birth arose because the 1990 Act—at §37 (4), below—removed the link between the Abortion Act 1967 and the Infant Life (Preservation) Act 1929, which had specified that it was a crime of "child destruction" to kill a child "capable of being born alive."]

§ 37 Amendment of law relating to termination of pregnancy

(1) For paragraphs (a) and (b) of section 1(1) of the [1967 c. 87.] Abortion Act 1967 (grounds for medical termination of pregnancy) there is substituted—

"(a) that the pregnancy has not exceeded its twenty-fourth week and that the continuance of the pregnancy would involve risk, greater than if the pregnancy were terminated, of injury to the physical or mental health of the pregnant woman or any existing children of her family; or

(b) that the termination is necessary to prevent grave permanent injury to the physical or mental health of the pregnant woman; or

(c) that the continuance of the pregnancy would involve risk to the life of the pregnant woman, greater than if the pregnancy were terminated; or

(d) that there is a substantial risk that if the child were born it would suffer from such physical or mental abnormalities as to be seriously handicapped."

(2) In section 1(2) of that Act, after "(a)" there is inserted "or (b)."
(3) After section 1(3) of that Act there is inserted—

"(3A) The power under subsection (3) of this section to approve a place includes power, in relation to treatment consisting primarily in the use of such medicines as may be specified in the approval and carried out in such manner as may be so specified, to approve a class of places."

(4) For section 5(1) of that Act (effect on [1929 c. 34.] Infant Life (Preservation) Act 1929) there is substituted—

"(1) No offence under the Infant Life (Preservation) Act 1929 shall be committed by a registered medical practitioner who terminates a pregnancy in accordance with the provisions of this Act."

(5) In section 5(2) of that Act, for the words from "the miscarriage" to the end there is substituted

"a woman's miscarriage (or, in the case of a woman carrying more than one foetus, her miscarriage of any foetus) is unlawfully done unless authorised by section 1 of this Act and, in the case of a woman carrying more than one foetus, anything done with intent to procure her miscarriage of any foetus is authorised by that section if—

(a) the ground for termination of the pregnancy specified in subsection (1)(d) of that section applies in relation to any foetus and the thing is done for the purpose of procuring the miscarriage of that foetus, or

(b) any of the other grounds for termination of the pregnancy specified in that section applies."

BIBLIOGRAPHY

Documents of the Magisterium

Full publication details are not provided of recent major magisterial documents where the Vatican has provided a standard English translation. Many publishers have reproduced these translations, including St. Paul Books in Boston, Massachusetts, and the Catholic Truth Society (CTS) in London. The texts are also available at the Vatican website: http://www.vatican.va.

Second Vatican Council. Dogmatic Constitution on the Church. *Lumen Gentium* (1964). In *Vatican Council II: The Conciliar and Post Conciliar Documents,* ed. Austin Flannery, O.P. Dublin: Dominican Publications, 1992.

———. Decree on the Church's Missionary Activity. *Ad Gentes* (1965). In *Vatican Council II: The Conciliar and Post Conciliar Documents,* ed. Austin Flannery, O.P. Dublin: Dominican Publications, 1992.

———. Pastoral Constitution on the Church in the Modern World. *Gaudium et Spes* (1965). In *Vatican Council II: The Conciliar and Post Conciliar Documents,* ed. Austin Flannery, O.P. Dublin: Dominican Publications, 1992.

The Catechism of the Catholic Church (1992). London: Geoffrey Chapman, 1994.

Leo XIII. Encyclical Letter, *Libertas praestantissimum* (1888). *Acta,* tom. 20, fasc. 240, 593–613. English translation in *The Pope and the People.* London: CTS, 1943.

———. Encyclical letter, *Rerum novarum* (1891). Centenary Study Edition, trans. Joseph Kirwan. London: CTS, 1992.

Pius XII. Address to the Italian Medical-Biological Union of St. Luke (12 Nov. 1944). In *The Human Body* (papal teachings selected and arranged by the monks of Solesmes), 51–65. Boston: St. Paul Editions, 1960.

———. Address to Delegates at the Twenty-sixth Congress of Urology (8 Oct. 1953). In *The Human Body* (papal teachings selected and arranged by the monks of Solesmes), 277–81. Boston: St. Paul Editions, 1960.

———. Discourse to the Fifth Convention of Italian Catholic Jurists (6 Dec. 1953). *Catholic Mind* (April 1954): 244–51.

———. Address to the Second World Congress on Fertility and Sterility (19 May 1956). In *The Human Body* (papal teachings selected and arranged by the monks of Solesmes), 384–94. Boston: St. Paul Editions, 1960.

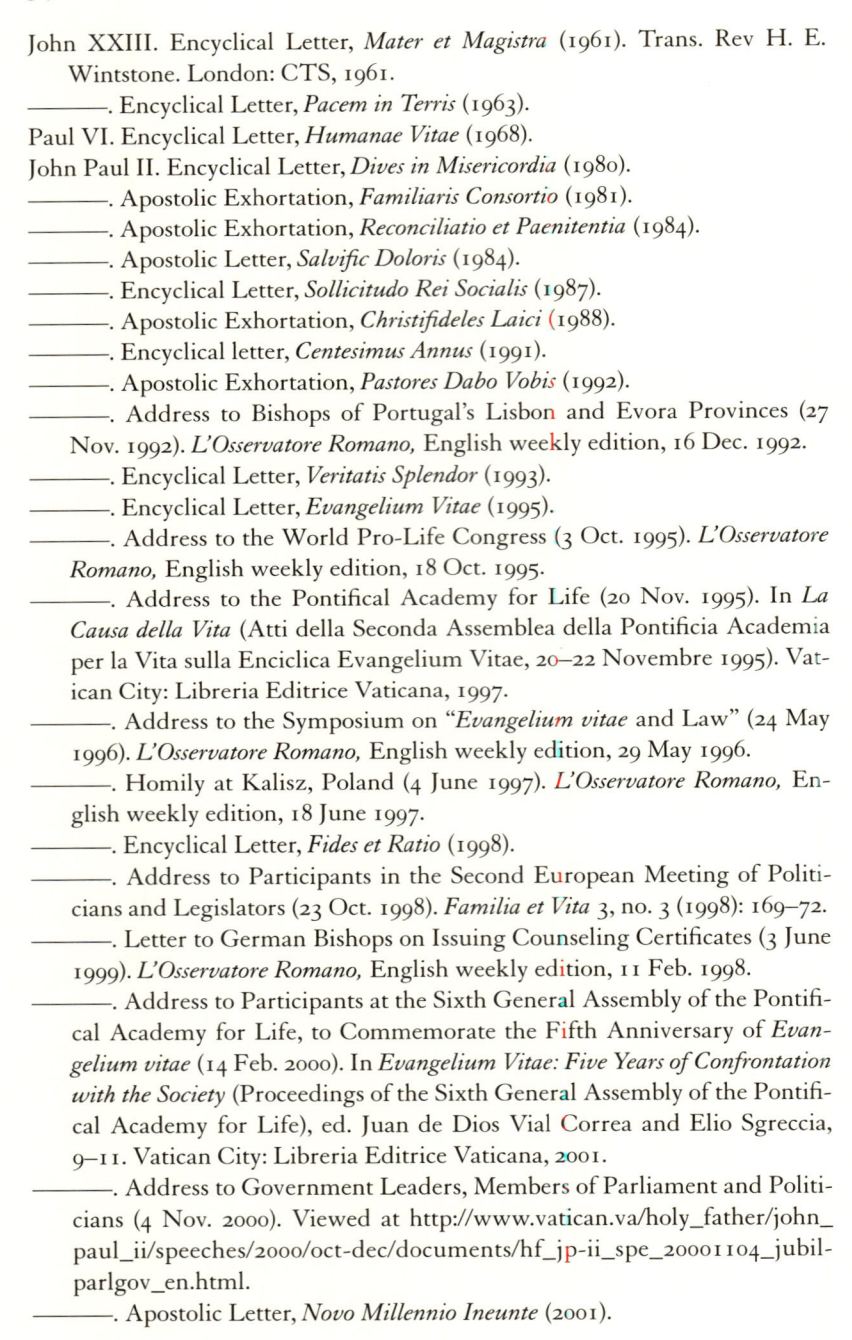

John XXIII. Encyclical Letter, *Mater et Magistra* (1961). Trans. Rev H. E. Wintstone. London: CTS, 1961.

———. Encyclical Letter, *Pacem in Terris* (1963).

Paul VI. Encyclical Letter, *Humanae Vitae* (1968).

John Paul II. Encyclical Letter, *Dives in Misericordia* (1980).

———. Apostolic Exhortation, *Familiaris Consortio* (1981).

———. Apostolic Exhortation, *Reconciliatio et Paenitentia* (1984).

———. Apostolic Letter, *Salvific Doloris* (1984).

———. Encyclical Letter, *Sollicitudo Rei Socialis* (1987).

———. Apostolic Exhortation, *Christifideles Laici* (1988).

———. Encyclical letter, *Centesimus Annus* (1991).

———. Apostolic Exhortation, *Pastores Dabo Vobis* (1992).

———. Address to Bishops of Portugal's Lisbon and Evora Provinces (27 Nov. 1992). *L'Osservatore Romano,* English weekly edition, 16 Dec. 1992.

———. Encyclical Letter, *Veritatis Splendor* (1993).

———. Encyclical Letter, *Evangelium Vitae* (1995).

———. Address to the World Pro-Life Congress (3 Oct. 1995). *L'Osservatore Romano,* English weekly edition, 18 Oct. 1995.

———. Address to the Pontifical Academy for Life (20 Nov. 1995). In *La Causa della Vita* (Atti della Seconda Assemblea della Pontificia Academia per la Vita sulla Enciclica Evangelium Vitae, 20–22 Novembre 1995). Vatican City: Libreria Editrice Vaticana, 1997.

———. Address to the Symposium on "*Evangelium vitae* and Law" (24 May 1996). *L'Osservatore Romano,* English weekly edition, 29 May 1996.

———. Homily at Kalisz, Poland (4 June 1997). *L'Osservatore Romano,* English weekly edition, 18 June 1997.

———. Encyclical Letter, *Fides et Ratio* (1998).

———. Address to Participants in the Second European Meeting of Politicians and Legislators (23 Oct. 1998). *Familia et Vita* 3, no. 3 (1998): 169–72.

———. Letter to German Bishops on Issuing Counseling Certificates (3 June 1999). *L'Osservatore Romano,* English weekly edition, 11 Feb. 1998.

———. Address to Participants at the Sixth General Assembly of the Pontifical Academy for Life, to Commemorate the Fifth Anniversary of *Evangelium vitae* (14 Feb. 2000). In *Evangelium Vitae: Five Years of Confrontation with the Society* (Proceedings of the Sixth General Assembly of the Pontifical Academy for Life), ed. Juan de Dios Vial Correa and Elio Sgreccia, 9–11. Vatican City: Libreria Editrice Vaticana, 2001.

———. Address to Government Leaders, Members of Parliament and Politicians (4 Nov. 2000). Viewed at http://www.vatican.va/holy_father/john_paul_ii/speeches/2000/oct-dec/documents/hf_jp-ii_spe_20001104_jubilparlgov_en.html.

———. Apostolic Letter, *Novo Millennio Ineunte* (2001).

Congregation for the Doctrine of the Faith. *Declaration on Procured Abortion* (1974). London: CTS, 1974. Latin text in *Acta Apostolicae Sedis* 66 (1974): 730–47.

———. *Haec Sacra Congregatio* (On sterilization in Catholic hospitals) (1975). In *Vatican Council II: More Post Conciliar Documents*, ed. Austin Flannery, O.P. Northport, N.Y.: Costello Publishing Co., 1982.

———. *Donum Vitae* (1987). Quebec: Editions Paulines, 1987.

———. *Letter to the Bishops of the Catholic Church Concerning the Reception of Holy Communion of Divorced and Remarried Members of the Faithful* (1994).

———. *Doctrinal Note on Some Questions Regarding the Participation of Catholics in Political Life* (2002).

———. *Considerations Regarding Proposals to give Legal Recognition to Unions between Homosexual Persons* (2003).

Pontifical Council for the Family. *In the Service of Life* (Instrumentum Laboris) (1992).

———. *Vademecum for Confessors Concerning Some Aspects of the Morality of Conjugal Life* (1997).

Catholic Bishops' [of the UK and Ireland] Joint Committee on Bio-Ethical Issues. "Imperfect Laws: Some Guidelines." *Briefing* 19, no. 14 (7 July 1989): 298–300.

Books and Articles

Alton, David. *Whose Choice Anyway?* Basingstoke: Marshall Pickering, 1988.

Anscombe, G. E. M. *Intention*. Oxford: Basil Blackwell, 1958.

Aquinas, Thomas. *Summa Theologiae*. English translation by the Fathers of the English Dominican Province. London: Burns, Oates and Washbourne, 1920. Latin text published at Madrid by Biblioteca de Autores Cristianos, 1955.

———. *Selected Political Writings*. Ed. A. P. D'Entrèves. Oxford: Basil Blackwell, 1948.

Austin, John. *The Province of Jurisprudence Determined*. 1832. Reprint, Cambridge: Cambridge University Press, 1995.

Bailey, Ruth. "Prenatal Testing and the Prevention of Impairment: A Woman's Right to Choose?" In *Encounters with Strangers: Feminism and Disability*, ed. Jenny Morris, 143–67. London: Women's Press, 1996.

Baker, Michael. "Evangelium Vitae 73 and the Supreme Principle of Morals" (2003). Viewed at http://www.superflumina.org/ev73suprempr_final.html (12 Dec. 2003).

Bertone, Tarcisio, S.D.B. "Catholics and Pluralist Society: 'Imperfect laws' and the Responsibility of Legislators." In *Evangelium Vitae: Five Years of Confrontation with the Society* (Proceedings of the Sixth Annual Assembly of the Pontifical Academy for Life, 11–14 Feb. 2000), ed. Juan de Dios Vial

Correa and Elio Sgreccia, 206–22. Vatican City: Libreria Editrice Vaticana, 2001.

Boyle, Joseph. "Double-Effect and a Certain Type of Embryotomy." *Irish Theological Quarterly* 44 (1977): 303–18.

———. "The Principle of Double Effect: Good Actions Entangled in Evil." In *Moral Theology Today: Certitudes and Doubts,* ed. Donald McCarthy, 243–60. St. Louis, Mich.: Pope John Centre, 1984.

Bristow, Peter. *The Moral Dignity of Man.* Dublin: Four Courts Press, 1997.

Callahan, Daniel. *Abortion: Law, Choice and Morality.* London: Collier-Macmillan, 1970.

Caparros, Ernest. "Some Myths and Some Realities in the Contemporary World of Law." *American Journal of Jurisprudence* 35 (1990): 87–104.

Compagnoni, Francesco, O.P. "La Responsabilità dei Politici nella *Evangelium Vitae.*" In *Scienza Medicina Etica 13: Evangelium Vitae e Bioetica: Un Approccio Interdisciplinare,* 97–112. Milan: Vita e Pensiero, Pubblicazione dell'Universita Cattolica, 1996.

Curran, Charles E. *Ongoing Revision: Studies in Moral Theology.* Notre Dame: Fides, 1975.

Damich, Edward J. "The Essence of Law According to Thomas Aquinas." *American Journal of Jurisprudence* 30 (1985): 79–96.

Davis, Alison. "Ofiara, Na Którą Można Się Zgodzić?" (An acceptable sacrifice?). *Ethos* 61–62 (2003): 214–31.

Delaney, Patrick. "Compromise or Principle?" *Latin Mass Magazine* 12, no. 1 (2003): 76–78.

Drinan, Robert F., S.J. "The Jurisprudential Options on Abortion." *Theological Studies* 31 (1970): 149–69.

———. "Strategy on Abortion." *America* 116 (4 Feb. 1967): 179.

Fedoryka, Damian P. "Thoughts towards a Clarification of *Evangelium Vitae* #73." In *Life and Learning XII* (Proceedings of the Twelfth University Faculty for Life Conference at Ave Maria Law School 2002), ed. Joseph W. Koterski, S.J., 311–32. Washington, D.C.: University Faculty for Life, 2003.

Finnis, John. "Three Schemes of Regulation." In *The Morality of Abortion: Legal and Historical Perspectives,* ed. John T. Noonan Jr., 172–207. Cambridge: Harvard University Press, 1970.

———. *Natural Law and Natural Rights.* Oxford: Clarendon Press, 1980.

———. *Fundamentals of Ethics.* Oxford: Clarendon Press, 1983.

———. "The Act of the Person." In *Persona, Verita e Morale* (Atti del Congresso Internazionale di Teologia Morale, Roma 7–12 Aprile 1986), 159–74. Rome: Citta Nuova Editrice, 1987.

———. "Intention and Side-Effects." In *Liability and Responsibility: Essays in Law and Morals,* ed. R. G. Frey and Christopher W. Morris, 32–64. Cambridge: Cambridge University Press, 1991.

———. *Moral Absolutes.* Washington, D.C.: Catholic University of America Press, 1991.

———. "Object and Intention: Moral Judgments According to Aquinas." *Thomist* 55 (1991): 1–27.

———. "The Legal Status of the Unborn Baby." *Catholic Medical Quarterly* (Aug. 1992): 5–11.

———. "Unjust Laws in a Democratic Society: Some Philosophical and Theological Reflections." *Notre Dame Law Review* 71, no. 4 (1996): 595–604.

———. "Is Natural Law Theory Compatible with Limited Government?" In *Natural Law, Liberalism, and Morality,* ed. Robert P. George, 1–26. Oxford: Clarendon Press, 1996.

———. "Natural Law—Positive Law." In *"Evangelium Vitae" and Law* (Acta Symposii Internationalis in Civitate Vaticana Celebrati, 23–25 Maii, 1996), ed. Alfonso Lopez Trujillo, Gonzalo Herranz, and Elio Sgreccia, 199–209. Vatican City: Libreria Editrice Vaticana, 1997.

———. "The Catholic Church and Public Policy Debates in Western Liberal Societies: The Basis and Limits of Intellectual Engagement." In *Issues for a Catholic Bioethic,* ed. Luke Gormally, 261–73. London: Linacre Centre, 1999.

———. "Public Good: The Specifically Political Common Good in Aquinas." In *Natural Law and Moral Inquiry,* ed. Robert P. George, 174–209. Washington, D.C.: Georgetown University Press, 1998.

———. *Aquinas: Moral, Political, and Legal Theory.* Oxford: Oxford University Press, 1998.

———. "Restricting Legalised Abortion Is Not Intrinsically Unjust." In *Cooperation, Complicity and Conscience,* ed. Helen Watt. London: Linacre Centre, 2005.

Finnis, John, Germain Grisez, and Joseph Boyle. "'Direct' and 'Indirect': A Reply to Critics of our Action Theory." *Thomist* 65 (2001): 1–44.

Fisher, Anthony, O.P. "On the Duties of a Catholic Politician with Respect to Abortion Law Reform, with Particular Reference to *Evangelium Vitae* 73" (1998). Viewed at http://www.priestsforlife.org/articles/imperflefisher.html.

———. "Some Problems of Conscience in Bio-lawmaking." In *Culture of Life—Culture of Death,* ed. Luke Gormally, 195–226. London: Linacre Centre, 2002.

Flannery, Kevin L., S.J. "What Is Included as a Means to an End?" *Gregorianum* 74, no. 3 (1993): 499–513.

———. "Practical Reason and Concrete Acts." In *Natural Law and Moral Inquiry,* ed. Robert P. George, 107–34. Washington, D.C.: Georgetown University Press, 1998.

———. *Acts amid Precepts.* Edinburgh: T. & T. Clark, 2001.

George, Robert P. "The Gospel of Life: A Symposium." *First Things* 56 (Oct. 1995): 32–38.

———. "Natural Law and Positive Law." In *The Autonomy of Law,* ed. Robert P. George, 321–34. Oxford: Clarendon Press, 1996.

———. "Bioethics and Public Policy: Catholic Participation in the American Debate." In *Issues for a Catholic Bioethic,* ed. Luke Gormally. London: Linacre Centre, 1999.

———. *In Defense of Natural Law.* Oxford: Clarendon Press, 1999.

———. "Political Action and Legal Reform in *Evangelium Vitae.*" Viewed at http://www.nccbusc.org/prolife/programs/rlp/96rlpgeo.htm (25 May 2000).

———, ed. *Natural Law, Liberalism, and Morality.* Oxford: Clarendon Press, 1996.

———. *The Autonomy of Law.* Oxford: Clarendon Press, 1996.

Gleeson, Gerald. "Is the 'Medical Management' of Ectopic Pregnancy by the Administration of Methotrexate Morally Acceptable?" In *Issues for a Catholic Bioethic,* ed. Luke Gormally, 359–70. London: Linacre Centre, 1999.

Glendon, Mary Ann. *Abortion and Divorce in Western Law.* Cambridge: Harvard University Press, 1987.

Gormally, Luke, ed. *Issues for a Catholic Bioethic.* London: Linacre Centre, 1999.

Griffin, Leslie C. "*Evangelium Vitae:* Abortion." In *Choosing Life: A Dialogue on Evangelium Vitae,* ed. by Kevin Wm. Wildes, S.J., and Alan C. Mitchell, 159–73. Washington, D.C.: Georgetown University Press, 1997.

Grisez, Germain. *Abortion: The Myths, the Realities, and the Arguments.* New York: Corpus Books, 1970.

———. "Towards a Consistent Natural-Law Ethics of Killing." *American Journal of Jurisprudence* 15 (1970): 64–96.

———. *Christian Moral Principles.* Vol. 1 of *The Way of the Lord Jesus.* Quincy, Ill.: Franciscan Herald Press, 1983.

———. *Living a Christian Life.* Vol. 2 of *The Way of the Lord Jesus.* Quincy, Ill.: Franciscan Herald Press, 1994.

———. *Difficult Moral Questions.* Vol. 3 of *The Way of the Lord Jesus.* Quincy, Ill.: Franciscan Herald Press, 1997.

Grześkowiak, Alicja. "Difesa della Famiglia e della Vita nell'Est dell'Europa." *Familia et Vita* 3, no. 3 (1998): 66–81.

Hannigan, E. T., S.J. "Is It Ever Lawful to Advise the Lesser Evil?" *Gregorianum* 30 (1949): 104–29.

Harte, Colin. "Inconsistent Papal Approaches towards Problems of Conscience?" *National Catholic Bioethics Quarterly* 2, no. 1 (2002): 99–122.

———. "Challenging a Consensus: Why *Evangelium Vitae* Does Not Permit Legislators to Vote for 'Imperfect Legislation.'" In *Culture of Life—*

Culture of Death, ed. Luke Gormally, 322–42. London: Linacre Centre, 2002.

———. "*Evangelium Vitae* 73 and Intrinsically Unjust Laws." *National Catholic Bioethics Quarterly* 3, no. 2 (2003): 241–43.

———. "Problems of Principle in Voting for Unjust Legislation." In *Cooperation, Complicity and Conscience,* ed. Helen Watt. London: Linacre Centre, 2005.

———. "The Opening Up of a Discussion: A Response to John Finnis." In *Cooperation, Complicity and Conscience,* ed. Helen Watt. London: Linacre Centre, 2005.

Huxley, Aldous. *Brave New World.* 1932. Reprint, Harmondsworth: Penguin Modern Classics, 1975.

Jensen, Steven J. "A Defense of Physicalism." *Thomist* 61 (1997): 377–404.

Joblin, Joseph. "I Cattolici Nella Società Pluralista: Attualità del Problema." In *I Cattolici Nella Società Pluralista: Il Caso delle "Leggi Imperfette,"* ed. Joseph Joblin and Réal Tremblay, 7–28. Bologna: Edizioni Studio Domenicano, 1996.

Joblin, Joseph, and Réal Tremblay, eds. *I Cattolici e la Società Pluralista: Il Caso delle "Leggi Imperfette."* Bologna: Edizioni Studio Domenicano, 1996.

Johnstone, Brian V., C.Ss.R. "Life in a Culture of Death." *Priests and People* 9, no. 11 (Nov. 1995): 409–13.

Kaczor, Christopher. "Is the 'Medical Management' of Ectopic Pregnancy by the Administration of Methotrexate Morally Acceptable?" In *Issues for a Catholic Bioethic,* edited by Luke Gormally, 353–58. London: Linacre Centre, 1999.

Kaveny, M. Cathleen. "Towards a Thomistic Perspective on Abortion and the Law in Contemporary America." *Thomist* 55 (1991): 343–96.

———. "The Limits of Ordinary Virtue: The Limits of the Criminal Law in Implementing *Evangelium Vitae.*" In *Choosing Life: A Dialogue on Evangelium Vitae,* ed. Kevin Wm. Wildes, S.J., and Alan C. Mitchell, 132–49. Washington, D.C.: Georgetown University Press, 1997.

Kiely, Bartholomew, S.J. "The Impracticality of Proportionalism." *Gregorianum* 66, no. 4 (1985): 655–86.

———. "Formation in Chastity: The Need and the Requirements." In *Issues for a Catholic Bioethic,* ed. Luke Gormally, 134–47. London: Linacre Centre, 1999.

Kretzmann, Norman. "Lex Iniusta Non Est Lex: Laws on Trial in Aquinas' Court of Conscience." *American Journal of Jurisprudence* 33 (1988): 99–122.

Kriele, Martin. "Influsso della Legislazione sulla Coscienza dei Cittadini." *I Cattolici e la Società Pluralista: Il Caso delle "Leggi Imperfette,"* ed. Joseph Joblin and Réal Tremblay, 84–98. Bologna: Edizioni Studio Domenicano, 1996.

Lawler, Ronald, Joseph Boyle, and William E. May. *Catholic Sexual Ethics.* Huntington, Ind.: Our Sunday Visitor, 1996.

Lobo, George V., S.J. *Guide to Christian Living.* Westminster, Md.: Christian Classics, 1991.

Lombardi, Joseph. "Obstetrical Dilemmas and the Principle of Double Effect." *American Journal of Jurisprudence* 37 (1992): 197–211.

Lotstra, Hans. *Abortion: The Catholic Debate in America.* New York: Irvington Publishers, 1985.

Luño, Angel Rodríguez. "*Evangelium Vitae* 73: The Catholic Lawmaker and the Problem of a Seriously Unjust Law." *L'Osservatore Romano,* English weekly edition, 38 (18 Sept. 2002): 3–5.

———. "The Dilemma of Catholic Legislators Faced with Proposals Seeking to Ameliorate Unjust Laws Promoting Artificial Procreation." In *The Dignity of Human Procreation and Reproductive Technologies: Anthropological and Ethical Aspects* (Proceedings of the Tenth General Assembly of the Pontifical Academy for Life, 19–22 Feb. 2004). Vatican City: Libreria Editrice Vaticana, 2005.

Lysaght, Gary. "The Lesser Evil: A Moral Quagmire?" *Catholic Medical Quarterly* (May 1997): 7–13.

Maestri, William F. "The Abortion Debate after Webster: The Catholic-American Moment." *Linacre Quarterly* 57, no. 1 (1990): 46–57.

———. "Abortion in Louisiana: Passion over Prudence." *Linacre Quarterly* 57, no. 4 (1990): 36–45.

Maritain, Jacques. *The Things That Are Not Caesar's.* London: Sheed and Ward, 1930.

May, William E. "Theologians and Theologies in the Encyclical [Veritatis Splendor]." *Anthropotes* (1994): 39–59.

———. "The Management of Ectopic Pregnancies: A Moral Analysis." In The *Fetal Tissue Issue: Medical and Ethical Aspects,* ed. Peter J. Cataldo and Albert S. Moraczewski, O.P., 121–47. Braintree, Mass.: Pope John Center, 1994.

———. "Unjust Laws and Catholic Citizens: Opposition, Cooperation and Toleration." *Homiletic and Pastoral Review* (Nov. 1995): 7–14.

———. "*Evangelium Vitae* 73 and the Problem of the Lesser Evil." *National Catholic Bioethics Quarterly* 2, no. 4 (2002): 577–79.

Mayer-Maly, Theo. "Il Diritto alla Vita e la Trasmissione della Vita." In *"Evangelium Vitae" and Law,* ed. Alfonso Lopez Trujillo, Gonzalo Herranz, and Elio Sgreccia, 77–97. Vatican City: Libreria Editrice Vaticana, 1997.

McCormick, Richard, S.J. "Notes on Moral Theology: The Abortion Dossier." *Theological Studies* 35 (1974): 312–59.

———. "The Gospel of Life: How to Read It." *Tablet* (22 April 1995): 492–95.

McCullagh, Peter. *The Foetus as Transplant Donor: Scientific, Social and Ethical Perspectives*. Chichester: J. Wiley & Son, 1987.

McInerny, Ralph. "*Humanae Vitae* and the Principle of Totality." In *Why Humanae Vitae Was Right: A Reader*, ed. Janet E. Smith, 329–41. San Francisco: Ignatius Press, 1993.

Melina, Livio. "La Cooperacion en Acciones Moralmente Malas Contra la Vida Humana." In *Commentario Interdisciplinar a la "Evangelium Vitae,"* ed. Ramon Lucas Lucas, 467–90. Madrid: Biblioteca de Autores Cristianos, 1996.

Merecki, Jarosław, and Tadeusz Styczeń. "Denying Equal Legal Protection to Weakest Undermines the State Itself." *L'Osservatore Romano*, English weekly edition 44 (1 Nov. 1995): 10.

Myers, John. "The Obligations of Catholics and the Rights of Unborn Children." *Origins* 20, no. 4 (14 June 1990): 65–72.

Newman, John Henry. *Apologia Pro Vita Sua*. 1864. Reprint, London: Collins, Fontana, 1959.

Prümmer, Dominic, O.P. *Handbook of Moral Theology*. Cork: Mercier Press, 1956.

Quinn, Kevin P., S.J. "Whose Virtue? Which Morality? The Limits of Law as a Teacher of Virtue—A Comment on Cathleen Kaveny." In *Choosing Life: A Dialogue on Evangelium Vitae*, ed. Kevin Wm. Wildes, S.J., and Alan C. Mitchell, 150–55. Washington, D.C.: Georgetown University Press, 1997.

Ratzinger, Joseph. *Church, Ecumenism and Politics*. Slough: St. Paul Publications, 1988.

———. Presentation of *Evangelium Vitae* to Journalists (30 March 1995). *L'Osservatore Romano*, English edition (5 April 1995): 1–2.

———. *Salt of the Earth*. San Francisco: Ignatius Press, 1997.

———. *Milestones: Memoirs, 1927–1977*. San Francisco: Ignatius Press, 1998.

———. "Contemporary Crisis of Law." Address given on the occasion of his receiving the degree of Doctor Honoris Causa from the LUMSA Faculty of Jurisprudence in Rome, 10 Nov. 1999. Viewed at http://www.culture-of-life.org/law_crisis.htm (29 Oct. 2000).

———. *The Winning Side*. Mishawaka, Ind.: St. Brendan's Institute, 1999.

Rhonheimer, Martin. "Fundamental Rights, Moral Law, and the Legal Defense of Life in a Constitutional Democracy." *American Journal of Jurisprudence* 43 (1998): 135–83.

———. "Intentional Actions and the Meaning of Object: A Reply to Richard McCormick." In *Veritatis Splendor and the Renewal of Moral Theology*, ed. J. A. DiNoia, O.P., and Romanus Cessario, O.P., 241–70. Princeton: Scepter Publishers/Our Sunday Visitor, 1999.

———. "Intrinsically Evil Acts and the Moral Viewpoint: Clarifying a Central Teaching of Veritatis Splendor." In *Veritatis Splendor and the Renewal of Moral Theology,* ed. J. A. DiNoia, O.P., and Romanus Cessario, O.P., 161–93. Princeton: Scepter Publishers/Our Sunday Visitor, 1999.

———. *Natural Law and Practical Reason.* New York: Fordham University Press, 2000.

Rice, Charles. *No Exception: A Pro-Life Imperative.* Notre Dame: Tyholland Press, 1990.

Rock, John J., S.J. "*Evangelium Vitae:* Some Highlights." *Linacre Quarterly* 64, no. 1 (Feb. 1997): 5–15.

Rodriguez, Pedro. "Pastori e Laici: Distinzione dei Loro Ruoli nella Dottrina Sociale della Chiesa." In *I Cattolici e la Società Pluralista: Il Caso delle "Leggi Imperfette,"* ed. Joseph Joblin and Réal Tremblay, 158–97. Bologna: Edizioni Studio Domenicano, 1996.

Sadler, Bernard. *Legislating for Life: A Commentary on Evangelium Vitae 73.* Sydney: Newman Graduate Education, 2003.

Saunders, William L., and Brian C. Robertson, eds. *Building a Culture of Life Thirty Years after Roe v. Wade.* Washington, D.C.: Family Research Council, 2002.

Sgreccia, Elio, Tadeusz Styczeń, S.D.S., Dorota Chabrajska, and Jarosław Merecki, S.D.S., eds. *Medicine and Law: For or Against Life?* Vatican City: Libreria Edictrice Vaticana, 1999.

Smith, Janet E. *Humanae Vitae: A Generation Later.* Washington, D.C.: Catholic University of America Press, 1991.

———. "Natural Law: Does It Evaluate Choices or Acts?" *American Journal of Jurisprudence* 36 (1991): 177–201.

———, ed. *Why Humanae Vitae Was Right: A Reader.* San Francisco: Ignatius Press, 1993.

Society for the Protection of Unborn Children (SPUC). *Facts on the Abortion (Amendment) Bill.* London: SPUC, 1987.

———. *Legal Abortion Examined: Twenty-one Years of Abortion Statistics.* London: SPUC, 1992.

———. *Our Aims, Ethics and Activities.* London: SPUC, 1997.

Springer, Robert H., S.J. "Notes on Moral Theology." *Theological Studies* 28 (1967): 308–55.

Styczeń, Tadeusz, S.D.S. "Le Leggi Contro la Vita: Analisi Etico-Culturale." In *"Evangelium Vitae" and Law,* ed. Alfonso Lopez Trujillo, Gonzalo Herranz, and Elio Sgreccia, 213–27. Vatican City: Libreria Editrice Vaticana, 1997.

———. "Ethics as the Theory of Natural Law Facing the 'Law Against Life.'" In *Medicine and Law: For or Against Life?* ed. Elio Sgreccia, Tadeusz Styczeń, S.D.S., Dorota Chabrajska, and Jarosław Merecki, S.D.S., 217–37 Vatican City: Libreria Edictrice Vaticana, 1999.

Trujillo, Alfonso Lopez, Gonzalo Herranz, and Elio Sgreccia, eds. *"Evangeli-*

um Vitae" and Law (Acta Symposii Internationalis in Civitate Vaticana Celebrati, 23–25 Maii, 1996). Vatican City: Libreria Editrice Vaticana, 1997.

Ulshafer, Thomas R., S.S. "On the Morality of Legislative Compromise: Some Historical Underpinnings." *Linacre Quarterly* 59, no. 2 (1992): 10–26.

Utz, Arthur F., O.P. "Das Unheil der Nr. 73/74 der Enzyklika *Evangelium Vitae.*" *Theologisches* 28, no. 6 (June 1998): 307–10.

Waldstein, Wolfgang. "Natural Law and the Defense of Life in *Evangelium Vitae.*" In *Evangelium Vitae: Five Years of Confrontation with the Society,* ed. Juan di Dios Vial Correa and Elio Sgreccia, 223–42. Vatican City: Libreria Editrice Vaticana, 2001.

Watt, Helen. *Abortion.* London: CTS/Linacre Centre, 2001.

Wojtyła, Karol. *Love and Responsibility.* London: Fount Paperbacks, 1982.

Woodall, George. "The Use of the Condom to Prevent the Transmission of HIV." *Medicina e Morale* 3 (1998): 545–79.

Zimmerman, Anthony, S.V.D. *Allowing Exceptions in Abortion Laws* (1990). Viewed at http://zimmerman.catholic.ac/1–23-except.htm (12 March 2001).

INDEX

Abortion Act 1967, 6, 18, 25–26, 42, 45, 65–66, 243, 248, 271, 325–27, 337–40
abortion laws: primary and secondary aspects of, 18, 218–19, 223, 224–34, 299, 302, 325; United Kingdom, 18–47, 335–46; United States, 5, 6, 8, 17, 62, 66, 73, 82–83, 171–72, 317; Poland, 82, 201–2, 317–18, 320, 323–24, 327; Germany, 82, 125, 163; Northern Ireland, 243, 271, 327–28
acts, interior and exterior, 145–47, 150
adultery, 78, 80, 83, 88, 91, 98, 100–101, 163, 182, 184–85, 280
"age-of-consent" legislation, 198
Alton, David, xi, xv, 1–3, 6, 7, 11, 20–33, 35–40, 47–51, 90, 318, 341, 343
amendment bills, judging the justness of, 224–30
Amos, Alan, 43
Anscombe, G. E. M., 183
anti-abortion politics, 159, 161–62, 168, 183, 185, 205–6
Aquinas, Thomas: definition of law, 92–93, 155, 291; on purpose of law, 15, 83, 208, 290; on function of law, 73, 78; on just and unjust laws, 94–100, 102–5, 113, 115, 157, 209, 291, 322; on legal permission and legal toleration, 79–80, 86–87, 103; distinguishing the "political" and the "moral", 96–98, 134, 162; on good and evil, 135; on object and intention, 140–42, 146; on interior and exterior acts, 145–47, 150, 184
Association of Lawyers for the Defence of the Unborn (ALDU), 30–31, 90

Augustine, 87, 99
Austin, John, 98–99, 108

Bailey, Ruth, xv, 50–51, 53–54
Baker, Michael, xv, 216–17
Benyon, William, 26
Bertone, Tarcisio, 193–201, 212, 311
Blair, Tony, 7
Bottomley, Virginia, 39
Bourne, Aleck, 336
Bowman, Phyllis, xvi, 28, 30, 32, 39, 41–42
Boyle, Joseph, 61, 129–31, 142, 145, 182
Braine, Bernard, 26, 34, 38
Bristow, Peter, xv, 146
Bruinvels, Peter, 240
Bush, George, 329

Caiaphas, 11, 202, 330
Callahan, Daniel, 65, 70
Campbell-Savours, Dale, 24
Caparros, Ernest, 105
Catholic hospitals, prohibiting abortion in, 244
chemical abortions, 7, 24, 238, 249, 280
collaboration, 127, 166, 193–94, 199, 253–54. *See also* cooperation in evil
Compagnoni, Francesco, 211–12
compromise, 37, 62–71, 167, 178–79, 193, 220, 311–14, 326–29; just compromise, 220–22; political and moral compromise, 134, 162–64; restrictive abortion legislation viewed as, 2, 22–23, 59–60, 63, 65–66, 82, 178, 253, 327

359

INDEX

Congregation for the Doctrine of the Faith (CDF), 94, 108, 164, 193, 311; on legal toleration, 81, 85; on legal protection of human life; 84–85, 221, 293; on intrinsically unjust law, 102, 104–5, 116, 297–98, 329; on cooperation, 124; and n. 73 of *Evangelium vitae (EV 73)*, 297–98, 313–16
conscience, non-participation in abortion on grounds of, 235, 246–47
consent to abortion, 8; informed consent, 239–40, 246; consent of child's father, 239–40; parental consent, 168, 239–40, 299
consequences. *See* restrictive abortion legislation
Conservative Party (UK) on abortion, 7
contraception, 149, 160, 181, 183, 186–90, 200–206, 209–11
cooperation in evil, 121–28, 134, 161, 165–67, 207, 251–52, 282, 304–7, 323. *See also* collaboration
"cooling-off" periods, 18, 239–40, 247, 299, 325
Corrie, John, 26
counseling: prior to abortion, 8, 239–40, 269, 275, 278, 299, 325; issuing of counseling certificates, 124–25, 163
craniotomy, 61, 129–30
Croshaw, Theresa, xv
Curran, Charles, 71

Damich, Edward, 93, 99
Davies, Keith, 27
Davis, Alison, xi–xii, xv, 3, 47–49
Dawson, J. G., 104–5
Delaney, Patrick, xvi, 313
democracy, 164, 173; establishment of right to life as a pre-condition of, 16, 84, 173, 292–94
Denney, M., 1
disability, xi, 19, 22–23, 25–55, 69–70, 94, 124, 232–33, 237, 328
double-effect principle, 61, 112, 128–33. *See also* side effect

Drinan, Robert, 59–61, 70–73, 76–78, 319
ectopic pregnancies, 128–30, 132
embryo experimentation, 11, 46, 281–82
euthanasia laws: sharing features with abortion laws, 11, 86, 102–4, 114, 221, 297, 314
exclusions: as a feature of restrictive abortion legislation, 15–55, 67–70; incompatibility of "no exceptions" approach with enactments of restrictive legislation, 178–81

Fedoryka, Damian, xv, 216
Ferriman, Annabel, 29
finis operantis, 146
finis operis, 146–49
Finnis, John: on n. 73 of *Evangelium vitae (EV 73)*, 115, 139, 165, 296, 304–6, 308; on cooperation, 122–28, 134, 161, 165–66, 251, 304, 323; on object/intention, 121, 131–34, 140–42, 145, 323; on side-effect, 112, 251–52; on schemes to regulate abortion, 59–61, 64, 72–73, 76, 78; on law, 92–93, 98, 99–101, 104, 107, 114–15, 155; on just abortion law, 106, 260; on restrictive legislation as permitting abortion, 175; on restrictive legislation as being just, 323–25; on bishops declining to call restrictive laws acceptable, 252–54; on restrictive legislation as rescuing, 3; on voting, 151–53, 165, 177; on craniotomy, 62, 127
Fisher, Anthony, 139, 143–45, 236, 238–39
Flannery, Kevin, xv, 129–30, 156, 182
Fletcher, Agnes, xv, 51, 54
Fletcher, Martin, 37
forced abortions, 246, 249–50; in China, 74, 249

George, Robert, xv, 70, 79–80, 94, 97, 102, 171–72, 187, 205, 320, 322

Gleeson, Gerald, 130
Glendon, Mary Ann, 63–65, 67–70
gradualness, law of, 206–11
Griffin, Leslie, 300
Grisez, Germain, 61, 123, 125, 129–30, 142, 145–47, 190–91
Grześkowiak, Alicja, 82, 327

Hannigan, E. T., 166
Harman, Harriet, 39
Harte, Colin, 95, 321, 323, 325
homosexual acts, 150, 182–83, 206, 210, 315
Human Fertilisation and Embryology Act 1990, 27, 39–40, 248, 327, 345–46
human person, value of, 211–12
Humanae vitae, 160, 187–88, 200, 202–5
Hurst, Rachel, xv, 50–51, 53–54
Huxley, Aldous, 74

in vitro fertilization (IVF), 238, 249, 279–82
infanticide, 236, 260
intention *v* object, 140–42, 181
intention. *See* restrictive abortion legislation; Finnis, on intention/object
intrinsically unjust law, 22, 88–89, 100–110, 113–16, 134–35, 137–38, 155–60; 283–85, 297–301, 308, 319–27; identification of, 215–37, 239–43, 245, 247–50, 259–60, 262, 265–67, 270–71, 274, 276, 280, 282
ius civile and *ius gentium*, 96–98, 100–101, 134, 162, 221, 226, 253

Janiak, Kazimierz, 82
Jensen, Steven, 147
Joblin, Joseph, 94, 122, 191
John XXIII, 163, 170, 204
John Paul II: *Evangelium vitae*, 15–16, 66, 81, 84–86, 102–4, 122, 136, 155, 157, 211, 289–92, 294, 308–10, 317, 330; n. 73 of *Evangelium vitae* (*EV* 73), 3, 82, 102, 104–5, 113–16, 125, 139, 144, 160–61, 164, 165–66, 171, 175, 186–87, 189, 193, 204–5, 211, 216, 289–90, 294–316, 321–22, 326, 329, 331; *Familiaris consortio*, 108, 204, 207, 210; *Centesimus annus*, 293; *Veritatis splendor*, 117, 121, 140–45, 147–50, 157–58, 181, 184–85, 187–88, 192, 202
Johnstone, Brian, 309
justice, 16, 78, 209, 290, 311–13, 317, 319; definition of, 88

Kaczor, Christopher, 130
Kaveny, M. Cathleen, 62–63, 68–70, 207–9
Kiely, Bartholomew, 190–92, 206
Knight, Jill, 37, 48–49
Kretzmann, Norman, 93, 98–99
Kriele, Martin, 253

Labour Party (UK) on abortion, 7
"last and least, the" 5, 19, 53, 312–13, 318, 320
law: definition of, 92, 155; essence of, 92–95, 209, 221, 314, 320; criteria for enacting, 154; "imperfect" law, 94–95, 175, 193, 300–301, 321; (extrinsically) unjust law, 88, 100–101, 103, 156, 250; purpose of human (civil) law, 208, 290, 292; validity of, 86, 102, 104, 106–7, 110, 113–15, 284, 292, 310; enactment of, 126–27, 154, 157–58; *see also* intrinsically unjust law, legal permission and legal toleration, natural law, restrictive abortion legislation
Lawler, Ronald, 182
legal permission and legal toleration, 73–89
legalism, 156
Leigh, Edward, 243
Leo XIII, 79–80, 130, 188
lesser evil, 8, 63, 81, 85, 137, 186–202, 211–12, 253, counseling the, 166–67
lex iniusta non est lex, 98–99, 103–4, 106–8, 113, 320

Lobo, George, 204
Lombardi, Joseph, 129
Lotstra, Hans, 66
Luño, Angel Rodríguez, 175–76, 320–22
Lysaght, Gary, 125, 202

MacKay, Andrew, 33–34
Macnaughten, Justice, 336
Maestri, William, 1, 6
Maritain, Jacques, 163
marriage, instantiation of, 108–12
masturbation, 83, 181–83
May, William, xv, 128–30, 148–49, 182, 321
Mayer-Maly, Theo, 186
McCormick, Richard, 63–64, 81–82, 84–85, 199
McCullagh, Peter, 31
McInerny, Ralph, 204
McLean, Peter, xv, 49–50
Melina, Livio, 175, 296
Merecki, Jaros?aw, xv, 293
Moonie, Lewis, 33
morning-after pill, 7, 280
Myers, John, 124

natural law: as foundation of pro-life position, 69, 71–72; and human law, 78, 81, 96–102, 105, 115, 157, 173, 290, 316; legal protection of unborn as requirement of, 101–2
Newman, John Henry, xi
non impedire. *See* toleration

oath swearing by lawmakers, 5, 154, 168–73; *see also* truth-telling under oath
Owen, Jane, 28

Pajak, Sandra, 28
partial-birth abortion, 9, 237–38, 249, 280, 329
Paul VI, 116, 160, 187–88, 202–4, 298
Paul, Ron, 329
peace, 15, 16, 83–84, 96, 101, 164, 208, 290, 292

Perry, C., 33
physicalism, 143, 146–50, 181–83
Pius XII, 16, 75, 80–81, 116, 182, 203
Poland. *See* abortion laws
Poole, David, 30–31, 90
Powell, Enoch, 282
prostitution, 83, 87–88, 107, 280, 319
Prümmer, Dominic, 123
public-funding legislation, 9, 86, 195–96, 229, 232–33, 245, 299, 322, 325–26
public-funding of abortion, 86, 195–96, 218, 229, 232–33, 245, 249, 270, 299, 303, 322, 326
punishment: as function of law, 73–74; for performing abortion, 76, 102, 260; toleration as absence of punishment, 81–82, 84–85, 319

Quinn, Kevin, 208

Rafferty, Cathy, 52–54
Ratzinger, Joseph, 95, 209, 221, 315, 328; on n. 73 of *Evangelium vitae* (*EV* 73), 311–12
registration of abortions, 247–48
repeal, 2, 174, 200, 224, 228, 315–16; of unjust law, 2, 200, 224, 226, 228, 236, 307, 313–16
rescuing in emergency situation, 1–5, 136, 211
restrictive abortion legislation, 9, 324–26; rationale of saving lives, 2, 10–11, 302; seen as unjust; 94, 175, 300, 320–22; seen as a "legal evil," 199; seen as just, 323–25; seen as justified by consequences, 90–91, 131, 136–40, 201–2, 248–49; seen as justified by intention, 131–36, 143–45, 181–83
Rhonheimer, Martin, xv, 54, 82–84, 97, 101, 145–48, 159–64, 166, 174–76, 181–82, 208, 292, 320, 322
Rice, Charles, xv, 178–81
Richardson, Jo, 34
Ripamonti, Robert, 47
Rock, John, 176, 302–3

Rodriguez, Pedro, 207
Roe v. Wade, 5–6, 8, 171–72, 317
RU 486. *See* chemical abortions

Sadler, Bernard, xv, 216
Saunders, William, 329
saving lives, 1–3, 5, 48, 52, 110, 123, 135–36, 144, 248, 299
Seller, Amanda, 52
Short, Clare, 33, 39
side effect, 112, 121–23, 128, 131–34, 149–50, 165, 218, 235, 248–52, 323. *See also* double-effect principle
Sidoli, Paul, 46
Smeaton, John, xv–xvi, 1–2, 27, 46, 90–91
Smith, Janet, 75, 187, 191–92, 204–5
Society for the Protection of Unborn Children (SPUC), xi–xii, xv–xvi, 1–2, 23, 26–28, 30, 32, 35–52, 90, 91, 240, 302
solidarity, 5, 15–20, 47–55, 227–28, 313, 318, 327–28, 331
Solidarity, 82
speed limits, legislating for, 65, 176–77, 217
Springer, Robert, 66
St. John Stevas, Norman, 65–66
Steel, David, 33, 42
Stell, P. M., 46
Styczeń, Tadeusz, xv, 106–7, 157, 292–93
Sunstein, Cass, 171–72

Thomas, Janet, 52
Thurnham, Peter, 30, 37

toleration, 75, 81, 187–89, 262. *See also* legal permission and legal toleration
totality, principle of, 160, 202–5, 211
Toynbee, Polly, 29
Tremblay, Réal, 94, 122
truth-telling under oath, 154, 168–70, 173

Ulshafer, Thomas, 66
Utz, Arthur, 125

voting: based on consequences, 136–40; based on intention, 131–36, 161; enactment votes signifying the willing of an enactment, 126–27; in elections, 45–46; objective meaning of enactment votes, 110, 176; purposes of different legislative votes, 151–54, 180–81; voting opportunities during a bill's passage, 255–85

Waldstein, Wolfgang, 102
Wałęsa, Lech, 201
Watt, Helen, xv, 94
White, James, 25–26, 39
Whitehouse, Christopher, 27, 40–41
Widdecombe, Ann, 1, 7, 21, 22, 38, 50
Wigley, Dafydd, 33
witness to the right to life, 60, 180, 251–52, 315, 326, 328
Wojtyła, Karol, 25
"women and children first," 3–4
Woodall, George, 189

Zimmerman, Anthony, 87

Changing Unjust Laws Justly: Pro-Life Solidarity with "the Last and Least" was designed and composed in Granjon by Kachergis Book Design, Pittsboro, North Carolina; and printed on sixty-pound Natural Offset and bound by McNaughton & Gunn, Inc., Saline, Michigan.

Printed in Great Britain
by Amazon